Cool Colleges 101

PETERSON'S

A nelnet COMPANY

About Peterson's Publishing

To succeed on your lifelong educational journey, you will need accurate, dependable, and practical tools and resources. That is why Peterson's is everywhere education happens. Because whenever and however you need education content delivered, you can rely on Peterson's to provide the information, know-how, and guidance to help you reach your goals. Tools to match the right students with the right school. It's here. Personalized resources and expert guidance. It's here. Comprehensive and dependable education content—delivered whenever and however you need it. It's all here.

For more information, contact Peterson's, 2000 Lenox Drive, Lawrenceville, NJ 08648; 800-338-3282 Ext. 54229; or find us online at www.petersonspublishing.com.

Stephen Clemente, Managing Director, Publishing and Institutional Research; Bernadette Webster, Director of Publishing; Mark D. Snider, Editor; Christine Lucas, Research Project Manager; Ward Brigham, Operations Manager; Matthew Gazda, Research Associate; Jim Ranish, Research Associate; Ray Golaszewski, Manufacturing Manager; Linda M. Williams, Composition Manager; Kelly Gibson, Interior Design; Victoria O'Malley, Content Editor

Cover photos from left to right: Hollins University (VA), Mills College (CA), New England College (NH). Divider page photos: The Eastern Region of the United States: Cabrini College (PA); The Midwestern Region of the United States: Carleton College (MN); The Western Region of the United States: Menlo College (CA); International: The American University in Paris (France); Getting Into College: Assumption College (MA); Cool Colleges Index: Delaware Valley College (PA)

ISBN-13: 978-0-7689-3397-0
ISBN-10: 0-7689-3397-8

Printed in the United States of America

10 9 8 7 6 5 4 3 2 1   12 11 10

First Edition

Sustainability—Its Importance to Peterson's, a Nelnet company

What does sustainability mean to Peterson's? As a leading publisher, we are aware that our business has a direct impact on vital resources—most especially the trees that are used to make our books. Peterson's is proud that its products are certified by the Sustainable Forestry Initiative (SFI) and that this book is printed on paper that is 10 percent post-consumer waste.

Being a part of the Sustainable Forestry Initiative (SFI) means that all of our vendors—from paper suppliers to printers—have undergone rigorous audits to demonstrate that they are maintaining a sustainable environment.

Peterson's continually strives to find new ways to incorporate sustainability throughout all aspects of its business.

CONTENTS

THE MIDWESTERN REGION OF THE UNITED STATES

THE WESTERN REGION OF THE UNITED STATES

COOL COLLEGES INDEX

WELCOME TO COOL COLLEGES 101!

Peterson's Cool Colleges 101 is a brand new undergraduate guide featuring colorful, easy-to-read profiles of hundreds of "cool" colleges and universities across the United States and abroad. *Peterson's Cool Colleges 101* is designed for the ultimate decision maker—the student. It is not a typical four-year college guide: The layout reflects what *you* want—vibrant photos, essential information, and fast facts and figures—right at your finger tips!

Whether high school graduation is right around the corner or a year or two away, you need to consider which college or university is going to suit your needs and lifestyle best. After all, you're about to make one of the most important decisions of your life, and you need the best information possible.

Peterson's is here to help! For more than forty years, Peterson's has given students the most comprehensive, up-to-date information on undergraduate institutions in the United States and abroad. Now, we are offering this new, one-of-a-kind college search experience.

The profiles displayed in this guide serve as an introduction to the culture and lifestyle on college campuses throughout the United States and abroad. In each college profile, you'll find those attributes that make each school unique: its culture, tradition, social life, atmosphere, architecture, and environment. We hope that after reading *Peterson's Cool Colleges 101* you will have a richer sense of the experiences awaiting you at each individual college and university.

Cool College Profiles

Peterson's Cool Colleges 101 contains more than 240 college profiles. Each profile appears on a two-page spread and contains vivid campus photos, an informative description, fast facts and figures, and contact information. The colleges are divided up into four sections:

- The Eastern Region of the United States
- The Midwestern Region of the United States

- The Western Region of the United States
- International

The U.S. regions are further divided by state, and then schools appear alphabetically within their specific state. The International section is delineated by country. If the country contains more than one school, the schools are listed alphabetically.

COLLEGE DESCRIPTIONS

All of the colleges featured in this guide have provided Peterson's with a brief description of what they have to offer you—the incoming student. These descriptions have been provided exclusively by college officials and edited by Peterson's for consistency. The descriptions are designed to give students a better sense of the individuality of each institution in terms of campus environment, student activities, and college lifestyle. Peterson's believes that, in addition to the programs of study offered, these quality-of-life intangibles are often the deciding factors in the college selection process.

PHOTOS AND CAPTIONS

Throughout this college guide you will find colorful photos that provide a visual preview of life on campus. The photos may feature school grounds, sports arenas, dining facilities, campus events, important buildings and monuments, and student life in general. Whenever possible schools have provided captions to help contextualize the information in their photos and help students better understand what campus life may be like for them.

CONTACT INFORMATION

At the beginning of a college profile you will see the school name; school logo; the city, state (city, country in the International section); and the school's Web site. The name, title, phone numbers, and e-mail address of the person to contact for further information are given in a green box on the right-hand page of every cool college profile. Toll-free numbers may also be included as well as numbers for in-state and out-of-state callers.

FAST FACTS AND FIGURES

Peterson's Cool Colleges 101 offers fast facts and figures for prospective students who want basic data for quick review and comparison. At the end of the college description, you'll find bulleted information on school enrollment, selectivity, test scores, application deadlines, and expenses. Any item that does not apply to a particular college or for which no information was supplied is omitted from that college's profile.

Enrollment

The number of undergraduate and (if applicable) graduate students, both full-time and part-time, as of fall 2009.

Selectivity

The five levels of entrance difficulty *(most difficult, very difficult, moderately difficult, minimally difficult,* and *noncompetitive)* are based on the percentage of applicants who were accepted for fall 2009 freshman admission (or, in the case of upper-level schools, for entering-class admission) and on the high school class rank and standardized test scores of the accepted freshmen who actually enrolled in fall 2009. The colleges were asked to select the level that most closely corresponds to their entrance difficulty (according to the above guidelines) to assist prospective students in assessing their chances for admission.

Test Scores

The percentage of freshmen who took the SAT and received critical reading and math scores above 500, as well as the percentage of freshmen taking the ACT who received a composite score of 18 or higher.

Application Deadline

Deadlines and dates for notification of acceptance or rejection for both freshmen and transfer students are given either as specific dates or as rolling or continuous. *Rolling* means that applications are processed as they are received, and qualified students are accepted as long as there are openings. *Continuous notification* means that applicants are notified of acceptance or rejection as applications are processed up until the date indicated or the actual beginning of classes.

Expenses

Tuition is the average basic tuition and fees for an academic year presented as a dollar amount. *Room & Board* is the average yearly room-and-board cost presented as a dollar amount. For state-supported and state-related schools, figures are presented for the cost of in-state resident tuition and fees (*not* nonresident tuition and fees).

DATA COLLECTION AND INCLUSION

The data contained in these college profiles were researched between winter 2009 and spring 2010 through *Peterson's Annual Survey of Undergraduate Institutions.* All data included have been submitted by officials at the colleges. Some of the institutions that submitted data were contacted directly by the Peterson's research staff to verify unusual figures, resolve discrepancies, or obtain additional data. Due to Peterson's comprehensive editorial review, we believe the information presented in this guide is accurate. However, you should check with a specific college or university at the time of application to verify such figures as tuition and room & board, which may have changed since the publication of this guide.

The absence of any college or university from this guide does not constitute an editorial decision on the part of Peterson's, nor do we attempt to portray one school as being "cooler" than any other. In essence, these profiles are an open forum for colleges and universities, on a voluntary basis, to communicate their particular message to a cool new generation of prospective students.

Getting Into College

For advice and guidance on searching for the right college, getting your application ready, or planning your education, take a glance at these enlightening articles—written for students like you. "Exploring Possible Career Paths in High School" will show you how you can test various career paths by exploring your interests. "Planning Your Education" will help you plan what you should be doing to prepare for college. "The College Search" illuminates those resources at your disposal to locate the right cool college for you. "Applying to College" helps you figure out what's involved in the application process and what schools look for in prospective students. "What to Expect in College" helps you answer some of the big questions you may have, such as how to choose your classes or major and how you can make the most of your life outside the classroom?

Cool Colleges Index

For a quick look-up, check out the "Alphabetical Listing of Colleges." Here you'll find an easy-to-use index of colleges and universities in alphabetical order.

YOUniversityTV.com

Want to see a lot of cool colleges and universities without leaving home? Check out the videos and educational resources on YOUniversityTV.com. In many of the cool college profiles throughout this book, you'll find easy-to-use links to YOUniversityTV.com videos that look like this:

 http://bit.ly/collvid55

YOUniversityTV.com assists students with the college-selection process by providing access to videos and educational resources for colleges across the United States. YOUniversityTV.com is free-of-charge and does not receive compensation from any of the universities it features.

Find Us On Facebook®

Join the cool college conversation on Facebook® at www.facebook.com/find.colleges and receive additional college search tips and advice. Peterson's wide array of resources is available to help you succeed in finding the right school!

Peterson's publishes a full line of books—college and grad guides, education exploration, financial aid, and test and career preparation. Peterson's publications can be found at high school guidance offices, college libraries and career centers, and your local bookstore and library. Peterson's books also available as eBooks.

We welcome any comments or suggestions you may have about this publication. Your feedback will help us make educational dreams possible for you—and others like you.

Colleges will be pleased to know that Peterson's helped you in your selection. Admissions staff members are more than happy to answer questions, address specific problems, and help in any way they can. The editors at Peterson's wish you great success in your college search!

THE EASTERN REGION OF THE UNITED STATES

Connecticut
District of Columbia
Florida
Georgia
Maine
Maryland

Massachusetts
New Hampshire
New Jersey
New York
North Carolina
Pennsylvania

Rhode Island
South Carolina
Vermont
Virginia
West Virginia

Rosary Hall Library

ALBERTUS MAGNUS COLLEGE

NEW HAVEN, CONNECTICUT
www.albertus.edu/

Students become leaders through the liberal arts education they receive at Albertus Magnus College. Here the focus is not only on the intellectual but also on the physical and moral status of each person. Undergrads live and learn on the beautiful 50-acre campus in the Prospect Hill neighborhood of New Haven. About 60 percent of the students live on campus in dorms that are renovated mansions from the early 1900s. Recently, the College has expanded its graduate-level offerings to include the Master of Science in Management, Master of Arts in Art Therapy, Master of Arts in Leadership and Master of Business Administration. Students head to the Campus Center to catch comedy shows, live music and contests. The variety of on-campus organizations includes the Student Government Association, the Campus Activities Board, the multicultural student union, a dance team, the Psychology Club, the Art Club, the Environmental Club, the Business Club and numerous creative writing options, such as

Breakwater literary magazine and the English Club. Albertus has recently added a new cyber lounge, the Common Ground, where students can check e-mail, work on homework and drink a cup of coffee. Students may also share in the excitement of live drama through the College's professionally managed ACT 2 Theatre. The active Campus Ministry provides opportunities to organize campus events and participate in community service projects. The Cosgrove, Marcus, Messer Athletic Center houses a 25-yard pool, a Jacuzzi, three racquetball courts, a weight and cardio room, a dance studio and a gymnasium. There are also soccer and softball fields, an outdoor track and several tennis courts. Albertus fields intercollegiate athletic teams in baseball, basketball, cross-country, soccer, tennis and volleyball for men and basketball, cross-country, soccer, softball, tennis and volleyball for women. These teams compete in the NCAA Division III/Great Northeast Athletic Conference (GNAC) and the Eastern College Athletic Conference (ECAC). New Haven is a multicultural city with a population of more than 130,000 people. The city has some of the finest theaters in the country, including the Long Wharf and Shubert theaters. Designer shopping, excellent restaurants and several recreational areas are only a short distance from the Albertus Magnus College campus.

CONTACT INFORMATION

Ms. Jessica Van Deren, Dean of Admissions

☎ 203-773-8501 or toll-free 800-578-9160

✉ admissions@albertus.edu

- **Enrollment:** *2,023*
- **Selectivity:** *moderately difficult*
- **Test scores:** *SAT—critical reading over 500, 43%; SAT—math over 500, 34%*
- **Application deadline:** *8/20 (freshmen), rolling (transfer)*
- **Expenses:** *Tuition $23,126; Room & Board $9914*

Athletic Center

The Duquès Center for Academic Success

Mitchell College

NEW LONDON, CONNECTICUT
www.mitchell.edu/

The professors and administrators of Mitchell College want students to know they care. In fact, Mitchell College has turned this philosophy into its mission: (CARES)—Character, Achievement, Respect, Engagement and Self-Discovery. The CARES model focuses on character development, personal and social responsibility, respect for others and community service. Mitchell College's innovative program, Thames Academy, continues to grow and strengthen. Launched in 2006, Thames Academy is a postgraduate/precollege program—a year of academic preparation for students between the end of their high school education and the start of their college studies. Students at Mitchell love the variety of living choices. In addition to traditional residence halls, Mitchell offers four historic Victorian and Colonial waterfront halls housing between 20 and 35 students each. A new suite-style, 120-bed residence hall opened in fall 2008. The college campus has a fully equipped gymnasium, a new fitness center, new dining hall and cafe, athletic fields, a sailing dock and indoor recreation areas. Biking, business, communications, community service, choir, Hillel, music, the newspaper, the yearbook, skiing, multi-cultural affairs, psychology and history are just some of the clubs students enjoy. Weekends are filled with guest comedians, bands and organized trips to Boston and New York City. The tradition of the scholar-athlete is strong at Mitchell. A provisional member of the NCAA Division III, Mitchell College recently joined the New England Collegiate Conference. Men play baseball, basketball,

cross-country, golf, lacrosse, sailing, soccer and tennis; women play basketball, cross-country, golf, sailing, soccer, softball, tennis and volleyball. New London, Connecticut, where Mitchell College makes its home, is a major center of activity in southeastern Connecticut. This small but sophisticated city, also home to Connecticut College and the U.S. Coast Guard Academy, is a maritime and resort center located midway between Boston and New York City. Bordered by a long stretch of sandy beach, the campus consists of 68 acres of gently sloping hillside and forest. Places for shopping, dining and fun are within easy walking distance. Major shopping malls, factory outlets and fine and casual dining are minutes from the campus. The region is also home to major tourist attractions, such as the U.S.S. Nautilus and Submarine Museum, Mystic Marinelife Aquarium, Mystic Seaport, Olde Mystic Village, Ocean Beach Park, Stonington Vineyards, Foxwoods Resort and Casino, the Mohegan

Students have the option to study right on the Mitchell College Beach.

Sun Casino and the Essex Steam Train.

- **Enrollment:** *961*
- **Selectivity:** *moderately difficult*
- **Application deadline:** *Rolling (freshmen), rolling (transfer)*
- **Expenses:** *Tuition $25,627; Room & Board $11,548*

CONTACT INFORMATION

Ms. Kimberly Hodges, Director of Admissions

☎ 860-701-5038 or toll-free 800-443-2811

🖳 admissions@mitchell.edu

Post University Men's Soccer

POST UNIVERSITY

WATERBURY, CONNECTICUT
www.post.edu/

Post University is known for its quality academic programs, small classes, award-winning student activities and competitive NCAA Division II athletics. In 2009, it added a Collegiate Sprint Football team and extended its commitment to serving military students by adding an ROTC program. Its students come from the United States and abroad and are supported by faculty whose mission is to prepare students to compete and succeed in today's global workplace. Post University attracts students from all races, cultures, geographies and socioeconomic backgrounds. This allows Post students to benefit from sharing varied viewpoints and experiences. The smaller campus also means more opportunities to take on leadership roles within and beyond the classroom. Post University undergrads can also get involved in various on-campus activities or take a trip into two of the nation's most exciting cities, New York and Boston. Post University also has an Honors College designed to meet the needs of highly motivated and academically accomplished students. Approximately two thirds of Post University's students live on campus in one of six up-to-date residence halls that range from single rooms to suites with private rooms that have a shared living and eating space. Post students participate in year-round intercollegiate and intramural athletics. The Post University Eagles compete in the National Collegiate Athletic Association (NCAA) Division II and the Central Atlantic Collegiate Conference (CACC). Men's intercollegiate sports teams include baseball, basketball, cross-country, golf, soccer, swimming and tennis. In 2010, Post University will compete in the Collegiate Sprint Football League against well-known universities such as Army, Navy, Princeton and Cornell. Women's teams include basketball, cross-country, lacrosse, soccer, softball, swimming, tennis and volleyball. The University also sponsors an active coed equestrian team and an International Dressage team. Intramural sports include everything from softball and volleyball to basketball and flag football. Students enjoy working out in the Drubner Fitness Center, which has a gymnasium, swimming pool, tennis and racquetball courts, fitness club and weight-training rooms. Post University offers students the best of both worlds. Located midway between New York City and Boston, Post University

CONTACT INFORMATION

Mr. Jay Murray, Director of Admissions

☎ 203-596-4500 or toll-free 800-345-2562

✉ admiss@post.edu

sits on a 58-acre hilltop in the suburbs of Waterbury, Connecticut.

- **Enrollment:** *2,590*
- **Selectivity:** *minimally difficult*
- **Test scores:** *ACT—over 18, 50%; SAT—critical reading over 500, 30%; SAT—math over 500, 31%*
- **Application deadline:** *Rolling (freshmen), rolling (transfer)*
- **Expenses:** *Tuition $25,050; Room & Board $9700*

Equine student with her horse.

QUINNIPIAC UNIVERSITY
HAMDEN, CONNECTICUT
www.quinnipiac.edu/

Quinnipiac University is big enough to support a wide variety of people and programs but small enough to keep students from getting lost in the shuffle. This coed university offers four-year and graduate-level degree programs leading to careers in health sciences, business, communications, natural sciences, education, liberal arts and law. Life on campus is exciting. The approximately seventy-five student organizations and extracurricular activities include intramural and intercollegiate (NCAA Division I) athletics. The University has a student newspaper, TV station, an FM radio station (WQAQ) and nineteen intercollegiate teams in men's baseball, basketball, cross-country, ice hockey, lacrosse, soccer and tennis, and in women's basketball, competitive cheer, cross-country, field hockey, ice hockey, lacrosse, soccer, softball, tennis, indoor/outdoor track and volleyball. The University has three distinct campuses. The 250-acre

Follow the music and you'll find the clock tower and Quinnipiac's state-of-the-art library!

Mount Carmel campus has fifty buildings including the Arnold Bernhard Library, an athletic and recreation center and twenty-five residence halls with traditional rooms, suites and multilevel suites with kitchens. The nearby 250-acre York Hill campus includes the TD Bank Sports Center with twin 3,500-seat arenas for ice hockey and basketball; a new suite-style 1,800-bed residence hall for juniors and seniors; student center; and multi-level parking garage. Just 4 miles away is the 104-acre North Haven campus with state-of-the-art facilities for graduate and upper division programs in the School of Health Sciences. There are plans for a proposed medical school. The Athletic and Recreation Center includes a 24,000-square-foot rec-reation/fitness facility with a free-weight room; an exercise machine center; aerobics studios; basketball, volleyball and tennis courts; and a sus-pended indoor track. There are also lighted tennis courts, playing fields and routes for running and biking. Career

Planning takes place in each of the schools with assistance from the deans' offices in health sciences, communica-tions, education, business and the college of arts and sciences. Approximately 30 percent of Quinnipiac under-grads remain at Quinnipiac for their graduate degrees in education, business, physi-cal and occupational therapy and physician assistant programs. Several of the graduate degree programs are offered online or in a hybrid format. The Quinnipiac University School of Law offers programs leading to a J.D. degree or J.D./M.B.A. degree in combination with the School of Business. Quinnipiac provides the best of the suburbs and the city. The University is only 8 miles from New Haven and less than 2 hours from New York

City and Boston. Bordering the campus is the 1700-acre Sleeping Giant State Park, for walking and hiking. The free campus shuttle takes students to nearby shopping and restaurants.

CONTACT INFORMATION

Ms. Joan Isaac Mohr, Vice President and Dean of Admissions

☎ 203-582-8600 or toll-free 800-462-1944

📠 admissions@quinnipiac.edu

- **Enrollment:** *7,758*
- **Selectivity:** *moderately difficult*
- **Test scores:** *ACT—over 18, 100%; SAT—critical reading over 500, 82%; SAT—math over 500, 87%*
- **Application deadline:** *2/1 (freshmen), 4/1 (transfer)*
- **Expenses:** *Tuition $34,250; Room & Board $12,730*

QU students collaborating in one of several Biology labs.

*Sacred Heart University
Library Waterfall*

SACRED HEART UNIVERSITY

FAIRFIELD, CONNECTICUT
www.sacredheart.edu/

Sacred Heart University draws students committed to academic excellence, cutting-edge technology, career preparation and community service. Founded in 1963, Sacred Heart University (SHU) is the second-largest Catholic university in New England and the first in America to be led and staffed by lay people. With endless opportunities for hands-on education through research, internships, independent study, work-study and study abroad programs worldwide, Sacred Heart University students are consistently challenged to apply their skills outside the classroom. These learning opportunities are enhanced by an active student life program that includes 31 Division I athletic teams and more than 80 student organizations. Students can join fraternities and sororities, student government, the newspaper, the yearbook, radio and television stations, academic clubs, political organizations, community service organizations, multicultural organizations, the performing arts, intramural programs and eighteen competitive sports programs. Sacred Heart University has thirty-one NCAA Division I men's and women's sports, making it one of the largest Divison I programs in the country. Varsity teams include baseball, basketball, bowling, crew, cross-country, equestrian, fencing, field hockey, football, golf, ice hockey, lacrosse, soccer, softball, swimming and diving, tennis, indoor/outdoor track and field, volleyball and wrestling. Students also participate in the University's twenty-five intercollegiate teams, competing against teams from top schools in the Northeast, including Ivy League schools. In addition to the more than 30 under-graduate degree programs, the University offers several graduate degree programs including Master of Science (M.S.) in computer science and information science (with a new concentration in computer game design and development), a nationally ranked Master of Science in Occupational Therapy (M.S.O.T.), a new Master of Science (M.S.) in exercise science and nutrition and a Doctor of Physical Therapy (D.P.T.) program ranked first in the State of Connecticut and among the five best in the Northeast accord-ing to *U.S. News & World*

Report. Located on 67 acres along the coast in Fairfield, Connecticut, Sacred Heart University is just 1 hour north of New York City and 2 hours south of Boston with international campuses in County Kerry, Ireland and Luxembourg. Rated ninth in the nation and best in the Northeast on a recent *Money Magazine* list of "Best Places to Live," Fairfield is an ideal location for work and play. SHU students can take full advantage of intern or career opportunities at the many companies headquartered in Fairfield, Connecticut such

CONTACT INFORMATION

Ms. Karen N. Guastelle, Dean of Undergraduate Admissions

☎ 203-371-7880

✉ enroll@sacredheart.edu

as the world headquarters for General Electric and the Discovery Museum of Science and Industry.

- **Enrollment:** *6,023*
- **Selectivity:** *moderately difficult*
- **Test scores:** *SAT—critical reading over 500, 63%; SAT—math over 500, 71%*
- **Expenses:** *Tuition $30,298; Room & Board $11,684*

Sacred Heart University students

SAINT JOSEPH COLLEGE
CONNECTICUT

SJC will inspire you to explore and expand your potential in a welcoming community that offers each student a personalized academic experience.

WEST HARTFORD, CONNECTICUT
www.sjc.edu/

Career-focused, leading women make their way to Saint Joseph College. The core values of compassionate service, Catholic identity, commitment to women through academic excellence and diversity are evident in the College's curriculum and daily life. Faculty members and students emphasize leadership in academics, career and community. Women lead every organization on campus, from the Business Society and Student Government to the Campus Ministry and honors societies. Saint Joseph College students shine in artistic performances, as coordinators of community service projects and on the athletic fields. The College's women compete in eight NCAA Division III sports: basketball, cross-country, lacrosse, softball, soccer, swimming/diving, tennis and volleyball. The O'Connell Athletic Center features a six-lane pool, gymnasium, suspended track, dance studio, fitness center, outdoor track, softball field and tennis courts. Saint Joseph College has a beautiful residential campus in the active town of West Hartford. Approximately 75 percent of the first-year students in The Women's College live on campus. Special student services include career planning, alumni mentoring, internship placement, counseling, health services, academic advisement and campus ministry. Saint Joseph College alumni have great impact on their communities; they are leaders in the fields of aerospace research, business, education, environmental science, law, medicine and politics. SJC is proud of its first doctoral program in pharmacy (pending accreditation). The chemistry program is accredited by the American Chemical Society, and the social work program is accredited by the Council on Social Work Education. The coordinated undergraduate program in dietetics is accredited by the American

Dietetic Association. The nursing program is accredited by the Commission on Collegiate Nursing Education. The College is located in suburban West Hartford, 4 miles from the state capitol. Among the nearby attractions are the XL Center and Coliseum, Bushnell Performing Arts Center and the Wadsworth Atheneum (the oldest public art gallery in the United States). Hartford is also home to the Tony Award-winning Hartford Stage Company, the Hartford Symphony Orchestra, the Connecticut Opera Company, the Hartford Ballet and the Dodge Music Center, which holds indoor and outdoor concerts.

CONTACT INFORMATION

Office of Admissions

☎ 866-442-8752 or toll-free 866-442-8752

🖥 admissions@sjc.edu

Students step out to West Hartford Center, just minutes from campus, to enjoy coffee bars, boutiques, restaurants and a state-of-the-art movie theater in the newly built Blue Back Square.

- **Enrollment:** *1,935*
- **Test scores:** *SAT—critical reading over 500, 40%; SAT—math over 500, 44%*
- **Application deadline:** *Rolling (freshmen), rolling (transfer)*
- **Expenses:** *Tuition $27,202; Room & Board $12,437*

Students at SJC benefit from working with engaging faculty in small classes that promote discussion-based learning in an academically rigorous program.

Through the applications of nanotechnology, Professor Christine Broadbridge introduces Southern Physics students to the microcomponents driving modern technology.

Southern Connecticut State University

NEW HAVEN, CONNECTICUT
www.southernct.edu/

The academic and social environment at Southern Connecticut State University encourages students to discover who they are, who they want to be and how to realize their dreams. This public, coed university offers 117 undergraduate and graduate programs, fascinating internships, unique research opportunities, a challenging faculty and an energetic campus. Southern has six academic schools: Arts and Sciences; Business; Education; Communication, Information and Library Sciences; Health and Human Services, including nursing, public health, recreation and leisure studies and social work; and Graduate Studies. Southern offers several honors programs for highly motivated students. The Honors College is a four-year alternative program featuring team-taught interdisciplinary courses, symposia and a written thesis. The Office of Student Supportive Services provides tutoring support and includes services and programs for veterans, international students and students with learning, physical and emotional/psychiatric disabilities. The student body represents diverse ethnic and socio-economic groups; students from thirty-eight states and thirty-nine countries enroll at Southern. Students live on campus in eight modern residence halls and town-houses. Competitive athletes and eager amateurs enjoy the unique sports programs at Southern. Intramural and club sports include coed basketball, cheerleading, flag football, coed floor hockey, a golf tournament, ice hockey (men), karate, rugby (men and women), skiing and snowboarding, coed softball, Ultimate Frisbee, coed soccer, a tennis tournament, Wiffle ball and coed volleyball. A member of the National Collegiate Athletic Association (NCAA), the Eastern College Athletic Conference and the Northeast-10 Conference, Southern has a long tradition of athletic excellence. It ranks among the top ten NCAA Division II colleges

and universities with its nine NCAA team championships and sixty-seven individual championships. Southern offers intercollegiate competition in men's baseball, basketball, cross-country, football, soccer, swimming and track and field. Southern holds six national championships in men's soccer and three in men's gymnastics. Intercollegiate programs for women include basketball, cross-country, field hockey, gymnastics, lacrosse, soccer, softball, swimming, track and field and volleyball. Outstanding facilities are available to all athletes in Moore Fieldhouse, Pelz Gymnasium and the Jess Dow Field outdoor sports complex. New Haven, Connecticut, is a sophisticated city of 130,000 people and a classic college town; about 35,000 students attend its half-dozen universities

Student life at Southern integrates classroom learning with extracurricular experience to foster a climate in which each student can achieve higher levels of intellectual, personal, and social growth.

CONTACT INFORMATION

Ms. Paula Kennedy, Associate Director of Admissions

☎ 203-392-5651

✉ joyners2@southernct.edu

and colleges. Only 75 miles from New York City and 3 hours from Boston, New Haven provides students with easy access to movies, restaurants, clubs, concerts, seaside activities, sports, museums and world-famous theater at the Yale Repertory, the Shubert and Long Wharf.

- **Enrollment:** *11,815*
- **Selectivity:** *moderately difficult*
- **Test scores:** *SAT—critical reading over 500, 39.2%; SAT—math over 500, 41.4%*
- **Application deadline:** *4/1 (freshmen), 8/1 (transfer)*
- **Expenses:** *Tuition $8050; Room & Board $9983*

The Quad is a beautiful, park-like gathering space for faculty and staff alike.

WESTERN CONNECTICUT STATE UNIVERSITY

DANBURY, CONNECTICUT
www.wcsu.edu/

Western Connecticut State University (WestConn) provides its students with a high-quality education and a memorable campus experience—all at an affordable cost. With programs in the arts and sciences, business and professional studies, this accredited university offers degrees through its five progressive schools. The most popular majors include communication, theater arts, education, business, justice and law administration, music and nursing. The Ancell School of Business offers the Master of Business Administration, Master of Health Administration and Master of Science in justice administration. The School of Arts and Sciences offers the Master of Arts in biological and environmental sciences, earth and planetary

CONNECTICUT

sciences, English, history and mathematics; the Master of Fine Arts is offered in professional writing. The School of Professional Studies offers the Master of Science in counselor education, elementary education, nursing and secondary education; also offered is WestConn's Doctor of Education (Ed.D.) in instructional leadership. WestConn's newly formed School of Visual and Performing Arts offers the Master of Fine Arts in visual arts and the Master of Music Education. The University also is rich with a number of learning and social activities beyond the classroom. Students run academic clubs and fraternities, publish an award-winning newspaper and yearbook and operate a radio station. They stage theater and musical productions, participate in cooperative education and internship programs and administer their own campus government association. The University provides services for learning-disabled students, study abroad, a University Scholars program and international students. A variety of NCAA Division III men's and women's sports are represented on campus. Students enjoy intramural sports and a premier recreation center that includes a swimming pool, an indoor track and weight-lifting machines. The campus also features a child-care center, a counseling center and campus ministries. WestConn offers two campuses in Danbury, in the heart of western Connecticut, as well as a satellite campus in Waterbury. Danbury is a major city in the foothills of the Berkshire Mountains, just 65 miles north of Manhattan and 50 miles west of Hartford. In Danbury, the 34-acre Midtown campus has an interesting mix of old and new architecture, and it offers easy access to entertainment, restaurants and shopping. The 364-acre Westside campus is ideal for hikers and nature buffs who want to explore the outdoors while enjoying state-of-the-art facilities. The WestConn-at-Waterbury campus offers a convenient location closer to the center of the state, with

CONTACT INFORMATION

Office of University Admissions

☎ 203-837-9000 or toll-free 877-837-WCSU

🖳 admissions@wcsu.edu

the same level of excellent service.

- **Enrollment:** *6,617*
- **Selectivity:** *moderately difficult*
- **Test scores:** *SAT—critical reading over 500, 50%; SAT—math over 500, 48%*
- **Application deadline:** *Rolling (transfer)*
- **Expenses:** *Tuition $7909; Room only $5858*

Fairfield Hall is a residence hall on the university's historic midtown campus.

Engaged. Respected. Connected. American University faculty bring the best of Washington, D.C., and the world to their students.

AMERICAN UNIVERSITY
WASHINGTON, DC

WASHINGTON, D.C.
www.american.edu/

At American University (AU), students learn from award-winning authors, policymakers, artists, researchers, filmmakers, lawyers, scientists and journalists. AU faculty members are committed teachers, and 94 percent have the highest degree in their fields. Here, students achieve the necessary balance between theory and practice with the nation's capital serving as their laboratory for learning. An AU education is more than just what students learn—it's what they do with that knowledge. Undergraduates at AU are active citizens and strive to serve the world around them via hands-on research, internships, community service and study abroad. Hailing from across the United States and more than 140 countries, AU students share a desire to shape tomorrow's world. AU actively promotes international understanding; this is reflected in the University's curriculum, its faculty research and the regular presence of world leaders on campus. AU students enjoy the convenience of EagleBuck$, a cashless way to pay on and off campus at the area's most popular businesses. A prepaid, stored-value account that is part of the AU identification card, EagleBuck$ are an easy way for students to buy food and services 24 hours a day. Almost all first-year students and a majority of all students live in on-campus housing. The University's seven smoke-free residence halls have been recently renovated and offer single-sex or coed floors and special interest options, such as an honors floor. Most rooms house 2 students and have two complete sets of furniture and computer network and telephone access points. AU has implemented a fully computerized laundry service called eSUDS. Students can

use a Web application to check if washers and dryers are available in the nearest laundry room. Students activate and pay for laundry service by swiping their student ID card. When the wash or dry cycle is complete, the student receives notification via e-mail or text message. Students also have a variety of meal plans from which to choose. AU has a main dining room close to the residence halls as well as many small cafes. On-campus restaurants include Subway, McDonald's and Einstein Bros. Bagels. Fraternities and sororities, more than 200 student-run organizations, NCAA Division I championship athletics and intramural sports offer students countless ways to get involved. American University is located in the residential "Embassy Row" neighborhood of Washington, D.C. where students enjoy a safe, suburban environment with easy access to Washington's various cultural highlights via the Metrorail subway system.

Representing all 50 states and 140 countries, American University students bring views from every angle and perspective.

- **Enrollment:** *6,648*
- **Selectivity:** *very difficult*
- **Test scores:** *ACT—over 18, 100%; SAT—critical reading over 500, 97%; SAT—math over 500, 95%*
- **Application deadline:** *1/15 (freshmen), 3/1 (transfer)*
- **Expenses:** *Tuition $36,697; Room & Board $13,468*

CONTACT INFORMATION

Greg Grauman, Director of Admissions

✉ admissions@american.edu

BARRY UNIVERSITY

MIAMI SHORES, FLORIDA
www.barry.edu/

Why choose Barry University? Its students will tell you because here they experience a high-quality education in a caring environment with a religious dimension. Classes are small (14:1), so students receive personal attention from faculty members. The palm-tree lined main campus featuring Spanish-style architecture is in Miami Shores. The University also offers adult and continuing education programs at more than twenty-five additional sites from South Miami to Tallahassee. Students come from all age groups, ethnicities and faiths, representing nearly all fifty states and close to 120 countries. Barry offers more than sixty undergraduate majors and more than fifty graduate degree programs in the arts and sciences, business, education, health sciences, human performance and leisure sciences, law, podiatric medicine and social work. Some are five-year bachelor's-to-master's programs. Barry's resident students live in eight air-conditioned residence halls and three apartment buildings. Each room includes cable and high-speed Internet access. All students may keep cars on campus. Barry holds membership in

Find yourself at Barry University in Miami Shores, Florida, the second-largest Catholic university in the Southeast. Our tropical campus is a few miles from the ocean and the dynamic city of Miami.

twenty honor societies and hosts more than sixty student organizations, including the dance club, gospel choir, the Campus Activities Board, and the student newspaper as well as fraternities and sororities. Barry also encourages community service through programs including Best Buddies, Habitat for Humanity, Alternative Spring Break and Pals-4-Paws animal rescue. The 78,000-square-foot R. Kirk Landon Student Union houses offices for student services and organizations as well as a bookstore, dining room, snack bar and game room. A fully equipped fitness center features state-of-the-art weight and cardio equipment. The University fields twelve intercollegiate teams that participate in the NCAA Division II and the Sunshine State Conference. The Buccaneers have won seven national championships and nearly 60 percent of Barry's student-athletes achieve grade point averages above 3.0. Intramural sports include basketball, flag football, soccer, softball and table tennis. Barry University is located just 5 miles from the ocean and minutes from Miami. Area highlights include Urban Beach Week, the Calle Ocho street festival, the Miami International Book Fair and the Art Basel Miami Beach contemporary art festival. South Florida also hosts the Miami Dolphins football team, the Miami Heat basketball team, the Florida Marlins baseball team and the Florida Panthers hockey team. Students at Barry University enjoy year-round swimming, sailing, scuba diving, golf, tennis, soccer and other outdoor activities and the natural beauty of the Florida Keys and the Everglades are just a day trip away.

CONTACT INFORMATION

Ms. Magda Castineyra, Director of Undergraduate Admissions

☎ 305-899-3100 or toll-free 800-695-2279

🖳 admissions@mail.barry.edu

- **Enrollment:** *8,846*
- **Selectivity:** *moderately difficult*
- **Test scores:** *ACT—over 18, 77%; SAT—critical reading over 500, 37%; SAT—math over 500, 35%*
- **Application deadline:** *Rolling (freshmen), rolling (transfer)*
- **Expenses:** *Tuition $25,500; Room & Board $8486*

At Barry, learning comes from everything around you. We offer more than 50 bachelor's degrees, an honor program, study abroad opportunities, and personal career counseling to prepare you for the future you want.

Apartments with appliances (including washer/dryer) are conveniently located next to Main Street restaurants, shops, and classes.

BEACON
COLLEGE

LEESBURG, FLORIDA
www.beaconcollege.edu/

Beacon College offers innovative academic programs exclusively for students with learning disabilities (LD), attention-deficit hyperactivity disorder (ADHD) or gifted LD. Students are not defined by their learning disabilities—they are people with interests, concerns and wishes about what they want to do during college and beyond. Beacon offers a fun, supportive atmosphere that aids in academic success, recognizes personal accomplishments and fosters lifelong friendships. Beacon combines educational support services with a student life program geared toward the social and intellectual development of students. New technologies enable students to manage many problems inherent with learning disabilities. Students receive proactive academic mentoring, appropriate test accommodations and a variety of classroom teaching techniques. The College also provides support services outside the classroom through the Writing Center, field placement opportunities in all majors as well as an emphasis on small classes and supplemental instruction from outstanding faculty and academic advisers. Out-of-the-classroom experiences are key to the personal development of well-rounded students. Activities include global/cultural awareness events, social outings, health and wellness programs, leadership education and community service. The College hosts on- and off-campus activities that include outdoor/nature experiences, sporting events, cultural/ethnic festivals, musical and arts entertainment, relationship and leadership building and fitness programs. The Beacon Activities Council, along with the Coordinator of Student Activities, schedules cocurricular activities. The activities calendar is available online and updated regularly. In addition, the Student Services Office maintains a current list of all student-run organizations and encourages the start-up of new clubs. The unique housing system allows students to live in apartment-style facilities and develop independent living skills while attending college. The Beacon Village Apartments are equipped with a full-size kitchen, a washer/dryer, television and Internet access. The complex is within walking distance of the education building and all campus buildings. Recreational highlights include a swimming pool, a basketball court, a tennis/volleyball court and a gazebo. Situated in the city of Leesburg, Beacon College is approximately 50 miles northwest of Orlando. Central Florida is one of the most beautiful and popular vacation destinations in the state—at Beacon, students are within minutes of the theme parks of nearby Orlando and Tampa. Central Florida is also known for its outdoor activities and wildlife, with more than 550 freshwater lakes, making it an ideal spot for anglers, boaters, water-skiers, bicyclists, hikers, bird watchers and nature buffs.

CONTACT INFORMATION

Ms. Celia Corrad, Coordinator of Admissions

☎ 352-787-7660

✉ ccorrad@beaconcollege.edu

- **Enrollment:** *128*
- **Selectivity:** *minimally difficult*
- **Application deadline:** *Rolling (freshmen), rolling (transfer)*
- **Expenses:** *Tuition $28,710; Room & Board $8150*

Small classes build students' self-esteem.

EMBRY-RIDDLE
Aeronautical University™

DAYTONA BEACH, FLORIDA
www.embryriddle.edu/

With the nation's first and only Ph.D. program in aviation, Embry-Riddle Aeronautical University is clearly a worldwide leader in aviation and aerospace education. The University, which dates back almost to the time of the Wright brothers, offers programs in aviation, aerospace, engineering, business and related fields. Residential campuses in Daytona Beach, Florida, and Prescott, Arizona, provide education in a traditional setting, while the Worldwide Campus provides instruction through more than 170 centers in the United States, Europe, Canada and the Middle East as well as through online learning. Embry-Riddle's premier aeronautical science (professional pilot) program and award-winning aerospace engineering program are the largest on campus and among the largest of their type in the nation. Embry-Riddle conducts applied research valued at approximately $10 million per year, and is leading the development of the Next Generation Air Transportation System along with the Federal Aviation Administration, Lockheed Martin, Boeing and other high-tech organizations. Alumni are leaders in aviation and aerospace industries and serve as a strong network and resource for students. At the Daytona Beach campus, students enjoy activities and clubs focused on aviation and aerospace, as well as fraternities, sororities and recreational sports. Embry-Riddle's award-winning precision flight demonstration teams compete nationally in air and ground events. Embry-Riddle also has the largest all-volunteer Air Force ROTC detachment in the country and among the fastest-growing Navy ROTC units and Army ROTC battalions. Embry-Riddle athletes participate in

Embry-Riddle is recognized worldwide as the leader in aviation and aerospace education. Our state-of-the-art facilities, including our fleet of 60+ aircraft, prepare our grads for a variety of careers.

FLORIDA

intercollegiate and intramural sports including baseball, basketball, crew, cross-country, golf, soccer, tennis, volleyball and ice hockey. The 68,000-square-foot ICI Center contains two full-size NCAA basketball courts, a fitness center and a weight room. The University sports complex also includes a soccer field, the Sliwa Stadium ballpark, the Ambassador William Crotty Tennis Center and the Track and Field Complex. The Tine Davis Fitness Center is adjacent to the pool and features fitness services and wellness programs. The 5,300-square-foot interfaith chapel has a 140-seat nondenominational worship area and four prayer rooms (Catholic, Jewish, Muslim and Protestant). The year-round clear flying weather surrounding Daytona Beach offers an excellent environment in which to study and fly. The campus, which is located adjacent to the Daytona Beach International Airport, is only 3 miles from

what is called the world's most famous beach. The high-technology industries located in nearby Orlando provide Embry-Riddle students with an outstanding support base. In addition, the Kennedy Space Center is less than a 2-hour drive away.

- **Enrollment:** *4,935*
- **Selectivity:** *moderately difficult*
- **Test scores:** *ACT—over 18, 92%; SAT—critical reading over 500, 63%; SAT—math over 500, 74%*

CONTACT INFORMATION

Mr. Robert J. Adams, Director of Undergraduate Admissions

☎ 386-226-6100 or toll-free 800-862-2416

🖨 dbadmit@erau.edu

- **Application deadline:** *Rolling (freshmen), 5/1 (transfer)*
- **Expenses:** *Tuition $29,724; Room & Board $8840*

http://bit.ly/collvid37

Ranked as one of the top engineering schools by U.S. News and World Report, the curriculum allows students to gain hands-on experience working in teams on complex projects.

Captain of the Florida Tech Surf Team (#1 in Florida in 2010) leading the team to the nationals; making waves is part of our campus culture.

Florida Institute of Technology
High Tech with a Human Touch™

MELBOURNE, FLORIDA
www.fit.edu/

Founded in 1958 by visionary physicist Jerome P. Keuper for area professionals working on the U.S. space program, Florida Institute of Technology got its start with an initial donation of 37 cents. Today, Florida Tech offers more than 130 bachelor's, master's and doctoral degree programs in science and engineering, aviation, business, humanities, psychology, education and communication. The only independent technological university in the southeastern United States, Florida Tech offers hands-on and technology-focused majors and unique personal and professional opportunities. More than 100 student organizations represent the interests of Florida Tech's students and include student government; fraternities and sororities; political and religious groups; radio and television stations; dance, music, science fiction, choral and theater performance; and academic organizations. Florida Tech competes in fifteen NCAA Division ll intercollegiate sports. Women's teams include basketball, cross-country, golf, rowing, soccer, softball, tennis and volleyball. Men's teams include baseball, basketball, cross-country, golf, rowing, soccer and tennis. The Panthers have earned regional titles in baseball, men's soccer and women's basketball; and Sunshine State Conference championships in men's soccer, men's and women's cross-country, men's and women's basketball and women's rowing. Florida Tech is listed as a *Barron's Guide* "Best Buy" in college education. The University was also ranked as a "Best Southeastern College" by the *Princeton Review* in 2009–10. Alumni surveys of recent Florida Tech graduates report a 97 percent placement rate in jobs, graduate schools or military service within six months of graduation. Of those employed, 99 percent work in a field related to their major and 68 percent earn starting salaries of over $50,000. Florida Tech is located along the Atlantic coastline of central Florida, better known as the Space Coast. Situated within Florida's High Tech Corridor, it is home to Kennedy Space Center and the United Space Alliance. The area has the nation's fourth-largest high-tech workforce and supports hundreds of high-tech companies. The surrounding natural resources are ideal for scientific research, including the estuarine habitats of the Indian River Lagoon, the Atlantic Ocean marine ecosystem, beaches and wetlands, thousands of acres of protected wildlife habitats and a variety of tropical/sub-tropical Gulf Stream weather phenomena. With the Indian River Lagoon and the Atlantic Ocean less than 5 miles from the campus, students enjoy swimming, sailing, surfing, diving, fishing and boating year-round. Central Florida attractions such as Walt Disney World are within a 1-hour drive and Miami is only 3 hours from campus.

Looking further: Students work with Florida Tech's Ortega Telescope, the largest research-grade telescope in Florida.

- **Enrollment:** *8,227*
- **Selectivity:** *moderately difficult*
- **Test scores:** *ACT—over 18, 98%; SAT—critical reading over 500, 77%; SAT—math over 500, 87%*
- **Application deadline:** *Rolling (freshmen), rolling (transfer)*
- **Expenses:** *Tuition $31,520; Room & Board $10,630*

CONTACT INFORMATION

Michael J. Perry, Director of Undergraduate Admission

☎ 321-674-8030 or toll-free 800-888-4348

🖳 admission@fit.edu

FLORIDA SOUTHERN COLLEGE

LAKELAND, FLORIDA
www.flsouthern.edu/

The oldest private college in the state, Florida Southern College today is a nationally ranked, coed college. Students choose Florida Southern because of its reputation for hands-on learning and guaranteed internships and study abroad. The atmosphere is friendly and personal, with a close-knit student body and faculty. All members of the academic community take pride in the beautiful campus, a historic landmark and home to the world's largest single-site collection of buildings designed by renowned architect Frank Lloyd Wright. Students live in contemporary on-campus housing, including the state-of-the-art Barnett Residential Life Center, which features stunning views of Lake Hollingsworth; modern student lounges, kitchens and bathrooms; and wireless Internet access. The George Jenkins Field House, which seats 3,000, includes a three-court gymnasium, a weight room and an athletic training room. Facilities for tennis, racquetball, dance, swimming and waterskiing are available at the Nina B. Hollis Wellness Center, which offers a fully

Guaranteed internships enable our students to land great jobs upon graduation. Merrill-Lynch, ESPN, Lockheed Martin, and Walt Disney World are among the companies who pursue FSC graduates.

equipped fitness center, an aerobics/dance studio, an intramural gymnasium, an Olympic swimming pool and a wide-screen TV/lounge area. There are branches of seven national Greek fraternities and seven national Greek sororities on campus. Popular student activities include intercollegiate and intramural sports, drama and music groups, publications and more than seventy clubs and organizations of academic, political, religious and social interest. Most students are involved in volunteer programs and internships in the surrounding community, statewide and internationally. Florida Southern's campus sits on approximately 100 acres on the shore of Lake Hollingsworth in Lakeland, Florida, a dynamic suburban community of about 120,000 residents in the heart of Florida's high-tech corridor. The campus is within walking or biking distance of Lakeland's historic downtown, and is just 45 minutes from Tampa and an hour from Orlando. With its proximity to Walt Disney World as well as gorgeous beaches, the College is ideally situated for internships and job opportunities with leading corporations that tap into one of the largest markets in the United States.

- **Enrollment:** *2,059*

- **Selectivity:** *moderately difficult*

- **Test scores:** *ACT—over 18, 100%; SAT—critical reading over 500, 71%; SAT—math over 500, 67%*

CONTACT INFORMATION

Mr. Bill C. Langston, Director of Admissions

☎ 863-680-4131 or toll-free 800-274-4131

🖥 fscadm@flsouthern.edu

- **Application deadline:** *3/1 (freshmen), rolling (transfer)*

- **Expenses:** *Tuition $24,662; Room & Board $8310*

http://bit.ly/collvid40

With sunshine 330 days per year and beautiful Lake Hollingsworth just steps away, Florida Southern students have unlimited opportunities to enjoy the great outdoors.

Students celebrate Civility Week.

Lynn University

BOCA RATON, FLORIDA
www.lynn.edu/

Lynn University is a private, liberal arts university that offers an innovative and individualized approach to learning. Specialized programs include a Conservatory of Music, a School of Aeronautics and the Institute for Achievement and Learning, which is a pioneer in developing successful teaching strategies for students with learning differences. Lynn's five colleges and two schools offer twenty-eight undergraduate majors as well as four master's degrees representing eight majors. A doctoral program in educational leadership began in fall 2009. The campus offers wireless coverage for classrooms, labs, residence halls, the library and other public spaces. All residence halls include study and computer lounges. Campus recreation areas include two pools, athletic fields, tennis and basketball courts, outdoor grills, a sand volleyball court and a newly remodeled fitness center.

The Lynn Student Center houses an auditorium and a snack bar with flat screen TVs and pool tables. Christine's, an on-campus coffee bar, serves Starbucks coffee, smoothies and snacks. The campus also has a newly renovated library, a concert hall and an international student center. The 750-seat Keith C. and Elaine Johnson Wold Performing Arts Center opened in spring 2010 and is the main venue for the world-renowned Lynn University Conservatory of Music. As a learning-centered community, Lynn University expects students to embrace decision-making and leadership opportunities that will translate into the workplace. Lynn has more than thirty-five campus organizations including student government and Greek life as well as a Leadership Academy. The career center's services include vocational and personality testing, a mentoring program and internship placements. Alumni receive lifetime job placement assistance. Lynn also has a top-ranked NCAA athletic program, which has earned nineteen national championships, twenty-five Sunshine State Conference championships and three NCAA coaches of the year. Lynn University has had ninety-five Academic/Scholar All-America honors in its history. The Fighting Knights intercollegiate athletic program includes men's and women's basketball, golf, soccer and tennis; men's baseball; and women's softball and volleyball. Located on Florida's southeastern coast, the Lynn campus is only 50 minutes from Miami, 30 minutes from West Palm Beach and 30 minutes from Fort Lauderdale. Because of its location in the heart of one of the world's leading business, sports, media and hospitality industry centers, Lynn students benefit from a wide variety of internship opportunities. The 123-acre campus sits three miles from the Atlantic Ocean and only a few minutes from first-class shopping and restaurants.

CONTACT INFORMATION

Juan Camilo Tamayo, Director of Undergraduate Admissions

☎ 561-237-7304 or toll-free 800-888-5966

✉ jtamayo@lynn.edu

- **Enrollment:** *2,224*
- **Selectivity:** *moderately difficult*
- **Test scores:** *ACT—over 18, 67.91%; SAT—critical reading over 500, 37.46%; SAT—math over 500, 40.72%*
- **Application deadline:** *Rolling (freshmen), rolling (transfer)*
- **Expenses:** *Tuition $30,100; Room & Board $10,900*

One-on-one attention from faculty is a hallmark of Lynn University.

While New College students are devoted to their studies, they also know how to live fully.

NEW COLLEGE OF FLORIDA

SARASOTA, FLORIDA

www.ncf.edu/

New College of Florida offers serious students the opportunity to study in an environment designed to promote in-depth thinking and the free exchange of ideas. Study is focused in the arts and sciences and is accelerated and independent. Nearly two thirds of the College's graduates go on to graduate or professional study at Harvard, Yale, MIT, Brown, Georgetown and Berkeley. The College's national reputation was further enhanced in 2001 when New College was designated as the official honors college in the arts and sciences for the State University System of Florida. Students at New College receive a private honors college experience at a public college cost. As a result, the College is regularly featured in guidebooks as being among the nation's leading educational values. First-year and second-year students must live on campus, but many continuing students choose to live on campus as well. In fact, five state-of-the-art residence halls opened in the fall of 2007 and they all incorporate the latest in green building technology. Architecture for the new buildings complements the existing dorms, such as the historic Pei Residence Halls, which were designed by architect I. M. Pei in the 1960s. The 131-room Pei complex has rooms with individual entrances, private baths, central air and combinations of large picture windows, sliding glass doors and/or balconies. The Dort and Goldstein Residence Halls provide apartment-style housing with four single rooms, two bathrooms and a common living room and kitchenette in each unit. New College student life is informal. The College's 110-acre bay front location on the Gulf of Mexico includes basketball, racquetball, tennis, and volleyball courts;

a multipurpose soccer and athletic field; a running trail; a 25-meter swimming pool; and a full fitness center. Sailboats, sailboards and canoes are also available for students and faculty free of charge. Situated along the Gulf of Mexico in southwest Florida, New College is located 50 miles south of Tampa in Sarasota, which is noted for its beautiful white-sand beaches and professional theater, art and music venues. Notably, New College sits adjacent to the world-famous John and Mable Ringling Museum of Art, which offers students free entry to view its Baroque and Renaissance art collections. Within the city, buses link the campus to shopping malls, parks and beaches but most students at New College simply hop on their bikes. The College's Office of Student Affairs offers group outings on a regular basis to the Sarasota Downtown Farmers Market and other spots around town.

Our students enjoy a healthy balance of academics and extracurricular activities.

- **Enrollment:** *825*

- **Selectivity:** *very difficult*

- **Test scores:** *ACT—over 18, 100%; SAT—critical reading over 500, 100%; SAT—math over 500, 99%*

- **Application deadline:** *4/15 (freshmen), 4/15 (transfer)*

- **Expenses:** *Tuition $4784; Room & Board $7783*

CONTACT INFORMATION

Office of Admissions

☎ 941-487-5000

✉ admissions@ncf.edu

SAINT LEO, FLORIDA
www.saintleo.edu/

Saint Leo University gives its students an education that prepares them for the future. The goal of the University is to develop the whole person, both academically and personally, by providing a values-based education in the Benedictine tradition. In a recent satisfaction survey, 95 percent of Saint Leo graduates said they would recommend Saint Leo to a friend. Nontraditional students take advantage of Saint Leo's weekend and evening program for working adults and traditional students earn undergraduate and graduate degree programs through seventeen education centers in seven states and through the Center for Online Learning, which houses the University's cutting-edge online degree programs. In addition to associate and bachelor's degrees, Saint

Students from all walks of life come together to study and live in a dynamic and supportive community.

Leo University offers a Master of Business Administration (M.B.A.) degree; a Master of Education (M.Ed.) degree; a Master of Science (M.S.) degree in criminal justice, critical incident management and instructional design; a Master of Arts (M.A.) degree in theology; a Master of Social Work (M.S.W.); and an education specialist degree. Students can participate in the nationally recognized honors program and the more than fifty different clubs and organizations on campus, including national fraternities and sororities. Many Saint Leo students catch movies, concerts, art exhibits, lectures, dances and other special events throughout the year. Saint Leo is a member of the Sunshine State Conference and competes in NCAA Division II intercollegiate athletics for men and women. Men's sports include baseball, basketball, cross-country, golf, lacrosse, soccer, swimming and tennis. Women compete in basketball, cross-country, golf, soccer, softball, swimming, tennis and volleyball. The campus has lighted racquetball and tennis courts; soccer, baseball and softball fields; a weight room/fitness center; and a heated outdoor Olympic-sized swimming pool. The campus is bordered by a 154-acre lake and an eighteen-hole golf course. Saint Leo is located 35 minutes north of Tampa and 90 minutes west of Orlando. The lakeside campus occupies 186 acres of rural rolling hills and wooded grounds, but the University is located near enough to metropolitan areas for students seeking internship opportunities or a night out.

CONTACT INFORMATION

Ms. Christine O'Donnell, Associate Director for Enrollment

☎ 352-588-8283 or toll-free 800-334-5532

✉ admissions@saintleo.edu

- **Enrollment:** *4,127*
- **Selectivity:** *moderately difficult*
- **Test scores:** *ACT—over 18, 98%; SAT—critical reading over 500, 44%; SAT—math over 500, 50%*
- **Application deadline:** *8/15 (freshmen), 8/1 (transfer)*
- **Expenses:** *Tuition $17,646; Room & Board $8724*

The Saint Leo experience...you'll love the person you become here.

An intentionally Christian university, Shorter stands at the intersection where faith meets learning. Shorter's aim is to help students become fully prepared to embrace God's plan for their lives.

Shorter University

ROME, GEORGIA
www.shorter.edu/

Shorter University combines a high-quality education with an intentionally Christian atmosphere. The University is a pioneer in both traditional semester programs and innovative continuous programs for working adults. And Shorter is proud of its statistics—an overall graduate school acceptance rate of 80 percent and an impressive 82 percent acceptance rate to medical colleges over the past twenty-one years. Each year, the campus is visited by Christian leaders, scholars and outstanding musicians. The dean of the chapel works together with the campus minister to provide a wide range of opportunities for spiritual growth. The largest religious organization on campus is the Baptist Collegiate Ministries (BCM), which includes Christians of many denominations. Student publications include a newspaper, a yearbook and a literary magazine. Music and drama groups take center stage at Shorter. They include the Shorter Chorale, the Shorter Chorus, the Shorter Theater Company, the Opera Workshop and the Shorter Marching Band. The Shorter Chorale was selected to represent the United States in choral festivals held in Yugoslavia, France and Austria and it performed in St. Petersburg, Russia to represent the University. The Chorale was also selected in 2008 to perform mass at the Vatican during a tour of Italy. Shorter has also been the home of numerous National Metropolitan Opera Audition winners and finalists. The University has three fraternities and three sororities as well as chapters of two national music fraternities and honor societies for majors in biology, communication, English,

music, religion and social sciences. Shorter University is a member of the Southern States Athletic Conference of the NAIA. The University also has a competitive cheerleading program and competes in the Mid-South Conference of the NAIA in football and track and field. Varsity teams compete in men's baseball, basketball, cross-country, football, golf, soccer, tennis and track and field and in women's basketball, cheerleading, cross-country, fast-pitch softball, golf, soccer, tennis, track and field and volleyball. Wrestling and men's and women's lacrosse are scheduled to be added in fall 2010. The University has 150 acres atop Shorter Hill, in Rome, Georgia and is located just 65 miles northwest of

CONTACT INFORMATION

Mr. John Head, Vice President for Enrollment Management

☎ 706-233-7342 or toll-free 800-868-6980

✉ admissions@shorter.edu

Atlanta and 65 miles south of Chattanooga, Tennessee. In Rome, students can enjoy the Symphony Orchestra, Rome Little Theatre, Rome Area Council for the Arts events, popular concerts and attractions at The Forum and the 334,859-volume modern library.

- **Enrollment:** *1,205*
- **Selectivity:** *moderately difficult*
- **Test scores:** *ACT—over 18, 79.5%; SAT—critical reading over 500, 60.5%; SAT—math over 500, 48.4%*
- **Application deadline:** *8/25 (freshmen), 8/25 (transfer)*

Freshmen thrive in Learning Communities that combine 3 core courses around a theme, building connections between classwork and understanding.

WESLEYAN

MACON, GEORGIA

www.wesleyancollege.edu/

Wesleyan College became the world's first college chartered to grant degrees to women. Today, Wesleyan is still dedicated to educating women and is regarded as one of the nation's finest liberal arts colleges. According to the seventh annual report of the National Survey of Student Engagement (NSSE), Wesleyan outperformed the top 10 percent of colleges and universities in all five categories studied: active and collaborative learning, enriching educational experiences, level of academic challenge, student-faculty interaction and supportive campus environment. The acceptance rate of Wesleyan students into medical, law, business and other graduate programs is excellent. Beyond the

Candler Building on the Wesleyan College campus

academic, Wesleyan offers an exciting residence life program, NCAA Division III athletics and a championship IHSA equestrian program. The College's beautiful 200-acre wooded campus, along with thirty historic buildings, is listed in the National Register of Historic Places as the Wesleyan College Historic District. White-columned, Georgian-style buildings surround a classic quadrangle that plays host to many College events. All residence halls have been recently renovated and offer single rooms and suites. Many students take advantage of the state-of-the-art equestrian center as well as the athletic complex (with fitness center, tennis courts, track and lighted softball and soccer fields). Other students hit the gym with heated pool or lace up for a jog on the trail around the lake. The Campus Activities Board plans concert-dance weekends, events with nearby colleges, international fashion shows, holiday trips and special dinners. The Student Recreation Council coordinates competitive activities in basketball, fencing, golf, soccer, softball and swimming. Wesleyan is a member of the National Collegiate Athletic Association (NCAA) Division III. There are intercollegiate basketball, cross-country, soccer, softball, tennis, volleyball and IHSA equestrian teams. The Council on Religious Concerns encourages volunteer work at the Georgia Industrial Children's Home, Macon Outreach, the Methodist Children's Home and neighborhood schools and churches. Wesleyan students also participate in interest clubs, student publications, performing arts groups, honor societies and professional fraternities. Wesleyan is located in a suburb of Macon, the third-largest city in the state, and about an hour's drive south of Atlanta. The city of Macon offers many entertainment opportunities, including the Georgia Music and Sports Halls of Fame. Wesleyan students also enjoy other special events associated with Macon's renowned Cherry Blossom Festival.

CONTACT INFORMATION

Mr. Stephen Farr, Vice President for Enrollment Services

☎ 478-757-3700 or toll-free 800-447-6610

✉ admissions@ wesleyancollege.edu

- **Enrollment:** *671*
- **Selectivity:** *moderately difficult*
- **Test scores:** *ACT—over 18, 97%; SAT—critical reading over 500, 81%; SAT—math over 500, 60%*
- **Application deadline:** *Rolling (freshmen), rolling (transfer)*
- **Expenses:** *Tuition $17,500; Room & Board $8000*

"At first, I was hesitant about an all-women's environment. But I quickly discovered that in a small campus community, there are so many leadership opportunities." —Juliana Cabrales

Students at College of the Atlantic are educated by more than the professors and staff. The engaged and diverse student body offers a wealth of knowledge in and outside of the seminar-based classes.

College of the Atlantic
life changing. world changing.

BAR HARBOR, MAINE
www.coa.edu/

Students at College of the Atlantic learn by doing—recent COA students have created first-in-the nation legislation for Maine, lobbied on the international stage, completed novels and presented independent research at international conferences. Located between the Atlantic Ocean and Acadia National Park, College of the Atlantic offers two degrees: a B.A. and a M.Phil., both in human ecology. In pursuit of this degree, students aim to investigate and improve relationships between humans and our social, natural, built and virtual communities. Seminar-style classes are encouraged. Faculty-student interchanges are as common in the college's dining room as they are during office hours. With one major, there are no departments, education is truly interdisciplinary, and all students design their course of study to suit their academic and personal goals. This unique curriculum has

MAINE

led some to describe COA as a graduate school for undergraduates. COA is also a democratic college, with students involved in all levels of government. Major decisions must be brought to an All-College Meeting; students are involved in most committees. COA has a strong international student presence, with nearly 20 percent of its student body from outside the United States. The College sponsors films, speakers, concerts and dances, and students hold informal parties, musical get-togethers and open mics. COA is located in the town of Bar Harbor on Mount Desert Island, Maine, also home to Acadia National Park. Connected to the mainland by a causeway, the scenic, mountainous island lies 300 miles north of Boston and 40 miles east of Bangor. In the summer, Bar Harbor teems with tourists. When students return in the fall, the traffic reverses direction and Bar Harbor becomes a quiet, coastal village. The Atlantic Ocean and Acadia National Park provide ample

COA's approach to education is centered around experience. Students frequently immerse themselves into the surrounding natural landscape, community organizations, and international destinations.

opportunities for swimming, fishing, canoeing, kayaking, rock climbing, hiking, biking, cross-country skiing and snowshoeing. Cooperative programs with the Jackson Laboratory, the Mount Desert Island Biological Laboratory, the national park and the local public school system broaden the scope of COA's educational activities on the island. The College's two island research stations and 73-acre organic farm expand COA's local resources. A new Trans-Atlantic Partnership in Sustainable Food Systems links College of the Atlantic with an organic research farm in the United Kingdom and a German graduate school.

- **Enrollment:** *341*
- **Selectivity:** *very difficult*
- **Test scores:** *ACT—over 18, 100%; SAT—critical reading over 500, 95%; SAT—math over 500, 78%*
- **Application deadline:** *2/15 (freshmen), 4/1 (transfer)*
- **Expenses:** *Tuition $34,380; Room & Board $8250*

CONTACT INFORMATION

Ms. Sarah Baker, Dean of Admission

☎ 207-801-5640 or toll-free 800-528-0025

✉ inquiry@coa.edu

UMM students enjoy hands-on learning opportunities along the coast of Maine.

THE UNIVERSITY OF MAINE AT
MACHIAS
Naturally!

MACHIAS, MAINE
www.umm.maine.edu/

Where you learn has great impact on what you learn. That's the philosophy of the faculty at the University of Maine at Machias. Located on the spectacular coast of Downeast Maine, the University of Maine at Machias (UMM) is a small, environmental liberal arts university that lends itself to amazing out-of-classroom experiences. Small classes (the average is 17 students) and a faculty-student ratio of 1:13 contribute to an academic atmosphere that is intimate and intense

MAINE

and where independent thinking is encouraged. The University's environmental emphasis, unique programs and desirable location draw students from all parts of the United States. Students come here for courses they won't find anywhere else—Book Arts, Adventure Recreation and Wildlife Biology to name a few. They also enjoy the numerous ways to get involved in clubs and organizations; choices range from Greek life to the Ukulele Club. Machias, Maine, is a classic New England town located on the tidal Machias River, with a town center that includes retail stores, restaurants, a natural foods store and churches of various denominations. The area is a popular outdoor destination because of its ocean beaches, inland lakes and streams and miles of mountains, forests and trails. Downeast Maine has been a source of inspiration for generations of artists, outdoorsmen, mariners and environmentalists. UMM's coastal location offers excellent opportunities for fieldwork, hands-on learning and cooperative education and internship experiences.

CONTACT INFORMATION

Mr. David Dollins, Director of Admissions

☎ 207-255-1318 or toll-free 888-GOTOUMM (in-state); 888-468-6866 (out-of-state)
✉ ummadmissions@maine.edu

- **Enrollment:** *964*
- **Selectivity:** *moderately difficult*
- **Test scores:** *ACT—over 18, 56.5%; SAT—critical reading over 500, 39.1%; SAT—math over 500, 23%*
- **Application deadline:** *8/15 (freshmen), rolling (transfer)*
- **Expenses:** *Tuition $6871; Room & Board $6574*

UMM students can take advantage of the endless opportunities for study and fun that the area provides.

The coastal area of southern Maine is a beautiful, livable part of the country, and the people are friendly and welcoming.

UNIVERSITY OF NEW ENGLAND

BIDDEFORD AND PORTLAND, MAINE
www.une.edu/

Research. Scholarship. Service. Leisure. All are important to students at the University of New England (UNE). Students enroll in more than forty undergrad programs in UNE's four colleges: the College of Arts and Sciences, the Westbrook College of Health Professions, the College of Pharmacy and the College of Osteopathic Medicine (Maine's only medical school). Here, students focus on business management, education, health sciences, the humanities, the natural sciences and social sciences. Internships, co-ops, clinicals and student teaching allow UNE students to apply skills learned in the classroom to real job situations. The University of New England has two campuses. The Biddeford Campus sits on the southern coast of Maine, 90 miles north of Boston and 20 miles south of Portland. UNE's Portland Campus is located in Portland, Maine. In addition to academics, the University encourages students to get involved in activities, clubs and sports. Popular interests include scuba diving, skiing, hiking, biking, swimming, community service programs and photography. The University of New England Athletic Department participates in NCAA Division III varsity sports. Men's teams are basketball, cross-country, golf, lacrosse, soccer and ice hockey. Women's teams are basketball, cross-country, field hockey, lacrosse, soccer, softball, swimming and volleyball. Intramural teams in basketball, floor hockey, softball, skiing and volleyball are popular with students. The Biddeford Campus contains a fitness center, bookstore, gym, pool, racquetball courts and an indoor track. The Harold Alfond Center for Health Sciences has biology and chemistry labs as well as lecture halls, a gross anatomy lab and UNE's medical school facilities. The Marine Science Education and Research Center features wet labs, aquaculture labs and a marine mammal rehabilitation wing. There are three recent additions to the Biddeford campus—the state-of-the-art Pickus Center for Biomedical Research; the Peter and Cecile Morgane Hall with laboratories for biology, chemistry and physics; and the George and Barbara Bush Center where students study and socialize on the outdoor terraces of Windward Cafe. On the Portland Campus, there are two residence halls, the Alexander Hall Student Union, the Finley Recreation Center and Ludcke Auditorium. The new College of Pharmacy building welcomed the first professional pharmacy class in September of 2009. The 540-acre Biddeford Campus sits on a beautiful coastal site where the Saco River flows into the Atlantic Ocean. Located 20 miles to the north is the 41-acre Portland Campus. Students at both campuses can enjoy the social life of nearby Boston or Portland and the dynamic outdoor activities that have made Maine a prime tourist destination.

UNE academic programs ensure that students have plenty of opportunities for extensive fieldwork, clinical experiences, research and internships through University partnerships.

- **Enrollment:** *4,493*

- **Selectivity:** *moderately difficult*

- **Test scores:** *ACT—over 18, 97.87%; SAT—critical reading over 500, 66.78%; SAT—math over 500, 70.76%*

- **Application deadline:** *2/15 (freshmen), rolling (transfer)*

- **Expenses:** *Tuition $27,920; Room & Board $10,870*

CONTACT INFORMATION
Mr. Robert J. Pecchia,
Associate Dean of
Admissions

☎ 207-283-0170 Ext. 2297 or
toll-free 800-477-4UNE
✉ admissions@une.edu

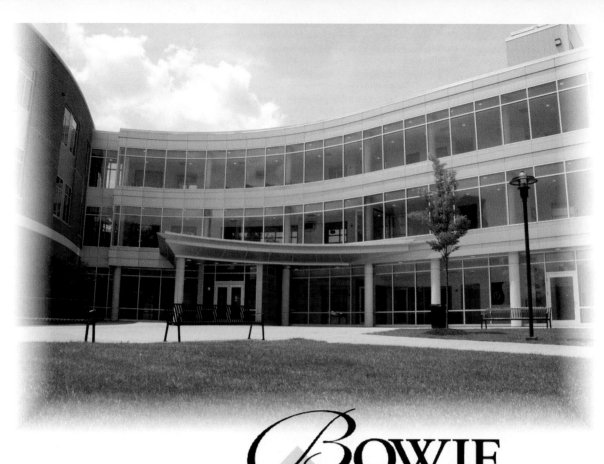

BSU College of Business and Graduate Studies Building

BOWIE STATE UNIVERSITY

BOWIE, MARYLAND
www.bowiestate.edu/

"New" is the key word at Bowie State University. Between campus improvements and the building of new halls and complexes, Bowie State University's physical plant is valued at more than $225 million. The University has twenty-two buildings on its 500-acre campus with the addition of the $21-million state-of-the-art Center for Learning and Technology that opened in 2000, the $11.8-million Computer Science Center that opened in 2002 and the new $19-million Center for Business and Graduate Studies that opened in 2007. The seven residence halls include Goodloe Hall and Alex Haley Hall, a high-tech building that houses honors students. In addition, a 460-bed apartment-style residence hall, Christa McAuliffe, was completed in 2004. The $2.6-million physical education complex houses a 3,000-seat basketball arena, an Olympic-size swimming pool with underwater viewing windows and room for 200 spectators, a dance studio, a wrestling room, a weight-training room, eight handball/squash courts and a therapy room. Bowie State has broken ground for its new $79 million Fine and Performing Arts Center. The 123,000-square-foot building will include a 400-seat main theater, a 200-seat black box theater, a 200-seat recital hall, an art gallery and labs. Bowie State University encourages involvement in the more than forty student activities on campus. These include student government, intercollegiate athletics, eight fraternities and sororities, departmental clubs and preprofessional organizations and music and drama clubs. The Graduate School grants the Master of Arts in counseling psychology, English, human resource development, mental health counseling, organizational communications, school psychology and teaching (M.A.T.); the Master of Business Administration; the Master of Education in elementary education, reading education, school administration and supervision, school counseling, secondary education and special education; the Master of Public Administration; and the Master of Science in applied computational mathematics, computer science, management information systems and nursing. The Doctor of Education is granted in educational leadership and the Applied Doctor of Science is granted in computer science. The Adler-Dreikurs Institute of Human Relations at Bowie State University is the first fully accredited master's-degree-granting Adlerian institute in the United States. Bowie, Maryland, is in a triangle formed by Annapolis (20 miles east), Baltimore (25 miles north) and Washington, D.C. (17 miles southwest). The suburban setting provides an ideal, safe environment for students, with easy access to all of the important and exciting cultural,

CONTACT INFORMATION

Don Kiah, Director of Admissions

☎ 301-860-3415 or toll-free 877-772-6943

🖳 sholt@bowiestate.edu

governmental and business activities in any of the three metropolitan areas.

- **Enrollment:** *5,617*
- **Selectivity:** *minimally difficult*
- **Test scores:** *SAT—critical reading over 500, 21%; SAT—math over 500, 17.7%*
- **Application deadline:** *4/1 (freshmen), 4/1 (transfer)*
- **Expenses:** *Tuition $6040; Room & Board $7536*

BSU Spring graduates

College of Notre Dame
OF MARYLAND

BALTIMORE, MARYLAND
www.ndm.edu/

Innovative change and forward thinking is what sets the College of Notre Dame of Maryland apart from others. Established in 1895, it was the first Catholic college for women to award a four-year degree. In 1972, the College initiated the Continuing Education (CE) program, offering women age 25 and older the opportunity to study and earn bachelor's degrees. In 1975, the Weekend College opened to working students with conveniently scheduled classes. In 1984, Graduate Studies began offering master's programs. In 2003, the College launched its Accelerated College for working professionals, establishing partnerships with business and health-care organizations throughout the area. Most recently, the College created its first doctoral program, a Ph.D. in instructional leadership for changing populations. The College opened its School of Pharmacy in fall 2009. This commitment to its students and their changing needs has not gone unnoticed—College of Notre Dame of Maryland was named to the 2010 "Great Schools, Great Prices" listing published

Tapping your unique gifts is a fulltime undertaking on our beautiful 58-acre suburban campus located in bustling Baltimore, Maryland. At Notre Dame, excellence has no limits.

by *U.S. News & World Report*. Today's students are achievement-oriented and deeply involved in their college and their community. Notre Dame's mission is to educate women as leaders. The English Language Institute (ELI) offers English as a second language and American culture classes. The Renaissance Institute, a noncredit membership program for students age 50 and older, rounds out the College's offerings. Students join many campus groups, including student media, performing arts, service and honor societies. Notre Dame's Gators participate in eight NCAA Division III sports: basketball, field hockey, lacrosse, soccer, softball, swimming, tennis and volleyball. The Marion Burk Knott Sports and Activities Complex has a gym, a fitness center, a dance and exercise studio and several racquetball courts. There also are two residence halls: Doyle Hall for first-year students and sophomores and Mary Meletia Hall for juniors and seniors. The recently renovated Marikle Chapel of the Annunciation is the spiritual center of the campus. Daily masses and special events are held in this beautiful chapel. Located on the North Charles Street college corridor in northern Baltimore, Notre Dame's campus sits on 58 wooded and landscaped acres. The College is just 15 minutes from downtown Baltimore and its Inner Harbor, which features shops and restaurants, the National Aquarium in Baltimore and Maryland Science Center. Annapolis and D.C. are also nearby. Notre Dame is part of the Baltimore Collegetown Network, a group of fifteen colleges that work together to encourage students to participate in social and academic events and programs on one another's campuses.

CONTACT INFORMATION

Sharon Bogdan, Associate Vice President for Enrollment

☎ 410-532-5332 or toll-free
   800-435-0200 (in-state)
   800-435-0300 (out-of-state)
✉ sbogdon@ndm.edu

- **Enrollment:** *2,971*
- **Selectivity:** *moderately difficult*
- **Application deadline:** *2/15 (freshmen), 2/15 (transfer)*
- **Expenses:** *Tuition $28,350; Room & Board $9500*

A sense of community, bonds that form between classmates and with faculty, an atmosphere that encourages you to strive to be your best in all things—these are just some of what sets Notre Dame apart.

One of the highlights of our green, 140-acre campus is "the Beach," a grassy area outside of the library and a popular spot for students to unwind.

JOHNS HOPKINS
U N I V E R S I T Y

BALTIMORE, MARYLAND
www.jhu.edu/

What is it about a place that makes it special? At The Johns Hopkins University (JHU) it's the idea that knowledge should be discovered, rather than merely transmitted. Johns Hopkins stresses creative thinking by providing research-oriented education for undergrads. Students in all majors are encouraged to ask questions and discover new ideas within a supportive environment. Johns Hopkins seeks diversity in its students, who come from all fifty states and from seventy-one other countries. Johns Hopkins has thirteen fraternities and seven sororities in the Inter-Fraternity Council and the Panhellenic Council. The Student Council runs a number of activities, including an annual Spring Fair featuring outdoor concerts, arts and crafts booths, food, carnival rides and exhibits. Men's varsity teams compete in twelve sports. In the fall, it's cross-country, football, soccer and water polo. In the winter, they compete in basketball, fencing, swimming and wrestling. The big sports season at Johns Hopkins is spring, with baseball, lacrosse, tennis and track and field. The men's and women's lacrosse teams compete at the Division I level, and the men have won forty-four national championships. Women's varsity sports also include basketball, cross-country, fencing, field hockey, soccer, swimming, tennis, track and field and volleyball. The O'Connor Recreation Center contains basketball and volleyball courts, a running track, racquetball

courts, a rock-climbing wall, a weight room and fitness and aerobic areas. In addition to the sports programs, there are more than 320 student-run clubs that hold events throughout the year. Johns Hopkins offers the best of both worlds—a quiet campus near an exciting urban area. Two museums are owned by the University: Homewood Museum, on campus, and Evergreen Museum & Library, located nearby on North Charles Street. The Baltimore Museum of Art is on the southwest corner of the campus. The Walters Art Museum, a 10-minute drive away, has a collection that spans civilization from Egypt to the nineteenth century, and many smaller museums, galleries and outdoor show-ings feature local artists. The University is located just three miles from the heart of down-town Baltimore; the theater, symphony and opera are 10 minutes away, as are Oriole Park at Camden Yards and M&T Bank Stadium. Weekend activities include shopping at Harborplace, visiting the National Aquarium, enjoying

At Johns Hopkins, students enjoy small classes in a gorgeous setting but with the resources of a large university.

an ethnic festival by the water, sailing on the Chesapeake Bay and hiking. Washington, D.C. is a 50-minute drive by car or a 1-hour train ride.

- **Enrollment:** *6,782*
- **Selectivity:** *most difficult*
- **Test scores:** *ACT—over 18, 99.79%; SAT—critical reading over 500, 99.12%; SAT—math over 500, 99.6%*
- **Application deadline:** *1/1 (freshmen), 3/15 (transfer)*
- **Expenses:** *Tuition $39,150; Room & Board $12,040*

CONTACT INFORMATION

Dr. John Latting, Dean of Undergraduate Admissions

☎ 410-516-8341
🖷 gotojhu@jhu.edu

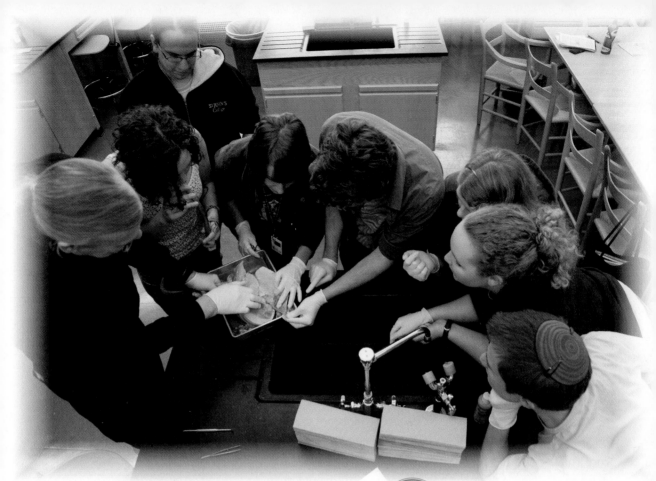

In a freshman laboratory class, students explore the motion of the heart and blood after reading a paper by William Harvey. Students read only original works at St. John's; there are no textbooks.

ST·JOHN'S
College

ANNAPOLIS · SANTA FE

ANNAPOLIS, MARYLAND
www.stjohnscollege.edu/

St. John's College breaks the mold on what students typically expect of a four-year school. For starters, St. John's maintains two widely separated campuses—one in Annapolis, Maryland, and another in Santa Fe, New Mexico. The campuses are alike in curriculum and methods, but their settings and moods are as different as sailing on the Chesapeake Bay and skiing in the Sangre de Cristo Mountains. Each has its own admissions and financial aid offices as well. A common curriculum, however, enables students and faculty members to move from one campus to the other. Students enjoy the small class sizes and the unique course offerings, everything from Ancient Greek to Musical Composition. Students at both campuses also get involved in publications, dance, drama, photography, art and wilderness exploration. The social climate is informal and lively. Facilities are available for almost any intramural sport; most students participate. The students on both campuses are outstanding, yet they fit no pattern. Though their backgrounds are varied geographically, academically and otherwise, they are, most typically, young people who read good books and value good

conversation. Their commitment to ideas and their enthusiasm for the St. John's program are well illustrated by the fact that about one fifth of them on each campus have transferred to St. John's as freshmen after a year or more of college somewhere else. St. John's is the third-oldest college in the United States. It has been located since 1696 in the Colonial seaport city of Annapolis, the capital of Maryland, just 30 miles from Washington, D.C. In 1964, a second campus was opened at the foot of the mountains surrounding Santa Fe, a cultural center and the capital of New Mexico. Students at the Annapolis campus have easy access to boating, sailing and crew, while those at the Sante Fe campus enjoy martial arts, yoga and rafting.

St. John's historic McDowell Hall is characteristic of the colonial architecture on the college's Annapolis campus. The building was originally constructed as a mansion for a colonial governor.

CONTACT INFORMATION

Mr. John Christensen, Director of Admissions

☎ 410-626-2522 or toll-free 800-727-9238

✉ admissions@sjca.edu

- **Enrollment:** *562*
- **Selectivity:** *moderately difficult*
- **Test scores:** *ACT—over 18, 100%; SAT—critical reading over 500, 98%; SAT—math over 500, 97%*
- **Application deadline:** *Rolling (freshmen), rolling (transfer)*
- **Expenses:** *Tuition $42,192; Room & Board $9984*

Mustang fans have a lot to cheer about! Among Stevenson's Division III teams are the nationally top-ranked men's lacrosse team and a new football team which will compete for the first time in 2011.

STEVENSON
UNIVERSITY

Imagine your future. Design your career.®

STEVENSON, MARYLAND
www.stevenson.edu/

Stevenson University (SU) doesn't just focus on the four years students spend on campus. It prepares undergraduates to survive and thrive in the working world after graduation. Stevenson University (SU), formerly Villa Julie College, offers a career-focused, liberal arts education. With a student-faculty ratio of 13:1, it is easy to understand why students often cite the easygoing, personal relationship with

MARYLAND

faculty members as one of the University's strong points. Through Stevenson University's concept of Learning Beyond, students step outside of the classroom to take their learning to the next level. Experiential learning opportunities include study abroad, service learning, field placements and independent research.

In addition, through an approach known as Career Architecture[SM], each student develops a professional career plan based on their values, skills and strengths. Stevenson's graduates maintain a placement rate that tops 95 percent each year, with students landing jobs or going on to graduate school within six months of graduation. At SU, students enjoy more than forty-five clubs and organizations, multiple honor societies and NCAA Division III athletics. The following sports are offered: men's and women's basketball, cross-country, golf, lacrosse, soccer, tennis and volleyball; men's baseball;

At Stevenson, the classroom is only the beginning. From clubs and organizations to opportunities in the performing and visual arts, there is something here for everyone.

and women's field hockey and softball. Cheerleading, dance and intramural sports are also extremely popular. Stevenson will add football in 2010 and will compete as a member of the NCAA in Division III in 2011. In addition to its undergraduate programs, the University offers the following master's degree programs: business and technology management, forensic science and forensic studies. Stevenson University has two beautiful campuses in the heart of Maryland, in Stevenson and Owings Mills. SU students truly appreciate the beauty of a rural campus as well as the convenience and appeal of a more urban setting. The original 60-acre Greenspring Campus sits among the rolling hills in Stevenson,

Maryland. The Owings Mills Campus is a booming center of student activity. Classes are held on both campuses, and the University provides a free shuttle service that runs between the locations.

- **Enrollment:** *3,432*

- **Selectivity:** *moderately difficult*

- **Test scores:** *ACT—over 18, 79.72%; SAT—critical reading over 500, 53.2%; SAT—math over 500, 55.14%*

- **Application deadline:** *Rolling (freshmen), rolling (transfer)*

- **Expenses:** *Tuition $20,644; Room & Board $10,296*

CONTACT INFORMATION

Mr. Mark Hergan, Vice President, Enrollment Management

☎ 410-486-7001 or toll-free 877-468-6852 (in-state) 877-468-3852 (out-of-state)
🖃 admissions@stevenson.edu

Assumption's 2,113 undergraduates enjoy a close-knit, supportive community. Dedicated faculty know the students as individuals, mentor them and encourage them to achieve their full potential.

ASSUMPTION COLLEGE

WORCESTER, MASSACHUSETTS
www.assumption.edu/

Assumption College invites students to define their own success. The College's undergrads choose from thirty-nine majors and forty-four minors, with strong programs in business and professional studies. This traditional, Catholic college encourages students to make the connection between faith and reason. With a student-faculty ratio of just 12:1, Assumption's professors challenge students to ask questions, find their own answers and grow—intellectually, socially and spiritually. Assumption students gain hands-on experience through internships and develop their own research projects. Within six months of graduation, 97 percent of Assumption graduates have jobs or are in graduate school. Assumption is no "suitcase college" either. The campus is alive seven days a week with programming, student-run activities, community service outings, campus ministry programs and intercollegiate, intramural and club sports. The Information Technology Center, completed in 2002, has four computer labs and eight computerized classrooms and offers students free laser printing. All dorms and academic areas are connected wirelessly, as well as public areas like the library and dining hall. The College's state-of-the-art recreation center has racquetball

Assumption is always active—90 percent of the students live on campus. Housing is guaranteed all 4 years. Located in Worcester, Massachusetts, there are many social, cultural and internship opportunities.

courts, a six-lane pool, a new jogging/walking track, an aerobics/dance studio and locker rooms with saunas. The Assumption Greyhounds participate in NCAA Division II and over 50 percent of these players earn 3.0 or greater grade point averages. The 185-acre campus is located in a residential neighborhood just minutes from downtown Worcester, Massachusetts. Worcester, the second largest city in New England, is a classic college town and is home to 30,000 students. Assumption students head off campus to hit great restaurants, shopping spots and professional sports events. Worcester is also centrally located, with

Boston, Providence and Hartford each an hour's drive away.

- **Enrollment:** *2,601*
- **Selectivity:** *moderately difficult*
- **Test scores:** *ACT—over 18, 88.2%; SAT—critical reading over 500, 71.5%; SAT—math over 500, 72.5%*
- **Application deadline:** *2/15 (freshmen), 7/1 (transfer)*
- **Expenses:** *Tuition $30,171; Room & Board $6340*

CONTACT INFORMATION

Ms. Kathleen Murphy, Dean of Enrollment

☎ 508-767-7110 or toll-free 888-882-7786

✉ admiss@assumption.edu

Collaboration and teamwork in a variety of venues are key ingredients to being a Babson student.

BABSON
COLLEGE

WELLESLEY, MASSACHUSETTS
www.babson.edu/

Once again, Babson College has been ranked the #1 college for entrepreneurship by both *U.S. News & World Report* (2010's "Best Colleges in America") and *Entrepreneurship* magazine. Students come to Babson with big ideas of initiating and managing change and solving the problems of today and tomorrow. They leave here as confident, capable business leaders. But entrepreneurship isn't all Babson College has to offer; its twenty-five different concentrations range from Gender Studies to Real Estate. This independent, coed college is a 24-hours-a-day, seven days-a-week community alive with lots to do and see. Students can hit a DJ party in Knight Auditorium, watch a game at Roger's Pub or see a movie at the Sorensen Center. In between studying, students head to the Serenity Room in the Reynolds Campus Center to relax in a massaging chair. Most undergrads live on campus in unique, themed residence halls for students interested in coed halls, fraternity and sorority housing, or substance-free, multicultural or entrepreneurial housing. Babson College is an NCAA Division III school, and most of the College's intercollegiate teams compete in the New England Women's and Men's Athletic Conference (NEWMAC). There are twenty-two men's and women's varsity sports teams, with club and intramural sports open to all students. The Webster Center features an indoor, 200-meter, six-lane track; a field house; a gym with three basketball courts; a racquetball court; a 25-yard, six-lane pool with 1- and 3-meter diving boards; a fitness center; squash courts; and a dance/aerobics studio.

The Babson Skating Center features a 600-seat skating arena. Outdoor, students enjoy the eight tennis courts, a new AstroTurf field, a game field, a renovated softball diamond, a baseball field, two sand-based varsity fields and a club rugby field. Babson's beautiful 370-acre campus is in Wellesley, Massachusetts, 14 miles west of Boston, a city famous for its culture and nightlife. More than sixty colleges and universities bring more than 250,000 college students to the Boston area, making it one of the world's best college towns for diversity and research.

CONTACT INFORMATION

Ms. Adrienne Ramsey, Senior Assistant Director of Undergraduate Admission

☎ 781-239-5522 or toll-free 800-488-3696

✉ ugradadmission@babson.edu

- **Enrollment:** *3,445*
- **Selectivity:** *very difficult*
- **Test scores:** *ACT—over 18, 97%; SAT—critical reading over 500, 95%; SAT—math over 500, 98%*
- **Application deadline:** *1/15 (freshmen), 4/1 (transfer)*
- **Expenses:** *Tuition $37,824; Room & Board $13,500*

http://bit.ly/collvid1

Babson College Undergraduate Dean Dennis Hanno talks with students at the Campus Center.

"I have met so many different people from so many different places and different countries—everybody brings something different, says something different," student, Abdul Samad Sadri.

BARD COLLEGE AT SIMON'S ROCK

THE EARLY COLLEGE

GREAT BARRINGTON, MASSACHUSETTS
www.simons-rock.edu/

Should you have to be 18 years old and finished with your senior year of high school in order to head off to college? Simon's Rock doesn't think so. In fact, the average age of entering students is 16. This is the only four-year college of liberal arts and sciences specifically designed to provide bright, highly motivated students with the opportunity to begin college after the tenth or eleventh grade when their interest, energy and curiosity are at a peak. Students who complete

"Living at Simon's Rock and being surrounded by the students and faculty has changed the way that I think; it's changed who I am."
—Faisa Sarif, student

the requirements receive the Associate of Arts (A.A.) degree after two years of study and the Bachelor of Arts (B.A.) degree after four. For more than forty years, Simon's Rock has proven that exceptional students of high school age are fully capable of taking on college-level work; that they learn best in a small-college environment; that these students require a faculty committed to teaching and scholarship; and that a general education in the liberal arts and sciences should be the foundation for early college students. Simon's Rock students stay busy outside the classroom, too. Some tend to the community organic garden; others join the jazz ensemble. And all students get moving—part of the curriculum requires students to take four courses in such activities as yoga, rock climbing, martial arts, scuba or volleyball (just to name a few). The College is built on over 200 rolling and wooded acres in the Berkshire Hills of western Massachusetts. Boston and New York City are 140 miles away; Albany and Springfield are 40 miles away. The Berkshires' natural beauty and wide variety of attractions make the area a great place in which to live. The countryside has excellent terrain for hiking, bicycling, cross-country and Alpine skiing, canoeing and climbing. The Tanglewood Music Festival, Jacob's Pillow Dance Festival and a number of summer theaters take place annually in nearby towns.

- **Enrollment:** *431*
- **Selectivity:** *very difficult*
- **Application deadline:** *5/31 (freshmen), 7/15 (transfer)*
- **Expenses:** *Tuition $40,170; Room & Board $10,960*

CONTACT INFORMATION

Steven Coleman, Director of Admissions

☎ 413-528-7312 or toll-free 800-235-7186

🖳 admit@simons-rock.edu

The opportunities our internships provide will prove to be invaluable and give you a great advantage as you apply for your first position out of school.

Bay State College

From Passion to Profession.

BOSTON, MASSACHUSETTS
www.baystate.edu/

Bay State College is a different kind of college. Here, students take what they love to do and make a career out of it. The College offers associate and bachelor's degrees in many fields you won't find at other schools—Fashion Merchandising, Entertainment Management and Medical Assisting. Personalized attention is key at Bay State College. In fact, with First-Year Experience, a mandatory 1-credit course, students learn the concept of "action planning"—identifying their goals and setting a course of action to achieve them. Students review their action plan each semester with their academic adviser and evaluate how they are progressing. For college life outside the classroom, Bay State College students create clubs and organizations such as the Criminal Justice Society, the Early Childhood Education Club, the Student Government Association and the Entertainment Management Association. Students also attend the College's fashion shows or catch a Boston Celtics or Boston Red Sox game. Bay State has partnered with the Body Evolver Fitness Club, where students can access fitness equipment and classes at a discounted rate. One of the unique aspects of Bay State College is the residence halls. With their location in the historic Back Bay, the buildings are original Victorian town houses and brownstones. All buildings have computer labs with free Internet access, laundry machines, vending machines, a house phone with free local calling and a lounge with cable TV. Each student room has access to a wireless network. The Career Services office offers lifetime career assistance to current students and alumni through counseling, workshops, guest speakers, resume and cover letter reviews, interview prep and job listings. Located in Boston, and surrounded by dozens of colleges and universities, Bay State College is an ideal place to live and learn. The College is within walking distance of several major-league sports franchises, concert halls, museums, the Freedom Trail, Boston Symphony Hall, the Boston Public Library and the Boston Public Garden. World-class shopping and major cultural events help make college life an experience that students will always remember.

Turn a love of fashion into a career with Fashion Merchandising and Fashion Design. Experience your very own Fashion Show as part of your class work.

CONTACT INFORMATION

Kim Olds, Director of Admissions

☎ 617-217-9115 or toll-free 800-81-LEARN
🖥 admissions@baystate.edu

BENTLEY UNIVERSITY

WALTHAM, MASSACHUSETTS
www.bentley.edu

With 23 varsity teams and over 100 clubs and organizations, there are plenty of reasons to cheer.

Bentley University is a national leader in business education. Its high-tech facilities are unmatched. Students have access to real-time data from Reuters, Bloomberg and Bridge. They use leading-edge software applications such as MultexNet, DataStream and FirstCall. Other campus buildings are stocked with up-to-the-minute tools for learning advertising creation to accounting. In addition, Bentley has a master's candidate program that allows students to earn a bachelor's degree and a master's degree in only five years. Bentley also offers two doctoral programs: accountancy and business. About 97 percent of Bentley freshmen live on campus in the twenty-three dorms and apartment-style buildings. The constantly updated residence halls are air-conditioned and carpeted and have common areas that include study lounges, exercise rooms, TV lounges and game rooms. The Student Center is home to Seasons Dining Room and Mongolian Grill; the Blue Line pub, with nightly entertainment; and more than 100 student clubs and organizations. Bentley students get involved in everything from academic groups to the performing arts, from campus media to fraternities and sororities. The Miller Center for Career Services (CSS) has an on-campus recruiting program involving 500 national and international companies; an online job-listing service available to Bentley students and alumni; an electronic database of student and alumni resumes; career fairs; and workshops on resume writing, interviewing and job-search strategies. Thanks to these and other programs, 98 percent of Bentley students find employment or enroll in graduate school within six months of graduation. The median annual salary for 2009 graduates was over $50,000. Students choose among intramural and recreational sports and twenty-three varsity teams in NCAA Divisions I and II. The Dana Athletic Center houses a weight and fitness complex; an aerobics room; a full-service food court; a suspended track; basketball, volleyball and racquetball courts; a competition-size pool with a diving tank; and saunas.

Outdoor facilities include soccer and baseball fields, a track, lighted tennis courts and other grass and Astroturf fields. Bentley is located just minutes west of Boston. As the country's ultimate university town, Boston offers theater to art exhibits, dance clubs to alternative rock concerts and championship sports to world-class shopping. Students do not need a car to get around. The free Bentley shuttle makes regular trips to Harvard Square in Cambridge, which is a great area to explore and just a quick subway ride from the heart of Boston.

CONTACT INFORMATION

Admissions Office

☎ 781-891-2244 or toll-free 800-523-2354

✉ ugadmission@bentley.edu

- **Enrollment:** *5,616*
- **Selectivity:** *very difficult*
- **Test scores:** *ACT—over 18, 100%; SAT—critical reading over 500, 92%; SAT—math over 500, 97%*
- **Application deadline:** *1/15 (freshmen)*
- **Expenses:** *Tuition $35,828; Room & Board $11,740*

 http://bit.ly/collvid31

More than 80 percent of students live on campus, creating a community that lasts well beyond college.

Danilo Perez works with Berklee Global Jazz Institute students (by Jennifer Shanley).

Berklee college *of* music

BOSTON, MASSACHUSETTS
www.berklee.edu/

Berklee College of Music is a magnet for aspiring musicians from every corner of earth. With more than a dozen performance and non-performance majors and a music industry "who's who" of alumni, Berklee is the world's premier learning lab for the music of today—and tomorrow. Berklee embraces change. The musical landscape looks nothing like it did when Berklee was founded in 1945, but the college has remained current by introducing emerging musical genres and indispensable new technology. Berklee also responds to important developments in music education and music therapy, making good on its promise to improve society through music. At Berklee, students start with a foundation of contemporary music theory and technique, and then build upon that foundation by learning the practical, professional skills needed to sustain a career in music. Students earn degrees in majors such as music production and engineering, film scoring, music business/management, music synthesis, songwriting and music therapy, performance and composition. Berklee attracts students who reflect today's music, be it jazz, rock, hip-hop, country, gospel, electronica, Latin or funk. Of all U.S. colleges and universities, Berklee has one of the largest percentages of undergrads from outside the United States— 25 percent. Notable alumni include BT, Gary Burton, Terri Lyne Carrington, Bruce Cockburn, Juan Luis Guerra, Roy Hargrove, Quincy Jones, Diana Krall, Aimee Mann, Arif Mardin, Branford Marsalis, Danilo Perez, John Scofield, Howard Shore, Alan Silvestri, Luciana Souza, Susan Tedeschi and Gillian Welch. Berklee College of Music is located in Boston's Fenway

Cultural District. The neighborhood includes museums and galleries and world-class performing arts centers such as Symphony Hall, the Wang Center and the Berklee Performance Center. In addition to the music made at Berklee, there is a lively club and concert scene in the area with coffee houses featuring folk and bluegrass music; neighborhood clubs playing jazz, reggae and world music; and clubs specializing in rock, blues, dance, urban and country-western music. Berklee students join intramural sports and fitness programs at nearby schools; watch Boston's professional sports teams play in the new

CONTACT INFORMATION

Mr. Damien Bracken, Director of Admissions

☎ 617-747-2222 or toll-free 800-BERKLEE

✉ admissions@berklee.edu

TD Banknorth Garden or at Fenway Park; attend theater, club and concert hall events year-round throughout the city; and walk, skate or bike through the city's many parks.

- **Enrollment:** *4,145*
- **Selectivity:** *moderately difficult*
- **Application deadline:** *1/15 (freshmen), 1/15 (transfer)*
- **Expenses:** *Tuition $30,650; Room & Board $15,080*

Impromptu Jam Session (by Bill Gallery)

An aerial view of Boston University and the city of Boston

BOSTON, MASSACHUSETTS
www.bu.edu/

What *isn't* Boston University known for? Whether it's the more than 250 cutting-edge degrees available in its 17 schools and colleges, winning Division I sports programs or its prime location in one of the most exciting U.S. cities, BU has it all. Students here take biochemistry, broadcast journalism, business, mechanical engineering, elementary education, international relations, physical therapy, psychology and theater arts. Boston University was one of the first U.S. schools to offer a study abroad program; today, students can study ecology in the rainforests of Ecuador or learn Arabic in Morocco. There is no shortage of fun on the BU campus either. BU students love the more than 500 different student organizations— everything from ice broomball teams to performing arts groups, student government to the classic rock club, Alpine racing to Amnesty International. The Terriers compete and win in NCAA Division I sports every year. The state-of-the-art facilities at BU include the DeWolfe Boathouse along the Charles River, a 270,000 square foot Fitness & Recreation Center and Agganis Arena where the national championship men's ice hockey team plays. Boston University makes great efforts to go green. From the local, organic food in the dining halls to green cleaning supplies,

Boston University students outside the College of Arts & Sciences

BU proudly earned recognition from "The Princeton Review's Guide to 286 Green Colleges." The city of Boston is an international center of cultural and intellectual activity. Home to many museums, baseball's Fenway Park, an active theater district and the Boston Symphony Orchestra, Boston is the ultimate college town.

- **Enrollment:** *31,960*
- **Selectivity:** *very difficult*
- **Test scores:** *ACT—over 18, 100%; SAT—critical reading over 500, 96%; SAT—math over 500, 99%*
- **Application deadline:** *1/1 (freshmen), 4/1 (transfer)*
- **Expenses:** *Tuition $39,864; Room & Board $12,260*

CONTACT INFORMATION

Ms. Kelly Walter, Director of Undergraduate Admissions

☎ 617-353-2300

✉ admissions@bu.edu

On Red Square, the center of activity at Clark University, you'll find Jonas Clark Hall and a larger-than-life statue of Sigmund Freud who gave his only lectures on U.S. soil at Clark in 1909.

CLARK UNIVERSITY™
1887
CHALLENGE CONVENTION. CHANGE OUR WORLD.

WORCESTER, MASSACHUSETTS
www.clarku.edu/

Clark University students are no ordinary students. Whether they are studying climate change in Alaska or setting up a health clinic for women in Ecuador, Clark students leave their mark around the world. Eager, bright undergrads come to Clark for intense, rewarding research and educational opportunities and leave as leaders ready to make global changes. Clark's strong Ph.D. and master's-degree programs focus on such areas as urban education, environmental issues and policies, management, health care, child and family welfare, holocaust and genocide studies, and international development and social change. Clark students are guaranteed housing in one of nine residence halls for their first two years of school. Bullock and Wright Halls are undergoing renovations. Students entering in the fall of 2010 will have access to lounges with flat-screen TVs, smart rooms with data connections and flat-screen monitors, quiet rooms, new bathrooms and kitchens, bike storage and laundry rooms with kiosk and computer workstations. Outside the classroom, Clark students get involved in the more than 100 clubs and organizations on and off campus—everything from ballroom dancing to Shenanigans (a comedy/improv group). Students use L*IN*K (similar to Facebook) to search clubs and event information. The Clark University Cougars participate in NCAA Division III sports. Men compete in baseball, basketball, cross-country, hockey, lacrosse, rowing, soccer, swimming and diving, and tennis. Women compete in basketball, cross-country, field hockey, rowing, soccer, softball, swimming and diving, tennis and volleyball. Sixty-five percent of undergrads join intercollegiate, intramural, club, wellness or rec programs. Located about 40 miles west of Boston, Worcester (pronounced "wooster") is home to a broad mix of immigrants, from Armenian to French-Canadian to Vietnamese, who have lent their distinctive cultures to Worcester neighborhoods, restaurants and places of worship. Worcester is also recognized as one of the ten most livable cities in the United States by *Forbes* magazine. Nearby attractions include Old Sturbridge Village and the Worcester Horticultural Society's Tower Hill Botanical Garden. Students head to nearby Wachusett Mountain for skiing and hiking.

CONTACT INFORMATION

Mr. Donald Honeman, Dean of Admissions

☎ 508-793-7431 or toll-free 800-GO-CLARK

✉ admissions@clarku.edu

- **Enrollment:** *3,416*
- **Selectivity:** *moderately difficult*
- **Test scores:** *ACT—over 18, 99%; SAT—critical reading over 500, 89%; SAT—math over 500, 88%*
- **Application deadline:** *1/15 (freshmen), 4/15 (transfer)*
- **Expenses:** *Tuition $36,420; Room & Board $6950*

Academic Commons in Goddard Library features computer labs, study spaces and Jazzman's Café. The library is named for Dr. Robert Goddard, Clark University physicist and father of modern rocketry.

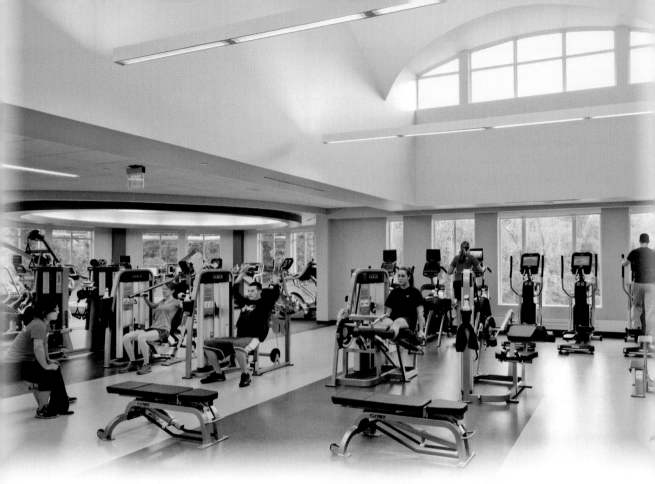

Curry College Student Center

Curry College

MILTON, MASSACHUSETTS
www.curry.edu/

Curry College challenges students to achieve greatness in all they do. This private, liberal arts school offers twenty majors with more than sixty-five minors and special concentrations in current fields like Entrepreneurship, Environmental Studies, Multimedia Journalism and Substance Abuse Counseling. Curry also offers four master's degree programs: a Master of Education (M.Ed.), an M.A. in Criminal Justice, an M.S. in Nursing and a Master of Business Administration (M.B.A.). The College's curriculum and programs focus on the two hallmarks of the Curry education: a high respect for student individuality and a developmental approach to learning that maximizes achievement.

 　　MASSACHUSETTS

Curry students enjoy many cocurricular activities, including the Student Government Association, the newspaper and yearbook, the *Curry Arts Journal*, performing arts clubs and the award-winning radio station. The Office of Student Activities and the Campus Activities Board schedule special events like Spring Weekend and Curry Up and Go! (weekly trips to Martha's Vineyard, Salem or other spots). The Curry Colonels play a full schedule of men's and women's Division III sports. Varsity sports for men are baseball, basketball, football, ice hockey, lacrosse, soccer and tennis; women's varsity sports are basketball, cross-country, lacrosse, soccer, softball and tennis. Intramural sports include Rugby and Ultimate Frisbee. Now well into its second century, Curry College was founded in Boston in 1879 and was moved to its present site in Milton in 1952. In 1974, Curry College absorbed the Perry Normal School, and, in 1977, it entered into a

collaborative relationship with Children's Hospital Medical Center, which resulted in the creation of Curry's Division of Nursing Studies. Curry sits on a wooded 135-acre campus in Milton, Massachusetts, a suburb of Boston. The greater Boston area is home to corporations, hospitals, agencies, broadcasting stations and schools that provide excellent internship and job opportunities for Curry students. The College operates a shuttle bus to the MBTA trains for easy access to Boston.

CONTACT INFORMATION

Ms. Jane P. Fidler, Dean of Admission

☎ 617-333-2210 or toll-free 800-669-0686

✉ curryadm@curry.edu

- **Enrollment:** *3,125*
- **Selectivity:** *moderately difficult*
- **Test scores:** *ACT—over 18, 77%; SAT—critical reading over 500, 28%; SAT—math over 500, 31%*
- **Application deadline:** *4/1 (freshmen), 7/1 (transfer)*

 http://bit.ly/collvid35

Academic Quad

A Christian college of the liberal arts & sciences, ENC challenges students to ponder the tensions and possibilities between Christian values and society, and embrace a global understanding of both.

Eastern Nazarene College
Discover your purpose

QUINCY, MASSACHUSETTS
www.enc.edu/

Eastern Nazarene College's (ENC) small size is one of its greatest assets. This Christian, liberal arts college sits on just 15 acres in Quincy, which was recently ranked as the second-safest city in the state. Also small are the class sizes—allowing easy interaction between students and professors. With an innovative curriculum, focused on global issues, ENC awards bachelor's and graduate degrees in over fifty areas. The newest additions to the College are

www.facebook.com/find.colleges   MASSACHUSETTS

the Cecil R. Paul Center for Business and the James R. Cameron Center for History, Law, and Government. But some of the most important lessons at ENC are learned outside the classroom. Eastern Nazarene is home to over seventy-five clubs and organizations in which students make a difference. ENC undergrads are eager to join programs like Big Brother, Big Sister or Open Hand/ Open Heart, a group that ministers to the local homeless with food, clothing and friendship. Other students get involved in STAND (Students Tackling AIDS kNeeling Down), an organization that focuses on prayer, awareness and outreach in the fight against AIDS. The ENC Lions participate in NCAA Division III sports; men compete in baseball, basketball, cross country, soccer and tennis, while women compete in basketball, cross country, soccer, volleyball, softball and tennis. Other extracurricular activities at ENC include a student-run literary magazine, the *Veritas News* newspaper, theatre, and several musical ensembles including the A Cappella Choir, Gospel Choir, Jazz Band and Quincy Bay Chamber Orchestra. A suburb of Boston, Quincy was the birthplace of John Adams and John Quincy Adams, as well as John Hancock. The main campus is located in Wollaston Park, just a quarter mile from beautiful Quincy Bay and Wollaston Beach, the largest of the Boston Harbor beaches. The Wollaston Park campus is home to a fine arts center, a prayer chapel, a student center, a college library, a physical education center, athletic fields, tennis courts, five residence halls and a college-owned apartment building. The Old Colony Campus is home to the Campus Kinder Haus Early Childhood Education Center; the James R. Cameron Center for History, Law, and Government; the Cecil R. Paul Center for Business; the Adams Executive Center; and the College's Leadership Education for Adults (LEAD) program for working adults and graduate students.

Professors, not teaching assistants, teach class here. ENC's size is also one of its greatest assets—small class sizes facilitate discussion and allow faculty members to engage students effectively.

- **Enrollment:** *1,075*

- **Selectivity:** *moderately difficult*

- **Test scores:** *ACT—over 18, 84%; SAT—critical reading over 500, 53%; SAT—math over 500, 53%*

- **Application deadline:** *Rolling (freshmen), rolling (transfer)*

- **Expenses:** *Tuition $23,772; Room & Board $8000*

CONTACT INFORMATION

Mr. Andrew R. Wright, Director of Admissions

☎ 617-745-3864 or toll-free 800-88-ENC88

✉ andrew.wright@enc.edu

One of four fabulous theaters on the Emerson campus, the historic 1,200-seat Cutler Majestic hosts several professional and student-staged performances each year.

1880

EMERSON COLLEGE

BOSTON, MASSACHUSETTS
www.emerson.edu

Emerson is a pioneer in the fields of communication and performing arts. It was one of the first colleges in the nation to establish a program in children's theater (1919), an undergraduate program in broadcasting (1937), professional-level training in speech pathology and audiology (1935), educational FM radio (1949), closed-circuit television (1955), and a B.F.A. degree program in film as early as 1972. In 1980, Emerson College created the country's first graduate program in professional writing and publishing. Today, Emerson invites students to come and create more "firsts." Students may choose from more than two-dozen undergrad programs supported by state-of-the-art facilities and a nationally renowned faculty. In addition to its

MASSACHUSETTS

undergraduate programs, Emerson College offers more than a dozen cutting-edge master's degree programs including Communication Disorders, Publishing & Writing and Integrated Marketing Communication. The campus is home to WERS-FM, the oldest non-commercial radio station in Boston; the historic 1,200-seat Cutler Majestic Theatre; and *Ploughshares*, the award-winning literary journal for new writing. Students can choose to live in special learning communities—the Writers' Block, Living Green and Digital Culture floors are popular among students. All of the College's residence halls are air conditioned with cable TV and Internet access. Wireless service is available in many campus locations. There is a fitness center, athletic field and a new fourteen-story campus center and residence hall. With dozens of colleges and universities, Boston is one of the country's best-known college towns. The city contains so many

off-campus options ranging from scenic harbor cruises and Boston Pops concerts to baseball's Fenway Park and the legendary Boston Marathon. Emerson's campus is located on Boston Common in the heart of the city's Theatre District—within sight of the Massachusetts State House and walking distance from the historic Freedom Trail, Boston Public Garden, Chinatown, the financial district as well as restaurants and museums.

CONTACT INFORMATION

Ms. Sara S. Ramirez, Director of Undergraduate Admission

☎ 617-824-8600

✉ admission@emerson.edu

- **Enrollment:** *4,546*
- **Selectivity:** *very difficult*
- **Test scores:** *ACT—over 18, 99%; SAT—critical reading over 500, 96%; SAT—math over 500, 93%*
- **Application deadline:** *1/5 (freshmen), 3/1 (transfer)*
- **Expenses:** *Tuition $29,918; Room & Board $12,280*

http://bit.ly/collvid38

Emerson College is located on Boston Common in the heart of the city's Theatre District. The gold dome on the Massachusetts State House can be seen from many vantage points on campus.

Student installing her work in the 2010 Senior Projects exhibition, "Departure."

BOSTON

School of the Museum of Fine Arts, Boston

BOSTON, MASSACHUSETTS
www.smfa.edu/

Forget what you think you know about college. Here at The School of the Museum of Fine Arts, Boston (SMFA) students do not take required art foundation classes and they don't have majors. Instead, students are given the freedom to design a program of study that best suits their needs and goals. SMFA is a division of the Museum of Fine Arts, Boston (MFA), and affiliated with Tufts and Northeastern Universities. In partnership with Tufts, SFMA offers the following degree programs: the Bachelor of Fine Arts, the five-year Combined-Degree program (B.A./B.F.A. or B.S./B.F.A.), the Master of Fine Arts and the Master of Arts in Teaching in Art Education. In partnership with Northeastern, SMFA offers a Bachelor of Fine Arts and a Master of Fine Arts in Studio Art. All students in degree programs are fully enrolled at the School of the Museum of Fine Arts and Tufts or Northeastern University and graduate with a Tufts or Northeastern degree. As in an artists' colony, the Museum School's focus is on creative investigation, risk taking and the exploration of an individual vision. SMFA continually incorporates new media and new approaches, concepts and theories. Exhibitions and visiting artists programs round out the curriculum. The state-of-the-art dorm, custom-built for artists, has ample studio space. The School of the Museum of Fine Arts, Boston, is within walking distance of numerous other colleges and major art museums. In addition to the Museum of Fine Arts, Boston, students also enjoy the nearby Isabella Stewart Gardner Museum and the Museum of the National Center of Afro-American Artists. Students can hop on the "T" subway system to go to The Institute of Contemporary Art as well as galleries on Newbury Street, the South End and Fort Point. Or the T can take them to Cambridge to explore the museums of Harvard University and the List Visual Arts Center at MIT. SMFA's campus is bordered on one side by parkland where students walk, jog, picnic or sketch the afternoon away. Harvard Square's eclectic

SMFA faculty consists of full- and part-time practicing artists of national or international reputation, who provide extensive opportunities for individual dialogue and consultation.

restaurants, shops, theaters and street performers are just across the Charles River. The Back Bay boasts a dizzying range of shops and eateries. Students can easily find a mix of theater—classical and experimental—some of the best independent movie houses around, comedy clubs, people-watching spots, poetry slams, lectures and great bookstores.

- **Enrollment:** *755*
- **Selectivity:** *moderately difficult*
- **Test scores:** *ACT—over 18, 88%; SAT—critical reading over 500, 79.8%; SAT—math over 500, 60.6%*
- **Application deadline:** *2/1 (freshmen), 3/1 (transfer)*
- **Expenses:** *Tuition $30,660; Room only $13,046*

CONTACT INFORMATION

Jesse Tarantino, Assistant Dean of Admissions

☎ 617-369-3626 or toll-free 800-643-6078

✉ admissions@smfa.edu

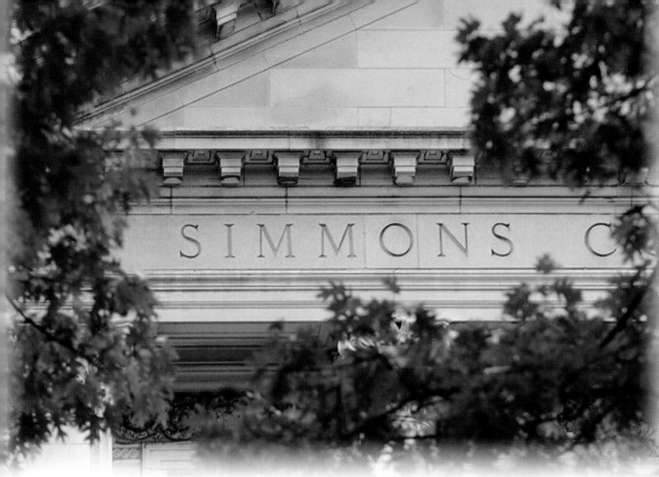

Simmons College provides an exceptional, student-centered learning experience in the thriving city of Boston.

SIMMONS COLLEGE

BOSTON, MASSACHUSETTS
www.simmons.edu/

Decades before women gained the right to vote, Boston businessman John Simmons had a revolutionary idea: women should be able to work and lead meaningful lives. Simmons College was the result. Founded in 1899, Simmons was the first college in the nation to offer women a liberal arts education. Simmons also created the world's first MBA program for women. Today, Simmons provides a strong education for women combined with professional career preparation, interdisciplinary study and global perspectives. The Simmons community encourages dialogue, respect and cooperation—making the Simmons experience as thoughtful as it is thought-provoking. First-year core courses focus on thinking and writing skills, while integrating two or more subjects—ranging from bioethics and Buddhist studies to computational linguistics and visual communication. Students learn outside the classroom through internships, fieldwork and research projects where they develop skills and a network of professional contacts. Many students intern for businesses and organizations such as Boston Public Schools, *The Boston Globe*, the Museum of Fine Arts, Smash Advertising or the World Affairs Council. On campus, students conduct research using state-of-the-art equipment in areas such as materials science, gene splicing and computer modeling. Professors often invite undergrads to collaborate on research projects and presentations or co-publish articles in academic journals. Gaining a global outlook is important at Simmons— including an understanding of languages, cultures and politics through programs such as Africana studies, East Asian studies and international relations. Simmons encourages students to spend an entire semester or year abroad. Short-term international courses enable students to learn journalism in South Africa, music in Austria or history and civilization in Japan. Students also take part in service-learning projects, ranging from education initiatives in Boston to health care in Nicaragua. The Simmons campus (named a top "Green College" by the *Princeton Review*) is home to the state-of-the-art Holmes Sports Center as well as libraries that feature wireless networks and laptops for loan. Simmons is located in Boston's Fenway neighborhood, which is alive with music and fine arts, medical care and research and the cheers of baseball fans at Fenway Park. From campus, it's an easy walk to other colleges as well as shops, cafes, clubs, museums, movie theaters, parks and public transportation. Students can hop aboard the "T" public transportation system and head to Downtown Crossing, the Italian North End, Chinatown or Harvard Square.

CONTACT INFORMATION

Catherine Capolupo, Director of Undergraduate Admissions

☎ 617-521-2057 or toll-free 800-345-8468

✉ ugadm@simmons.edu

- **Enrollment:** *5,003*
- **Selectivity:** *moderately difficult*
- **Test scores:** *ACT—over 18, 99%; SAT—critical reading over 500, 74%; SAT—math over 500, 73%*
- **Application deadline:** *2/1 (freshmen), 4/1 (transfer)*
- **Expenses:** *Tuition $31,450; Room & Board $12,050*

Simmons's residential campus is an oasis in the heart of the city.

UMass Boston's campus is located just a short subway ride from downtown Boston and overlooks Boston Harbor.

UMASS BOSTON

BOSTON, MASSACHUSETTS
www.umb.edu/

The University of Massachusetts Boston (UMass Boston) is the second-largest campus of the University of Massachusetts system. With over 150 academic programs for undergrads, graduates and non-degree seeking students, UMass Boston attracts students from an extraordinary range of backgrounds, talents and interests. Many come straight from high school, while others transfer from two- and four-year colleges. The UMass Boston student body shares a strong desire to succeed academically and turn their classroom instruction into a career.

The University Advising Center can help them do just that. Its team of professional counselors provides personalized assistance for students to design their course of study, use tutoring and mentoring services, choose a major and career path and develop their interviewing, resume writing and job-search skills. UMass Boston has an active student life. From student government to student publications; from a championship chess team to working with inner-city youth; from the Sailing Club and athletics to fraternities and sororities—there is a club or organization for every interest. The UMass Boston Beacons compete in NCAA Division III sports with fourteen varsity teams. The Beacons have been named All-Americans ninety-three times in seven sports and the women's indoor and outdoor track & field teams have won four NCAA Team Championships and

thirty-eight individual NCAA championships. The UMass campus is relaxed and fun. Students can grab a cup of Peet's coffee at The Atrium Café or workout at the state-of-the-art Beacon Fitness Center. From its peninsula on Boston Harbor, just south of downtown Boston, the University overlooks Dorchester Bay and the harbor islands. Its neighbors are the John F. Kennedy Presidential Library and the Massachusetts State Archives and Commonwealth Museum. UMass Boston students have easy access to everything from Fenway Park and the

15,000 undergraduate and graduate students enjoy over 175 majors, minors, and programs at Boston's public research university with a teaching soul.

CONTACT INFORMATION

Mrs. Liliana Mickle, Director of Undergraduate Admissions

☎ 617-287-6000

🖥 enrollment.info@umb.edu

Bank of America Garden to Symphony Hall and the Museum of Fine Arts.

- **Enrollment:** *14,912*
- **Selectivity:** *moderately difficult*
- **Test scores:** *SAT—critical reading over 500, 58%; SAT—math over 500, 68%*
- **Application deadline:** *6/1 (freshmen), 7/1 (transfer)*
- **Expenses:** *Tuition $10,611*

http://bit.ly/collvid68

Wheaton College is located in Norton, Massachusetts—just 35 miles from historic Boston and 20 miles of Providence, Rhode Island, within reach of many of the best opportunities and resources in the world.

WheatonCollege

NORTON, MASSACHUSETTS
www.wheatoncollege.edu/

Curious, career-minded students come to Wheaton College. Undergrads can choose from more than forty majors and fifty minors at the only coed, private liberal arts college in the Boston area. Excellence and innovation rule here. Since 2001, Wheaton students have won more than 120 scholarship awards, including three Rhodes Scholarships. And each year, Wheaton spends more than $350,000 on student research, travel and internships. The high energy on campus comes from student involvement in the many extracurricular activities and organizations. Popular clubs include the Black Students Association, student government, the Christian

Fellowship, the newspaper, yearbook and the campus radio station. Other students join musical groups, such as the Whims, Wheatones, Gentleman Callers and chamber music ensembles. Still others get up and get moving with the Modern Dance Group. The Wheaton Lyons compete and win in NCAA Division III athletics. Men's teams are baseball, basketball, cross country, lacrosse, soccer, softball, swimming and diving, tennis and track. Women's teams are basketball, cross country, field hockey, lacrosse, soccer, softball, swimming and diving, synchronized swimming, tennis, track and field and volleyball. Wheaton makes a solid commitment to sustainability in its buildings and across campus—students and faculty recently opened an apple orchard behind the President's house. Construction is underway for a new Science Center at Wheaton—students can check the progress of this $42 million campus addition through an online "construction cam." Also new is the Office of Service, Spirituality, and Social Responsibility where students gather to participate in community service, explore spirituality and initiate social activism. The 400-acre campus with its eighty-seven buildings is located in the suburb of Norton. South of Boston, north of Providence and just a train ride to NYC, Wheaton is at the center of it all.

CONTACT INFORMATION

Gail Berson, Vice President for Enrollment and Dean of Admission and Student Aid

☎ 508-286-8251 or toll-free 800-394-6003

🖥 admission@wheatoncollege.edu

- **Enrollment:** *1,632*
- **Selectivity:** *very difficult*
- **Application deadline:** *1/15 (freshmen), 3/1 (transfer)*
- **Expenses:** *Tuition $41,084; Room & Board $10,180*

Wheaton is a selective four-year liberal arts college with a student body of 1,550 from nearly every state and 69 countries. Since 2000, Wheaton students have won more than 130 national scholarships.

WPI Superfans and Gompei, the mascot

WORCESTER, MASSACHUSETTS
www.wpi.edu/

Worcester Polytechnic Institute (WPI) believes in the power of its students to make an impact. They may want to be on the first Mars mission, find alternative energy sources or work on cancer research. Students here do much more than study science and technology in the classroom. They complete projects on campus and around the world where they connect what they have learned in the lab with real-life challenges, from human health and the environment to business and engineering. Small classes and a flexible curriculum make learning at WPI an experience unlike any other. WPI is consistently ranked among the top national universities by *U.S. News & World Report*. In the National Survey of Student Engagement, WPI ranked number one for student-faculty interactions. More than thirty-five areas of study in engineering, science, business management, and the liberal arts give students the freedom to learn everything from molecular biology to music. Exciting new interdisciplinary programs are driven by real-world demand, such as interactive media and game development, robotics engineering, and environmental studies and engineering. WPI students have received some of the nation's highest academic honors: the prestigious Marshall Scholarship, the National Institute of Health Research Scholarship, the Fulbright Scholarship, the Goldwater Scholarship, the Rotary Ambassadorial Scholarship and the Society of Women Engineers Award. In addition, two students were recently named to the *USA Today* All-USA College Academic Team. WPI has twenty varsity (NCAA Division III) athletics teams and thirty-four club and intramural sports. There are thirteen fraternities and three sororities, fifteen music

or theater ensembles and more than 200 other student clubs and activities. On WPI's beautiful New England campus, students chat with their friends and professors on the grassy quad or play pool at the Campus Center. They study by the fountain in Reunion Plaza, go cosmic bowling, relax in the English garden behind Higgins House or catch a student play at the Little Theatre. Home to twelve other colleges and universities, Worcester is a great college town. Late-night diners, clubs, museums, concert venues and theaters are right down the hill from WPI. Boston is less than an hour away by commuter rail, and there are great skiing and snowboarding at nearby

Wachusett Mountain. WPI students have easy access to Providence, New York City, the Berkshires, the White Mountains and Cape Cod.

CONTACT INFORMATION

Mr. Edward J. Connor,
Director of Admissions

☎ 508-831-5286

✉ admissions@wpi.edu

- **Enrollment:** *4,978*

- **Selectivity:** *very difficult*

- **Test scores:** *ACT—over 18, 100%; SAT—critical reading over 500, 92%; SAT—math over 500, 100%*

- **Application deadline:** *2/1 (freshmen), 4/15 (transfer)*

- **Expenses:** *Tuition $38,920; Room & Board $11,610*

WPI students making a difference in Cape Town, South Africa.

Environmental Science students engage in University recycling efforts with Professors Catherine Owen Koning and Fred Lord.

FranklinPierce
UNIVERSITY

RINDGE, NEW HAMPSHIRE
www.franklinpierce.edu/

Why go to a one-size-fits-all college when you can come to Franklin Pierce University? This small, private university grounded in the liberal arts gives students the personal attention they need and the high-quality instruction they deserve. The University consists of the College at Rindge and the College of Graduate & Professional Studies. Students can earn bachelor's to doctoral degrees and take a host of interesting courses in everything from medieval history to web design. The College of Graduate & Professional Studies enrolls adult learners at its five campuses across the state, in Arizona and through distance learning. The main campus at Rindge has modern classrooms with state-of-the-art technology, a MAC computer lab, digital photo and print labs, a campus center, apartment and townhouse complexes (including an A-frame house on Pearly Pond with two decks overlooking the water), a field house, an air frame recreation complex (with a batting cage, two full tennis courts cardio/strength area and free personal training for students), a dance studio, a boat house, the Lakeside Educational Center, a glass-blowing facility and a theater. Franklin Pierce students find plenty of time to join campus activities including the *Pierce Arrow* (newspaper), the EMS squad, the Anthropology Club or the Raven Thunder Dance Club. The University's active Adventure Recreation program schedules camping, rock climbing and kayaking trips for students; off campus trips happen almost every weekend and all equipment is free for students to use. The Franklin Pierce Ravens compete at the NCAA Division II level. Men's teams are baseball, basketball, crew, golf, ice hockey, lacrosse, soccer and tennis. Women's teams are basketball, cross-country, rowing, lacrosse, field hockey, soccer, softball, tennis and volleyball. The University has earned national championships in men's and women's soccer and achieved top regional honors in baseball and women's basketball. The main campus in Rindge sits on 1,200 wooded acres on the shore of Pearly Pond near the base of Mount Monadnock. Rindge, which is 65 miles from Boston, 112 miles from Hartford and 236 miles from New York City. There are many lakes and streams for fishing, swimming and sailing. There are also a ton of trails for hiking, mountaineering, biking and cross-country skiing.

Anthropology Professor Robert Goodby examines an artifact with a student.

- **Enrollment:** *2,437*
- **Selectivity:** *moderately difficult*
- **Test scores:** *ACT—over 18, 76.9%; SAT—critical reading over 500, 46.2%; SAT—math over 500, 42%*
- **Application deadline:** *Rolling (freshmen)*
- **Expenses:** *Tuition $28,700; Room & Board $9800*

CONTACT INFORMATION

Office of Admissions

☎ 603-899-4050 or toll-free 800-437-0048
✉ admissions@fpc.edu

Keene State's Owl is the mascot for 18 varsity sports and other campus activities. KSC athletes compete in Division III's Little East Conference.

KEENE STATE UNIVERSITY

KEENE, NEW HAMPSHIRE
www.keene.edu/

Students come to Keene State College (KSC) for so many reasons— small classes, its location in the heart of New England, and a choice of more than 40 liberal arts majors. They stay and graduate for even more reasons—the unmatched facilities, the relaxed feel on and off campus and the belief that here they can and do make a differ- ence. The 170-acre campus has three buildings that are registered as National Historic Landmarks. They blend right in with Keene's state-of-the-art facilities. The newer buildings include a Recreation Center with racquetball court, swimming pool and an elevated track;

the Thorne-Sagendorph Art Gallery with skylit exhibit halls and climate control; and a new Media Arts Center housing the departments of communication, journalism, film studies and graphic design. The $23-million David F. Putnam Science Center opened in 2004; it has thirty-two labs with modern ventilation and safety features and an award-winning outdoor courtyard that serves as a living classroom. The $20-million Zorn Dining Commons was completed in 2005 and has made-to-order meals and wi-fi access. Pondside III, the College's newest residence hall, was awarded LEED® "silver" certification in 2008 for its green efforts that include motion-sensor lights and recycling rooms on each floor. Community service is a core value at Keene. In 2006, the College received a prestigious Carnegie Foundation Award for community engagement. In 2008, students contributed more than 15,000 hours of noncredit service to the local area and more than 400,000 hours of credited service

learning. Involvement on campus is high, too. Students can join everything from the Fishing Club to fraternities and sororities. Keene athletes compete in NCAA Division III sports. Men's teams are baseball, basketball, cross country, lacrosse, soccer, swimming/diving and track and field. Women's teams are basketball, cheerleading, cross country, field hockey, lacrosse, soccer, softball, swimming/diving, track and field and volleyball. Keene is located only 84 miles from Boston and 200 miles from New York City. The Keene State campus is bordered by Main Street on one side and the Ashuelot River on another and is only four blocks from the historic downtown district with its shops, restaurants and theaters. Mount Monadnock (the most-climbed mountain in the world) is only 18 miles southeast of Keene. Students can camp, hike, mountain climb, ski and swim all within a short drive from campus.

Keene State's campus bustles with 5,000 students engaged in academic study, extracurricular activities, and community service.

- **Enrollment:** *5,356*
- **Selectivity:** *moderately difficult*
- **Test scores:** *SAT—critical reading over 500, 49.5%; SAT—math over 500, 50.4%*
- **Application deadline:** *4/1 (freshmen), rolling (transfer)*
- **Expenses:** *Tuition $9334; Room & Board $8444*

CONTACT INFORMATION

Ms. Margaret Richmond, Director of Admissions

☎ 603-358-2273 or toll-free 800-KSC-1909
🖳 admissions@keene.edu

Students, faculty and staff support athletic events both on and off campus following their favorite NEC teams. There is nothing like Pilgrim Pride. Go Grims!

New England College

HENNIKER, NEW HAMPSHIRE
www.nec.edu/

New England College (NEC) is a place where students amaze themselves with what they learn and with what they can accomplish. NEC prepares students for the professional world with a focus on the liberal arts and hands-on learning in more than thirty cutting-edge majors from Environmental Sustainability to Sport and Recreation Management. The Pathways Center provides mentors and academic advisers. Through this program, NEC students begin developing real-world skills, planning for their future and building their resumes from the moment they arrive on campus. As a result, education majors have enjoyed 100 percent job placement over the last twelve years. Outside the classroom, students enjoy the many extracurricular activities at NEC ranging from outdoor recreation to theater productions and the student newspaper. There are thirteen Division III intercollegiate sports teams at NEC and popular club and recreational sports such as Ultimate Frisbee and Tae Kwon Do. The campus has 26 acres of playing fields, a fitness center with updated exercise and strength-building equipment, a gymnasium and an indoor field house. The Lee Clement Ice Arena, home to the NEC Pilgrims, provides some of the best hockey games in the region. The College's new outdoor artificial turf field is scheduled to be ready for the field hockey and lacrosse teams in fall 2010. Living on campus is fun and relaxed; the residence halls offer suites, Ethernet ports and

even a coffee house. New England College's location offers students the best of all worlds—easy access to cities and wilderness areas of New Hampshire. The College is located a short drive from the state capital, Concord, and about 30 minutes from the state's largest city, Manchester. Students hit Portsmouth, Boston and some of the best ocean beaches in New England in just 90 minutes. Pats Peak, located only 3 miles from the campus, provides free skiing and snowboarding to all NEC students. The College's 225-acre campus has excellent trails for cross-country skiing and hiking. Flowing through the center of campus, the Contoocook River has an historic covered bridge, a popular subject for photographers.

Experiential learning opportunities both in and outside of the classroom help students develop a strong foundation of professional skills.

- **Enrollment:** *1,916*
- **Selectivity:** *minimally difficult*
- **Test scores:** *ACT—over 18, 54.55%; SAT—critical reading over 500, 26.22%; SAT—math over 500, 27.71%*
- **Application deadline:** *9/7 (freshmen), 8/7 (transfer)*
- **Expenses:** *Tuition $27,450; Room & Board $9626*

CONTACT INFORMATION

Diane Raymond, Director of Admission

☎ 603-428-2223 or toll-free 800-521-7642
🖳 admission@nec.edu

Located in Nashua, New Hampshire, Rivier is just an hour away from the mountains, the seacoast, and Boston.

Rivier
COLLEGE

NASHUA, NEW HAMPSHIRE
www.rivier.edu/

Rivier College invites students to take a closer look. What they will see is a small, Catholic college committed to its students and located in one of the most beautiful areas of the United States. Rivier College offers more than sixty undergraduate, graduate and post-graduate degrees—and the only doctorate of education in the state of New Hampshire. Academic advisers, staff at the Writing and Resource Center and peer tutors help students meet their academic goals.

The Regina Library and Educational Resource Center include 91,000 volumes and access to more than 3 million volumes in twelve area libraries. And from 2006 through 2008, Rivier received a perfect score from the U.S. Department of Education for financial responsibility, which rates the economic stability of colleges and universities across the country. Life on campus is relaxed and comfortable. Students can choose from four modern residence halls that have suites, Internet connections in each room and lounges. All students can have cars on campus. Rivier College also has more than twenty-five active clubs and organizations—from the Riviera College Dance Team to the Psychology Club. The College hosts concerts, live entertainment, films, sporting events and a ton of trips. One weekend students may be visiting the museums of Boston or New York; the next weekend they may be house building for Habitat for Humanity in Kentucky. Rivier competes in NCAA Division III men's baseball,

basketball, cross-country, lacrosse, soccer and volleyball; and women's basketball, cross-country, field hockey, lacrosse, soccer, softball and volleyball. The men's volleyball team has been nationally ranked every year since 2001. The Muldoon Health and Fitness Center is home to the Rivier Raiders varsity athletics as well as intramural sports and activities that include volleyball, floor hockey, basketball, weight training, aerobics and self-defense. Also on campus are soccer and softball fields, a beach volleyball court and a cross-country trail. All students can use the on-campus rehabilitation clinic, which offers free injury assessment, physical and occupational therapy and athletic training. Nashua is located in southern New Hampshire. The city of Boston lies just 40 miles to the south. Students have easy access to nearby lakes and ski areas in the White Mountains to the north and at the coast, which is just an hour's drive to the east.

CONTACT INFORMATION

David Boisvert, Vice President of Enrollment

☎ 603-897-8507 or toll-free 800-44RIVIER

✉ rivadmit@rivier.edu

- **Enrollment:** *2,256*
- **Selectivity:** *moderately difficult*
- **Test scores:** *SAT—critical reading over 500, 34.7%*
- **Application deadline:** *Rolling (freshmen), rolling (transfer)*
- **Expenses:** *Tuition $25,050; Room & Board $9428*

Rivier offers hands-on learning in all its academic programs; students build confidence and knowledge that will help them in their future careers.

BFA Students prepare for their final exhibition.

UNIVERSITY
of NEW HAMPSHIRE

DURHAM, NEW HAMPSHIRE
www.unh.edu/

The University of New Hampshire (UNH) is a rising star among American research universities. Undergrads choose from more than 100 majors; popular ones are Business Administration, Biology and Psychology. The campus is a mix of classic and modern buildings that give way to 2,600 acres of woods, fields and farms. Students can live in on-campus apartment complexes and themed housing (honors, first-year experience or international housing is offered by dorm or floor). Holloway Commons, a dining and conference building with an after-hours cafe, opened in fall 2003. Kingsbury Hall, home of the engineering school, underwent a $50-million renovation in 2007. The Memorial Union Building (MUB) is the University's community center; it has two movie theaters, the Copy Center, the bookstore and specific lounge/study space for nontraditional and graduate students. The Games Room in MUB has fourteen Xbox360s, three PS3s, three Wiis, a Rock Band Rock Box and all the hottest video games. Students at the University can join one of the more than 160 clubs or organizations such as the Organic Garden Club, the Juggling Club, the Running Club or the Fencing Club. The Hamel Student Recreation Center has two multipurpose courts, a group exercise studio, a club/martial art studio, an 8,000-square-foot fitness center with more than 100 exercise stations, three basketball/volleyball courts, an indoor track and saunas. Campus Recreation offers group exercise classes such as step aerobics, Reebok cycling or cardio kickboxing. Other students head to Hamel for Pilates, yoga, tai chi, a climbing wall, racquetball, personal training or massage therapy. The intramural sports program has more than twenty different sports and activities for men's, women's and coed teams. Some clubs are intensely competitive; they compete either on an intercollegiate basis with New England teams or sponsor University tournaments. In

addition, Campus Recreation offers ice skating, manages a large outdoor recreation facility with its own sailing and canoe center, runs a children's camp (Camp Wildcat) in the summer and supports the men's and women's sport club crew boat house. Nestled in New Hampshire's seacoast region, UNH is an outdoor-lover's dream with ski and hiking mountains and working-port cities nearby. Popular road trips for students include Boston (about an hour), Portsmouth (about 20 minutes) and the White Mountains (about an hour). Durham is a classic college town that caters to students. Durham's Main Street includes restaurants, coffeehouses, a bookstore, pizza shops and other student hangouts.

- **Enrollment:** *15,311*
- **Selectivity:** *moderately difficult*
- **Test scores:** *ACT—over 18, 98%; SAT—critical reading over 500, 79%; SAT—math over 500, 84%*

Hamilton Smith Hall, University of New Hampshire

- **Application deadline:** *2/1 (freshmen), 3/1 (transfer)*
- **Expenses:** *Tuition $12,743; Room & Board $8874*

 http://bit.ly/collvid69

CONTACT INFORMATION

Admissions Office

☎ 603-862-0077

🖵 admissions@unh.edu

CALDWELL COLLEGE
CALDWELL, NEW JERSEY
www.caldwell.edu/

Students, faculty, and staff sorted food and packed boxes at the Community FoodBank of New Jersey in Hillside for distribution to soup kitchens, pantries, and families in need.

Caldwell College is linked to the 800-year history of the Dominican order, a worldwide community of preachers, scholars and educators. Today, this Catholic, coed school continues in the spirit of life-long learning and individual attention to its students. Caldwell has twenty-nine undergrad degrees, seventeen graduate programs and a Caldwell Scholars Program. The most popular degrees at Caldwell are in business, psychology and education. The adult undergraduate program encourages working adults to complete their degree, earn a new degree or simply learn for pleasure through convenient day, evening, Saturday and distance learning courses. Accelerated options combine the opportunities of the distance education program with on-campus courses. Master's degrees are offered in applied behavior analysis (ABA), which is a highly effective treatment for autism;

business administration (accounting, nonprofit management); counseling psychology (art therapy, mental health counseling, school counseling); curriculum and instruction (special education, supervisor certification); educational administration; pastoral ministry (church administration); and special education (general teacher and certification, learning disabilities). Caldwell College students take advantage of work-based internships to explore possible careers and obtain valuable contacts. Last year, students interned at CNN, Xerox and the New York Red Bulls professional soccer team. The College's Business Advisory Council, which includes about 40 members from major corporations throughout New Jersey, helps business leaders and educators share their resources so both students and the business community can prepare for the challenges of the global marketplace. The Caldwell campus is a home away from home for students.

A new 200-bed, apartment-style residence hall opened in August 2007. The food service has extended hours and an expanded menu that includes an omelet station and an upscale deli. Sports are an important part of campus life, too. Caldwell fields NCAA Division II teams in men's baseball, basketball, golf, soccer and tennis and in women's basketball, cross-country, soccer, softball, tennis and volleyball. The 60,000-square-foot George R. Newman Student Activities and Recreation Center opened in 2002; it has a 1,600 seat basketball arena, a fitness center, suspended track and bookstore. The 70-acre campus lies 20 miles west of New York City. Area attractions include theaters, museums, parks, ski resorts, professional sports arenas, the New Jersey Performing Arts Center and the Jersey shore.

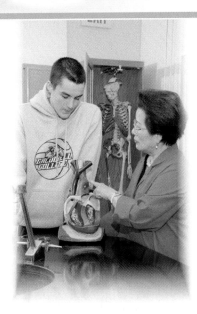

Our new B.S.N. program provides you with the chance to address the need for qualified nurses that currently exists, while giving back to society. You start with a strong foundation in the liberal arts and sciences and then spend time learning the clinical side of nursing at Mountainside Hospital. The B.S.N. degree is becoming the standard in nursing.

CONTACT INFORMATION

Ms. Kathryn Reilly, Director of Admissions

☎ 973-618-3226 or toll-free 888-864-9516

✉ admissions@caldwell.edu

Social Science Building

The College of New Jersey

EWING TOWNSHIP, NEW JERSEY
www.tcnj.edu/

Both *U.S. News & World Report* and *Barron's* cite The College of New Jersey (TCNJ) as one of the most competitive schools in the nation, public or private. Prepping students to be leaders in their fields, TCNJ has set the standard for higher education. That's why an exceptional 96 percent of first-year students return for their sophomore year. The College of New Jersey has more than 50 liberal arts and professional programs and study abroad programs in eighty cities around the world. While a very high percentage of graduates find immediate employment related to their fields of study, more than 20 percent go directly into graduate schools across the country. Rooming arrangements at TCNJ are flexible, from doubles in freshman halls to suites and single rooms in campus town houses or apartments for upperclass students. And students jump right into the mix of the more than 150 clubs and organizations on campus. Some play Manhunt in the dark (yes, Manhunt). Others join the Surf Club, the Astronomy Club or a fraternity or sorority. The arts come alive at TCNJ in two theaters, a recital hall and a gallery. Student health is important here, too. In Packer Hall, students use the large fitness center, a 25-meter swimming and diving pool and a basketball court. The Student Recreation Center has racquetball courts, four tennis courts that convert to basketball or volleyball courts, a weight room and an indoor track. Other facilities include a lighted Astroturf field, eight lighted outdoor tennis courts, an outdoor "beach" volleyball court and athletic fields. As a NCAA Division III member,

TCNJ students play twenty-one sports: eleven for men and ten for women. Since 1979, TCNJ student-athletes have earned thirty-six national championships and twenty-nine runner-up awards, more than any other Division III school in the country. TCNJ also offers tons of intramural sports from soccer to floor hockey. The College of New Jersey is set on 289 acres approximately 15 minutes from downtown Princeton and 5 miles from the state capital of Trenton. Woodlands and lakes surround the campus, which lies 30 miles from the

CONTACT INFORMATION

Ms. Lisa Angeloni, Dean of Admissions

☎ 609-771-2131 or toll-free l800-624-0967

✉ admiss@tcnj.edu

museums and nightlife of Philadelphia and 60 miles from New York City.

- **Enrollment:** *6,980*
- **Selectivity:** *very difficult*
- **Test scores:** *SAT—critical reading over 500, 99%; SAT—math over 500, 100%*
- **Application deadline:** *1/15 (freshmen), 2/15 (transfer)*
- **Expenses:** *Tuition $12,722; Room & Board $9996*

TCNJ Students

COLLEGE *of*
SAINT ELIZABETH

The College of Saint Elizabeth is an independent, four-year liberal arts college for women, located on 200 acres within Morris County, New Jersey. It is the oldest women's college in New Jersey and the first Catholic college in the United States to award degrees to women. In addition, CSE has undergraduate programs for non-traditionally aged adults, both men and women, as well as a comprehensive graduate program.

MORRISTOWN, NEW JERSEY
www.cse.edu/

The College of Saint Elizabeth (CSE), which celebrated its 110th anniversary in 2009, is the oldest college for women in New Jersey. Now open to men for weekend and evening classes, this Catholic-based college offers more than twenty-five bachelor's degree programs, ten master's degree programs, a three-year doctoral program in Educational Leadership and a number of professional certifications and certificates. Located on a 200-acre campus, CSE's buildings have gorgeous views of the surrounding hills. The two state-of-the-art residence halls have private and double rooms, kitchenettes, laundry rooms, lounges, convenient parking and Internet/email access in every room. The student center has an Olympic-size swimming pool, a gym, a fitness center, a drama studio, a newly renovated lounge and the College store. Annunciation Center, a multipurpose arts and education building opened in 2007, houses state-of the-art music, drama and art studios and a 560-seat performance center. Outside the classroom, students join extracurricular activities such as honor and professional societies, the Elizabeth Singers, the International/ Intercultural Club, the Nutrition and Wellness Club, Campus Ministry, Student Government and varsity athletics. Volunteerism is big, here, too. Most students take alternative spring break trips, organize Christmas toy drives or participate in disaster relief efforts. The College is affiliated with the North Eastern Athletic Conference (NEAC) and the Eastern Colleges Athletic Conference (ECAC); the Screaming Eagles compete in basketball, cross-country, lacrosse, soccer, softball, swimming,

tennis and volleyball at the NCAA Division III level. The College of Saint Elizabeth keeps a full calendar of social and cultural events. Recent visitors to the College have been Sister Helen Prejean (author of Dead Man Walking) and Dr. John Francis, who gave up riding in cars for 22 years out of concern for the environment. Students often hang with friends from Drew University and Fairleigh Dickinson University (FDU), two coed universities within walking distance of the campus. Morristown is located in the rapidly growing corporate center of historical

CONTACT INFORMATION

Ms. Donna Tatarka, Dean of Admissions

☎ 973-290-4700 or toll-free 800-210-7900

✉ apply@csa.edu

Morris County. The College is just an hour from New York City.

- **Enrollment:** *2,157*
- **Selectivity:** *moderately difficult*
- **Test scores:** *SAT—critical reading over 500, 27%; SAT— math over 500, 25%*
- **Application deadline:** *8/15 (freshmen), rolling (transfer)*
- **Expenses:** *Tuition $25,058; Room & Board $10,904*

Alyssa Kirby '10, a Business Administration major, is shown playing one of two sports she was involved in at the College. CSE offers eight NCAA Division III sports including basketball, cross-country, lacrosse, soccer, softball, swimming, tennis, and volleyball. CSE is a member of the North Eastern Athletic Conference (NEAC), North Atlantic Conference (NAC) and Eastern College Athletic Conference (ECAC).

FELICIAN COLLEGE
The Franciscan College of New Jersey

LODI, NEW JERSEY
www.felician.edu/

Students come first. That's the motto at Felician College, a Catholic/Franciscan liberal arts school that challenges students to reach their full potential while meeting the challenges of the new century. There are almost 55 undergrad majors in cutting-edge areas like Allied Health Technologies, Computer Information Services and Clinical Laboratory Sciences. In addition to its undergrad programs, Felician College offers the Master of Science in Nursing (M.S.N.), Master of Business Administration (M.B.A.), Master of Arts in Religious Education and Master of Arts in Teacher Education. Service to the community is an important part of the Felician experience. In fact, 2010 marks the third consecutive year that Felician has been named to the President's Honor Roll for community service. In 2009, 831

Felician students gather in front of the historic castle on the Rutherford campus.

NEW JERSEY

Felician students completed nearly 16,000 hours of community service at homeless shelters and food pantries, through tutoring at-risk kids and by working with environmental agencies. Students also learn outside the classroom at WRFC, Felician's own student-run radio station. It has state-of-the-art facilities offering digital broadcasts live 24 hours a day via streaming Web cast on the Internet. Felician College participates in NCAA Division II athletics. The Felician Golden Falcons compete in men's baseball, men's and women's basketball, men's and women's soccer, men's and women's cross-country, men's golf and women's softball and volleyball. The Athletics Department also sponsors a ton of intramural sports including indoor soccer, faculty-student softball and volleyball games on the quad. Felician College is located on two campuses in Lodi and Rutherford, in northern New Jersey. Both campuses are 12 miles from New York City and a few miles from the New Jersey Meadowlands sports complex. Students may choose to live in one of the spacious suites in Elliott Hall or Milton Court Residence, where they can grill in the courtyard or hit the game room. Both living units are located on the Rutherford Campus, a 10-minute shuttle bus ride from the campus in Lodi. The campuses offer comfortable student lounges, student meeting rooms, dining halls, a gym, a fitness center and grassy areas for picnicking or reading.

Small class sizes and personal attention are part of the Felician College experience!

- **Enrollment:** *2,088*
- **Selectivity:** *moderately difficult*
- **Test scores:** *SAT—critical reading over 500, 21.4%; SAT—math over 500, 23%*
- **Application deadline:** *Rolling (freshmen), rolling (transfer)*
- **Expenses:** *Tuition $25,050; Room & Board $9700*

CONTACT INFORMATION

College Admissions Office

☎ 201-559-6131

✉ admissions@felician.edu

Monmouth University's campus features modern buildings like the Jules L. Plangere Jr. Center for Communication. The center houses student radio station WMCX and the University's television studio.

MONMOUTH UNIVERSITY

WHERE LEADERS LOOK *forward*

WEST LONG BRANCH, NEW JERSEY
www.monmouth.edu/

Want it all? Monmouth University has it all. Location. Quality academics. Division I sports. Monmouth offers thirty-three undergraduate and twenty-one graduate degree programs in areas that are in demand in the workplace—business administration, corporate and public communication, criminal justice, financial mathematics, health-care management, nursing and software engineering to name a few. Special services ensure Monmouth students succeed, from the First Year at Monmouth Office to the Math Center, Writing Center and Peer Tutoring Office. Students can live in comfortable, air-conditioned halls with cable TV, microwaves and computer lounges or apartment complexes with full kitchens across the street from the beach. Popular activities include the Student Government Association; the campus newspaper *(Outlook)*, FM radio station (WMCX), and television station (Hawk TV); the African American Student Union; Hillel; intramurals; and sororities and fraternities. Special events run throughout the year including kayaking and whitewater rafting, trips to Philly and New York, concerts, student art exhibits and movie screenings. The University's NCAA Division I athletics program has nine men's teams—baseball, basketball, cross-country, football (FCS), golf, indoor track, outdoor track and field, soccer and tennis—and ten women's teams—basketball, cross-country, field hockey, golf, indoor track, lacrosse, outdoor track and field, soccer, softball and tennis. The 153,200-square-foot Multipurpose Activity Center (MAC) opened in fall 2009 and features a 4,100-seat arena with premium suites; 200-meter, six-lane indoor track; and fitness center. Outdoor facilities include tennis courts; an all-weather track; and baseball, football, soccer and softball fields. The University is located less than a mile from the beach and just over an hour's drive from New York City and Philadelphia. The University's 156-acre campus, considered to be one of the most beautiful in New Jersey, has Woodrow Wilson Hall as its centerpiece. This National Historic Landmark, made of the same limestone used in the Empire State Building, is where brides come to get photographed and magazines use as a backdrop for their ads. The Jules L. Plangere Jr. Center for Communication and Instructional Technology provides state-of-the-art studios and imaging rooms—and an Einstein Bagel Brothers coffee shop for hungry students. Restaurants, shops and theaters are within easy reach, and the PNC Bank

CONTACT INFORMATION

Ms. Victoria Bobik, Director of Undergraduate Admission

☎ 732-571-3456 or toll-free 800-543-9671

admission@monmouth.edu

Arts Center (for concerts and events) is only a few miles away. Also nearby are high-technology firms and financial institutions where graduates can find jobs and undergrads can intern.

- **Enrollment:** *6,499*
- **Selectivity:** *moderately difficult*
- **Test scores:** *ACT—over 18, 100%; SAT—critical reading over 500, 72%; SAT—math over 500, 81%*
- **Application deadline:** *3/1 (freshmen), 7/15 (transfer)*
- **Expenses:** *Tuition $25,013; Room & Board $9554*

http://bit.ly/collvid55

Students study, socialize, and snack together at Café Diem, Montclair State's wireless Internet café, which is open 24/7.

MONTCLAIR STATE
UNIVERSITY

MONTCLAIR, NEW JERSEY
www.montclair.edu/

Size matters at Montclair State University. As the second largest university in New Jersey, Montclair offers more than 250 undergraduate majors, minors and concentrations, and graduate programs in 100 fields of study. Size is important inside the classroom, too. With an average class size of 23, students get the personalized attention they need. Harry A. Sprague Library houses over 1.5 million books, periodicals and media—and allows students to borrow laptops for use throughout the wireless building. With this attention to detail, it's not surprising to its students and faculty that Montclair was recently named the top public university in New Jersey and number 54 in the nation by Forbes magazine. The University believes its students should be comfortable and happy living away from home. Here, students can choose from halls with central air and special interest communities (for example, arts students or international students grouped together) to garden apartments and even an apartment complex with a half basketball court and swimming pool. When not in class, students play Frisbee in the Quad, meet up for a Panini at Café Diem, catch a concert in one of MSU's six professionally equipped performance spaces or head to the newly built Recreation Center to play racquetball or swim. Students interested in working or interning at one of the many area businesses can simply access hundreds of listings online through the University's Career Directions site. The University's Center for Student Involvement provides countless clubs, organizations, activities and events to meet the needs of all students. Some join fraternities and sororities while others get active in the Cheerleading or Wrestling Clubs. With seventeen varsity sports for men and women, Montclair State University

competes in the highest of Division III conferences. To date, Montclair State has captured five NCAA Division III national championships and had over 260 of its athletes honored as all-Americans. And athletes needing treatment and rehab receive "Wiihab" at Montclair—trainers have been using the Nintendo Wii for therapy since 2007. Montclair State sits on a beautiful 246-acre suburban campus only 14 miles west of New York City. There are two New Jersey Transit train stations right on campus that provide easy access to Penn Station. Many students take day trips to nearby mountain resorts and beaches.

CONTACT INFORMATION

Jason Langdon, Director of Admissions

☎ 973-655-5116 or toll-free 800-331-9205

✉ undergraduate.admissions@montclair.edu

- **Enrollment:** *18,171*
- **Selectivity:** *moderately difficult*
- **Test scores:** *SAT—critical reading over 500, 45.94%; SAT—math over 500, 53%*
- **Application deadline:** *3/1 (freshmen), 6/15 (transfer)*
- **Expenses:** *Tuition $7042*

 http://bit.ly/collvid54

Seventeen varsity sports for men and women—and more than 100 clubs—make college life much more than the classroom.

For five years running, Ramapo College of New Jersey has been named to Kiplinger's list of the "100 Best Values in Public Colleges." Why? For starters, this liberal arts college offers about 700 courses each semester in forty different academic programs. That, combined with Ramapo's location near some of the world's major corporations, its state-of-the art facilities and its commitment to scholarship, grant and financial aid programs makes Ramapo an obvious choice for Kiplinger's list. Ramapo offers bachelor's degrees in the arts, business, humanities, social sciences and sciences as well as in professional studies that include nursing and social work. In addition, Ramapo offers programs leading to teacher certification at the elementary, middle school and secondary levels. The College offers the Master of Arts in Liberal Studies, the Master of Science in Educational Technology and the Master of Science in Nursing. In fall of 2010, Ramapo will welcome the first class of

RAMAPO COLLEGE
OF NEW JERSEY

MAHWAH, NEW JERSEY
www.ramapo.edu/

students into its Master of Arts in Sustainability Studies program—the only program of its kind in the Tristate area. This two-year program will create leaders of tomorrow in education, science and public policy. Life on campus is relaxed and fun. Students live in air-conditioned halls, with fridges, microwaves, cable television and high-speed Internet connections. The Robert A. Scott Student Center, with rec rooms, lounges and club offices, is the hub of on-campus activity. Students flock here during finals each year for "study break"—free refreshments, free copies of coursework, evening goodie bags and a quiet place to study. Most Ramapo students join a club or two—and they have more than 100 to pick from, everything from the Ski and Snowboard Club to the Bass Fishing Club. The 116,684-square-foot Bill Bradley Sports and Recreation Center opened in fall 2004. It has a 2,200-seat arena; fitness center, climbing wall; dance/aerobics studio; gym; and indoor pool. At Ramapo, sports facilities are open to all students, not just the varsity athletes. The Ramapo Roadrunners compete in twenty-two intercollegiate sports in one of the most challenging NCAA Division III conferences in the country. Ramapo College's barrier-free campus is located in the foothills of the Ramapo Mountains, just 25 miles from New York City.

CONTACT INFORMATION

Michael DiBartolomeo, Associate Director for Freshmen Admissions

☎ 201-684-7300 or toll-free 800-9RAMAPO

✉ admissions@ramapo.edu

- **Enrollment:** *6,026*
- **Selectivity:** *moderately difficult*
- **Test scores:** *SAT—critical reading over 500, 90%; SAT—math over 500, 96%*
- **Application deadline:** *3/1 (freshmen), 5/1 (transfer)*
- **Expenses:** *Tuition $11,416; Room & Board $11,290*

 http://bit.ly/collvid60

Students enjoy a game of billiards in the Overlook Residence Hall.

STOCKTON COLLEGE

THE RICHARD STOCKTON COLLEGE OF NEW JERSEY

POMONA, NEW JERSEY
www.stockton.edu/

At The Richard Stockton College of New Jersey (RSCNJ), students enjoy small class sizes, exceptional academics, an environmentally friendly campus, a great location and reasonable tuition. This public liberal arts school offers programs in the arts and humanities; business; education; health sciences; and social, behavioral and natural sciences. In addition to bachelor's degrees, Stockton offers graduate programs: Doctor of Physical Therapy; Master of Arts in criminal justice, Holocaust and genocide studies, education, and instructional technology; Master of Business Administration; and Master of Science in computational science, nursing, occupational therapy and social work; a Professional Science Master in environmental science, as well as certificate programs in education, ESL, NJ Standard Supervisor Endorsement and paralegal studies. Outside the classroom, students join intramural and club sports including aikido, crew, flag football, golf, ice hockey, soccer, softball, street hockey, swimming and volleyball. At the intercollegiate level, Stockton fields NCAA Division III teams in men's baseball, basketball, lacrosse and soccer; women's basketball, crew, field hockey, soccer, softball, tennis and volleyball; and men's and women's cross-country and track and field. The multipurpose Sports Center has fitness rooms, racquetball courts and weight rooms; outdoors is a field house, NCAA track and four lighted fields for soccer and lacrosse. The G-Wing College Center is the hub for clubs and organizations such as the Performing Arts Committee, the Social Work Club, the Accounting and Finance Society and twenty-one sororities and fraternities. The N-Wing College Center has a living room-space with a dining area, a wide-screen television, a game room and lounge areas where students can shoot pool or play foosball. Many students take advantage of the free Stockton After Hours programs—everything from karaoke to concerts and comedy shows. On-campus,

Stockton students live in completely furnished and air-conditioned dorms and apartments with cable TV, telephone service and Internet access (port-per-pillow) provided. Off-campus choices range from new townhouse complexes near campus to winter rentals in one of the local seashore towns. The Richard Stockton College of New Jersey is located on a 1,600-acre campus in the Pinelands National Reserve, just 12 miles from Atlantic City and an hour from Philadelphia. Stockton was "green" before it became trendy. The campus has one of the world's largest operating geo-thermal heating and cooling systems and innovative

environmental studies and marine science programs. Within a 15-minute drive of campus, students can fish, boat, hike and swim.

CONTACT INFORMATION

Mr. John Iacovelli, Dean of Enrollment Management

☎ 609-652-4261
🖥 admissions@stockton.edu

- **Enrollment:** *7,559*

- **Selectivity:** *very difficult*

- **Test scores:** *ACT—over 18, 92%; SAT—critical reading over 500, 68%; SAT—math over 500, 76%*

- **Application deadline:** *5/1 (freshmen), 6/1 (transfer)*

- **Expenses:** *Tuition $11,041; Room & Board $10,189*

At the University, you'll find a supportive environment that encourages you to gain confidence and acquire the knowledge that remarkable things are within your reach.

WILLIAM PATERSON UNIVERSITY

WAYNE, NEW JERSEY
www.wpunj.edu/

William Paterson University invites its students to turn what's possible into what's next. This forward-thinking University reflects the area's need for challenging, affordable education. William Paterson offers forty-four undergraduate and twenty-one graduate programs through its five colleges. The Center for Continuing and Professional Education offers everything from noncredit courses to corporate training and advanced computer skills training to today's working adults who require professional development and flexible scheduling.

William Paterson's 370-acre campus, with its wooded areas and waterfalls, is an ideal place to study and relax. On campus, undergrads live in state-of-the-art halls or apartments. High Mountain East and West, built in 2006, feature suite-style rooms, lounges equipped with wireless connectivity and two "smart" classrooms. The recently renovated University Commons complex is where the entire University community hangs out. This campus center has a 500-seat ballroom, outdoor patios and lounges, meeting and event rooms and a new student cafe all under one roof. Most students join at least one of the more than seventy clubs and organizations from fraternities and sororities to honor societies. Students staff the campus radio station (WPSC) and the television station (WPC-TV), which develops television programs for local and statewide cable networks. The Recreation Center has main courts for badminton, basketball, indoor tennis and volleyball; an exercise room; saunas; and Jacuzzis. Wrightman Stadium, where the Pioneer football and field hockey teams play, was renovated in 2004; upgrades included the installation of A-Turf—a state-of-the-art synthetic grass-like surface that provides excellent playing conditions even in the worst weather. The University has twelve intercollegiate sports teams, five for men and seven for women, including successful NCAA teams in men's baseball and women's softball. Popular club sports include bowling, rugby, horseback riding and ice hockey. The University has a competition-size indoor pool, outdoor tennis courts and a lighted athletics field complex. William Paterson University is located in northern New Jersey in the busy suburb of Wayne. New York City is just 20 miles to the east, the beach is an hour's drive south, skiing is 30 miles north, and the Meadowlands

At the University, you'll study in small classes taught by professors who are experts in their fields.

Sports Complex is a half-hour away.

- **Enrollment:** *10,819*
- **Selectivity:** *moderately difficult*
- **Test scores:** *SAT—critical reading over 500, 43.5%; SAT—math over 500, 50%*
- **Application deadline:** *5/1 (freshmen), 6/1 (transfer)*
- **Expenses:** *Tuition $10,838; Room & Board $10,280*

CONTACT INFORMATION

Mr. Anthony Leckey, Associate Director of Admissions

☎ 973-720-2903 or toll-free 877-WPU-EXCEL
✉ admissions@wpunj.edu

Named a Fiske Guide *"Best Buy" five years in a row.*

ADELPHI UNIVERSITY
GARDEN CITY, NEW YORK

GARDEN CITY, NEW YORK
www.adelphi.edu/

Discover Adelphi University—its students, its programs and its traditions—and you won't look anywhere else. The University's schools and programs include the College of Arts and Sciences; the Honors College; the Schools of Business, Nursing, and Social Work; the Ruth S. Ammon School of Education; the Gordon F. Derner Institute of Advanced Psychological Studies; and adult academic programs in University College. Besides the University's main location in Garden

City, it also has three off-campus centers: the Manhattan Center in New York City, the Hauppauge Center on Long Island, and the Hudson Valley Center in Poughkeepsie, New York. While universities around the country have been getting rid of faculty, Adelphi has been hiring—more than 280 new professors since 2001. Adelphi has also spent millions in recent years to build a new performing arts center, bring smart classrooms to campus, introduce state-of-the-art lasers to the physics labs and present new Steinway pianos to the music departments. Campus life is fun and fast-paced. Students can live in updated dorms with climate control, private bathrooms and patios—construction is underway on an eco-friendly residence hall to be completed by summer 2011. Students also join the many intramural and intercollegiate athletics at Adelphi. The Panthers play twenty-two intercollegiate sports at the Division II level—with the exception of the Division I men's soccer team. Intramural sports include dodgeball, flag

First team to win NCAA Lacrosse title for two consecutive years.

football and 5-on-5 basketball. The Rec Department hosts popular one-day tournaments in kickball, wiffleball and badminton, too. Woodruff Hall, renovated in the summer of 2008, includes a four-lane swimming pool (swimsuit dryers in the locker rooms); a three-court gym for basketball and volleyball; weight-training and exercise rooms; a large indoor running track; a café where students can grab a snack or smoothie; and fields for baseball, lacrosse, soccer and softball. In the Ruth S. Harley University Center (UC), Adelphi students browse in the bookstore, relax in one of the lounges (commuter students have a special lounge equipped with lockers), eat in the UC Cafeteria and enjoy movies,

comedy shows, dance parties and concerts. Adelphi's main campus is located in the suburb of Garden City, a village of stately homes, historic buildings and parks. New York City is only 20 miles east of campus.

- **Enrollment:** *7,951*

- **Selectivity:** *moderately difficult*

- **Test scores:** *ACT—over 18, 97.36%; SAT—critical reading over 500, 68.94%; SAT—math over 500, 76.1%*

- **Application deadline:** *Rolling (freshmen), rolling (transfer)*

http://bit.ly/collvid28

NYC is the laboratory where students apply theory. Theatre majors head to Broadway and art historians to world-class museums. Our location also means practical learning—2,500 internships in every field.

BARNARD

THE LIBERAL ARTS COLLEGE
FOR WOMEN
IN NEW YORK CITY

NEW YORK, NEW YORK
www.barnard.edu/

Barnard College was founded in 1889 as a liberal arts college for women. Barnard partnered with the Columbia University system in 1900 and today students at the two schools may cross-register for courses at either school. Barnard students have access to Columbia University libraries, and graduates receive their degree from the university. Despite this close connection, Barnard College remains a small, independent college that maintains its own Board of Trustees, faculty and staff; its own endowment; an independent admissions process; and sole ownership of its property. The self-contained Barnard campus sits on four acres in NYC along Broadway between 116th and 120th streets. The newly renovated Ethel S. LeFrak '41 and Samuel J. LeFrak Gymnasium has an indoor track, stage and a wide variety of phys ed courses—everything from archery and volleyball to yoga and aquatic exercise. The College's newest building, the seven-story glass Diana Center, is where students go to dine, relax and study. It houses a student café, a theater, lounges and a green roof. The green roof's pavilion and open patio provide outdoor classroom experience for Biology and Environmental Science students and is energy efficient since it reduces heat transfer and limits rainwater surges. Other students learn outside the classroom through Barnard's study abroad program; currently, Barnard undergrads study in 35 countries from Australia to Tibet. Athletes at Barnard have the unique opportunity to compete as teammates with Columbia undergrads. This arrangement, known as a "consortium" under NCAA rules, is one of just three in the nation—and the only one at the Division I level. Women compete in archery, basketball, fencing, field hockey, golf, lacrosse, rowing, soccer, softball, swimming and diving, tennis, track and field, cross country and volleyball. Undergrads are guaranteed housing all four years and they can choose from halls, suites and apartments; all residence halls have modern security systems and 24-hour desk coverage when classes are in session. Barnard is located on the upper west side of Manhattan, in the safe and quiet Morningside Heights neighborhood, directly across from Columbia University.

CONTACT INFORMATION

Ms. Jennifer Gill Fondiller, Dean of Admissions

☎ 212-854-2014

✉ admissions@barnard.edu

- **Enrollment:** *2,417*
- **Selectivity:** *most difficult*
- **Test scores:** *ACT—over 18, 100%; SAT—critical reading over 500, 99%; SAT—math over 500, 99%*
- **Application deadline:** *1/1 (freshmen), 4/1 (transfer)*
- **Expenses:** *Tuition $38,650; Room & Board $12,319*

A liberal arts college for women, a green campus in NYC, a partnership with an Ivy League university, Barnard is unique. Within a community as diverse as it is nurturing, Barnard is transformational.

The College of Saint Rose

ALBANY, NEW YORK
www.strose.edu/

Academics and career preparation are top priorities at The College of Saint Rose. In fact, *Money* magazine and *U.S. News & World Report* have ranked Saint Rose as one of the top colleges in the Northeast and the nation, based on affordability and academic quality. Students dive into the College's sixty-six undergraduate programs, most of which incorporate a field experience or internship component—and finding internships is easy when you have the capital of New York as your location. The College comprises eighty buildings that have the latest technology and are eco-friendly. The new, 46,000-square foot Massry Center for the Arts (one of the most energy efficient buildings in the region) has smart classrooms, practice and rehearsal rooms, performance space—and students enjoy wireless Internet throughout the building. The $15 million Thelma P. Lally School of Education is entirely wireless and each classroom is equipped with a multimedia station; it also has an educational and clinical services center with an on-site preschool and a speech and hearing clinic. The new Center for Communications and Interactive Media (CCIM) has a full HDTV/photography studio, multimedia labs for Mac and PC, a viewing and projection room and a high-tech music studio. Students of all faiths come to meditate and relax at The Hubbard Interfaith Sanctuary; it has a natural wood and interior garden and even a bubbling lily pond. Campus housing includes traditional and suite-style residence halls and town houses as well as more

than thirty Victorian homes. Each house has its own history and character, with unique wraparound porches and stained-glass windows. The College of Saint Rose participates in NCAA Division II and the Northeast-10 Conference. Intercollegiate teams include men's baseball and golf; men's and women's basketball, cross country, soccer, swimming, tennis and track and field; and women's softball and volleyball. Saint Rose students also belong to more than thirty groups and clubs from the Adventure Club to the student newspaper. Saint Rose is located in the historic Pine Hills neighborhood of Albany. With more than 60,000 college students in the area, there are always things to do and people to

CONTACT INFORMATION

Mr. Jeremy Bogan, Assistant Vice President of Undergraduate Admissions

☎ 518-454-5154 or toll-free 800-637-8556
✉ admit@strose.edu

meet. Off campus, students can walk or grab a bus to hit a ton of restaurants, shops, museums, malls and theaters.

- **Enrollment:** *5,158*
- **Selectivity:** *moderately difficult*
- **Test scores:** *ACT—over 18, 90%; SAT—critical reading over 500, 57%; SAT—math over 500, 60%*
- **Application deadline:** *5/1 (freshmen), 5/1 (transfer)*
- **Expenses:** *Tuition $24,135; Room & Board $9880*

CSI nursing student

COLLEGE OF STATEN ISLAND IS CUNY

STATEN ISLAND, NEW YORK
www.csi.cuny.edu/

The College of Staten Island (CSI) is a four-year senior college within the City University of New York (CUNY) and is Staten Island's only public college or university. Here, students choose from thirty exciting undergrad programs and nearly twenty graduate programs in everything from Chemistry to Performing and Creative Arts. CSI sits on 204 acres in the heart of Staten Island and is the largest college campus (public or private) within New York City. The campus is amazing and high-tech. The Division of Science and Technology operates the Advanced Imaging Facility complete with an atomic force microscope, a live cell imaging system and instruments for tissue processing. The College also has a High Performance Computing (HPC) Facility with cluster-based super-computers that support interactive and batch computing and visualization. The Astrophysical Observatory (funded by NASA and the NSF) has a Meade 16-inch computerized telescope and is open to students and the public monthly and during special celestial events. The two-story rotunda space in the campus center houses study and sleep lounges, a performance/cafe space, game rooms with the latest game consoles as well as the state-of-the-art studios of WSIA (the student-operated FM radio station). CSI's Sports and Recreation Center has an eight-lane pool with diving boards; five racquetball courts; courts for basketball, volleyball and badminton; and a full schedule of yoga and kick-boxing classes. Outdoors, students compete on twelve tennis courts, three softball fields and the football field. The CSI Dolphins participate in NCAA Division III sports; men's teams are baseball,

basketball, soccer, swimming, tennis and cross country and women's teams are basketball, soccer, softball, swimming, tennis, volleyball and cross country. And CSI's campus doesn't become a ghost town in summer. Students enroll in a number of summer courses and enjoy a ton of activities from ice cream and crafts at the fountain to sky watching at the observatory. CSI's location offers students the best of two worlds— the suburbs of Staten Island combined with Manhattan's city culture and nightlife just 25 minutes away.

CONTACT INFORMATION

Mr. Emmanuel Esperance Jr., Interim Director of Recruitment and Admissions

☎ 718-982-2010
✉ admissions@mail.cuny.csi.edu

- **Enrollment:** *13,858*
- **Selectivity:** *moderately difficult*
- **Test scores:** *SAT—critical reading over 500, 40.74%; SAT—math over 500, 53.19%*
- **Application deadline:** *Rolling (freshmen), rolling (transfer)*
- **Expenses:** *Tuition $4978*

Jose Saltos, Biochemistry major at CSI

With students of color representing more than 50% of the student body, and almost 20% from international backgrounds, Columbia is known as one of the most diverse institutions in the country.

COLUMBIA UNIVERSITY
IN THE CITY OF NEW YORK

www.columbia.edu/

In 1754, King George II granted a charter to a group of New York citizens to found King's College. In its early days, Alexander Hamilton, John Jay and Robert Livingston all studied there. After the Revolution, New York State issued the college a new charter with a patriotic name—Columbia. In 1897, Columbia moved to a site on the Upper West Side of Manhattan. The architectural firm of McKim, Mead and White designed an open central enclave six blocks long, with a majestic domed library at the center. To this day, it remains one of New York's most impressive settings. Today, Columbia College and The Fu Foundation School of Engineering and Applied Science offer students unique advantages; they are at the same time small, selective colleges while also parts of a major research university. Students come from all fifty states and over ninety countries. They represent a mix of ethnic, social, economic, cultural and religious backgrounds—just like the people of New York City itself. Columbia students take part in many groups: artistic (theater, musical and dance), athletic (thirty-one Division I varsity sports and dozens of club and intramural sports), communications (the *Columbia Daily Spectator*, WKCR-FM, a campus television station), community service (Amnesty International, Big Brother/Big Sister, a volunteer ambulance squad), and preprofessional (the Charles Drew Pre-Medical Society and the National Society of Black Engineers). There are also thirty-three fraternities and sororities. Columbia shares its Morningside Heights neighborhood with other famous institutions: Barnard College, the Cathedral of St. John the Divine, Union Theological Seminary, Jewish Theological Seminary and the Manhattan School of Music, to name a few. The area is known for bookstores, restaurants and stores that cater to student tastes, student budgets and student hours. Through the Columbia University Arts Initiative, students can receive discounted tickets to Broadway shows, film screenings and art galleries. Passport to NYC offers students free access to museums throughout the city. Columbia students can be found any day of the week exploring the Metropolitan Museum of Art, the Museum of Modern Art, the Guggenheim Museum, the Museum of African Art or the Museo del Barrio. At night, they might be attending the ballet at Lincoln Center; watching a movie on campus or in one of New York's 400-plus movie theaters; enjoying jazz in Greenwich Village or blues at the Apollo; sampling *pai gwat* in Chinatown; or biking or boating in Central Park.

- **Enrollment:** *5,766*
- **Selectivity:** *most difficult*
- **Test scores:** *SAT—critical reading over 500, 100%; SAT—math over 500, 100%*
- **Application deadline:** *1/2 (freshmen), 3/15 (transfer)*
- **Expenses:** *Tuition $39,296; Room & Board $10,228*

A passion for food is what brings students to the world's premier culinary college—The Culinary Institute of America (CIA). This private college provides the world's best undergraduate education in culinary arts and baking and pastry arts. At the CIA, students gain the general knowledge and specific skills they need to become leaders in the foodservice and hospitality industry, the largest private employer in the United States. All CIA degree programs emphasize professional, hands-on learning in the college's kitchens, bakeshops and restaurants—students typically log at least 1,300 hours in a kitchen or bakeshop. CIA classes span the culinary globe, exploring great cultures, cooking techniques and cuisines—everything from sushi to Cuban sandwiches to strawberry Napoleans, CIA students prepare and eat amazing dishes every day. Classes are taken in a progressive sequence in order to build skills, food knowledge and production experience. These studies culminate in operating courses that give students both

THE CULINARY INSTITUTE OF AMERICA®

THE WORLD'S PREMIER CULINARY COLLEGE

HYDE PARK, NEW YORK

www.ciachef.edu/

kitchen and front-of-the-house experiences in the college's famous restaurants. On campus, students have access to forty-one kitchens and bakeshops, five public restaurants and a huge culinary library. Bachelor's degree students also focus on foodservice management development, with a broad range of business management and liberal arts courses. CIA students enjoy an active campus life, with a variety of intramural and club sports, student clubs, and extracurricular activities such as ski and camping trips, live entertainment, presentations by leading chefs and industry executives and cook-offs. The college's Student Recreation Center includes a six-lane pool, a gym, racquetball courts, an aerobics studio, a fitness center and free-weight room, a game room, outdoor tennis courts, and the Courtside Cafe and Pub. Freshmen live in air-conditioned, wireless halls on the banks of the Hudson

River; upperclassmen can live in six Adirondack-style lodges with suites and private baths. The CIA's 170-acre campus in Hyde Park is just 1½–2 hours from New York City and Albany. There are a number of state parks and historic sites throughout the area. Students can taste wines at local vineyards, visit farmer's markets and pick apples at nearby orchards. To the west are the Catskill and Shawangunk Mountains, where CIA students go

CONTACT INFORMATION

Ms. Rachel Birchwood, Director of Admissions

☎ 845-451-1459 or toll-free 800-CULINARY

✉ admissions@culinary.edu

to hike, ski, rock climb, mountain bike and sightsee.

- **Enrollment:** *2,914*
- **Selectivity:** *moderately difficult*
- **Application deadline:** *Rolling (freshmen)*
- **Expenses:** *Tuition $24,550; Room & Board $8110*

Academics at Daemen College will challenge and inspire you.

DAEMEN
COLLEGE

AMHERST, NEW YORK
www.daemen.edu/

Daemen College prepares students for life and leadership in an increasingly complex world. This private, career-oriented liberal arts college offers more than thirty undergraduate programs and six graduate programs through the Division of Arts and Sciences and the Division of Health and Human Services. With a Daemen education, students don't just learn inside a classroom either. At least half the student body participates in community service activities, whether working in nursing homes or clinics or tutoring at-risk kids. Daemen is so committed to service that it was selected to host the 2010 Global

Youth Service Day—the largest annual service event in the world. This three-day event brought together 500-600 students for community gardening, clean-ups and environmental literacy projects. Assisted by a supportive faculty, Daemen students are encouraged to pursue goals beyond their initial expectations, to respond to academic challenges and to develop habits that enrich their lives and their community. On campus, the modern, apartment-style residence halls have kitchens, laundry facilities, lounges and in-room phone/Internet connections. Students head to the Wick Student Center to grab a bite at the Cyber Café or hang in the gameroom or lounge. The newest Daemen building, the Research and Information Commons, is innovative in its design and eco-friendly features. It is a beautiful and relaxing place to study in its library or computing center while at the same time being water and energy efficient.

Most Daemen students join at least one of the more than fifty student clubs and organizations, from the Environmental Club to the Lacrosse Club. The Daemen Wildcats play intercollegiate sports in men's and women's basketball, cross country and soccer. Men have a golf team and women also compete in volleyball. Other students enjoy the popular intramural program—some play touch football while others sign up for karate or yoga. The College hosts a ton of themed dinners, movie nights, musical theater and internationally famous speakers (Erin Brockovich spoke on environmental activism recently). Daemen's suburban 39-acre campus is located in Amherst. Daemen is just minutes away from the city of Buffalo, where students take in theater, music, art, restaurants and major league sports. The city is very close to scenic Niagara Falls and Canada.

Daemen College students taking a study break and enjoying a day in Italy.

- **Enrollment:** *2,921*
- **Selectivity:** *moderately difficult*
- **Test scores:** *ACT—over 18, 90.7%; SAT—critical reading over 500, 49.8%; SAT—math over 500, 59%*
- **Application deadline:** *Rolling (freshmen), rolling (transfer)*
- **Expenses:** *Tuition $20,720; Room & Board $9450*

CONTACT INFORMATION

Mr. Frank Williams, Director of Undergraduate Admissions

☎ 716-839-8225 or toll-free 800-462-7652

🖳 admissions@daemen.edu

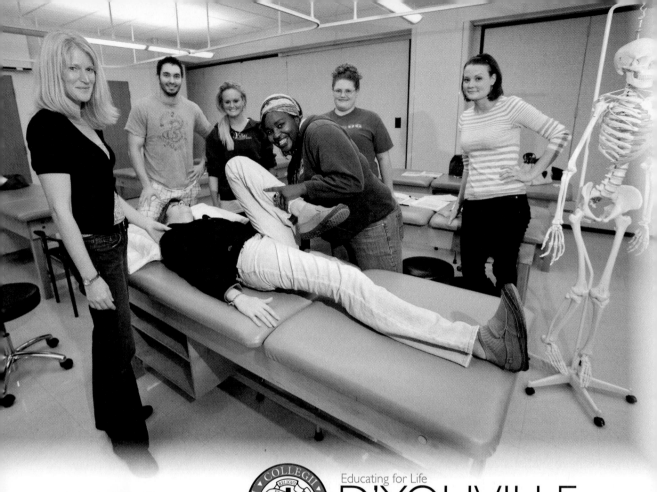

A leader in health care education D'Youville offers a wide array of programs including Nursing, Physician Assistant, Dietetics, Pharmacy, Chiropractic, Occupational and Physical Therapy.

Educating for Life

D'YOUVILLE COLLEGE

BUFFALO, NEW YORK
www.dyc.edu/

Deciding which college to go to is hard. D'Youville College makes your decision a lot easier. Here, students can choose from twenty-seven bachelor's, eight master's and five post-bachelor's degrees as well as advanced certificate programs in health-related professions. The multiple-option Nursing Degree Program is one of the largest four-year private-college nursing programs in the country. Available nursing programs include B.S.N., B.S.N./M.S. (five years) and RN to B.S.N. The College is committed to helping its students to grow not only academically but also socially and personally. Service learning programs are an important part of the D'Youville experience. Political Activism students have worked on campaigns and registered voters, Sociology students have developed an Adopt-a-Grandparent program and Occupational Therapy students have taught ceramics to children. Through the College's study abroad program, students head to Italy and England to earn credits while studying and exploring. Back home on campus, students live in Marguerite Hall or the new apartment complex where they have a scenic view of the Niagara River and Lake Erie, which separate the U.S. and Canadian shorelines. The Student Center has a new gym, a swimming pool, fitness and wellness area, a training room, a dance studio and a recreation center. D'Youville students know how to have fun. They regularly schedule activities such as psychic fairs and scavenger hunts, soul food luncheons and Easter egg hunts. They join intramural sports, NCAA Division III intercollegiate sports (baseball, basketball, crew, volleyball, golf, cross-country, soccer and softball), the ski club and the College newspaper. D'Youville is situated on Buffalo's residential west side. The College is close to many attractions, including shopping, night-clubs, Ralph Wilson Stadium (where the Buffalo Bills play) and the Buffalo Raceway. Buffalo is only 90 miles from Toronto and 25 minutes from Niagara Falls. Holiday Valley, a skier's paradise, is an hour's drive away. And D'Youville undergrads can meet friends from all walks—college students in the Buffalo area number more than 60,000.

CONTACT INFORMATION

Dr. Steve Smith, Director of Undergraduate Admissions

☎ 716-829-7600 or toll-free 800-777-3921

- **Enrollment:** *2,971*
- **Selectivity:** *moderately difficult*
- **Test scores:** *ACT—over 18, 98%; SAT—critical reading over 500, 64%; SAT—math over 500, 68%*
- **Application deadline:** *Rolling (freshmen), rolling (transfer)*
- **Expenses:** *Tuition $20,030; Room & Board $9800*

Student surveys at D'Youville show students consistently rank "small classes, friendly campus and great faculty" as key reasons they like the college.

EUGENE LANG COLLEGE
THE NEW SCHOOL
FOR LIBERAL ARTS

NEW YORK, NEW YORK
www.lang.edu/

Eugene Lang College is the undergraduate liberal arts division of The New School, a leading university in New York City with a tradition of innovative learning. The New School has long been a home for artists, educators and public figures. In fact, The New School was the first college or university to offer courses in fields such as black culture and race, taught by W. E. B. DuBois, and psychoanalysis, taught by Freud's disciple Sandor Ferenczi. Among the world-famous artists and performers who have taught at The New School are Martha Graham, Aaron Copland and Thomas Hart Benton. Eugene Lang College students take exciting, meaningful classes in Environmental Studies, Culture and Media, Economics and the Arts. At Lang, academic programs are closely connected with all that New York City has to offer:

its wealth of music, theater and arts; its vibrant international community; its history; and its energy. Always at the forefront, Lang co-sponsored the World Science Festival in June 2010. The festival presented programs ranging from astronomy, physics and genetics to neuroscience, robotics and mathematics. The festival's programs also featured traditional arts—dance, theatre, music and visual—to stress that science is everywhere. Internships are an important part of the college experience at Lang; recently, Lang undergrads have landed coveted spots at MTV, HBO, the *Village Voice*, the ACLU and the White House. Students start up and join a ton of different clubs and activities at Eugene Lang College, too. They organize outings to Broadway shows through the "Lang in the City" program. They meet up for group runs with the Lang Marathon Team. They write for the school newspaper. There is truly something for everyone here at Lang. The university is located in New York City's Greenwich Village. This legendary New York City neighborhood of town houses and tree-lined streets offers students a friendly and stimulating environment. Students can head to the Grey Dog Café for coffee and pancakes or visit the Rock and Roll Hall of Fame Annex. Students can take walks through Washington Square Park or shop in vintage clothing stores. Nowhere, except at Lang, can you get a small college, a bigger university and an even bigger city life.

CONTACT INFORMATION

Karen Williams, Director of Admissions

☎ 212-229-5665 or toll-free 877-528-3321

🖥 lang@newschool.edu

- **Enrollment:** *1,439*
- **Selectivity:** *very difficult*
- **Test scores:** *ACT—over 18, 97%; SAT—critical reading over 500, 87%; SAT—math over 500, 66%*
- **Application deadline:** *2/1 (freshmen), 5/15 (transfer)*
- **Expenses:** *Tuition $34,550; Room & Board $15,260*

FIT student in a textile class.

FASHION INSTITUTE OF TECHNOLOGY

NEW YORK, NEW YORK
www.fitnyc.edu/

The Fashion Institute of Technology (FIT) is New York City's urban college for creative and business talent. A selective State University of New York (SUNY) college of art and design, business and technology, FIT is a creative mix of innovative achievers, original thinkers and industry pioneers, with nearly forty programs leading to A.A.S., B.F.A. and B.S. degrees. The School of Graduate Studies also offers a Master of Arts (M.A.) or Master of Professional Studies (M.P.S.) degree. FIT's mission is to produce well-rounded graduates: doers and thinkers who raise the professional bar to become the next generation of business pacesetters and creative icons. FIT is flexible, too; students opt for full- or part-time study, evening/weekend degree programs and online studies. One of the things FIT students like best is that they can start major-area courses right away—they don't have to spend their first two years chipping away at general education courses like at other schools. The college has an active student and residential life. Throughout the David Dubinsky Student Center are lounges, a game room, a dining hall, a student radio station, the Style Shop (a FIT student-run boutique),

student government and club offices, a comprehensive health center, two gyms, a dance studio, a weight room and a counseling center. FIT students take their pick of more than sixty clubs and organizations, from The Ad Group to the Snow Club to the Merchandising Society. FIT is a member of the National Junior College Athletic Association and offers the following varsity sports: women's cheerleading, men's and women's cross country and half marathon, co-ed dance, men's and women's swimming and diving, co-ed table tennis, women's tennis, men's and women's track and field and women's volleyball. Occupying an entire block in Manhattan's Chelsea neighborhood, FIT's campus places students at the heart of the fashion, advertising, visual arts, design, business and communications industries. Students gain unparalleled exposure to their field through internship opportunities and professional connections. Students also have

Fashion Institute of Technology

access to hip restaurants, museums, art galleries and boutiques within walking distance of the campus.

- **Enrollment:** *10,413*
- **Selectivity:** *moderately difficult*
- **Application deadline:** *1/15 (freshmen), 1/15 (transfer)*
- **Expenses:** *Tuition $5618; Room & Board $11,248*

http://bit.ly/collvid39

CONTACT INFORMATION

Ms. Yamiley Saintvil, Director of Admissions

☎ 212-217-3760 or toll-free 800-GOTOFIT

✉ fitinfo@fitnyc.edu

This shot was taken on location in New York City's Central Park as part of a project for a film class.

FIVE TOWNS COLLEGE
When you're serious about Music, Business, Education, Media and the Performing Arts!

DIX HILLS, NEW YORK
www.ftc.edu/

Students serious about music, business, education, media and the performing arts look no further than Five Towns College. Located on Long Island's North Shore, this independent college lets students study in a suburban environment that is close to New York City. The College offers a number of associate, bachelor's, master's and doctoral degrees—notably, programs leading to the Master of Music (M.M.) degree in jazz/commercial music and in music education, the Master of Science in Education (M.S.Ed.) and the Doctor of Musical Arts (D.M.A.). The College's music programs are contemporary jazz in nature, although classical musicians are also part of this creative community. The most popular programs are audio recording technology, broadcasting, journalism, music performance, music business, music and elementary teacher education, theater, and film/video production. To support these majors, Five Towns is constantly upgrading its buildings and technology; the campus has three audio recording studios, a film/television studio, a piano lab, a ProTools/MIDI lab, a PC lab, a computer graphics lab and a number of other music rooms and studios. The state-of-the-art Dix Hill Performing Arts Center welcomes local and well-known musicians and comedians to campus. The Five Towns College Living/Learning Center is a brand-new complex containing four modern life residence halls. Each residence hall has single- and double-occupancy rooms equipped with private bathrooms, climate control, high-speed Internet access and cable television. The College's beautiful 35-acre campus, located in

the wooded countryside of Dix Hills, provides students with a quiet college setting. But just off campus is Long Island's bustling Route 110 corridor, home to national and multinational corporations—many places where Five Towns students can work and intern. Recently, students have interned at Sony, Def Jam, Cablevision, Disney and Madison Square Garden. New York City, with everything from Lincoln Center to Broadway, is just a train ride away. The College is located within the historic town of Huntington, which is home to the Cinema Arts Center, Hecksher Museum, Vanderbilt Museum, and numerous restaurants, coffeehouses

CONTACT INFORMATION

Mr. Jerry Cohen, Dean of Enrollment

☎ 631-424-7000 Ext. 2110
✉ jcohen@ftc.edu

and shops. Nearby, students hit the white sand beaches of Jones Beach State Park and Fire Island National Seashore.

- **Enrollment:** *1,447*
- **Selectivity:** *moderately difficult*
- **Application deadline:** *Rolling (freshmen), rolling (transfer)*
- **Expenses:** *Tuition $17,750; Room & Board $12,300*

Students are seen here mixing a song for an upcoming project using the SSL9000J 72 consol.

HilbertCollege

HAMBURG, NEW YORK
www.hilbert.edu/

A liberal arts education is the cornerstone of any Hilbert graduate's success. Since 1957, Hilbert College has provided challenging academic programs and close personal attention to its students. The College offers thirteen bachelor-level programs in majors that are in demand—Accounting, Forensic Science/Crime Scene Investigation and Rehabilitation Services—as well as more than fifty minors and concentrations. The Criminal Justice program is rated one of the top in New York State—it prepares students for careers in law enforcement at all levels (local, state and federal). In fact, Hilbert introduced the Institute for Law and Justice in 2000; it serves as a local, regional and national resource for law enforcement, crime prevention and community well-being. Hilbert's campus is modern and comfortable. Students live in suites and apartments with 24-hour computer labs and free laundry services. The Hafner Recreation Center was renovated in 2005. It now features a 2,000-square-foot fitness center with state-of-the-art aerobic and strength training equipment, an expanded athletic training room, six new televisions with Direct TV and four locker rooms (making it easy to host double header basketball games). The $6 million Paczesny Hall, Hilbert's newest building, has twelve networked classrooms with Smartboards and Sympodium tools and a connected 452-seat auditorium with state-of-the-art sound and lighting, a green room and rehearsal space. Students get involved in the tons of on-campus events (movie nights and quad parties) and clubs (Adventure Club and student newspaper). The College's NCAA Division III athletics program supports intercollegiate sports in men's baseball, basketball, cross-country, golf, lacrosse, soccer and volleyball. Women's sports are basketball, cross-country, lacrosse, soccer, softball and volleyball. Competitive lacrosse is new to the College in the 2010–11 school year. Hilbert College's nearly 50-acre campus is located in the town of Hamburg in western New York State. Hamburg is close to several ski and snowboard areas. The campus is also about 10 minutes south of Buffalo, and just minutes from the shores of Lake Erie. Downtown Buffalo attractions include Kleinhans Music Hall, the Albright-Knox Art Gallery, the Museum of Science, several professional sports stadiums and the Buffalo Zoo. Niagara Falls is just a 30-minute drive from the campus.

Students walking on the quad.

- **Enrollment:** *1,046*

- **Selectivity:** *minimally difficult*

- **Test scores:** *ACT—over 18, 71%; SAT—critical reading over 500, 27%; SAT—math over 500, 41%*

- **Application deadline:** *9/1 (freshmen), 8/1 (transfer)*

- **Expenses:** *Tuition $18,490; Room & Board $7990*

CONTACT INFORMATION

Mr. Timothy Lee, Director of Admissions

☎ 716-649-7900

🖥 tlee@hilbert.edu

HOBART AND WILLIAM SMITH COLLEGES

The nationally-ranked HWS sailing team practices on Seneca Lake. 80 percent of HWS students participate in an intramural, club or intercollegiate team.

GENEVA, NEW YORK
www.hws.edu/

At Hobart and William Smith Colleges, learning does not stop at the classroom door— or even at the boundaries of campus. HWS students put their education into practice through internships and through extensive service-learning programs in the local community. They are at home on six continents, with 59 percent of students spending at least one semester studying abroad. Through these carefully designed programs, HWS students develop confidence and gain the necessary skills to be competitive in the workplace. They win prestigious fellowships. They gain admittance into the best graduate programs in the world. They go on to lead lives of consequence. With more than forty majors and sixty minors to choose from, students here have no limits. Some enroll in Africana Studies, Geoscience or Public Policy. Others take on Architectural Studies or Dance. At Hobart and William Smith, your education is just that—yours. The whole college community is also committed to living green. The Colleges launched a Yellow Bike program; any given day, students leave their cars parked and instead zip around campus on a borrowed bike. From the Buildings and Grounds' utility carts that run on rechargeable batteries to the main dining room's composting efforts, students and staff are inspired to find new ways to do their part. Students also take part in the more than 70 clubs and organizations on campus; from traditional (yearbook, fraternities and sororities) to unique (Bodybuilding Club, Glass Blowing Club, Trap Shooting Team), HWS has something for everyone. Hobart and William Smith are located on a spectacular 188-acre campus along the northern tip of Seneca Lake in the City of Geneva, New York. There are over 1,500 trees on campus (including a 200-year-old red oak and 150-year-old Austrian pine)—a nod to nurseryman and founder William Smith. Two programs, Outdoor Recreation Adventure (ORAP) and Waterfront, take advantage of the Colleges' beautiful location. ORAP funds and schedules weekend and day trips to ice and rock climb, snowshoe and cross country ski. The Waterfront program features the Bozzuto Boathouse, which houses the Colleges' nationally ranked sailing team. The Colleges have twenty-two intercollegiate teams and dozens of club sports.

CONTACT INFORMATION

Don W. Emmons, Dean of Admissions and Vice President of Enrollment

☎ 315-781-3622 or toll-free 800-245-0100

✉ emmons@hws.edu

HWS students pose on the Great Wall of China during a semester study abroad program in Beijing. Nearly 60% of HWS students study abroad in more than 30 countries across the globe.

Find your future by choosing from about 150 undergraduate programs. Hofstra's student-faculty ratio of 14 to 1 and a priority on teaching excellence ensures you're part of creating your own success.

HOFSTRA UNIVERSITY®

find your edge

HEMPSTEAD, NEW YORK
www.hofstra.edu/

Hofstra University is where students find their edge to succeed in about 140 undergraduate and 150 graduate programs of study. With an outstanding faculty, advanced technology and state-of-the-art facilities, Hofstra enjoys a growing national reputation. Hofstra has five undergraduate colleges: the Hofstra College of Liberal Arts and Sciences; the School of Communication; the Frank G. Zarb School of Business; the School of Education, Health, and Human Services; and Honors College. Campus life is exciting, with more than 170 student clubs and organizations, about thirty local and national fraternities and sororities, seventeen NCAA Division I teams for men and women and more than 500 cultural events on campus each year. Recreational and athletic facilities include a

NEW YORK

15,000-seat stadium, a 5,000-seat arena, a 1,600-seat field turf soccer stadium and a new field hockey stadium. Students also have access to a physical fitness center, a swim center with an indoor Olympic-sized swimming pool and high-dive area, a softball stadium and a rec center with a multipurpose gym, an indoor track, a fully equipped weight room, a cardio area and a mirrored aerobics/martial arts room. Students are not limited to one main dining hall at Hofstra. From Starbucks to Subway, from late-night tapas at Kate and Willie's to sushi at Taro 13, they never get hungry or bored. Hofstra students show that they care what happens off campus, too. Throughout the year, students organize blood drives and walks to raise money for breast cancer research. Human Action, a new student group, recently organized Refugee Campus. Students, faculty and people from the community camped out for four nights and five days to bring attention to, and raise funds for, refugees around the world. A nationally recognized arboretum, Hofstra's 240-acre campus sits just 25 miles east of New York City. Students have easy access by train or car to NYC as well as to the corporate headquarters of some of the world's leading companies where many students intern. The surrounding Long Island area offers excellent beaches and parks, golf courses, restaurants and theaters. Students head just off campus to Long Island's Nassau Veterans Memorial Coliseum to catch a NHL Islanders game or concert.

CONTACT INFORMATION

Mr. Sunil Samuel, Director of Admissions

☎ 516-463-6700 or toll-free 800-HOFSTRA

✉ admission@hofstra.edu

- **Enrollment:** *12,068*
- **Selectivity:** *moderately difficult*
- **Test scores:** *ACT—over 18, 100%; SAT—critical reading over 500, 93%; SAT—math over 500, 96%*
- **Application deadline:** *Rolling (freshmen)*
- **Expenses:** *Tuition $30,130; Room & Board $11,330*

 http://bit.ly/collvid44

Hofstra offers students the opportunity to live and learn on our beautiful, 240-acre campus on Long Island and have easy access to the academic, cultural and career opportunities in the New York City.

HUNTER
The City University of New York

NEW YORK, NEW YORK
www.hunter.cuny.edu/

Hunter College has been named the #2 "Best Value Public College for 2010" by the *Princeton Review* and *USA Today*. How did it earn this distinction? For starters, Hunter offers top-notch academic programs that cover more than a hundred fields ranging from anthropology to nursing, women's studies to Arabic. Hunter is also the home of world-renowned research centers, including the Center for Study of Gene Structure and Function, the Center for Puerto Rican Studies and the Brookdale Center on Aging, to name a few. Look a little closer to see the exciting changes happening at Hunter. Recently, billionaires Patricia Phelps de Cisneros and husband Gustavo gave $1

Hunter's men's volleyball is extremely competitive.

million to Hunter to boost the Latin American Art program. In 2011, the CUNY School of Public Health at Hunter College will open its doors, officially making Hunter a Ph.D.-granting school. Taking a cue from the Hunter motto—Mihi Cura Futuri—"the care of the future is mine"—the College's Sustainability Council has planted trees, installed sensors in the residence halls to automatically turn off lights and set up a number of bike racks to encourage cycling around the city. For fun, students join special interest clubs (Animal Rights Team, Gay Men's Alliance), recreational clubs (Billiards Club, Ultimate Frisbee) and visual and performing arts groups (Hip Hop-ology, Jazz Improv Club). The Hunter Hawks compete in NCAA Division III sports. Men and women have teams in basketball, cross country, fencing, indoor and outdoor track, tennis and volleyball. Men also compete in soccer and wrestling and women have swimming and softball teams. The Hunter College Sportsplex is the premier athletic and recreational center in the New York City area. It lies completely underground on the corner of 68th and Lexington and is the deepest building in NYC. The Sportsplex is completely climate controlled and has multiple gyms, racquetball courts, a weight room and a training room. Hunter students get to live and study in the heart of Manhattan. Many of the world's finest museums, libraries, concert halls and theaters are just a quick walk away.

- **Enrollment:** *22,168*
- **Selectivity:** *moderately difficult*

CONTACT INFORMATION

Mr. William Zlata, Director of Admissions

☎ 212-772-4490

✉ bill.zlata@hunter.cuny.edu

- **Test scores:** *SAT—critical reading over 500, 84%; SAT—math over 500, 89%*
- **Application deadline:** *3/15 (freshmen), 3/15 (transfer)*
- **Expenses:** *Tuition $4999; Room only $5500*

A busy day in Hunter's courtyard.

Jesuit education stresses development of the whole person, and student clubs and activities like theater are abundant at Le Moyne College

LE MOYNE

SPIRIT. INQUIRY. LEADERSHIP. JESUIT.

SYRACUSE, NEW YORK
www.lemoyne.edu/

Le Moyne College is the perfect choice for undergrads who know exactly what they want to be and for those who want to discover the world first. This second youngest of the twenty-eight Jesuit colleges and universities in the United States uniquely balances a comprehensive liberal arts education with preparation for a career or graduate study. Students choose from more than thirty bachelor's programs in the humanities, science, nursing, business and education. Master's degrees are offered in business administration, education, nursing and physician assistant studies. The College's newest building, a

$20 million science center, will open in 2011. The 48,000-square-foot facility will have research labs, a computer lab and simulation rooms—all using solar heating. Le Moyne athletes are champions on the field (110 All-Americans, four NCAA championships since 2004), in the classroom (received *USA Today*/NCAA award for highest graduation rate in Division II) and in their communities (student athletes volunteered 1,000 hours in 2009). The Le Moyne Dolphins compete in seventeen intercollegiate sports—eight for men and nine for women. Intramural sports are very popular with Le Moyne students, too; nearly 85 percent of the students play wallyball, basketball, indoor soccer and more. Athletic facilities include soccer/lacrosse, softball and baseball fields; tennis, basketball and racquetball courts; a weight-training and fitness center; practice fields; and two gyms. A recreation center houses an Olympic-size indoor swimming pool, jogging track, indoor tennis and volleyball

courts and additional basketball, racquetball and fitness areas. Most students live in residence halls, apartments and town houses on campus. The Residence Hall Councils and the Le Moyne Student Programming Board organize a variety of campus activities, including concerts, dances, a weekly film series, student talent shows and off-campus trips. Le Moyne's 160-acre, tree-lined campus is located 10 minutes from downtown Syracuse, which offers year-round entertainment in the form of rock concerts at the Landmark Theatre, professional baseball and hockey, Bristol Omnitheatre, the Syracuse Symphony Orchestra, Everson Museum of Art as well as one-of-a-kind restaurants, pubs and coffeehouses in Armory Square.

CONTACT INFORMATION

Mr. Dennis J. Nicholson, Director of Admission

☎ 315-445-4300 or toll-free 800-333-4733

✉ admission@lemoyne.edu

Just a few miles outside the city are hills and miles of open country for swimming, boating, hiking, skiing, snowboarding and golf.

- **Enrollment:** *3,524*
- **Selectivity:** *moderately difficult*
- **Test scores:** *ACT—over 18, 96%; SAT—critical reading over 500, 71%; SAT—math over 500, 79%*
- **Application deadline:** *2/1 (freshmen), 6/1 (transfer)*
- **Expenses:** *Tuition $25,830; Room & Board $9990*

http://bit.ly/collvid48

At Le Moyne, students benefit by small class sizes that allow them to get to know their professors.

Manhattanville College's NCAA Division III Men's and Women's Hockey Teams are nationally ranked.

MANHATTANVILLE COLLEGE

PURCHASE, NEW YORK
www.manhattanville.edu/

On its 100-acre campus 30 minutes north of New York City, Manhattanville College has created a small global village. This private college offers more than fifty bachelor's degree programs, ranging from Liberal Arts to Environmental Science and professional concentrations in areas such as Business and Museum Studies. Many students choose to spend a "semester abroad" living, interning and studying in the city; others head a bit farther away to explore Spain, South Africa, Germany or Japan. Back home on campus, students enjoy the many clubs (Irish Step Dancing to Nature Nomads), as well as the chocolate fountain in the dining hall and the cheese fries in the pub. In between classes, students meet up with friends in the Game Zone, Manhattanville's own arcade and rec center that opened in 2006. With its Olympic-size ping pong table, arcade games, foosball table, Jukebox, gaming kiosk and video wall with seven TV monitors, this is truly a gamer and techie paradise. Manhattanville students know how to have fun, but they also have a sense of purpose. Last year, undergrads logged 30,000 hours of community service through the College's close ties with organizations such as the American Cancer Society, local Humane Societies and Habitat for Humanity. Manhattanville's global perspective is enriched by its role as a Non-Government Organization of the United Nations. Select students have an opportunity to intern at the UN and to study with an ambassador on Manhattanville's faculty. In addition, the College offers a Meet the Ambassadors Series on campus, where students attend lectures by leading ambassadors followed by dinner at the home of the College's president. Manhattanville's campus lies in the heart of Westchester County, bordered on the east by Long Island Sound and on the west by the Hudson River. From the roof of the castle that serves as the campus' main hall, students have a clear view of Manhattan's skyline. The College provides transportation to the city on weekends and to Manhattan-bound commuter trains during the week so students can take advantage of all New York City has to offer.

Reid Castle, a beautiful replica of a 19th century Norman castle, is the centerpiece of Manhattanville College.

 http://bit.ly/collvid53

- **Enrollment:** *2,890*

- **Selectivity:** *moderately difficult*

- **Application deadline:** *3/1 (freshmen), 3/1 (transfer)*

- **Expenses:** *Tuition $34,350; Room & Board $13,920*

CONTACT INFORMATION

Ms. Erica Padilla, Director of Admissions

☎ 914-323-5129 or toll-free 800-328-4553

✉ admissions@mville.edu

THE NEW SCHOOL

MANNES COLLEGE THE NEW SCHOOL FOR MUSIC

NEW YORK, NEW YORK
www.mannes.edu/

Mannes College The New School for Music in New York City is one of the world's top conservatories of classical music. Here, aspiring artists learn and play music with scholars, composers, conductors and performing artists from some of the world's most admired orchestras, ensembles and opera companies. Most of the more than 400 concerts produced by the School each year at its two concert halls or at venues throughout the New York metropolitan region feature Mannes students. With an average class size of only ten to twelve students, Mannes provides an intimate, supportive atmosphere. Part of The New School, a leading urban university, Mannes offers its own undergraduate curriculum focused on classical music. Students may choose to supplement this curriculum by taking courses at the other divisions of The New School. In addition, throughout their time at Mannes, students learn the techniques of music. This program includes studies in ear training, sight singing, keyboard skills, theory, analysis and dictation. Graduate degrees include the Master of Music (M.M.), a two-year degree program offered in all orchestral instruments (violin, viola, cello, bass, flute, oboe, clarinet, bassoon, saxophone, horn, trumpet, trombone, tuba, harp and percussion), piano, harpsichord, guitar, vocal accompaniment for pianists, voice, composition, conducting and theory. Students receive private lessons in their major field and take performance classes such as orchestra, opera and chamber music. Mannes also offers the Professional Studies Diploma (P.S.D.), an advanced course designed to enhance performance or compositional skills. Orchestral instrument majors join the Mannes Orchestra, which performs at Lincoln

Center and other major venues. Through The New School, Mannes students live in apartment-style suites (equipped with full kitchens, air conditioning, 24-hour security and Internet service) in Chelsea, Greenwich Village, Union Square and lower Manhattan. Mannes is located in Manhattan's Upper West Side. It is within walking distance of the Museum of Natural History and Lincoln Center for the Performing Arts (home to the New

CONTACT INFORMATION

Ms. Georgia Schmitt, Director of Admissions

☎ 212-580-0210 Ext. 4862 or toll-free 800-292-3040

✉ mannesadmissions@ newschool.edu

York Philharmonic and the Metropolitan Opera).

- **Enrollment:** *384*
- **Selectivity:** *very difficult*
- **Application deadline:** *12/1 (freshmen), 4/1 (transfer)*
- **Expenses:** *Tuition $33,600; Room & Board $15,260*

THE NEW SCHOOL

THE NEW SCHOOL FOR JAZZ AND CONTEMPORARY MUSIC

NEW YORK, NEW YORK

www.jazz.newschool.edu

Part of The New School, a leading university in New York City, The New School for Jazz and Contemporary Music guides talented students to develop their individual, creative voice. The School's primary goal is to give students a technical, conceptual and historical grasp of jazz and contemporary music. The curriculum is based on the tradition of artist-as-mentor and is taught by accomplished, active musicians with links to the history and evolution of jazz, blues, pop and new genres. Students do their core work in high-tech classrooms and private studios with exceptional musician-educators. Students can cross-register in classes ranging from classical theory, composition, counterpoint and musicology to music therapy, management and liberal arts. And students here have the opportunity to take courses at Mannes College The New School for Music, a classical music conservatory. Learning takes place in three environments: in the classroom (all classrooms are equipped with Yamaha grand pianos, drum kits, amps, PA systems and full component stereo systems); in traditional, tutorial instrumental study, where students meet one-on-one with jazz and classical performers who live, work and teach in New York City; and in master classes. These scheduled lectures/performances/workshops have featured such artists as Jon Faddis, Jim Hall, Barry Harris, Lee Konitz, Wynton Marsalis and Jimmy McGriff. Some students work while attending classes through

The New School for Jazz Gig Office where they get hired to play at weddings and corporate events. Activities and clubs at The New School for Jazz are quirky and fun; they include Adventure Force (a club for nerds), The New Jew, the Sketch Comedy Group and the Wes Anderson Enthusiasts Society. The New School maintains several residence halls as well as university-leased apartments, most located within six blocks of the campus. The New School is located in Greenwich Village, home to many of the city's famous jazz nightclubs, such as the Village Vanguard, Blue Note, Smalls and Jazz

CONTACT INFORMATION

Ms. Terri Lucas, Jazz Admissions

☎ 212-229-5896

⌨ jazzadm@newschool.edu

Standard. The area is also home to design and art studios, galleries, shops and restaurants. Carnegie Hall and Lincoln Center are just a short subway ride away.

- **Enrollment:** *253*
- **Selectivity:** *very difficult*
- **Application deadline:** *1/1 (freshmen), 1/1 (transfer)*
- **Expenses:** *Tuition $33,600; Room & Board $15,260*

Entrance to East 70th Street building on Manhattan's Upper East Side, and a recent M.F.A. Thesis project.

New York School of Interior Design

founded 1916

NEW YORK, NEW YORK

www.nysid.edu/

Throughout its history, the New York School of Interior Design (NYSID) has devoted all of its resources to a single field of study—interior design—and has played a significant role in the development of the interior design profession. NYSID's curriculum reflects the complex yet sophisticated world of interior design. Courses stress the health, safety and welfare of the public while also focusing on functionality and beauty. The college offers three undergraduate degree programs: a B.A. in the History of the Interior and Decorative Arts, a B.F.A. in Interior Design and an A.A.S. in Interior Design. NYSID also offers three graduate programs: a professional-level Master of Fine Arts (M.F.A.) degree in interior design, a post-professional-level M.F.A. degree in interior design and a Master of Professional Studies (M.P.S.) degree in sustainable interior environments. Through these programs, NYSID students learn not only the right colors and materials to use but also how to design environmentally sound and accessible hospitals, offices, schools and restaurants. Whether learning the importance of historic preservation or the latest programs in computer-aided design, NYSID students gain a wide range of skills and techniques taught by faculty members who work in the field. The area's art and antique shops, museums, professional design studios

and showrooms are all an exciting part of the college's "campus." Because of its select faculty and established reputation, the School continues to maintain a close relationship with the interior design industry. This translates into phenomenal internship opportunities and valuable contacts for after graduation. The New York School of Interior Design is located on Manhattan's Upper East Side, where several major interior design studios are located. Many of the world's finest galleries, museums and showrooms are within walking distance. The campus consists of two, 100-year-old Renaissance and Colonial-Revival

buildings. The light-filled atelier is a favorite spot for students to work between classes and the roof garden (with panoramic views of the city) is a great place to relax.

CONTACT INFORMATION

**Cassandra Ramirez,
Admissions Associate**

☎ 212-472-1500 Ext. 204 or
   toll-free 800-336-9743 Ext. 204
✉ admissions@nysid.edu

- **Enrollment:** *714*
- **Selectivity:** *moderately difficult*
- **Test scores:** *SAT—critical reading over 500, 21%; SAT— math over 500, 52%*
- **Application deadline:** *3/1 (freshmen), 3/1 (transfer)*
- **Expenses:** *Tuition $22,895; Room only $15,600*

A view of the tranquil atelier, an open studio where students work independently on projects.

Overlooking the lower Niagara, Niagara University is located just a few miles north of the world famous Falls and a few minutes from the quaint village of Lewiston, New York. Nearby metropolitan areas include Buffalo, New York, and Toronto, Canada.

NIAGARA UNIVERSITY

Education That Makes a Difference

NIAGARA UNIVERSITY, NEW YORK
www.niagara.edu/

Niagara University (NU) takes its Catholic and Vincentian tradition of serving others and making a difference in the world very seriously. Service learning is offered in nearly every academic department. Some students work with the Niagara County District Attorney's Office in the domestic violence program. Other students help people in the community with tax preparation. During the 2008–09 academic year alone, Niagara students recorded almost 60,000 hours of community service. It's no surprise then that Niagara was one of only thirty schools across the nation named as a *U.S. News & World Report* "Top College" in the area of Service Learning. NU has four colleges: Arts and Science, Business Administration, Education and Hospitality and Tourism Management. Here, students choose from more than fifty majors, six preprofessional options and two, five-year combined master's programs. Between classes, students join the more than eighty extracurricular activities from ROTC to N ZONE (the University spirit club) to a number of fraternities and sororities. University teams compete on the Division I level. Intercollegiate sports for men include baseball, basketball, cross country, golf, ice hockey, soccer, swimming and diving, and tennis. Women's teams are basketball, cross country, golf, ice hockey, lacrosse, soccer, softball, swimming

and diving, tennis and volleyball. Club sports include cheerleading, danceline, hockey, martial arts, rugby and skiing. The updated Kiernan Rec Center has four basketball courts, a six-lane swimming and diving pool, an indoor track, racquetball courts, free-weight and Nautilus rooms and aerobics rooms. Outside, students have two basketball courts, a turf athletic field and tennis courts. Students live in five residence halls, small cottages or apartments. They meet friends in the Jazzman's Café for coffee and a muffin or head off campus for a hike down Niagara Gorge. In every season, there is something to do or see here. Niagara University is situated on Monteagle Ridge overlooking the lower Niagara River, which connects the two Great Lakes of Erie and Ontario. Students are just a few miles from the world-famous Niagara Falls, 20 minutes from Buffalo (which has a number of sports and entertainment venues) and just 90 minutes from Toronto, Canada.

A popular place for students to meet before, after or in-between classes is at Jazzman's—Niagara University on-campus coffee shop.

- **Enrollment:** *4,255*

- **Selectivity:** *moderately difficult*

- **Test scores:** *ACT—over 18, 91%; SAT—critical reading over 500, 57%; SAT—math over 500, 65%*

- **Application deadline:** *8/1 (freshmen), 8/15 (transfer)*

- **Expenses:** *Tuition $24,700; Room & Board $10,250*

CONTACT INFORMATION

Ms. Christine M. McDermott, Associate Director of Admissions

☎ 716-286-8700 Ext. 8715 or toll-free 800-462-2111

✉ admissions@niagara.edu

THE NEW SCHOOL

PARSONS THE NEW SCHOOL FOR DESIGN

NEW YORK, NEW YORK
www.parsons.edu/

Parsons The New School for Design in New York City is one of the premier colleges of art and design in the nation. Parsons has supported outstanding artists, designers, scholars, businesspeople and community leaders for more than a century. Today, when design is increasingly called upon to solve complex global problems like environmental degradation and poverty, Parsons is leading new approaches to art and design education. Parsons has five schools—Art, Media, and Technology; Fashion; Constructed Environments; Art and Design History and Theory; and Design Strategies—and the programs within each span contemporary art and design practices. As part of The New School, a leading university in New York City, Parsons students also weave the liberal arts, social sciences, performance, management and urban policy into a comprehensive education. Parsons uses pioneering technology and collaboration to predict trends and respond to society's needs. Graduates and faculty members appear on the short list of leaders in every area of art and design—creative, management and scholarly. Like New York City itself, Parsons never sleeps. Some 2,000 continuing education students take individual courses or are enrolled in certificate programs. More than 700 children and young people attend weekend and summer precollege programs. And at any given time, Parsons students are involved in a ton of social clubs and activities from publications to athletics to political activism. Students live in the university's residence halls in the Greenwich Village and Wall

Street areas. Parsons' main campus is located downtown in Greenwich Village, a historic neighborhood with a style and atmosphere found nowhere else in New York City. The area is home to design and art studios, galleries, shops and restaurants as well as avant-garde artists, musicians and writers. With its international sophistication and cutting-edge attitude, New York City is a vibrant environment that has inspired and challenged artists and designers throughout history. Not surprisingly, Parsons faculty members use New York City as an urban design laboratory. The city has more than eighty museums, such

CONTACT INFORMATION

Director of Admissions

☎ 212-229-8989 or toll-free 877-528-3321

✉ parsadm@newschool.edu

as the Metropolitan Museum of Art, the Museum of Modern Art, and Cooper-Hewitt, National Design Museum.

- **Enrollment:** *4,598*
- **Selectivity:** *very difficult*
- **Test scores:** *ACT—over 18, 96%; SAT—critical reading over 500, 66%; SAT—math over 500, 72%*
- **Application deadline:** *2/1 (freshmen), 2/1 (transfer)*
- **Expenses:** *Tuition $36,010; Room & Board $15,260*

MetroTech Center is not only a hotbed of innovation and business, it's also an inspirational environment set to the backdrop of beautiful Brooklyn Heights.

NYU·poly

POLYTECHNIC INSTITUTE OF NEW YORK UNIVERSITY

BROOKLYN, NEW YORK
www.poly.edu/

As a leading technological university and research center, Polytechnic Institute of NYU offers degrees in computer science, digital media, engineering, humanities, the sciences and technology management. The Institution's research and education programs focus on i2e–invention, innovation and entrepreneurship. This is the second-oldest independent technological university in the United States. Polytechnic has a main campus in the MetroTech Center in downtown Brooklyn and graduate centers in Long Island, Manhattan and Westchester. Students have access to a variety of research centers where they work with world-renowned faculty members and are involved in innovative fields including telecommunications, electronics, robotics, digital systems, wireless communications and integrative digital media, among others. The Institute offers a wide variety of student activities, as it ranks

NEW YORK

among the top five universities in the nation in social diversity (undergrads come from forty states and fifty-five countries). From the Jewish Student Union to the Cyber Security Club and from fraternities/sororities to PolyRadio, there are clubs and organizations to satisfy every interest. The Fighting Blue Jays participate at the NCAA Division III level. Athletics for men and women—from basketball to lacrosse to volleyball—are popular on both intercollegiate and intramural levels. The state-of-the-art Jacobs Gymnasium has the Skybox with "club box" style seating. Polytechnic offers on-campus housing in the Othmer Residence Hall, located across the street from the MetroTech campus in downtown Brooklyn. It features suites and apartments that are fully wired for personal computers, laptops, cable TV and telephone access; study rooms; student lounges; 24-hour security; a laundry room; and a modern dining hall. Students can use the central computer labs and various specialized labs, connect wirelessly with a laptop or dial in from home. Polytechnic is located in the heart of historic downtown Brooklyn in MetroTech Center, a 16-acre, $1-billion academic/professional park in New York City. Situated at the foot of the famous Brooklyn Bridge, the campus is the gateway to Wall Street, Broadway and the South Street Seaport on one side of the river and the Brooklyn Museum and Prospect Park on the other. Polytechnic is just a 10-minute subway ride from Manhattan, too. Exceptional careers begin with exceptional locations, and Polytechnic has an unrivaled one in the greater New York area. The career opportunities are virtually everywhere—from Wall Street to New York's new media industry, affectionately dubbed "Silicon Alley."

Digital Media student Nikkisha Persad came to NYU-Poly to gain the skills to make the next big 3D movie. NYU-Poly is helping Nikkisha reach her goal through hands-on interaction with 3D technology.

- **Enrollment:** *4,514*
- **Selectivity:** *very difficult*
- **Test scores:** *SAT—critical reading over 500, 96%; SAT—math over 500, 99%*
- **Application deadline:** *2/1 (freshmen), rolling (transfer)*
- **Expenses:** *Tuition $34,420; Room & Board $9000*

CONTACT INFORMATION

Joy Colelli, Dean of Admissions and New Students

☎ 718-260-5917 or toll-free 800-POLYTECH
✉ uadmit@poly.edu

*Pratt Institute Hall Street Entrance
(© 2010 Bob Handelman)*

Pratt

PRATT INSTITUTE

BROOKLYN, NEW YORK

www.pratt.edu/

Industrialist and philanthropist Charles Pratt founded Pratt Institute in 1887 to educate students on a non-degree level. Today's Pratt Institute has a wide variety of highly ranked programs in art, design and architecture and Pratt continues to evolve by adding programs at all levels, including undergraduate programs in creative writing and critical and visual studies, undergraduate and graduate programs in art history and art education, and graduate programs in arts and cultural management, historic preservation and design management. Standards are high, modeled after the professional world. Pratt offers four-year bachelor's, two-year associate and master's degrees. In educating more than five generations of students to be creative, technically skilled and adaptable professionals as well as responsible citizens, Pratt has gained a national and international reputation that attracts undergrads and graduate students from more than forty-nine states, the District of Columbia, Puerto Rico, the Virgin Islands and sixty countries. Unlike the typical American college student, most students who choose Pratt already have career objectives, or at least they know they want to study art, design, architecture or creative writing. A short subway or bus ride from the museums, galleries and design centers of both Manhattan and Brooklyn, Pratt Institute has twenty-four buildings spread across a 25-acre campus. The campus includes a contemporary sculpture garden (ranked among the top ten campus art collections by *Public Art*

Review), an athletic center (with the largest indoor track in Brooklyn), outstanding studio facilities and historic buildings. Six buildings are for student housing, including the Stabile Hall freshman residence, which provides studio space on each floor. The more than sixty active student organizations include fraternities and sororities, honorary societies and professional societies. And Pratt students give back to the community in so many ways—two such examples are the Saturday Art School (undergrads and graduate students hold art classes for more than 300 kids) and the Liberty Partnership Program (students tutor at-risk middle school students). Pratt Institute is located in the Clinton Hill section of Brooklyn. Here, students find a green oasis just minutes from the art capital of the world, Manhattan. Within

CONTACT INFORMATION

Ms. Olga Burger, Visit Coordinator

☎ 718-636-3779 or toll-free 800-331-0834

🖥 visit@pratt.edu

walking distance of campus are the Brooklyn Museum, the Brooklyn Academy of Music and many ethnic restaurants.

- **Enrollment:** *4,707*
- **Selectivity:** *very difficult*
- **Test scores:** *ACT—over 18, 99%; SAT—critical reading over 500, 86%; SAT—math over 500, 84%*
- **Application deadline:** *1/5 (freshmen), 2/1 (transfer)*
- **Expenses:** *Tuition $34,880; Room & Board $9756*

Pratt Institute Main Building (© 2010 Bob Handelman)

Traditionally styled stucco and tile buildings border the campus's grassy, tree-lined quad, an ideal place for strolling, reading, and relaxing between classes.

QUEENS
COLLEGE

FLUSHING, NEW YORK

www.qc.cuny.edu/

Often referred to as "the jewel of the City of New York (CUNY) system," Queens College has a national reputation for its liberal arts and sciences and preprofessional programs. Students come from more than 140 different nations; the result is a diverse education and experience that gives Queens College graduates a competitive edge in today's global society. The 77-acre campus surrounds a quad that has a fantastic view of the Manhattan skyline. The campus also blends old with new. Still standing are original Spanish-style stucco and tile buildings from the early 1900s, including Jefferson Hall, which houses the Welcome Center. Powdermaker Hall has state-of-the-art technology throughout its classrooms, and the College's science labs recently underwent a $30-million renovation. The entire campus has Wi-Fi capability and students may relax and meet friends in the Student Union and the College's many cafes, lounges and dining areas. With the opening of the College's first residence hall, The Summit, in August 2009, Queens College shed its commuter school identity. The low-rise building has individually climate-controlled single- and double-room suites with shared kitchen and lounge areas. It also has its own exercise room. Queens College goes to great lengths to accommodate its many commuter students; the

Child Development Center, staffed by professionals, provides inexpensive child-care services to students with children. There are more than 100 clubs on campus, from the Accounting Honors Society and Alliance of Latin American Students to clubs for theater, fencing, environmental science, science fiction and the fine arts. Queens, the only CUNY college that participates in Division II sports, has twenty men's and women's teams. Ongoing cultural events include readings by known authors such as Margaret Atwood, Toni Morrison and Salman Rushdie; concerts by world-famous artists; and theater and dance performances. QC is home to the Godwin-Ternbach Museum, the only comprehensive museum in the borough of Queens, with art from ancient times to the present. Queens College has had a chapter of Phi Beta Kappa since 1950 (less than 10 percent of U.S. liberal arts colleges are members of Phi Beta Kappa, the nation's oldest and most respected undergraduate

honors organization). In 1968, Queens College became a member of Sigma Xi, the national science honor society. The College is located in a residential area of Flushing and is only 20 minutes from Manhattan.

- **Enrollment:** *20,711*
- **Selectivity:** *very difficult*
- **Test scores:** *SAT—critical reading over 500, 68%; SAT—math over 500, 85%*
- **Application deadline:** *5/15 (freshmen)*
- **Expenses:** *Tuition $5047; Room & Board $11,125*

CONTACT INFORMATION

Mr. Vincent Angrisani, Executive Director of Enrollment Management and Admissions

☎ 718-997-5600

✉ vincent.angrisani@qc.cuny.edu

ROBERTS
WESLEYAN COLLEGE
Education for Character Since 1866

ROCHESTER, NEW YORK
www.roberts.edu/

Roberts Wesleyan College (RWC) was founded in 1866 as the first Free Methodist college or university in North America. Today, RWC remains a leader among liberal arts colleges with a Christian worldview. Roberts Wesleyan offers more than fifty undergraduate programs, as well as graduate programs in education, health administration, nursing, nursing leadership and administration, school psychology, school counseling, social work and management marketing.

Northeastern Seminary at Roberts Wesleyan College offers the Master of Arts in Theological Studies, Master of Divinity, Master of Divinity/ Master of Social Work (with RWC) and Doctor of Ministry degree programs. Student life at RWC is inspiring and fun. In April 2010, 100 RWC students spent "One Day Without Shoes" to raise awareness about world poverty; still other students skipped a meal at the dining hall to raise $700 for the cause (http://my.toms.com). There are also many student clubs and activities on campus from the Ecology Club to the Jazz Ensemble, the Ballroom Dance Club to the newspaper. The College's intramural program offers flag football, water polo, dodgeball, ultimate Frisbee and even an annual decathlon. Varsity sports for men are basketball, cross-country, golf, soccer, tennis and indoor and outdoor track and field. Women's varsity teams are in basketball, cross-country, golf, soccer, tennis, indoor and outdoor track and field and volleyball. All RWC students use the Voller Athletic Center, which includes a pool, four basketball courts, an indoor track, racquetball courts, a weight room, saunas and BT's Cafe. An outdoor stadium, constructed in 2002, has a full-size soccer field, Olympic style track and field, 1,200-seat stadium and state-of-the-art lighting. Roberts Wesleyan College is located 8 miles southwest of Rochester in the suburb of North Chili. Rochester, with a metropolitan-area population of more than 1 million, is home to the Eastman School of Music, the Rochester Philharmonic Orchestra and many leading corporations (Eastman Kodak, Xerox, Paychex, Bausch & Lomb and PAETEC) where students can intern or work after graduation. Lake Ontario, Niagara Falls, Watkins Glen, Letchworth Park and the Finger Lakes are all nearby.

Roberts Wesleyan student athletes are fierce competitors and astute scholars.

- **Enrollment:** *1,928*
- **Selectivity:** *moderately difficult*
- **Test scores:** *ACT—over 18, 92%; SAT—critical reading over 500, 64%; SAT—math over 500, 66%*
- **Application deadline:** *2/1 (freshmen), rolling (transfer)*
- **Expenses:** *Tuition $23,780; Room & Board $8520*

CONTACT INFORMATION

Ms. Linda Kurtz Hoffman, Admissions and Marketing Specialist

☎ 585-594-6400 or toll-free 800-777-4RWC

✉ admissions@roberts.edu

Teaching and learning takes center stage on a dynamic and connected campus.

R·I·T
ROCHESTER INSTITUTE OF TECHNOLOGY

ROCHESTER, NEW YORK
www.rit.edu/

Rochester Institute of Technology (RIT) is one of the world's leading career-oriented, technological universities. RIT's eight colleges offer more than ninety undergraduate programs in areas such as engineering, computing, information technology, engineering technology, business, hospitality, science, art, design, photography, biomedical sciences and game design and development. Students may choose from more than ninety different minors, too. With dozens of smart classrooms, a $7 million web printing press, a laser optics laboratory, a blacksmithing area, a microelectronics "clean room" and art galleries, RIT students work with the most up-to-date equipment to prepare themselves for future careers. Experiential education is integrated into many programs through cooperative education (last year, co-op students combined on-campus study with paid employment at more than 1,900 firms across the United States and overseas); internships at places like ESPN, Microsoft and the CIA; study abroad in amazing locales like Croatia, New Zealand and Ireland; and undergraduate research.

As home to the National Technical Institute for the Deaf (NTID), RIT is a leader in providing access services for deaf and hard-of-hearing students. Undergrads live on campus in apartments, townhouses, Greek houses or residence halls where students with shared interests (art, photography) can live and learn together. Park Point is located on the northeast corner of the campus; the building has more than 100 apartments and a mix of restaurants and shops including Barnes & Noble and Abbot's Ice Cream. There are so many different activities, clubs, organizations and sports students can join here. From fraternities and sororities to the radio station and a biweekly student magazine, RIT gives students a taste of everything. RIT offers twenty-three varsity sports, including Division I men's hockey. More than 50 percent of students play an intramural sport such as golf or indoor soccer. RIT's recreational facilities include an ice rink, an aquatics center, the $25 million field house with an indoor track, eight racquetball courts and athletic fields. The campus sits on 1,300 acres in suburban Rochester, the third largest city in New York. Rochester is the world center of photography, the largest producer of optical goods in the United States, and among the leaders in production of electronic equipment and precision instruments.

CONTACT INFORMATION

Dr. Daniel Shelley, Assistant Vice President

☎ 585-475-6631

✉ admissions@rit.edu

- **Enrollment:** *16,773*
- **Selectivity:** *moderately difficult*
- **Test scores:** *ACT—over 18, 100%; SAT—critical reading over 500, 88%; SAT—math over 500, 94%*
- **Application deadline:** *2/1 (freshmen)*
- **Expenses:** *Tuition $29,283; Room & Board $9642*

http://bit.ly/collvid61

The annual Imagine RIT Festival attracts more that 25,000 visitors and includes more that 400 creative and innovative student and faculty displays and exhibits.

The Brooklyn Campus is located in Historic Clinton Hill surrounded by tree-lined blocks and architecturally stunning campus buildings. This campus is only ten minutes away from NYC.

St. Joseph's College
NEW YORK
1916

BROOKLYN AND PATCHOGUE, NEW YORK
www.sjcny.edu/

St. Joseph's College inspires students to transform their lives. A private, liberal arts college with campuses in Brooklyn and Long Island, St. Joseph's enrolls undergrads and graduate students in its School of Arts and Sciences and School of Professional and Graduate Studies. St. Joseph's students learn in ways that go far beyond the classroom, through independent projects, team-building assignments, internships, community service and study-abroad programs designed to suit every schedule. And with just 15 students for every professor on campus, St. Joseph's students easily find mentors to guide them in everything from academics to focusing on future careers and life goals. Both campuses are alive with social events, athletics and a Common Hour that encourages students to explore new possibilities for fun, leadership and friendship. On any given day at St. Joseph's, students might come to campus to hear a Pulitzer Prize-winning author, enjoy a jazz concert, join a community service effort, view an art exhibit, watch a basketball game or debate over dinner with other students and professors. Each campus supports over thirty student clubs and activities, including intercollegiate basketball; women's softball, swimming, tennis and volleyball; men's baseball, basketball, tennis and volleyball; and coed cross country. The Long Island campus also offers men's soccer and a coed equestrian team. For undergraduates, St. Joseph's offers fast tracks to advanced degrees through special affiliated programs in accounting, podiatry and computer science. The School of

Professional and Graduate Studies at St. Joseph's College offers a wide range of graduate programs in education, human services, management and nursing, including the Executive M.B.A., an M.B.A. in accounting, an M.B.A. in health care management and the MS in nursing. The Brooklyn campus is located in the Clinton Hill Historic District, a neighborhood where many of New York's wealthiest citizens lived in the 1920s. Today this area is home to several schools, including the Pratt Institute of Art and the Brooklyn Academy of Music. Here, students like the freedom of a safe, well-landscaped campus combined with close proximity to New York City. St. Joseph's Long Island campus is located in the village of Patchogue on

Great South Bay, about 50 miles from Manhattan and 60 miles from Montauk Point. Patchogue offers plenty to do, with fine harbors, shops, restaurants and tennis courts right in the village. There are parks nearby as well as museums, golf courses, hiking and ski trails and beaches.

- **Enrollment:** *1,358*
- **Selectivity:** *moderately difficult*
- **Test scores:** *SAT—critical reading over 500, 45%; SAT—math over 500, 55%*
- **Application deadline:** *8/15 (freshmen), 8/15 (transfer)*
- **Expenses:** *Tuition $16,765*

CONTACT INFORMATION
Ms. Theresa LaRocca Meyer, Director of Admissions
☎ 718-636-6868
✉ asinfob@sjcny.edu

St. Joseph's College maintains small class sizes and individualized attention from professors who are very engaged in the growth of each student's success.

ST. LAWRENCE UNIVERSITY

CANTON, NEW YORK
www.stlawu.edu/

St. Lawrence University invites students see the world in a new way, voice their ideas and connect with others. Founded in 1856, St. Lawrence is the oldest continuously coed degree-granting college or university in New York State. Initially established as a theology school for the Universalist Church, it quickly evolved into the liberal arts college that it is today. St. Lawrence is known for its residential/academic First-Year Program, its international study and area studies programs, its students' strong interest in the environment and its friendliness. The self-designed major is popular, intramural sports leagues are always full and more than 100 student organizations bring students together for community service, creativity and fun. Concerts, plays and films are regulars on the weekly events calendar. A 60,000-square-foot Student Center opened in winter 2004. Students come here to sit by the stone fireplace or catch a bite in the Northstar

Café. The University's freshmen live and learn together in groups of about 30–35 students. Upperclass students can choose to live in dorms, townhouses, Greek houses and suites and theme cottages that focus on student interests (e.g., low-impact living and community service).St. Lawrence students place high value on athletics; most students join varsity, intramural or club sports. The thirty-two varsity men's and women's teams compete at the NCAA Division III level, except for men's and women's ice hockey, which compete in Division I. Recreational facilities include cross-country ski and running trails, indoor and outdoor tennis courts, an athletic complex, two field houses, a 133-station fitness center, a three-story climbing wall, a pool, an ice rink, an equestrian center, a boathouse, a golf course, a nine-lane all-weather track, an artificial-turf field for lacrosse and field hockey, ten squash courts and newly renovated fields for soccer, football, baseball and softball. St. Lawrence sits on a 1,000-acre campus on the edge of the village of Canton. Canton, with its Victorian homes, tree-lined streets, village green and small shops, is typical of college towns throughout the Northeast. Students and residents often mix in stores, at athletic events and in community projects. Ottawa, Canada's capital, is 75 minutes north, while Lake Placid, one of America's hiking and skiing meccas, is 90 minutes southeast.

CONTACT INFORMATION

Ms. Terry Cowdrey, Vice President and Dean of Admissions and Financial Aid

☎ 315-229-5261 or toll-free 800-285-1856

📧 tcowdrey@stlawu.edu

- **Enrollment:** *2,401*
- **Selectivity:** *very difficult*
- **Test scores:** *ACT—over 18, 98.4%; SAT—critical reading over 500, 93.5%; SAT—math over 500, 95.3%*
- **Application deadline:** *2/1 (freshmen), 4/1 (transfer)*
- **Expenses:** *Tuition $39,765; Room & Board $10,160*

Sarah Lawrence has concentrations, not "majors," with small classes in nearly 50 disciplines. So you'll have enormous flexibility in building an individualized, interdisciplinary program of study.

SARAH
•
LAWRENCE
•
COLLEGE

BRONXVILLE, NEW YORK
www.sarahlawrence.edu/

Sarah Lawrence College is a model for individualized education among liberal arts colleges. It offers an innovative program of study that encourages students to take risks and explore highly challenging topics as they take an active role in planning their own education. Some students attend the Center for Continuing Education, which is a flexible, supportive program for returning adult students. On the graduate level, the College offers programs in writing, theater, dance, human genetics, health advocacy, art of teaching, child development and women's history. A dual degree in child development and social work is offered with the New York University School of Social Work, and a joint degree in women's history and law is offered in cooperation with Pace University Law School. The College also offers a 3-2 program in which a student receives a Bachelor of Arts in the Liberal Arts from Sarah Lawrence College and a Bachelor of Science in Engineering from Columbia University. There are also 3-2 master's programs with the College's Art of Teaching and Women's History graduate departments. About one-third of Sarah Lawrence students take on an internship in the arts, business, communications, law, medicine, publishing, social services, theater, and non-profit sector. Other students opt to study abroad in Italy, France or Cuba. Back home, Sarah Lawrence has an active campus with many opportunities for involvement in clubs, student organizations, dramatic productions, musical performances, literary societies,

student publications, student government and athletics. The College has intercollegiate teams in men's and women's crew, cross country, equestrian and tennis; men's basketball and soccer; and women's softball, swimming and volleyball. The 48,000 square foot Campbell Sports Center has an elevated track, three squash courts, a rowing tank, a swimming pool and studio space for everything from dance to fencing. The College's 44-acre campus combines the charm of a rural English village with award-winning contemporary buildings. The Frances Ann Cannon Workshop Theatre was the first permanent environmental theatre built in the United States. The Heimbold Visual Arts Center, built in 2004, has six studios, a photography suite and darkroom and a digital imaging lab. Sarah Lawrence is located in southern Westchester County, 15 miles north of midtown Manhattan.

- **Enrollment:** *1,701*
- **Selectivity:** *very difficult*
- **Application deadline:** *1/1 (freshmen), 3/1 (transfer)*

CONTACT INFORMATION

Mr. Stephen M. Schierloh, Acting Dean of Admission

☎ 914-395-2510 or toll-free 800-888-2858

🖥 slcadmit@sarahlawrence.edu

Creative and collaborative, Sarah Lawrence's community of scholars, scientists, and artists are all strong communicators—able to articulate their thoughts both in writing, and in person.

STATE UNIVERSITY OF NEW YORK COLLEGE OF ENVIRONMENTAL SCIENCE AND FORESTRY

SYRACUSE, NEW YORK

www.esf.edu/

Students study the environment through "hands-on" research.

Since its 1911 founding as the New York State College of Forestry, the SUNY College of Environmental Science and Forestry (ESF) has expanded both its role in education and its campus. In fact, *Forbes Magazine* recently placed ESF at #21 in its listing of "America's Best Public Colleges." The College has grown from its initial focus on forestry to include professional education in environmental science, landscape architecture, environmental studies and engineering in addition to programs in the biological and physical sciences. All in all, ESF offers twenty-two undergraduate and thirty graduate degree programs. Throughout its history, the College has addressed the environmental issues of the time through instruction, research and public service. The College is dedicated to educating future

www.facebook.com/find.colleges

NEW YORK

scientists and managers who, through specialized skills, will be able to use a holistic approach to solving the environmental and resource problems facing society. A leader in its field, ESF is the top-rated doctoral degree-granting college in the State University of New York System. Graduate programs lead to the Master of Science (M.S.), Master of Landscape Architecture (M.L.A.), Master of Professional Studies (M.P.S.), and Doctor of Philosophy (Ph.D.) degrees. ESF's research program has attracted a worldwide clientele, and support currently amounts to $14.5 million per year. And ESF's research facilities are unmatched. Whether students are taking Field Ornithology or Animal Behavior classes at ESF's remote, forested Cranberry Lake Biological Station or studying aquatic ecology at the Thousand Islands Biological Station, learning happens in the real world. ESF's main campus is located on 12 acres adjacent to Syracuse University and the SUNY Upstate Medical

University. The College's longstanding partnership with Syracuse University lets ESF students take classes there, as well as participate in SU's events, honorary societies, social fraternities and sororities and professional and academic organizations. Syracuse, a metropolitan area of more than 730,000 people, is a leader in the manufacture of china, air-conditioning equipment, medical diagnostic equipment, drugs, automotive parts and lighting equipment. Syracuse is about five hours from New York City, Philadelphia, Boston, Toronto and Montreal and about

CONTACT INFORMATION

Ms. Susan Sanford, Director of Admissions

☎ 315-470-6600 or toll-free 800-777-7373

✉ esfinfo@esf.edu

three hours from Buffalo and Albany.

- **Enrollment:** *2,199*
- **Selectivity:** *moderately difficult*
- **Test scores:** *ACT—over 18, 100%; SAT—math over 500, 95%*
- **Application deadline:** *Rolling (freshmen), rolling (transfer)*
- **Expenses:** *Tuition $5891; Room & Board $12,460*

Where else can you find a Timber Sports team?

OSWEGO
STATE UNIVERSITY OF NEW YORK

Oswego provides students hands-on learning opportunities through classes, the summer scholars program, and our Global Laboratories project providing research opportunities on the seven continents.

OSWEGO, NEW YORK
www.oswego.edu/

Founded in 1861, SUNY Oswego is well into its second century of meeting the needs of today's students. Although it started out focusing on teacher education, Oswego has evolved into a comprehensive college with an excellent academic reputation and a commitment to undergraduate education. More than 110 liberal arts and career-oriented programs are offered through the College of Liberal Arts and Sciences; the School of Business; the School of Communication, Media, and the Arts; and the School of Education. Located on 696 acres on the southern shore of Lake Ontario, the tree-lined campus opened a $56-million Campus Center with a convocation center/ice arena in 2006. Oswego has also committed over $300 million to current and planned construction and renovations. This includes developing a $35-million, on-campus townhouse village for 350 students (opening fall 2010); renovating several academic buildings and residence halls; and investing more than $110 million in new and environmentally friendly science facilities.

The campus is also alive with more than 150 extracurricular organizations covering a wide range of social, academic, cultural and intellectual interests. Theater, art, film, music and dance events fill the campus cultural calendar. SUNY Oswego also offers a full slate of twenty-four NCAA Division III intercollegiate sports for men and women, along with a ton of club sports and intramurals. During the last several years, SUNY Oswego has been cited for excellence and selectivity in *The Princeton Review*'s *Best Northeastern Colleges* and *U.S. News & World Report*'s *Best Colleges Guide*. Oswego was also honored as one of the "Top Up-and-Coming Colleges" *in America's Best Colleges 2010*. The city of Oswego is the country's oldest freshwater port and one of the leading ports on the Great Lakes and St. Lawrence Seaway. The city and its surrounding area are well known for all kinds of summer and winter fun, including camping, boating, sailing, fishing, tennis, golf, ice skating, cross country skiing and sledding. The campus is conveniently located 35 miles northwest of Syracuse and 65 miles east of Rochester.

CONTACT INFORMATION

Dr. Joseph Grant, Vice President for Student Affairs and Enrollment

☎ 315-312-2250
📧 admiss@oswego.edu

- **Enrollment:** *8,119*
- **Selectivity:** *moderately difficult*
- **Test scores:** *ACT—over 18, 100%; SAT—critical reading over 500, 78%; SAT—math over 500, 83%*
- **Application deadline:** *Rolling (freshmen), rolling (transfer)*
- **Expenses:** *Tuition $6256; Room & Board $10,870*

http://bit.ly/collvid63

Oswego is experiencing a facilities renaissance with $400 million in recently completed projects, including the $56 million campus center and over $300 million in current and planned projects.

Syracuse University's residential campus features historical and modern architecture. Students enjoy diverse academic and extra-curricular opportunities, along with a community-oriented campus.

SYRACUSE UNIVERSITY

SYRACUSE, NEW YORK
www.syracuse.edu/

Explore, discover, break boundaries and leave your mark at Syracuse University (SU). This private university with an international reputation draws students from every state and from more than 100 other countries. The University offers a unique mix of academic programs—more than 200 majors and ninety minors—through its nine liberal arts and professional colleges. With one of the oldest study abroad programs in the nation, Syracuse sends students to study and live in more than thirty amazing places around the globe—Hong Kong, Madrid, Florence, Beijing and London, to name a few. Students at SU live in modern residence halls, apartments and town houses and all are connected to the University's high-speed wired or wireless networks. Social life is centered on the campus through the more than 300 extracurricular groups and clubs and a full events calendar that is regularly updated online. The Syracuse Orangemen dominate in the classroom and on the playing fields in NCAA Division I sports. Men's intercollegiate sports are basketball, cross country, football, lacrosse, rowing, soccer, swimming and diving and track and field. Women have teams in basketball, cross country, field hockey, ice hockey, lacrosse, rowing, soccer, softball, swimming and diving, tennis, track and field and volleyball. The 50,000-seat world-famous Carrier Dome is the site of concerts and sports events. It's the only domed stadium in the Northeast and the country's largest structure of its kind on a college campus. The city of Syracuse is the business, educational and cultural hub of central New York. The 200-acre campus sits on a hill overlooking the downtown area of Syracuse. The city offers professional

theater and opera, as well as visiting artists and performers. Highlights of the downtown area include the Everson Museum of Art, the Milton J. Rubenstein Museum of Science and Technology (MOST), the impressive Civic Center and the Armory Square shopping area. Syracuse is within easy driving distance of Toronto, Boston, Montreal and New York City.

CONTACT INFORMATION

Office of Admissions

☎ 315-443-3611

🖥 orange@syr.edu

- **Enrollment:** *19,638*

- **Selectivity:** *moderately difficult*

- **Test scores:** *ACT—over 18, 99%; SAT—critical reading over 500, 80.5%; SAT—math over 500, 88.3%*

- **Application deadline:** *1/1 (freshmen), 1/1 (transfer)*

- **Expenses:** *Tuition $34,926; Room & Board $12,374*

http://bit.ly/collvid10

SU's vision of Scholarship in Action allows academic exploration to extend far beyond the classroom. Above, current students apply their knowledge in meaningful ways within the Syracuse community.

An architecture class at UB.

University at Buffalo
The State University of New York

BUFFALO, NEW YORK
www.buffalo.edu/

The University at Buffalo (UB) is a major public research university where undergraduate and graduate education focus on cutting-edge technology. With more than 100 bachelor's degree programs and minors, 184 master's programs and ninety doctoral programs, UB offers more academic choices than any other public university in New York and New England. In addition to twenty-nine departments in the College of Arts and Sciences, the University has schools of architecture and planning, dental medicine, education, engineering and applied sciences, law, management, medicine and biomedical sciences, nursing, pharmacy, public health and health professions and social work. Because UB is a research-intensive university, undergrads study and work with faculty members who are leaders in their

www.facebook.com/find.colleges

NEW YORK

fields in top academic and research labs and organizations. UB undergrads—not just graduate students—can collaborate with faculty on groundbreaking research and creative projects. UB's undergrads also have an opportunity to combine several fields or design their own bachelor's degree programs. Graduates of UB's Honors College have won Fulbright, Marshall, Guggenheim and other distinguished awards. As a large university, UB offers an exciting student life full of events and programs. The University has men's and women's sports programs at the intramural and NCAA Division I levels, more than 200 student organizations and a busy calendar of lectures, concerts and films. UB's North Campus in suburban Amherst is one of the most modern campuses in the nation, with more than 5 million square feet of academic space, laboratories, libraries, residence halls and recreation facilities. A mathematics building and a state-of-the-art earthquake engineering simulation laboratory were

recently completed. The University has added five apartment-style complexes on or near campus. The South Campus, 3 miles away, is largely devoted to the health sciences and architecture. Buffalo's rapid transit line connects that campus with the city center and the waterfront. Recently, UB has expanded its presence in downtown Buffalo. The area is already home to the New York State Center for Excellence in Bioinformatics and Life Sciences, the Ross Eye Institute and the Jacobs Executive Development Center. Buffalo is a Great Lakes city with a population of more than 1 million. It is a city of friendly neighborhoods and has recreation for every interest: professional sports, the Buffalo Philharmonic Orchestra, the Albright-Knox Art Gallery and a club scene. It also has a dramatic setting on Lake Erie and the Niagara River. Skiing, hiking, camping, beaches and the natural wonder of Niagara Falls are all nearby.

Laboratory for Spintronics Research in Semiconductors (LSRS). (© 2008 University at Buffalo / Douglas Levere)

- **Enrollment:** *28,881*
- **Selectivity:** *moderately difficult*
- **Test scores:** *ACT—over 18, 99%; SAT—critical reading over 500, 91%; SAT—math over 500, 98%*
- **Expenses:** *Tuition $7013; Room & Board $9648*

 http://bit.ly/collvid66

CONTACT INFORMATION

Ms. Patricia Armstrong, Director of Admissions

☎ 716-645-6900 or toll-free 888-UB-ADMIT

✉ ub-admissions@buffalo.edu

The library collections in Rush Rhees date from 1850 and have been built over the course of more than 150 years in support of teaching and research at the University of Rochester.

UNIVERSITY *of* ROCHESTER

ROCHESTER, NEW YORK
www.rochester.edu/

The University of Rochester stands out in a lot of ways. It's one of the leading private universities in the country, one of sixty-two members of the prestigious Association of American Universities and one of eight national private research institutions in the University Athletic Association. Students in the College of Arts, Sciences, and Engineering at The University of Rochester also have access to resources at the Eastman School of Music, the William E. Simon Graduate School of Business Administration, the Margaret Warner Graduate School of Education and Human Development, the School of Medicine and Dentistry and the School of Nursing. Special opportunities include the Take Five program, which allows selected undergraduates a tuition-free fifth year or semester of academic study; Rochester Early Medical Scholars (REMS), an eight-year combined B.A. or B.S./M.D. program; Rochester Early Business Scholars (REBS), a six-year combined B.A. or B.S./M.B.A. program; Graduate Engineering at Rochester (GEAR), a 3-2 BS/MS program; Guaranteed Rochester Accelerated Degree in Education (GRADE), a five-year B.A. or B.S./M.S. program; study abroad; Quest courses, first-year classes that encourage collaborative research between faculty and students; seven certificate programs; Senior Scholars Program; and employment opportunities that include a national summer jobs program and paid internships. Set on a bend in the Genesee River, the River Campus is home to undergrads who live in modern halls, fraternity houses and special-interest housing. Most of the campus buildings have neoclassical architecture, yet all academic buildings are wireless, and all residence halls are wired for Internet and cable television. Facilities include Wilson Commons, the student union; the multipurpose Goergen Athletic Center; and a new research facility—the Goergen Hall of Biomedical Engineering and Optics. Rochester students participate in more than 220 clubs and organizations, including eighteen fraternities and thirteen sororities, performing arts groups, musical ensembles, WRUR radio, URTV, campus publications as well as twenty-two varsity sports and thirty-six intramural and club sports. With Lake Ontario on its northern border, the scenic Finger Lakes to the south, and more than a million people, Rochester is rated among the most livable cities in the United States. Students take day trips to museums, parks, orchestras, the planetarium, theater companies and professional sports arenas.

CONTACT INFORMATION

Office of Admissions

☎ 585-275-3221 or toll-free 888-822-2256

✉ admit@admissions.rochester.edu

- **Enrollment:** *9,976*
- **Selectivity:** *very difficult*
- **Test scores:** *ACT—over 18, 100%; SAT—critical reading over 500, 96%; SAT—math over 500, 98%*
- **Application deadline:** *1/1 (freshmen), 6/1 (transfer)*
- **Expenses:** *Tuition $38,690; Room & Board $11,200*

 http://bit.ly/collvid70

The University celebrated the Fourth of July with a series of photos for the University homepage.

Wagner not only offers extraordinary access to NYC but also a traditional campus experience, including student clubs, athletic programs and residence hall living. Over 80% of students live on campus!

WAGNER COLLEGE

BE PART OF THE CITY

STATEN ISLAND, NEW YORK
www.wagner.edu/

In New York City's borough of Staten Island, Wagner College sits atop Grymes Hill on the nineteenth-century estate of the Cunard family—founders of the famous shipping line. This private college rooted in the liberal arts offers more than thirty majors; the most popular majors are Biological Sciences, Business, Psychology, Sociology and Theatre. In addition to undergraduate programs, Wagner offers master's degree programs in business administration (M.B.A.), education, microbiology, nursing and physician assistant studies. Recently, the College received attention for its nationally recognized curriculum, the

Wagner Plan for the Practical Liberal Arts, which integrates courses across disciplines and directly connects coursework to field experiences and internships. For the second year in a row, the College was named to *U.S. News & World Report*'s list of "Top Up-and-Coming Schools", and it was also ranked first among master's degree-granting schools in the North. Only seventy-seven schools nationwide were included on this list. Most Wagner undergrads live on campus in four residence halls; a new residence hall for seniors offers spectacular views of the New York Harbor, Manhattan and the Atlantic Ocean. Students choose Wagner because it offers excellent academic preparation, great access to professional and cultural opportunities and a traditional campus setting. Wagner strongly believes that career development is an important part of a student's education—one that begins in a student's first year at Wagner and ends in a senior year practicum in a specific field of study. Student life is active on the campus with more than sixty different clubs and

organizations, including both national and local fraternities and sororities. Campus Life arranges trips to museums, concerts, Yankee Stadium, Broadway shows, Six Flags— any and all spots in the New York area. The College also offers outstanding athletics programs, which include NCAA Division I standing in twenty areas, many intramurals and an excellent coaching staff. Athletic teams offered are men's baseball, basketball, football, golf, lacrosse, tennis and track/cross-country and women's basketball, golf, lacrosse, soccer, softball, swimming, tennis, track/cross-country and water polo; club sports are cheerleading and men's ice hockey. Wagner's location offers students the best

CONTACT INFORMATION

Ms. Leigh-Ann Nowicki, Dean of Admissions

☎ 718-420-4242 or toll-free 800-221-1010

✉ leigh-ann.nowicki@wagner.edu

of both worlds; they get to live on a wooded, suburban campus but they can also hop on a ferry and be in Manhattan in 25 minutes.

- **Enrollment:** *2,265*
- **Selectivity:** *moderately difficult*
- **Test scores:** *ACT—over 18, 99%; SAT—critical reading over 500, 89%; SAT—math over 500, 93%*
- **Application deadline:** *2/15 (freshmen), 5/1 (transfer)*
- **Expenses:** *Tuition $32,580; Room & Board $9700*

The Wagner Plan not only connects students to real-world experiences across the city and beyond, it also connects you to your professors in meaningful ways.

Wells College

AURORA, NEW YORK
www.wells.edu/

Wells College is consistently ranked among the nation's top liberal arts colleges. Here, students receive a high-quality education at an affordable price on one of the most beautiful campuses in the United States. Wells College was established in 1868 by Henry Wells, who also founded the Wells Fargo and American Express companies. At Wells, professors are dedicated to teaching, and students frequently collaborate with their professors on original research and creative projects. At most other schools, these opportunities are only available to graduate students. Because faculty members at Wells know their students so well, they are especially effective advisers and mentors. Another aspect of the Wells tradition is hands-on learning. In addition to dynamic classroom teaching, Wells students explore experiential learning through internships, service, study abroad and off-campus study. Wells

Thanks to the shelter of beautiful Cayuga Lake, students enjoy a more mild fall.

fields intercollegiate teams at the NCAA Division III level in men's and women's cross country, lacrosse, soccer, swimming and golf. Women also have field hockey, softball and tennis teams and men also play basketball. Women's basketball will be added during the 2010–11 academic year. Intramural sports are also popular here; students join basketball, soccer, swimming, skiing, tennis and volleyball teams throughout the year. Athletic facilities include indoor and outdoor tennis courts, a gym, a newly renovated fitness center, a nine-hole golf course and a campus boathouse and dock used for teaching and enjoying sailing, canoeing and lifeguarding. Wells has a number of active student organizations, including a literary magazine and newspaper, music and drama groups, environmental groups and political organizations. Students at Wells live in comfortable residence halls with wireless Internet and lounges

In addition to soccer, Wells boasts nine women's Division III sports and six men's sports. Volleyball for both men and women will become a new intercollegiate sport in the fall of 2011.

with cable TV. Wells is located in the village of Aurora on the eastern shore of Cayuga Lake—part of New York's scenic Finger Lakes region. The area is well known for its high concentration of colleges and universities, including Cornell University, Ithaca College, Hobart and William Smith Colleges, Colgate University, Hamilton College and Syracuse University. Aurora is 25 miles from Ithaca and 60 miles from both Rochester and Syracuse. Students just have to step outside to access the area's outdoor recreation

and sports, including sailing, swimming, horseback riding, skiing and hiking.

- **Enrollment:** *568*
- **Selectivity:** *moderately difficult*
- **Test scores:** *ACT—over 18, 95%; SAT—critical reading over 500, 77%; SAT—math over 500, 71%*
- **Application deadline:** *3/1 (freshmen), rolling (transfer)*
- **Expenses:** *Tuition $29,680; Room & Board $9000*

CONTACT INFORMATION

Ms. Susan Raith Sloan, Director of Admission

☎ 315-364-3264 or toll-free 800-952-9355

✉ admissions@wells.edu

inspiring futures

Barton College

WILSON, N.C. • WWW.BARTON.EDU

Our alumni are proof that a Barton degree can take you places. Recent alumni work for the Harlem Globetrotters, Walt Disney World, BB&T, Merck Pharmaceuticals, the U.S. Department of Defense...

Barton College takes advantage of its smaller size to create a unique undergraduate experience. Barton offers more than forty majors and programs through its five schools: Arts and Sciences, Behavioral Sciences, Business, Education and Nursing. The College has an innovative freshman advising program; all freshmen meet with their adviser three times a week in a classroom seminar setting. Outside the classroom, the First-Year Seminar program offers a ton of events to involve students and make the transition from home to college easier; events center around concerts, sports, art and theater. In addition, Barton also has fifty clubs and organizations for students to join, including academic organizations, specialty clubs, fraternities and sororities. The Career Services Center provides an on-campus recruiting program that brings about 100 recruiters to Barton's campus each year, representing corporations, government and education. In fact, Barton's graduates rank exceptionally well in landing jobs in their chosen field of study. Students live in five residence halls on campus: East Campus Suites, Hilley, Hackney, Waters and Wenger. All five buildings feature cable television and Internet access in each room. Barton College's Bulldogs compete in the NCAA Division II and the Conference Carolinas. The intercollegiate sports program includes women's basketball, cross country, fast-pitch softball, soccer, tennis, and volleyball and men's baseball, basketball, cross country, golf, soccer and tennis. In 2007, the Barton College men's basketball team won the NCAA Division II National Championship. All students—not just the ones involved in Barton's intramural, physical education and athletic programs—benefit from the Kennedy Recreation and Intramural Center that features an indoor swimming pool, walking/jogging areas, an auxiliary gym and a weight/fitness room. Barton also has a twelve-court tennis

Here at Barton, you'll find an ideal combination for success: a strong academic foundation with opportunities to make personal connections.

complex. The 30-acre Barton College Athletic Complex is comprised of the award-winning Nixon Baseball Field, the Jeffries Softball Field, a newly lighted soccer field, several practice fields and the Scott Davis Field House. Wilson is in the coastal plain region of eastern North Carolina. The state capital of Raleigh is a 35-minute drive to the west; to the north, Richmond, Virginia, is 2 hours away and Washington, D.C., is 4 hours away. The beautiful Atlantic coast of North Carolina is 100 miles from the campus, and many students head to the scenic Blue Ridge Mountains for hiking and camping.

Theaters, shopping centers and restaurants are close to campus.

- **Enrollment:** *1,150*
- **Selectivity:** *minimally difficult*
- **Test scores:** *ACT—over 18, 66%; SAT—critical reading over 500, 26%; SAT—math over 500, 33%*
- **Application deadline:** *Rolling (freshmen), rolling (transfer)*
- **Expenses:** *Tuition $20,648; Room & Board $7012*

CONTACT INFORMATION

Mrs. Amanda Metts, Director of Admissions

☎ 800-345-4973 or toll-free 800-345-4973

✉ ahmetts@barton.edu

Main Building

GREENSBORO

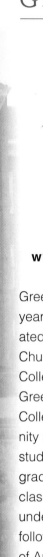

COLLEGE

SINCE 1838

**GREENSBORO,
NORTH CAROLINA**
**www.greensborocollege
.edu/**

Greensboro College is a four-year liberal arts college affiliated with the United Methodist Church. It is located in the College Hill Historic District of Greensboro, North Carolina. The College enjoys a small-community atmosphere and maintains a student-faculty ratio of 11:1—and graduate assistants do not teach classes here. Greensboro offers undergraduate degrees in the following programs: Bachelor of Arts, Bachelor of Business Administration, Bachelor of Music Education and Bachelor of Science. The College also offers graduate programs in these areas: Master of Arts degree in Teaching English to Speakers of Other Languages and the

Master of Education degree in Elementary Education and Special Education. The environmentally friendly campus features an indoor athletic center, a chapel, a performing arts center that recently underwent $4 million in renovations and a completely wireless library where students can borrow laptops. At the Royce Reynolds Family Student Life Center, students access squash, racquetball and basketball courts; a fitness facility; an indoor pool; an aerobics room; a Jacuzzi; a steam room; and a sauna. Intercollegiate sports include baseball, basketball, cross country, football, golf, lacrosse, soccer and tennis for men as well as basketball, cross country, lacrosse, soccer, softball, swimming, tennis and volleyball for women. Greensboro College is a member of the NCAA Division III and competes in the U.S.A. South Athletic Conference. Intramural sports draw even more students to play dodge ball, 3v3 basketball, ping pong and more. Many Greensboro graduates have earned distinction in graduate and professional schools in all parts of the United States and abroad. Recent Greensboro College graduates have been accepted into graduate programs at the College of William and Mary as well as Duke, Emory, Georgetown, Johns Hopkins, North Carolina State, Princeton, St. Andrews (Scotland), Temple, Vanderbilt and Wake Forest Universities and the Eastman School of Music. Most graduates pursue careers in business, education, health care and the arts. The 60-acre campus is only six blocks from downtown Greensboro. With a population of more than 1 million people in the Triad region, the city is a thriving business center that offers excellent internship opportunities. More than 45,000 college students study at the six colleges and universities within the city. Greensboro College is at the heart of this community.

CONTACT INFORMATION

Mr. Timothy L. Jackson, Dean of Enrollment Management

☎ 336-272-7102 or toll-free 800-346-8226

✉ admissions@greensborocollege.edu

- **Enrollment:** *1,264*
- **Selectivity:** *moderately difficult*
- **Test scores:** *ACT—over 18, 63%; SAT—critical reading over 500, 44%; SAT—math over 500, 46%*
- **Application deadline:** *Rolling (freshmen), rolling (transfer)*
- **Expenses:** *Tuition $23,616; Room & Board $8721*

Back Campus

*One journey ends as
another one begins.*

Guilford
COLLEGE

**GREENSBORO, NORTH
CAROLINA**

www.guilford.edu/

Founded in 1837, Guilford is one of the oldest coed colleges in the nation. With its long-standing commitment to the liberal arts and to its Quaker values, Guilford College prepares men and women for a lifetime of learning, work and social responsibility. The College's size lends itself to personalized education—95 percent of classes have fewer than 30 students. Students choose from thirty-nine majors and more than fifty minors and Guilford students can take courses at seven other colleges and universities in the area including at Elon University and the University of North Carolina at Greensboro. Guilford has received recent attention as one of only forty colleges featured in Loren Pope's book *Colleges that Change Lives* and also as one of the nation's most "underappreciated colleges" in Jay Matthews' book, *Harvard Schmarvard*. Guilford students take an active part in extracurricular activities on campus, including seminars and lecture series, interest and service clubs, as well as intercollegiate and intramural sports. Many students participate in community service projects and volunteer programs, too. The Bryan Distinguished Visiting Professorship in the Arts, Humanities, and Public Affairs at Guilford College (www.guilford.edu/bryan-series) brings to campus experts in their given fields. Past speakers include Mikhail Gorbachev, Madeleine Albright, Cokie Roberts, Archbishop Desmond Tutu and Sidney Poitier. Guilford College students attend Bryan Series lectures free of charge. Guilford's intercollegiate athletic teams compete at the NCAA Division III level and in the Old Dominion Athletic Conference (ODAC). Women's teams are basketball, cross country, lacrosse, soccer, softball, swimming,

tennis, track and volleyball; men's teams are baseball, basketball, cross country, football, golf, lacrosse, soccer, tennis and track. Sports programs are coupled with special academic opportunities in sports medicine, sport management and physical education. Guilford's athletic facilities include basketball courts, cardio and weight-training facilities, racquetball courts and multi-purpose courts. Greensboro is located midway between Washington, D.C., and Atlanta, Georgia. Local, state and national parks are within day-trip distance of the College. And Greensboro's central location in the state allows easy access to the

CONTACT INFORMATION

Ms. Tania Johnson, Associate Director of Admissions

☎ 336-316-2100 or toll-free 800-992-7759

✉ admission@guilford.edu

state's beautiful beaches and to several major ski areas in the mountains.

- **Enrollment:** *2,833*
- **Selectivity:** *moderately difficult*
- **Test scores:** *ACT—over 18, 91%; SAT—critical reading over 500, 65%; SAT—math over 500, 62%*
- **Application deadline:** *2/15 (freshmen), 4/1 (transfer)*
- **Expenses:** *Tuition $27,450; Room & Board $7560*

 http://bit.ly/collvid41

We really do have classes outside!

HIGH POINT UNIVERSITY

Extraordinary education. It's holistic and extremely experiential. HPU is ranked as the #1 School to Watch by U.S. News & World Report and in the top 6% of "America's Best Colleges" by Forbes.com.

HIGH POINT, NORTH CAROLINA
www.highpoint.edu/

The time to be at High Point University (HPU) is now. This private university is changing and expanding in so many ways. With fourteen new buildings, two new stadiums and $120 million in contributions from friends and alumni in the last four years, High Point is undergoing the greatest period of growth in its 84-year history. The new University Center has a theatre, a convenience store, housing for 500 students, dining spots and an entire floor of study rooms—all under one roof. The Plato S. Wilson Family School of Commerce has an investment trading room with a stock ticker and Reuters trading software. The new Jerry & Kitty Steele Sports Center has training and weight rooms, new soccer and baseball stadiums and an eight-lane track. Here, student athletes shine in NCAA Division I sports. Men compete in baseball, basketball, cross-country, golf, soccer and indoor/outdoor track.

Women compete in basketball, cross-country, lacrosse, soccer, indoor/outdoor track and volleyball. High Point offers sixty-eight majors, thirty-three minors and four master's degrees (the Master of Business Administration; the Master of Education in elementary education, educational leadership and special education; the Master of Science in international management, management and sport studies; and the Master of Arts in history and nonprofit management). The University's faculty and staff members believe that education alone is not enough, so the University encourages personal responsibility and values through its programs and services including a required ethics course, the President's Seminar on Life Skills, and the University chapel, where services are offered each week. Although attendance is voluntary, chapel services are packed each Wednesday. Together, High Point, Greensboro and Winston-Salem form the Piedmont Triad of North Carolina, a metropolitan area of about 1.5 million people. Both Winston-Salem and Greensboro are 20 minutes from the campus. Raleigh and Charlotte are 1½ hours away, the Appalachian Mountains are 2 hours away and the Atlantic Ocean and beaches are 4 hours from campus. The region is known nationally and internationally for the quality of its colleges and universities. Within a 60-mile radius are Duke University, the University of North Carolina at Chapel Hill and Wake Forest University, along with twenty-eight other colleges and universities.

Caring people. From the first-class concierge service to the open door policy of professors, students find the attention and resources to succeed.

- **Enrollment:** *3,603*
- **Selectivity:** *moderately difficult*
- **Test scores:** *ACT—over 18, 95%; SAT—critical reading over 500, 65%; SAT—math over 500, 69%*
- **Application deadline:** *8/15 (freshmen), 8/15 (transfer)*
- **Expenses:** *Tuition $35,900*

http://bit.ly/collvid43

CONTACT INFORMATION

Ms. Beth McCarthy, Director of Admissions

☎ 336-841-9148 or toll-free 800-345-6993

✉ jmcilrat@highpoint.edu

MEREDITH
COLLEGE

RALEIGH, NORTH CAROLINA
www.meredith.edu/

Meredith College is one of the largest private women's colleges in the U.S. Students receive a comprehensive liberal arts education with 32 majors including business, psychology and biology.

Meredith College is the largest private women's college in the Southeast. With a focus on the liberal arts, students choose from more than forty fields (including preprofessional studies) leading to Bachelor of Arts, Science, Music and Social Work degrees. The College also offers Master of Business Administration, Master of Education, Master of Arts in Teaching and Master of Science in nutrition degrees. Through Meredith's Laptop Program, all full-time undergrads are given laptops loaded with software that they get to keep once they graduate. The College focuses heavily on leadership development for women. Students are encouraged to join a wide variety of campus activities, including performing groups, sports, publications, academic and personal interest clubs and student government. More than 500 leadership positions are available for women to fill. A member of NCAA Division III, Meredith fields intercollegiate teams in six sports: basketball, cross-country, softball, soccer, tennis and volleyball. The College

NORTH CAROLINA

joined the USA South Athletic Conference in 2007. The campus residence halls are modern and comfortable—all are air conditioned and have voicemail, free laundry and kitchens. One highlight of the campus is the beautiful McIver Amphitheatre. This outdoor venue for concerts and events stays busy year-round in Raleigh's mild climate. Any given day, students lounge here to study or relax with a cup of coffee from the Beehive Café. The Science and Mathematics Building is Meredith's newest and largest academic building. It houses all the science, mathematics and computer science programs, including biological sciences (one of the most popular majors). Meredith's beautiful 225-acre campus is on the western edge of Raleigh, North Carolina's capital city, and is adjacent to the booming Research Triangle area of Raleigh, Durham and Chapel Hill. A total of eleven colleges and universities

are found here. Raleigh, a city of 350,000 people, is centrally located between the North Carolina coast and the mountain ranges of the western part of the state. The Raleigh-Durham International Airport is just 15 minutes from the campus.

- **Enrollment:** *2,262*

- **Selectivity:** *moderately difficult*

- **Test scores:** *ACT—over 18, 77%; SAT—critical reading over 500, 58%; SAT—math over 500, 61%*

- **Application deadline:** *2/15 (freshmen), 2/15 (transfer)*

CONTACT INFORMATION

Ms. Christan Trahey Harris, Director of Admissions

☎ 919-760-8581 or toll-free 800-MEREDITH

✉ admissions@meredith.edu

Meredith College opened a semester-long study-abroad site in Sansepolcro, Italy, in 2009. Students immerse themselves in an intensive language program while enjoying cultural perspectives courses.

WARREN WILSON COLLEGE

ASHEVILLE, NORTH CAROLINA
www.warren-wilson.edu/

Warren Wilson College stands out among American colleges and universities. For starters, the College's 1,100-acre campus includes a 300-acre working farm, 600 acres of managed forest, a 6-acre fruit and vegetable garden and 20 miles of hiking trails. Since its founding in 1894, the College has educated students with its unique blending of a strong liberal arts program, work for the College and service to those in need—a combination that makes Warren Wilson unlike any other college. Students choose from twenty-one majors; Art, English, creative writing, biology, outdoor leadership and the nationally recognized environmental studies program are the most popular majors. Students are integral to the day-to-day operation of the College. Each student works 15 hours a week at a job that is essential to running the school. Juniors and seniors usually have work assignments that relate to their majors and students receive pay in the amount of $3480 each year for the work they do. Service is also essential to the College's way of thinking. Warren Wilson is one of only a few colleges in the country that requires student participation in community service before graduating. Students must put in an average of at least 25 hours of service to the community each year. The campus and surrounding area are havens for outdoor activities such as white-water sports, hiking, camping, mountain biking and rock climbing. The College offers men's and women's intercollegiate basketball, cross-country, soccer and swimming, and its mountain bike team has finished in the top three nationally (Division II) for the past seven years. The College also offers intramural sports, a wellness program and a ton of outdoor programs. Warren Wilson, on the edge of the city of Asheville, North Carolina, is in the heart of the Blue Ridge Mountains. Asheville is considered one of the most livable cities in the United States. Surrounded by more than 1 million acres of national forest, Asheville is an ideal setting in which to live and learn. In the spring and summer, dogwood, wildflowers, rhododendron, mountain laurel and azaleas cover the mountains. The beauty of the autumn colors attracts photographers and artists from the world over. During the winter, natural snow is enhanced by machine-made snow, producing excellent downhill skiing. A short drive from the Warren Wilson campus are Great Smoky Mountains National Park,

CONTACT INFORMATION

Mr. Richard Blomgren, Dean of Admission

☎ 828-771-2073 or toll-free 800-934-3536

✉ admit@warren-wilson.edu

Pisgah National Forest and the Blue Ridge Parkway, offering great views, excellent camping spots and a perfect setting for class field trips.

- **Enrollment:** *1,002*
- **Selectivity:** *moderately difficult*
- **Test scores:** *ACT—over 18, 98%; SAT—critical reading over 500, 89%; SAT—math over 500, 69%*
- **Application deadline:** *3/15 (freshmen), 3/15 (transfer)*
- **Expenses:** *Tuition $24,196; Room & Board $7770*

Before, between, and after classes, Alvernia students take advantage of the Adirondack chairs scattered all across campus.

 ALVERNIA UNIVERSITY

READING, PENNSYLVANIA
www.alvernia.edu/

Design your future the way you want it at Alvernia University, a caring learning community rooted in the Catholic, Franciscan and liberal arts traditions. Students here choose from over fifty programs in both liberal arts and professional programs ranging from Accounting to Addiction Studies, from Forensic Science to Political Science. Alvernia participates in a number of intercollegiate sports: baseball, basketball, cross-country, field hockey, golf, ice hockey, lacrosse, soccer, softball, tennis, track and field and volleyball. The University is a member of the NCAA Division III, the ECAC and the Commonwealth

Conference of the Middle Atlantic States Collegiate Athletic Corporation (MAC), a highly competitive Division III intercollegiate conference. A state-of-the-art turf field and track opened in 2009. Alvernia's full schedule of student events, activities and organizations offers something for everyone. From ballroom dancing to Spring Fling, from philosophical debates to three-on-three basketball, from improvisational theatre to community service, there's a club for every interest—and if there isn't, students can start one. The Student Government Association and the Campus Activities Board plan plenty of on-campus entertainment and social events, including comedians, bands and film series, as well as trips. Students log 40 hours of volunteer service as a graduation requirement, and Alvernia helps them find opportunities to fit their interests, schedule and talents. Students can tutor schoolchildren, shovel sidewalks for the elderly, stock groceries at a food bank or practice Spanish language skills on alternative spring break mission trips to Ecuador or Santo Domingo. Giving back, pitching in, helping out, getting involved, making a difference—no matter what it's called, at Alvernia, all that matters is that everyone does it. On-campus housing includes suite-style residence halls and town houses. New residence halls opened in 2003, 2005 and 2009. Students head over to the 24/7 student center to catch a bite at the new Crusader Cafe, study with wireless Internet access and relax in the lounge with a big-screen television and game room. Located in the scenic Blue Mountain area of eastern Pennsylvania, Alvernia's 121-acre campus overlooks Angelica Park,

CONTACT INFORMATION

Mr. Jeff Dittman, Vice President for Enrollment Management

☎ 610-796-8269 or toll-free 888-ALVERNIA

✉ admissions@alvernia.edu

noted for its rustic beauty. Beyond Reading lies Pennsylvania's famous Amish country. The University also has easy access to New York, Philadelphia, Baltimore and Washington, D.C.

- **Enrollment:** *2,856*
- **Selectivity:** *moderately difficult*
- **Test scores:** *ACT—over 18, 74%; SAT—critical reading over 500, 43%; SAT—math over 500, 44%*
- **Application deadline:** *Rolling (freshmen), rolling (transfer)*
- **Expenses:** *Tuition $24,350; Room & Board $9212*

Alvernia's Student Center is the hub of campus life, with a newly renovated dining hall and student-run café open 24/7 for late-night study breaks or hanging out between classes.

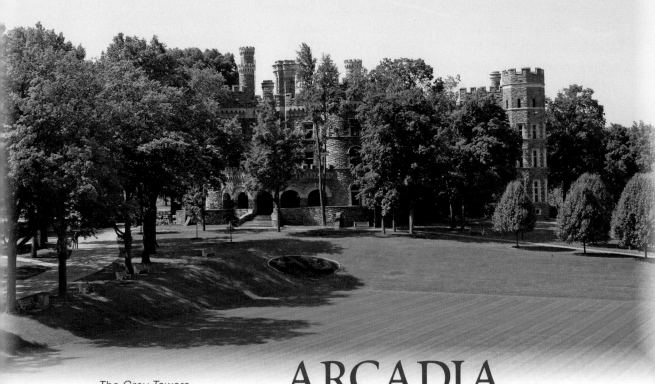

The Grey Towers Castle is not only the trademark and heart of Arcadia University, it is also a National Historic Landmark.

ARCADIA
UNIVERSITY

GLENSIDE, PENNSYLVANIA
www.arcadia.edu/

Arcadia is a top-ranked private university that invites students to get their passports ready. Why? Because Arcadia was ranked first in the nation for the percentage of undergrads studying abroad in the 2008 *Open Doors* report. Students here can choose from over 100 programs in more than fourteen countries from Tanzania to Ireland. Arcadia students also choose from among seventy-five cutting-edge fields of study. In fall of 2010, Arcadia is introducing five new three-year accelerated undergrad programs in business administration, communications, international business and culture, international studies and psychology—giving students a faster path to graduate school or a career. Arcadia offers master's programs in business administration, counseling psychology, education, English, forensic science, genetic counseling, health education, humanities, international peace and conflict resolution, international relations and diplomacy, physician assistant and public health—and *U.S. News & World Report* ranks Arcadia University among the top 25 master's universities in the North. Doctor of Physical Therapy (DPT) and Doctor of Education (EdD) in special education degrees are also offered. Arcadia students jump into the mix of more than forty-five clubs and organizations or a ton of community service programs. Students volunteer on neighborhood improvement projects, work at literacy or gerontology centers and assist disadvantaged or disabled children. Arcadia athletes participate in NCAA Division III intercollegiate sports in basketball, field hockey, lacrosse, soccer, softball, swimming, tennis and volleyball for women and

Arcadia University's Knight Madness!

baseball, basketball, golf, soccer, swimming and tennis for men. Cheerleading, men's lacrosse and equestrian are offered as club sports, while a number of other students play intramurals like Ultimate and flag football. Arcadia features a beautiful rolling campus built around the historic landmark Grey Towers Castle. The University is 12 miles from Center City Philadelphia and only 90 minutes from the Jersey shore and Pennsylvania's Pocono Mountains. Students have access to dozens of museums, galleries, performing arts centers and

nightspots and historic, government and commercial sites in the metropolitan area.

- **Enrollment:** *4,021*
- **Selectivity:** *moderately difficult*
- **Test scores:** *ACT—over 18, 96%; SAT—critical reading over 500, 81%; SAT—math over 500, 74%*
- **Application deadline:** *3/1 (freshmen), 6/15 (transfer)*
- **Expenses:** *Tuition $31,260; Room & Board $10,680*

CONTACT INFORMATION

Mr. Mark Lapreziosa, Assistant Vice President of Enrollment Management

☎ 215-572-2910 or toll-free 877-ARCADIA

✉ admiss@arcadia.edu

M. Carey Thomas Library

Bryn Mawr College

BRYN MAWR, PENNSYLVANIA
www.brynmawr.edu/

Bryn Mawr women are leaders in the classroom, in the studio, in the laboratory and on the field. They engage with the world beyond the campus, too, through advanced research projects, summer internships and collaborative research with faculty members. Bryn Mawr's innovative programs—the Katherine Houghton Hepburn Center for Women in Public Life, Office of Civic Engagement and the Praxis Program—provide many internship opportunities in Philadelphia and Washington, D.C. Recent interns worked for Governor Rendell, the Smithsonian Institute and the Arden Theatre Company. Students can choose from thirty-six majors and thirty-eight minors and many students opt for independent and interdepartmental majors. Joint academic programs also exist with Haverford, Swarthmore and the

University of Pennsylvania. Bryn Mawr ranks among the top ten schools in graduates going on to earn their Ph.D. Bryn Mawr's alumnae include the first woman president of Harvard University, one of the first women to receive the Nobel Peace Prize, the first woman neurosurgeon and the first and only woman to receive four Academy Awards for acting. Above all else, Bryn Mawr women share a tremendous respect for individual differences, not just a passive tolerance of other lifestyles and points of view. Bryn Mawr is home to twelve NCAA Division III varsity teams. Students compete in badminton, basketball, crew, cross-country, field hockey, lacrosse, soccer, swimming, tennis, indoor track and field, outdoor track and field and volleyball. A $7-million upgrade and renovation of the Bern Schwartz Gymnasium, due to be ready for fall 2010 students, will offer students and athletes enhanced spaces for training, fitness and aquatics. Students live on campus in thirteen unique halls; some rooms have fireplaces, window seats and hardwood floors while others have private bathrooms and outdoor patios (two of the buildings are listed on the National Register of Historic Places). The $19 renovations to the Goodhart Theatre were completed in the fall of 2009 to include wireless access and upgraded facilities for music and theatre majors. Bryn Mawr College is located on a 135-acre suburban campus, 11 miles from Philadelphia. Students can hop on a train and be in Philadelphia's funky art galleries or eclectic restaurants or bookstores in just 25 minutes.

Students on Erdman Path

- **Enrollment:** *1,771*

- **Selectivity:** *most difficult*

- **Test scores:** *ACT—over 18, 100%; SAT—critical reading over 500, 97.54%; SAT—math over 500, 97.53%*

- **Application deadline:** *1/15 (freshmen), 3/15 (transfer)*

- **Expenses:** *Tuition $38,034; Room & Board $12,000*

CONTACT INFORMATION

Ms. Marjorie Torchon, Director of Admissions

☎ 610-526-5152 or toll-free 800-BMC-1885

🖳 admissions@brynmawr.edu

The Academic Quad and Bertrand Library form the hub of academic life on a quintessential college campus.

Bucknell
UNIVERSITY

LEWISBURG, PENNSYLVANIA
www.bucknell.edu/

Bucknell is a top-ranked university offering a comprehensive liberal arts education to exceptionally talented students. With academic programs in the arts, engineering, humanities, management and social and natural sciences, Bucknell University is a place that prepares students for success in an increasingly complex and interconnected global society. Bucknell's undergrads can choose from more than fifty majors and sixty minors. Students have the freedom to build robots, write and perform in their own plays or debate solutions to the environmental crisis in the Gulf. Engineers can make art, artists can analyze DNA and philosophers can make music. Each student chooses his or her own pathway, but what unites everyone is a shared passion for learning. Bucknell's award-winning professors (not graduate assistants) teach every class, getting to know students personally

PENNSYLVANIA

and challenging them to do their best. Often, they engage students in research and creative projects outside of class. Student athletes participate in NCAA Division I sports along with intramural and club sports, active Greek life programs and more than 150 student-run clubs and organizations. These clubs focus on anything from social and environmental causes to cultural awareness, poetry slams, dance, pottery or politics. Students perform service work in places as close as the local nursing home and as far away as Nicaragua. They secure summer internships with nonprofit organizations and corporations. They study abroad through one of University's own "in" programs or 130 other approved programs in Africa, Asia, Europe and South America. And after they graduate, they live and work all over the world. Alumni of Bucknell succeed in their careers because they offer a combination of skills, knowledge and flexibility of mind that employers seek. To prepare students, the University offers

career services including advising, networking, mock interviews, internship support and employer fairs. The placement rate is consistently high: 93 percent of the class of 2008 was employed or in graduate school within six months of graduation. With its green spaces, red brick buildings and striking views, Bucknell's campus sits in the heart of scenic central Pennsylvania. The shops of downtown Lewisburg lie within walking distance of campus. The University is about a 3 to 4 hour drive from

CONTACT INFORMATION

Dean Robert Springall, Dean of Admissions

☎ 570-577-1101

✉ admissions@bucknell.edu

New York City, Washington, D.C. and Philadelphia.

- **Enrollment:** *3,673*
- **Selectivity:** *most difficult*
- **Test scores:** *ACT—over 18, 100%; SAT—critical reading over 500, 98%; SAT—math over 500, 98%*
- **Application deadline:** *1/15 (freshmen), 3/15 (transfer)*
- **Expenses:** *Tuition $42,342; Room & Board $9938*

Nine months after graduation, 95 percent of the Class of 2009 was employed, in graduate school, volunteering, or traveling. Bucknell alumni rank among the highest for earnings potential.

Cabrini College students learn by doing. The Communication Department offers a strong and varied major for students interested in careers in communication, convergent media, and theater.

CABRINI
COLLEGE

RADNOR, PENNSYLVANIA
www.cabrini.edu/

Cabrini College is a forward-thinking Catholic college that stresses the importance of service and experience. Cabrini offers more than thirty undergraduate programs in the liberal arts and sciences and professional studies. At the graduate level, Cabrini has a Master of Education degree, numerous teacher certifications and a Master of Science degree in organization leadership. The campus is centered on four core values: community, respect, vision and dedication to excellence. The National Survey of Student Engagement consistently shows that Cabrini first-year students and seniors score higher than those at more than 700 colleges and universities in several benchmarks—level of academic challenge, student-faculty interaction, enriching educational experiences and supportive campus environment. Cabrini was one of the first colleges or universities to add community service into the curriculum and the first in Pennsylvania to require community service of all undergrads. Students have helped homeless people write resumes, raised money for anti-malaria nets, planted trees in the community and brought fair-trade bananas and coffee to campus—whatever the cause or interest, students here get involved. Many Cabrini students also land paid internships at leading business and organizations from *The Philadelphia Inquirer* to the U.S. Secret Service. Many study abroad programs are offered at Cabrini, including its popular Semester at Sea program. New short-term courses will allow students to study science in Switzerland and France, explore British and American theatre in London and live and learn from host families in Castilla, Spain. Student athletes at Cabrini participate in sixteen intercollegiate sports at the NCAA Division III level as well as in a number of intramural sports like cricket and dodgeball. Men's varsity

Inside the classroom, a Cabrini College education stresses engagement. Students choose from more than 30 majors, or design their own.

teams are basketball, cross country, golf, lacrosse, soccer, swimming and tennis. Women compete in basketball, cross country, field hockey, lacrosse, soccer, softball, swimming, tennis and volleyball. Other popular extracurricular activities are the theater program, the College chorus, professional organizations like the Accounting Association and the American Institute for Graphic Arts and the campus radio station. Cabrini is located on a wooded 112-acre suburban campus, just minutes from the King of Prussia shopping mall and 30 minutes from Philadelphia. Students head to the city to check out museums,

historic sites, musical performances and sporting events. Cabrini is also close to other Philadelphia-area colleges.

- **Enrollment:** *3,514*
- **Selectivity:** *moderately difficult*
- **Test scores:** *SAT—critical reading over 500, 37%; SAT—math over 500, 35%*
- **Application deadline:** *Rolling (freshmen), rolling (transfer)*
- **Expenses:** *Tuition $31,030; Room & Board $11,400*

CONTACT INFORMATION

Mr. Stephen Colfer, Senior Associate Director of Admissions

☎ 610-902-8557 or toll-free 800-848-1003

🖥 admit@cabrini.edu

Carnegie Mellon

PITTSBURGH, PENNSYLVANIA
www.cmu.edu/

Carnegie Mellon is world-renowned for its unique approach to education and research. Left-brain and right-brain thinking unite within our collaborative culture and become the foundation of learning.

Carnegie Mellon students come away from their undergrad experience poised to be trendsetters, whether in the business world, the art community or in graduate school. Since its beginning more than 100 years ago, Carnegie Mellon has evolved into a school consistently ranked in the top 25 for its unique approach to education and research. Students become experts in fields ranging from business, the fine arts and computer science to humanities, the sciences and engineering—far more than businessman and philanthropist Andrew Carnegie first envisioned when he founded Carnegie Mellon as a technical school in 1900. Students here learn sound judgment, resourcefulness and professional ethics through interdisciplinary and hands-on experiences. Graduates go on to become the innovative leaders and problem solvers of tomorrow. Carnegie Mellon has more than 100 research centers and institutes. CyLab is one of the largest university-based cybersecurity education and research centers in the United States. High school juniors can participate in Carnegie Mellon's six-week summer Pre-College programs, in which students can take college course work, meet people from all over the country, live like true college students and explore the city of Pittsburgh. Students can enroll in two regular Carnegie Mellon courses for full credit in disciplines such as engineering, humanities, computer science or the sciences; immerse themselves in the fine arts studio or conservatory-based courses to figure out if they're really interested in architecture, art, design, drama or music; or attend the National High School Game Academy where students learn interactive digital game development through hands-on experience. Student activities at Carnegie Mellon include more than 150 clubs and

organizations, varsity and intramural sports (NCAA Division III), fraternities and sororities and student government. Most students live in University housing: traditional residence halls, special-interest housing, apartments and fraternity/sorority houses. Off campus, students can head to the largest public park in Pittsburgh or enjoy shopping, professional sports, art galleries and amusement parks. Carnegie Mellon is located 5 miles from the downtown area in the Oakland neighborhood of Pittsburgh. Although Carnegie Mellon's 150-acre campus has the collegiate feel of a suburban campus, the surrounding Pittsburgh community has a big city

Carnegie Mellon's unique approach to education gives students the opportunity to become experts in their chosen field while studying course work across disciplines.

CONTACT INFORMATION

Mr. Michael Steidel, Director of Admissions

☎ 412-268-2082

✉ undergraduate-admissions@andrew.cmu.edu

vibe. The University is about 1 hour from some of the best skiing in the East and is only a short plane ride from Boston, New York, Chicago, Philadelphia and Washington, D.C.

- **Enrollment:** *11,443*

- **Selectivity:** *most difficult*

- **Test scores:** *ACT—over 18, 100%; SAT—critical reading over 500, 99%; SAT—math over 500, 99%*

- **Application deadline:** *1/1 (freshmen), 3/1 (transfer)*

- **Expenses:** *Tuition $40,728; Room & Board $10,840*

CEDAR CREST COLLEGE

ALLENTOWN, PENNSYLVANIA
www.cedarcrest.edu/

Learning shouldn't stop outside of the classroom! Cedar Crest offers a large number of campus activities, from varsity sports to theatre and our college newspaper and radio club.

A liberal arts college by design, Cedar Crest College prepares women to lead in a global society. The College has more than thirty academic programs as well as faculty members who put a unique spin on traditional majors like business and marketing, communication, English and performing arts. In addition, Cedar Crest College has renowned programs in forensic science (one of fourteen accredited programs in the country and the only one affiliated with a women's college), social work (the only accredited program in the Lehigh Valley) and genetic engineering (one of the oldest programs in the country). The College's award-winning health and wellness program includes personal sports training; nutrition counseling; and a full schedule of dance, yoga and aerobics classes. The Rodale Aquatic Center for Civic Health—a state-of-the-art, two-pool complex—is open to all students. The campus also has tennis courts; regulation fields for field hockey, lacrosse, soccer and softball; and a fitness center. Cedar Crest students participate in eight NCAA Division III intercollegiate sports: basketball, cross-country, field hockey, lacrosse, soccer, softball, tennis and volleyball. The College offers two club sports: equestrian and swimming. Cedar Crest student-athletes successfully balance schoolwork with athletics. The Colonial States Athletic Conference (CSAC) recently awarded Cedar Crest student-athletes the first institutional achievement award for earning the highest grade point average in the Conference. Cedar Crest students can join more than forty clubs and organizations on campus ranging from student government to the Literary Club and Biology Club. The College prepares women to lead, not just in college, but for life. Leadership retreats are held throughout the year and students complete more than 20,000 hours in community service annually at schools, hospitals, animal shelters and through Habitat for Humanity. Some Cedar

Cedar Crest was recently named one of the top ten colleges for women by Forbes Magazine. *It is a smart choice for women who want to achieve at the highest levels.*

Crest upperclassmen opt for the College's living-learning communities. These communities bring together students who share a common interest (for example, the environment or social justice), regardless of major or career focus. These students live together, take a house class together, travel together and develop close relationships with a faculty member affiliated with the community. Students enjoy Cedar Crest's parklike campus in the heart of the Lehigh Valley. The campus is an 84-acre nationally registered arboretum with more than 130 species of trees. Cedar Crest is within easy distance of Allentown parks, high-end shopping,

restaurants and Pocono ski resorts. Cedar Crest is located in "College Valley," home to more than 32,000 students at eight colleges within 20 minutes of campus.

- **Enrollment:** *1,887*
- **Selectivity:** *moderately difficult*
- **Test scores:** *ACT—over 18, 100%; SAT—math over 500, 63%*
- **Application deadline:** *Rolling (freshmen), rolling (transfer)*
- **Expenses:** *Tuition $28,135; Room & Board $9321*

CONTACT INFORMATION

Andrea Stewart, Associate Director of Admissions

☎ 610-606-4666 or toll-free 800-360-1222
✉ astewart@cedarcrest.edu

chatham
UNIVERSITY

PITTSBURGH, PENNSYLVANIA
www.chatham.edu/

Undergraduate Closing Convocation is one of Chatham's oldest traditions. Seniors wear their "Tutorial Hats" which represent their senior research project and memories at Chatham.

Chatham University provides students with a solid education built upon strong academics, public leadership and global understanding. The University houses three distinctive colleges: Chatham College for Women offers academic and cocurricular programs for undergrad women; the College for Graduate Studies offers women and men master's- and doctoral-level programs; and the College for Continuing and Professional Studies provides online and hybrid degree programs for women and men as well as certificate programs and community programming. Chatham College for Women fields NCAA Division III sports in basketball, cross-country, ice hockey, soccer, softball, swimming and diving, tennis, volleyball and water polo. Chatham's Athletic and Fitness Center includes an eight-lane competition pool, a gym, squash courts, cardio rooms, a climbing wall, a running track and exercise and dance studios. Chatham University's campus is high-tech on so many levels. All incoming undergrads receive tablet PCs that can access the University's wireless network and are incorporated into the curriculum for in-class note-taking, research and online learning. Students lease the computers, which they then own upon graduation. All residence halls have computer labs and high-speed network printers as well as network ports in each room. Central computer equipment supports e-mail, computer-mediated courseware, personal Web pages and file and print servers. Chatham participates in campuswide software license agreements that permit students to install select productivity software on their personal machines at no extra cost. Chatham's Shadyside Campus is located minutes from downtown Pittsburgh and features towering trees and century-old mansions that have been converted into residence halls. The Shadyside Campus includes Chatham Eastside, a new LEED Silver facility that houses the University's

interior architecture, landscape architecture, occupational therapy, physical therapy and physician assistant studies programs. The University's Eden Hall Campus is located north of the city in Richland Township and is home to Chatham's new School of Sustainability and the Environment. Pittsburgh is one of the safest and most dynamic green cities in the country and is headquarters to major businesses in finance, health care and technology. Students have a free ride on public transportation within Allegheny County simply by flashing their Chatham ID. For sports enthusiasts, Pittsburgh has several professional sports teams: the

CONTACT INFORMATION

Ms. Lisa D. Meyers, Director of Admissions

☎ 412-365-1672 or toll-free 800-837-1290

✉ lmeyers@chatham.edu

Penguins, the Pirates and the Steelers. Pittsburgh has also been rated "America's Most Livable City" by *Places Rated Almanac* and "Most Livable City in the United States" and twenty-ninth "Most Livable City Worldwide" by *The Economist.*

- **Enrollment:** *2,219*

- **Selectivity:** *moderately difficult*

- **Test scores:** *ACT—over 18, 83.3%; SAT—critical reading over 500, 69.4%; SAT—math over 500, 58.1%*

- **Application deadline:** *8/1 (freshmen), rolling (transfer)*

Community service is integral to the Chatham experience, for undergraduates and graduates alike.

DELAWARE VALLEY COLLEGE
Founded 1896

DOYLESTOWN, PENNSYLVANIA
www.delval.edu/

Students come to Delaware Valley College (DVC), first and foremost, to prepare themselves for a professional career. The placement record of Delaware Valley College graduates is outstanding, proving that the time-honored philosophy of "scholarship with applied experience" works. This private college offers a broad range of programs in agriculture, business, science, education and liberal arts. On the graduate level, Delaware Valley College has a Master in Business Administration degree program, a Master of Business Administration in Food and Agribusiness and a Master of Educational Leadership. The College also offers a ton of extracurricular activities and events. Student publications include the weekly *RamPages* (newspaper), the *Cornucopia* (yearbook) and the *Gleaner* (literary magazine). Groups plan mixers, movies, concerts, field trips and workshops. A-Day, a campuswide fair, annually attracts 50,000 visitors who enjoy the festival, the entertainment, and the academically oriented projects. Such projects as livestock judging, plant sales, chemistry magic shows, computer-aided design demonstrations, a model rainforest habitat and equestrian events all showcase the talents of DVC students. DVC is big on technology—students meet in smart classrooms with Sympodium stations, finish research papers in computer labs with the latest software and printers and even configure their iPhones for Del Val's Microsoft exchange email server—all across a wireless campus. DVC fields seventeen intercollegiate teams for men and women (NCAA Division III, ECAC and MAC). Del Val's dining is getting a facelift. Students are going to be able to choose meals (during extended hours) made from fresh, locally grown ingredients—some grown at Del

Val's own farms. The College is located in historic Bucks County, about 30 miles north of Philadelphia and 70 miles southwest of New York City. Bucks County is one of the fastest-growing areas in the United States, yet it maintains its historical and agricultural history. The College enjoys a friendly relationship with its surrounding community. Many students find part-time work and internships with the local businesses, and the community benefits from the many events and activities that are held on campus.

CONTACT INFORMATION

Mr. Stephen Zenko, Director of Admissions

☎ 215-489-2211 or toll-free 800-2DELVAL

🖳 admitme@devalcol.edu

- **Enrollment:** *2,253*
- **Selectivity:** *moderately difficult*
- **Test scores:** *ACT—over 18, 97.92%; SAT—critical reading over 500, 51.84%; SAT—math over 500, 54.11%*
- **Application deadline:** *5/1 (freshmen)*
- **Expenses:** *Tuition $27,742; Room & Board $9836*

Students take advantage of a snowfall to do some sledding on one of the campus hills.

DeSales University

CENTER VALLEY, PENNSYLVANIA
www.desales.edu

DeSales University is a private university that aims to provide a high-quality education in a caring, Christian environment. DeSales' undergrads receive a broad-based liberal arts education through the more than thirty majors leading to the bachelor of arts, bachelor of science or bachelor of science in nursing degree. The University's graduate degree programs focus on the fields of business, criminal justice, education, technology and health care (including an innovative physician assistant program). Most undergrads live on campus and participate in the more than forty clubs and organizations that range from the Guitar Club to Best Buddies (which pairs up college students with mentally and physically challenged people). DeSales has sixteen intercollegiate teams that compete at the NCAA Division III level. Men's teams are baseball, basketball, cross country, golf, lacrosse, soccer, tennis and track and field. Women's teams are basketball, cross country, field hockey, soccer, softball, tennis, track and field and volleyball. The 82,500 square foot Billera Hall houses a fitness center with weights and aerobic areas, a gym with three full basketball courts, a track and a lounge with pool table and big screen TV. The popular Campus Ministry attracts students who want to participate in retreats and social justice groups. The Labuda Center for the Performing Arts houses the largest department in the University; it has three stages with full set construction and

design facilities, a dance studio and the Iacocca TV Studio and editing suite. The University Center (opened in 2003) has a 500-seat dining area, an outdoor patio and a bridge over the swale. Eight suite-style residence halls offer a range of living options, including living-learning communities, which allows students with common interests to live together. The Lehigh Valley offers year-round recreational activities, from skiing and skating in the winter to golf and swimming in the summer. The Lehigh Valley has a wide variety of museums, art galleries and concert venues, while farmers' markets are a common sight throughout the region. Amusement parks like Dorney Park and Wildwater Kingdom and the Crayola Factory are nearby, as are Kutztown Festival and other annual celebrations. The Promenade Shops at Saucon Valley offer more than sixty-five stores and restaurants

CONTACT INFORMATION

Mr. Derrick Wetzell, Director of Admissions

☎ 610-282-1100 Ext. 1711 or toll-free 877-4DESALES

✉ derrick.wetzell@desales.edu

and a state-of-the-art movie theater. The campus is less than 2 hours from New York City and 1 hour from Philadelphia.

- **Enrollment:** *3,150*
- **Selectivity:** *moderately difficult*
- **Test scores:** *ACT—over 18, 94%; SAT—critical reading over 500, 70%; SAT—math over 500, 70%*
- **Application deadline:** *8/1 (freshmen), 8/1 (transfer)*
- **Expenses:** *Tuition $27,200; Room & Board $9750*

The DeSales University Center is where students eat and attend events.

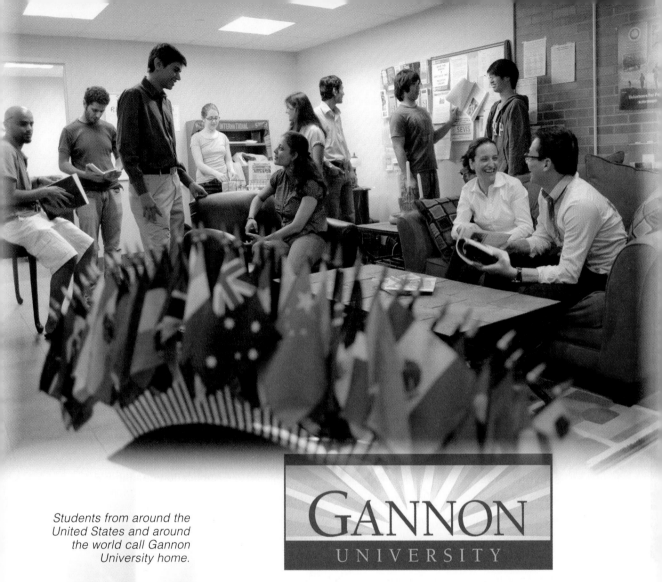

Students from around the United States and around the world call Gannon University home.

GANNON
UNIVERSITY

Believe in the possibilities.

ERIE, PENNSYLVANIA
www.gannon.edu/

Gannon University—consistently named one of America's Best Colleges by *U.S. News & World Report*—is dedicated to excellence in value-centered education. Students can choose from fifty-five bachelor's level programs, nineteen master's level programs and two doctoral degrees (counseling psychology, organizational learning and leadership). The campus maintains more than thirty buildings within six city blocks. The state-of-the-art Carneval Athletic Pavilion has a six-lane pool with diving boards and 250-seat observation deck; a suspended rubberized track; a 2,600-square-foot weight room; courts for racquetball, handball, volleyball and basketball; and a cardio room. Also on campus are two residence halls (with another one under construction), nine apartment buildings, classroom and faculty office buildings, an administration building and a multipurpose chapel building. The Waldron Campus Center is where students meet and eat between classes; it has everything from a big screen TV lounge to two food courts to a game room with multiple gaming systems—all in a wireless building. Students enjoy the intramural sports program that runs throughout the entire year. They play everything from co-ed badminton to handball. In Division II intercollegiate athletics, Gannon offers men's baseball, basketball, cross country, football, golf, soccer, water polo and wrestling and women's basketball, cross country, golf, lacrosse, soccer, softball,

volleyball and water polo. There is also an intercollegiate coed swimming and diving team. The University has a Career Development and Employment Services Office to aid students in locating internships and part-time work during school and full-time work after graduation. Gannon's campus is located in the heart of downtown Erie, giving students the benefit of internships with businesses, law and law-enforcement agencies, health-care facilities and social service organizations. It is also within walking distance of stores, shops, restaurants and theaters. Just six blocks from campus, Presque Isle State Park has seven miles of beaches, lagoons, hiking trails and biking paths. Erie is Pennsylvania's fourth-largest city and is located in the northwestern corner of the state on the shore of Lake Erie. Erie is approximately 120 miles north of Pittsburgh, 90 miles east of Cleveland and 90 miles southwest of Buffalo.

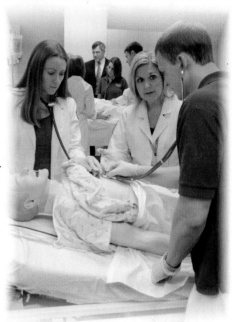

Our Health Professions students prepare for the real world by utilizing our state-of-the-art Patient Simulation Center, the largest in the region.

- **Enrollment:** *4,238*

- **Selectivity:** *moderately difficult*

- **Test scores:** *ACT—over 18, 84.5%; SAT—critical reading over 500, 52.4%; SAT—math over 500, 59.8%*

- **Application deadline:** *Rolling (freshmen), rolling (transfer)*

- **Expenses:** *Tuition $23,574; Room & Board $9330*

CONTACT INFORMATION

Office of Admissions

☎ 814-871-7240 or toll-free 800-GANNONU

🖳 admissions@gannon.edu

Ed Breen Student Union

GROVE CITY COLLEGE

ESTABLISHED 1876 · PENNSYLVANIA

GROVE CITY, PENNSYLVANIA
www.gcc.edu/

The campus of Grove City College (GCC) stretches more than 150 acres and includes twenty-seven neo-Gothic buildings valued at more than $100 million. The landscaped campus is considered one of the nicest in the nation. While the College has changed to meet business and societal needs, its basic philosophy has remained unchanged since its founding in 1876. It is a Christian liberal arts and sciences school dedicated to providing the highest-quality education at the lowest possible cost. Wanting to stay a private school governed by private citizens (trustees), it is one of the very few colleges in the country that does not accept any state or federal money. It is informally affiliated with the Presbyterian Church (USA)—the College believes that well educated students should be exposed to the central ideas of the Christian faith. A 20-minute chapel program offered

Tuesday and Thursday mornings, along with a Sunday evening worship service, challenges students in their faith. Students are required to attend sixteen out of the fifty scheduled chapel services per semester. The Physical Learning Center is one of the finest among the nation's small colleges and includes an eight-lane bowling alley; two swimming pools; handball/racquetball courts; fitness rooms with free weights, aerobic equipment and Cybex machines; a three-lane running track; and the basketball arena. The Grove City Wolverines participate in NCAA Division III sports. Mean's teams are baseball, basketball, cross country, golf, football, soccer, swimming and diving, tennis and track and field. Women's teams are basketball, cross country, golf, volleyball, soccer, softball, swimming and diving, tennis, track and field and water polo. There are also more than 130 organizations and special interest groups, including local fraternities and sororities. The College's placement services, ranked recently by *The Princeton Review* in the top 20 in the nation, help students land internships and jobs after graduation. A complete file of personal data, academic records and recommendations is kept for each registrant and potential employers who visit the campus have access to these files when interviewing graduating seniors. Grove City is 60 miles north of Pittsburgh and only a day's drive from Chicago, New York City, Toronto and Washington, D.C.

Fun group of students

- **Enrollment:** *2,530*
- **Selectivity:** *most difficult*
- **Test scores:** *ACT—over 18, 100%; SAT—critical reading over 500, 99%; SAT—math over 500, 98%*
- **Application deadline:** *2/1 (freshmen), 8/15 (transfer)*
- **Expenses:** *Tuition $12,590; Room & Board $6824*

CONTACT INFORMATION

Mr. Jeffrey Mincey, Director of Admissions

☎ 724-458-2100

✉ admissions@gcc.edu

JUNIATA COLLEGE

Founders Hall—in the spring, students study outside and professors hold outdoor classes on the quad.

HUNTINGDON, PENNSYLVANIA
www.juniata.edu/

Juniata College is an independent college of liberal arts and sciences that offers a flexible curriculum. In fact, about 30 percent of all students design their own major here. The most popular majors at Juniata are biology, chemistry, environmental science and education, health sciences, peace and conflict studies and prelaw. Recent studies rank the College highly in the percentage of graduates that eventually earn doctoral degrees; one, in fact, ranked Juniata in the top 10 percent in the nation among all four-year private undergraduate institutions. The College is known for the personal attention it gives to students. Each student is assigned two faculty advisers—not one. School spirit and campus activities are the heart and soul of the College. The 100 clubs and organizations (from Habitat for Humanity to the Skeet and Trap Club) have a positive impact on the entire Juniata campus. The College competes in nineteen NCAA

Division III sports. The Juniata Eagles have men's teams in baseball, basketball, cross country, football, soccer, tennis, track and field and volleyball. Women's teams are basketball, cross country, field hockey, soccer, softball, swimming, tennis, track and field and volleyball. Juniata is located in Huntingdon in the scenic Allegheny Mountains of central Pennsylvania. The 110 acres on College Hill overlook the historic architecture of a classic river town. Juniata's campus also consists of a 365-acre field station and a 315-acre nature preserve where students take hands-on classes such as conservation biology and vertebrate zoology.

The surrounding area has many spots for swimming, fishing, hunting, rock climbing and hiking. Raystown Lake, the largest recreational lake that lies completely in Pennsylvania, is 15 minutes from Juniata. Several major cities are within a short drive of the campus—3 hours to

Professor Goldstein teaching a Science Fiction English class.

Pittsburgh, Baltimore and Washington, D.C.; 4 hours to Philadelphia; and 5 hours to New York City.

- **Enrollment:** *1,468*
- **Selectivity:** *moderately difficult*
- **Test scores:** *SAT—critical reading over 500, 90.9%; SAT—math over 500, 92.8%*

- **Application deadline:** *3/15 (freshmen), 6/15 (transfer)*
- **Expenses:** *Tuition $32,820; Room & Board $8980*

CONTACT INFORMATION

Terry Bollman-Dalansky, Director of Admissions

☎ 814-641-3424 or toll-free 877-JUNIATA

✉ admissions@juniata.edu

At Keystone, students balance more than academics!

Keystone College

LA PLUME, PENNSYLVANIA
www.keystone.edu/

Keystone College was founded in 1868 as Keystone Academy in La Plume, Pennsylvania. Initially opened as the only high school between Binghamton, New York, and Scranton, Pennsylvania, Keystone operated as a secondary school for more than sixty-five years. Rechartered as Scranton-Keystone Junior College in 1934 and then Keystone Junior College in 1944, the College served as one of the premier two-year institutions in the Northeast until 1995. That year, the school was again renamed—as Keystone College. At today's Keystone, students can choose from over forty programs of study through six divisions: Business, Management and Technology; Communication Arts and Humanities; Education; Fine Arts; Natural Sciences and Mathematics; and Social and Behavioral Sciences. Students do not just sit in the back of a lecture hall at Keystone College—they learn by doing. Keystone has its own sugar shack—with a hobby-sized evaporator and sugarbush with 275 taps, students get to test their hand at maple sugaring. The Chef's Table restaurant in Hibbard Campus Center is where the culinary arts students create menus and prepare meals for people. The 165-acre Woodlands campus at Keystone has about 7 miles of walking trails; students can enjoy a self-guided hike or grab one of the interpretive guides and head out for an environmental education adventure. There's even an observatory on campus with a 9 ½" refracting telescope that is open to the public. Student athletes compete at the NCAA Division III level in basketball, soccer, baseball, softball, field hockey, cross country, tennis, golf and outdoor track. Located at the foot of the Endless Mountains in northeastern Pennsylvania, the 270-acre campus is both scenic and historic, with buildings dating back to 1870. Located 13 miles from Scranton, Pennsylvania, the campus offers easy access to major East Coast cities, including New York, Philadelphia and Baltimore.

CONTACT INFORMATION

Jessica Lopez, Senior Administrative Assistant

☎ 570-945-8111 or toll-free 877-4COLLEGE Ext. 1
🖥 admissions@keystone.edu

- **Enrollment:** *1,691*
- **Selectivity:** *minimally difficult*
- **Test scores:** *ACT—over 18, 50%; SAT—critical reading over 500, 20.5%; SAT—math over 500, 21.5%*
- **Application deadline:** *7/15 (freshmen), 8/1 (transfer)*
- **Expenses:** *Tuition $19,120; Room & Board $9250*

Just one of the many beautiful buildings on Keystone's 270-acre campus.

At KU, students can see the stars! Kutztown is one of the only campuses in Pennsylvania that houses an observatory and planetarium.

KUTZTOWN, PENNSYLVANIA
www.kutztown.edu/

In an independent survey, 93 percent of students and recent alumni rated their education at Kutztown University (KU) as excellent or good in regard to their overall college experience, the quality of instruction they received and the quality of the faculty. KU offers excellent academic programs through its undergraduate colleges—Liberal Arts and Sciences, Visual and Performing Arts, Business, and Education. In addition to its undergrad program, the University's graduate program awards master's degrees in a number of fields. Students can earn the

Master of Science in computer and information science and electronic media; the Master of Arts in counseling psychology and English; the Master of Education in art education, elementary education, elementary school counseling (certification and licensure), instructional technology, reading specialist, secondary education (with specializations), secondary school counseling (certification and licensure) and student affairs in higher education (administration and college counseling licensure). The Master of Library Science, Master of Business Administration, Master of Public Administration, and Master of Social Work are also awarded. Kutztown students take advantage of a well-rounded program of athletic, cultural and social events. There are clubs, organizations and activities to suit every need and hobby. Kutztown University's attractive 330-acre campus includes a mix of old and new buildings, including stately Old Main, the historic building known to generations

of Kutztown's students; University Place, a modern residence hall in a courtyard setting; and the McFarland Student Union. The Student Recreation Center opened in fall 2006, and the state-of-the-art Academic Forum opened in January 2007. Renovations of the Sharadin Arts Building and a new 865-bed suite-style residence hall were completed for fall 2008. All residence hall rooms are wired for Internet usage, and multistation computer labs are available in buildings across the campus. The University is located in a beautiful, rural Pennsylvania Dutch community, midway between the cities of Allentown and Reading. Kutztown borough, an easy walk from the campus, has a ton of stores that cater to KU students. Philadelphia is about 1½ hours away and New York City is about 2½ hours from campus.

- **Enrollment:** *10,634*
- **Selectivity:** *moderately difficult*

CONTACT INFORMATION

Dr. William Stahler, Director of Admissions

☎ 610-683-4060 or toll-free 877-628-1915

✉ admission@kutztown.edu

- **Test scores:** *ACT—over 18, 72.1%; SAT—critical reading over 500, 41%; SAT—math over 500, 42.5%*

- **Application deadline:** *Rolling (freshmen), rolling (transfer)*

- **Expenses:** *Tuition $7397; Room & Board $7698*

Reaching new heights: A rock climbing wall is one of the many fitness amenities available in the state-of-the-art Student Recreation Center.

Lafayette's picturesque campus features a blend of modern and Old World architecture.

LAFAYETTE COLLEGE

EASTON, PENNSYLVANIA
www.lafayette.edu/

Classified as one of the nation's most academically competitive colleges, Lafayette focuses exclusively on undergraduates by offering a ton of academic choices in the humanities, social sciences, natural sciences and engineering—without the distraction of graduate programs and graduate students. Lafayette's in-depth curriculum is unusual and unexpected in a college of its size. One of just a few undergraduate colleges with fully accredited programs in engineering, Lafayette draws strength from the diversity of its students who represent a wide range of interests, special talents and aspirations. Lafayette is a residential college where learning continues outside the classroom. Living in college housing is guaranteed and required for all four years. More than 95 percent of students live in College-owned residence halls, apartments, special-interest houses or fraternity/sorority houses. A number of student organizations, cultural events, social opportunities and varsity and intramural sports programs are open to all students. The Lafayette Leopards compete in men's baseball, basketball, cross country, football, golf, lacrosse, soccer, tennis, swimming and diving and track and field and in women's basketball, cross country, field hockey, lacrosse, soccer, softball, swimming and diving, tennis, track and field and volleyball. A strong internship program with alumni and parent mentors helps pave the way to successful careers. Recent interns worked in licensing for Jim Henson Enterprises in NYC and tested groundwater at the Marine Biological Laboratory in Cape Cod, Massachusetts. Lafayette is located atop a hill overlooking the Delaware and Lehigh rivers, just 70 miles from New York City and 60 miles from Philadelphia. Easton, Allentown and Bethlehem

are the principal cities of the Lehigh Valley, Pennsylvania's third-largest metropolitan area. Shops and restaurants are within walking distance of the campus. Just beyond Easton are great ski slopes, top fishing rivers and challenging hiking trails.

- **Enrollment:** *2,406*

- **Selectivity:** *most difficult*

- **Test scores:** *ACT—over 18, 99.5%; SAT—critical reading over 500, 96%; SAT—math over 500, 99%*

CONTACT INFORMATION

Ms. Carol Rowlands, Director of Admissions

☎ 610-330-5100

✉ admissions@lafayette.edu

- **Application deadline:** *1/1 (freshmen), 6/1 (transfer)*

- **Expenses:** *Tuition $37,815; Room & Board $11,799*

 http://bit.ly/collvid47

Lafayette College students celebrate Earth Day with a green picnic on the Quad.

College is like beginning a friendship. You'll know when it clicks. Take the time to learn more about the place that will help shape who you'll become. Take some time to learn more about Marywood.

Marywood
UNIVERSITY

SCRANTON, PENNSYLVANIA
www.marywood.edu/

Marywood University is a comprehensive Catholic University that is motivated by a pioneering, progressive spirit. Marywood helps its students master professional and leadership skills through its four colleges. Students choose from fifty undergraduate degrees in the arts, sciences, music, fine arts, social work and nursing. Students can opt for a double major, honors programs, independent study, internships or study abroad—the choices are endless. Marywood University is constantly upgrading and adding to its campus. Its Robert J. Mellow Center for Athletics and Wellness opened in the fall of 2006; it has a 5,000-square-foot fitness center, elevated jogging track, climbing wall, dance and aerobics studio and state-of-the-art hydro therapy room. The athletics program at Marywood provides students with opportunities to play on competitive intercollegiate, club and intramural teams. Marywood is a member of NCAA Division III and the Colonial States Athletic Conference (CSAC) and student athletes compete in baseball, basketball, cross-country, field hockey, lacrosse, soccer, softball, swimming/diving, tennis and volleyball. More than 300 microcomputers are found throughout the campus, giving students access to the library's online catalog, software and Internet. Situated on a hilltop, Marywood's scenic 115-acre campus is part of a residential area of Scranton—the fifth-largest city in Pennsylvania. Marywood is just 2½ hours from New York and Philadelphia; 4 hours from Washington, D.C.; and 5½ hours from Boston. The Pocono Mountains, offering spectacular scenery and a ton of outdoor recreational opportunities (including downhill skiing) are a short distance from the campus.

- **Enrollment:** *3,471*

- **Selectivity:** *moderately difficult*

- **Test scores:** *SAT—critical reading over 500, 65%; SAT—math over 500, 62.9%*

- **Application deadline:** *Rolling (freshmen), rolling (transfer)*

- **Expenses:** *Tuition $26,270; Room & Board $11,498*

CONTACT INFORMATION

Mr. Christian DiGregorio, Director of University Admissions

☎ 570-348-6234 or toll-free 866-279-9663

✉ yourfuture@marywood.edu

We believe in dreaming big. It is part of our heritage. Big dreams inspired the Rotunda, which is a magnificent symbol of what people can accomplish with passion, determination, and a shared purpose.

MESSIAH COLLEGE.

GRANTHAM, PENNSYLVANIA

www.messiah.edu/

Messiah College is a nationally-ranked, private Christian college that aims to sharpen students' talents, deepen their faith and inspire them to act. Messiah competes in twenty-two intercollegiate sports and maintains one of the most successful NCAA Division III athletics programs in the nation. Messiah teams have earned eleven national championships and regularly achieve national rankings and conference titles. Messiah athletes have been recognized as all-Americans and have been featured in *Sports Illustrated*, *USA Today* and on national network television. Messiah students participate in more than sixty student groups and organizations, including theater and music groups, a campus newspaper and a student-operated radio station. Students can grow in faith and fellowship at Messiah College through chapel and worship services, discipleship groups, ministry outreach teams, community service and mission trips. In April 2008, Messiah College was selected to host "The Compassion Forum," a nationally televised conversation with presidential candidates speaking on the integration of faith and public policy. The College has been widely recognized for its commitment to service-learning and civic engagement. In 2009, Messiah was named to the President's Higher Education Community Service Honor Roll, a distinction granted to only seven colleges in Pennsylvania. The College's service-learning program was nationally recognized by *U.S. News & World Report* as a 2010 "Program to Look For." In 2008, the College was awarded the Carnegie Foundation's prestigious Community Engagement Classification for curricular engagement and outreach and partnership. The College offers both traditional residence halls and apartment-style residences on campus; all residence halls have air conditioning, cable television,

Internet and on-site laundry. The College operates a number of campus safety services for students, such as an after-hours transport service; sixteen 24-hour emergency telephone alarm devices; and a 24-hour professional security patrol. A crisis management and response team, emergency text-messaging system, and emergency evacuation plan are also in place on the campus. Messiah College, named a 2008 Green College by the National Association of Independent Colleges and Universities, is situated on 471 scenic wooded acres, just 12 miles from Harrisburg. The College is approximately 2 hours from Philadelphia, Baltimore and Washington, D.C. For outdoor fun, students head to the Yellow Breeches Creek, which flows through the campus, the nearby Susquehanna River and the Appalachian Trail. The College also operates a satellite campus in Philadelphia in conjunction with Temple University.

- **Enrollment:** *2,801*
- **Selectivity:** *moderately difficult*
- **Test scores:** *ACT—over 18, 95.98%; SAT—critical reading over 500, 82.59%; SAT—math over 500, 81.68%*
- **Application deadline:** *Rolling (freshmen), rolling (transfer)*
- **Expenses:** *Tuition $27,480; Room & Board $8160*

CONTACT INFORMATION

Mr. John Chopka, Vice President for Enrollment Management

☎ 717-691-6000 or toll-free 800-233-4220

✉ admiss@messiah.edu

MU Students enjoy a high level of student-faculty interaction.

MISERICORDIA UNIVERSITY

DALLAS, PENNSYLVANIA
www.misericordia.edu/

Misericordia University is a high-quality liberal arts and professional studies university rooted in a foundation of service to others and committed to providing the personal attention students need in order to succeed both professionally and personally. In the National Survey of Student Engagement, Misericordia students say they are more involved in learning and have better relationships with faculty members and peers than students at other institutions. Misericordia is also ranked in the top tier of *U.S. News & World Report's* "America's Best Colleges 2010" in the Master's North category. Misericordia has comfortable residence halls and townhouses. Each hall offers study rooms, laundry facilities and lounges. The new dining hall is located in the Banks Student Life Center, which also houses the Cougar's Den coffeehouse and the newly renovated Student Union with its flat-screen televisions, pool table and foosball tables. Cultural events, Campus Ministry, intramural and intercollegiate athletics, performing arts shows and art exhibits in the Pauly Friedman Art Gallery all add to the academic experience. In keeping with the University's tradition of mercy, justice, service and hospitality, The University's Service Leadership Center engages students in the development of lifelong civic responsibility through course work.

On spring break, students have served those in need in rural Appalachia, the storm-ravaged Gulf Coast and the South Bronx. Misericordia was named a "Best School for Standing by Grads" in *Kiplinger's Personal Finance Magazine*'s December 2009 special edition, "The Best of Everything 2009." If a student fulfills the requirements of a program and is not employed in his or her field or enrolled in graduate or professional school within six months of graduation, a paid internship is assured. Misericordia has

special bachelor's, master's and doctoral programs for adults, including the Expressway Program, an accelerated degree program; Women with Children, which provides housing and support services for single women with children; and evening, online and weekend formats for people with families and full-time jobs. Master's degrees are available in education, nursing, occupational therapy, physical therapy, speech-language pathology, business administration and organizational management. A doctoral program in physical therapy is available to students and a doctoral program in occupational therapy is available for graduate students via part-time study. Located in northeastern Pennsylvania, Misericordia

CONTACT INFORMATION

Mr. Glenn Bozinski, Director of Admissions

☎ 570-675-6264 or toll-free 866-262-6363

✉ admiss@misericordia.edu

University is 9 miles from the city of Wilkes-Barre. The area offers shopping centers, malls, skiing and professional sports. Pennsylvania's largest natural lake and two state parks are nearby, as are Pocono ski resorts.

- **Enrollment:** *2,736*
- **Selectivity:** *moderately difficult*
- **Test scores:** *ACT—over 18, 93%; SAT—critical reading over 500, 58%; SAT—math over 500, 61%*
- **Application deadline:** *Rolling (freshmen), rolling (transfer)*
- **Expenses:** *Tuition $24,050; Room & Board $10,050*

MU students benefit from community service and guaranteed career placement.

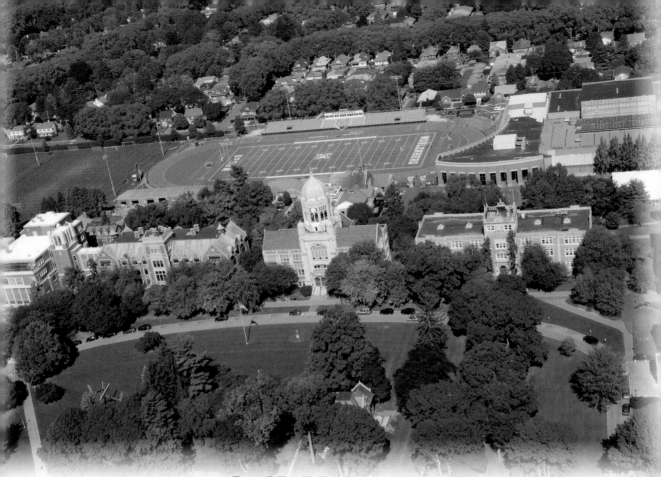

A bird's eye view of Muhlenberg College's 81 acre scenic suburban campus in Allentown, Pennsylvania.

MUHLENBERG

COLLEGE

ALLENTOWN, PENNSYLVANIA
www.muhlenberg.edu/

Muhlenberg College is a highly selective, private college that attracts independent critical thinkers. Students here choose from forty majors (and just as many minors) in the humanities, fine arts, social sciences and natural sciences. Muhlenberg's cutting-edge preprofessional programs prep student interested in pursuing pre-medicine and allied health, pre-law, business, education and pre-theological studies. About one third of Muhlenberg's graduates head immediately to graduate or professional school. Muhlenberg is big on service learning (academically-based community service projects); in fact, there are service learning courses available in nine different departments. For fun on the Muhlenberg campus, students jump right into the more than 100 student clubs and organizations from the special interest (Gaming Society) to the academic (History Club) and from media (WMUH Allentown 91.7 FM) to sports (fencing). Muhlenberg fields twenty-two intercollegiate teams at the NCAA Division III level. Men compete in baseball, basketball, cross country, football, golf, lacrosse, soccer, tennis, indoor/outdoor track and field and wrestling. Women compete in basketball, cross country, field hockey, golf, lacrosse, soccer, softball, tennis, indoor/outdoor track and field and volleyball. Even more students play intramural or club sports ranging from air hockey to ice hockey. Muhlenberg's state-of-the-art facilities include the solar-heated Life Sports Center with basketball, racquetball and squash courts; an

all-weather outdoor track with AstroTurf Gameday Grass 3D (resurfaced in 2008); and tennis courts built in 2003. Students are aided by an active Career Planning and Placement Service in relating academic and personal knowledge and skills to appropriate career goals and in obtaining positions upon graduation. Muhlenberg College makes its home in suburban west Allentown. The downtown area of Allentown is a 10-minute ride from the campus. The College is located 90 miles west of New York City and 60 miles north of Philadelphia. The College also maintains a 60-acre arboretum and a 40-acre environmental field station/wildlife sanctuary.

CONTACT INFORMATION

Mr. Christopher Hooker-Haring, Director of Undergraduate Admissions

☎ 484-664-3245

✉ adm@muhlenberg.edu

- **Enrollment:** *2,517*
- **Selectivity:** *very difficult*
- **Test scores:** *ACT—over 18, 100%; SAT—critical reading over 500, 91.4%; SAT—math over 500, 92.1%*
- **Application deadline:** *2/15 (freshmen), 6/15 (transfer)*
- **Expenses:** *Tuition $36,990; Room & Board $8440*

Students stroll down Muhlenberg College's picturesque academic row.

Penn State Behrend Lion Shrine. Penn State quality in a small university atmosphere.

PENN STATE ERIE, THE BEHREND COLLEGE

ERIE, PENNSYLVANIA
www.pserie.psu.edu/

Penn State Erie, The Behrend College, offers a high-quality, comprehensive education in business, engineering, the humanities and social sciences, science and nursing. The College offers thirty-four bachelor's degree programs, six associate degree programs and two graduate degree programs—a Master of Business Administration (M.B.A.) and a Master of Project Management (M.P.M.). Among all public colleges and universities in Pennsylvania, Penn State Behrend ranks in the top five in student-to-faculty ratio, SAT scores, first-year student retention and graduation rate. The historic core of Penn State Behrend's wooded hilltop campus features the original Glenhill Farmhouse given to Penn State by the Behrend family, founders of Hammermill Paper Company in Erie. More recent additions to the College's campus include an athletics and recreation complex, a research and development center, a chapel and carillon, an observatory, numerous residence halls and the new Metzgar Admissions and

Alumni Center. The campus and its surrounding area are home to woodlands, deep gorges, beautiful streams and cross-country skiing and fitness trails. Here, students attend classes in modern academic buildings and labs, and students live on campus in modern dorms, suites and apartments. A member of NCAA Division III and the Allegheny Mountain Collegiate Conference, Penn State Behrend fields twenty-two varsity sports: eleven teams for men (baseball, basketball, cross-country, golf, indoor track, soccer, swimming and diving, tennis, track and field, volleyball and water polo) and eleven for women (basketball, cross-country, golf, indoor track, soccer, softball, swimming and diving, tennis, track and field, volleyball and water polo). More than 65 percent of students join intramurals, too—everything from slow-pitch softball to coed volleyball and even horseshoes. Situated along Lake Erie's beautiful Presque Isle Bay, Erie is the fourth-largest city in Pennsylvania. The area

is alive with cultural, sports and recreational resources, including Presque Isle State Park, which offers 7 miles of sandy beaches, as well as boating and trails for walking, jogging and biking. Public transportation comes and goes from campus every half hour to points throughout the Erie area, including movie theaters, restaurants, museums, performing arts venues and a zoo. A convention center in downtown Erie features Broadway plays and top-name performers in rock, classical and country music. Erie is located within 2 hours of Buffalo, Cleveland and Pittsburgh and is a

CONTACT INFORMATION

Anne L. Rohrbach, Executive Director for Undergraduate Admissions

☎ 814-865-4700 or toll-free 866-374-3378

✉ admissions@psu.ed

comfortable 4-hour drive from Toronto.

- **Enrollment:** *4,400*
- **Selectivity:** *very difficult*
- **Test scores:** *SAT—critical reading over 500, 55.18%; SAT—math over 500, 68.49%*
- **Application deadline:** *Rolling (freshmen), rolling (transfer)*
- **Expenses:** *Tuition $12,750; Room & Board $8170*

 http://bit.ly/collvid58

Over 110 clubs and organizations, NCAA Division III athletics, intramurals, and opportunities for research and leadership development.

Graphic Design graduate showcases her talent during the Student Portfolio Exhibition in The Gallery at Penn College, located on the third floor of the Madigan Library.

Pennsylvania College of Technology

PENNSTATE
1855

WILLIAMSPORT, PENNSYLVANIA
www.pct.edu/

Pennsylvania College of Technology (Penn College) is a special-mission affiliate of Penn State dedicated to applied technology education. The College has a national reputation for "degrees that work"—advanced technology majors with hands-on instruction and access to the latest equipment. Students choose from more than 100 different majors through Penn College's eight schools. Partnerships with industry leaders, including Honda, Ford and Caterpillar, provide students with unique opportunities to build relationships and tackle internships. Excellent graduate placement rates exceed 95 percent annually (100 percent in some majors). State-of-the-art classrooms and laboratories reflect the expectations of the modern workforce. A number of campus buildings—including a conference center, a Victorian guest house, an athletic field house and a rustic retreat for professional gatherings—have been designed, constructed and maintained by students. Some men and women take part in noncredit classes, including customized business and industry courses offered through Workforce Development and Continuing Education. Most Penn College Wildcat sports teams compete regionally in the Penn State University Athletic Conference (PSUAC) and nationally in the United States Collegiate Athletic Association (USCAA). Varsity sports include archery, baseball, basketball, bowling, cross-country, dance team, golf, soccer, softball, team tennis and volleyball. Penn College is located in north-central Pennsylvania. The main campus is in Williamsport, a city known

around the world as the home of the Little League Baseball World Series. Penn College offers credit classes at three other locations: the Advanced Automotive Technology Center in the Wahoo Drive Industrial Park in Williamsport, the Aviation Center at the Williamsport Regional Airport in Montoursville and the Earth Science Center, 10 miles south of Williamsport near Allenwood. Noncredit classes

CONTACT INFORMATION

Mr. Dennis Correll, Associate Dean for Admissions/ Financial Aid

☎ 570-327-4761 Ext. 7337 or toll-free 800-367-9222

✉ dcorrell@pct.edu

are offered from locations in Williamsport and Wellsboro.

- **Enrollment:** *6,409*
- **Selectivity:** *noncompetitive*
- **Application deadline:** *7/1 (freshmen), rolling (transfer)*
- **Expenses:** *Tuition $12,480; Room & Board $8350*

Civic-minded students from a variety of campus organizations "Walk-It-Out" for a common goal—raising money for the American Cancer Society.

What if going to college meant getting to study things that you're interested in and good at with professors who know your long-term goals and understand how you learn? Welcome to Rosemont College.

ROSEMONT COLLEGE

ROSEMONT, PENNSYLVANIA
www.rosemont.edu/

Rosemont knows that students come to college with their eyes on their future. Here, their dreams are the starting point for an education that is truly their own. This Catholic liberal arts school has a reputation for academic excellence in a diverse setting. In fact, *U.S. News & World Report* has ranked Rosemont the second most diverse liberal arts college in the nation. Rosemont is one college with three schools: the Undergraduate College, the School of Graduate Studies and the School of Professional Studies. Rosemont's nationally acclaimed Undergraduate College offers the Bachelor of Arts, the Bachelor of Fine Arts and the Bachelor of Science degrees in twenty-three majors from Chemistry to Women's Studies. The School of Graduate Studies offers seven graduate degrees, including the Master of Arts in education, English literature and publishing

Rosemont offers students an exceptional and comprehensive learning experience. With 23 majors, 13 varsity sport teams, and numerous clubs, Rosemont develops your unique talents.

programs, as well as a Master of Fine Arts degree in creative writing, a Master of Science in management and a Master of Business Administration. The School of Professional Studies offers working adults the chance to earn a Bachelor of Science or Bachelor of Arts degree in three majors. Rosemont participates in NCAA Division III with varsity teams for men's basketball, cross-country, golf, lacrosse, soccer and tennis and women's basketball, cross-country, field hockey, lacrosse, softball, tennis and volleyball. Other popular activities and clubs at Rosemont include the Film Critics Guild, the Ram Squad (a club of dancers and steppers) and the *Thorn* literary magazine. Rosemont's 56-acre campus is located in the town of Rosemont, a suburban community with many shops, movie theaters, restaurants and bookstores. The city of Philadelphia is 11 miles east of Rosemont and just a 20-minute train ride from the campus. Philadelphia draws students in to experience the Philadelphia Museum of Art, the South Street nightlife and Phillies, Flyers and Eagles games. The Philadelphia area is home to about eighty other colleges and universities. Rosemont is just a short drive from both the Pocono Mountains and the New Jersey shore.

- **Enrollment:** *940*
- **Selectivity:** *moderately difficult*
- **Test scores:** *ACT—over 18, 100%; SAT—critical reading over 500, 29%; SAT—math over 500, 23%*
- **Application deadline:** *Rolling (freshmen), rolling (transfer)*
- **Expenses:** *Tuition $26,250; Room & Board $10,580*

CONTACT INFORMATION

Mr. Chuck Walz, Vice President for Enrollment Management

☎ 610-527-0200 Ext. 2905 or toll-free 800-331-0708
✉ admissions@rosemont.edu

Reach higher. Go far.

SAINT FRANCIS UNIVERSITY

LORETTO, PENNSYLVANIA
www.francis.edu/

Saint Francis University (SFU) is a small liberal arts school with big ideas. For more than 150 years, the University has emphasized two values: providing a high-quality education and respecting the student as an individual. And these guiding principles have not gone unnoticed—*U.S. News & World Report* recently named Saint Francis as a Best Value institution in its *America's Best Colleges 2010* edition. Saint Francis University has also received recognition for its advances in study abroad (Springtime in Italy, French in Quebec) and outreach in health care. Students can choose from a ton of majors and minors in SFU's four schools: Business, Health Sciences, Arts & Letters and Sciences. On the graduate level, Saint Francis awards a Master of Arts degree in human resource management and industrial relations. The University also offers the Master of Business Administration,

Master of Education, Master of Medical Science, Master of Science in physician assistant sciences and Master of Science in occupational therapy degrees. A doctoral degree in physical therapy is also available. Outside of class, undergrads find a number of outlets for their talents, interests and abilities. Departmental clubs, volunteer organizations and social and service fraternities/sororities are all a popular part of campus life. The Student Activities Organization packs a full calendar of lectures, films and concerts as well. Athletics play a major role here, too. The athletics program offers twenty-two NCAA Division I sports for men and women as well as intramural sports. Men's varsity teams are basketball, cross country, football, golf, indoor/outdoor track and field, soccer, tennis and volleyball. Women compete in basketball, cross country, field hockey, golf, lacrosse, indoor/outdoor track and field, soccer, softball, swimming, tennis and volleyball. The state-of-the-art facilities include SportExe artificial turf on DeGol Field, a six-lane swimming pool in the Stokes Natatorium, modern training and physical therapy rooms and study space for the student athletes who have accumulated an impressive twenty-two consecutive semesters of 3.0 GPAs or higher. The Southern Alleghenies Museum of Art, separately chartered, is located on the campus. Saint Francis University sits on 600 acres in the heart of the Allegheny Mountains. The campus is located in the borough of Loretto and is 6 miles from the county seat of Ebensburg. The University is a 90-minute drive east of Pittsburgh.

CONTACT INFORMATION

Robert Beener, Associate Dean for Enrollment Management

☎ 814-472-3100 or toll-free 800-342-5732

✉ rbeener@francis.edu

- **Enrollment:** *2,300*
- **Selectivity:** *moderately difficult*
- **Test scores:** *ACT—over 18, 92%; SAT—critical reading over 500, 66%; SAT—math over 500, 68%*
- **Application deadline:** *Rolling (freshmen), rolling (transfer)*
- **Expenses:** *Tuition $25,554; Room & Board $8716*

DiSepio Institute for Rural Health and Wellness

Hawk's view of the Barbelin Tower.

SJU SAINT JOSEPH'S UNIVERSITY

PHILADELPHIA, PENNSYLVANIA
www.sju.edu/

Saint Joseph's University (SJU) is not for spectators. Its students get involved in everything from research to community service, sports to study abroad. This nationally recognized Jesuit university is one of only 142 schools with a Phi Beta Kappa chapter and business school accreditation by AACSB International–The Association to Advance Collegiate Schools of Business. Saint Joseph's University offers more than seventy-five undergraduate programs, forty-seven graduate degree programs and an Ed.D. in Educational Leadership. SJU

PENNSYLVANIA

students make new friends and learn new cultures through the popular study abroad program—and they can choose from thirty different programs in eighteen countries including Belgium, Japan and South Africa. For on-campus fun and adventure, students start and join clubs and organizations of every kind—the Jazz Band, Up 'til Dawn (fundraiser for St. Jude), the Japanese Culture Club and fraternities/sororities to name a few. The SJU Hawks compete in twenty varsity sports at the NCAA Division I level. Men's teams are baseball, basketball, cross country, golf, lacrosse, rowing, soccer, tennis and track and field. Women's teams include basketball, cross country, field hockey, lacrosse, rowing, soccer, softball, tennis and track and field. Club sports draw even more students in with cricket, golf, martial arts, roller hockey and more. The new Michael J. Hagan '85 Arena (opened in 2009) is a fully air conditioned arena with top-notch basketball courts, a premium seating section with chairbacks, an upper-level concourse with concessions and a media room. SJU's state-of-the-art boathouse (opened in 2002) has four heated boat bays and a 750-square-foot deck for fans. On-campus housing is comfortable and unique; students can choose from traditional dorms, houses and apartments that offer everything from air conditioning and fitness rooms to solariums and private washers/dryers. Located on the edge of the city of Philadelphia, Saint Joseph's provides ready access to many career opportunities of America's sixth-largest city. Students enjoy direct access to internships (many paid), cooperative programs and an active nightlife to boot.

CONTACT INFORMATION

Admissions Department

☎ 610-660-1300 or toll-free 888-BEAHAWK

✉ admit@sju.edu

- **Enrollment:** *8,337*
- **Selectivity:** *moderately difficult*
- **Test scores:** *ACT—over 18, 98%; SAT—critical reading over 500, 80%; SAT—math over 500, 83%*
- **Application deadline:** *2/1 (freshmen), 3/1 (transfer)*
- **Expenses:** *Tuition $34,090; Room & Board $11,575*

Students enjoying the autumn weather as they stroll across the Maguire Campus.

Seton Hill captured its first West Virginia Intercollegiate Athletic Conference baseball title in 2010.

Seton Hill
U N I V E R S I T Y

GREENSBURG, PENNSYLVANIA
www.setonhill.edu/

Seton Hill University, a private liberal arts and sciences school, offers more than thirty undergraduate programs and twelve graduate degree programs through five academic divisions: Education, Humanities, Natural and Health Sciences, Social Sciences and Visual and Performing Arts. The most popular majors at Seton Hill are business, art, psychology, music and biology. At the graduate level, Seton Hill grants the Master of Arts degree in art therapy, elementary education, inclusive education (online), marriage and family therapy, special education and writing popular fiction; a Master of Business Administration; and a Master of Science in physician assistant studies. Seton Hill has graduate certificate programs in entrepreneurship, genocide and holocaust studies (online) and writing popular fiction. Seton Hill's orthodontics program—the newest addition to the health sciences program—provides cutting-edge research, teaching and clinical experiences through the Center for Orthodontics. Seton Hill's new

Performing Arts Center has everything a theatre major needs to go from student to professional—two mainstage performance spaces, a concert hall, rehearsal rooms and the latest in lighting, sound, video and acoustics. Seton Hill remains at the forefront of technology, too. Beginning in the fall of 2010, all first-year undergrads will receive a 13" MacBook Pro laptop and an iPad. After two years, Seton Hill will replace the laptop with a new one—one that students can take with them when they gradu-ate. Outside of class, many events and activities happen on and off campus from lectures to theater produc-tions to University-sponsored trips to Pittsburgh so students can tour museums or catch a Steelers game. Seton Hill fields varsity teams at the NCAA Division II level. Women compete in basket-ball, cross-country, equestrian competition, field hockey, golf, lacrosse, soccer, soft-ball, tennis, track and field

Administration Building at Seton Hill University

and volleyball. Men have teams in baseball, basketball, cross-country, equestrian competition, football, golf, lacrosse, soccer, tennis, track and field and wrestling. Seton Hill University's beautiful 200-acre campus is located in Greensburg in the Laurel Highlands, an area of south-western Pennsylvania known for its scenery and recreation. Just steps from campus, stu-dents can ski, cycle, hike and go whitewater rafting. Just 35 miles east of Pittsburgh,

Seton Hill students can easily head into the city for nightlife and entertainment yet come home to Greensburg's small-town atmosphere.

- **Enrollment:** *2,145*
- **Selectivity:** *moderately difficult*
- **Application deadline:** *8/15 (freshmen), rolling (transfer)*
- **Expenses:** *Tuition $26,622; Room & Board $8810*

CONTACT INFORMATION

Ms. Sherri Bett, Director of Admissions

☎ 724-838-4255 or toll-free 800-826-6234

✉ admit@setonhill.edu

Situated in the heart of the Cumberland Valley of southcentral Pennsylvania, Shippensburg's 200-acre campus offers a tranquil setting with many cultural and recreational opportunities.

SHIPPENSBURG UNIVERSITY

SHIPPENSBURG, PENNSYLVANIA
www.ship.edu/

Shippensburg University welcomes students to try the "Ship" experience. Because whatever the major and whatever the goals, Shippensburg sees to it that every student succeeds. This public university is divided into the College of Arts and Sciences, the College of Education and Human Services, the John L. Grove College of Business and the School of Graduate Studies. More than 200 student clubs and organizations are open to Shippensburg students. Organizations include academic clubs, community service groups, media organizations, performing arts troupes and fraternities and sororities. Many student-run programs bring nationally and internationally known people to campus, too. Pulitzer Prize-winning author David

McCullough, Archbishop Desmond Tutu, Rev. Jesse Jackson, Danny Glover, Maya Angelou, Vice President Dick Cheney, Wynton Marsalis and Buzz Aldrin have all appeared on campus. The residence halls have lounges, exercise rooms, music practice rooms, study rooms and computer connections to the online library catalog system. Each room has a cable television and two direct computer network connections. The University offers state-of-the-art athletic facilities for intercollegiate and intramural sports. These include a 2,768-seat field house, an 8,000-seat stadium, outdoor tennis courts, indoor and outdoor tracks, an indoor swimming pool, squash and handball courts, a rehabilitation center and sand volleyball courts. The 62,000-square-foot student recreation center includes thirty-nine cardiovascular machines with individual televisions, four multipurpose courts, a fitness studio and an elevated track. The University is a member of the Pennsylvania State Athletic Conference and NCAA Division II. Men's intercollegiate sports include baseball, basketball, cross-country, football, soccer, swimming, track and field and wrestling. Women's intercollegiate sports include basketball, cross-country, field hockey, lacrosse, soccer, softball, swimming, tennis, track and field and volleyball. There are also ten intramural sports, including street hockey, and thirteen club sports, including men's and women's rugby. Shippensburg University lies on 200 acres overlooking its namesake community in the Cumberland Valley. The University is about 40 minutes southwest of Harrisburg, 2 hours from both Baltimore and Washington, D.C. and 2½ hours from Philadelphia. The campus is within easy walking distance of the center of town.

CONTACT INFORMATION

Dr. Thomas Speakman, Dean of Enrollment Services

☎ 717-477-1231 or toll-free 800-822-8028

✉ admiss@ship.edu

- **Enrollment:** *8,253*

- **Selectivity:** *moderately difficult*

- **Test scores:** *ACT—over 18, 81.5%; SAT—critical reading over 500, 50.3%; SAT—math over 500, 56.2%*

- **Application deadline:** *Rolling (freshmen), rolling (transfer)*

- **Expenses:** *Tuition $7444; Room & Board $7086*

In each of Shippensburg's 75 undergraduate degree programs, you will find an emphasis on practical application, individual attention, and exposure to the latest ideas and methods.

The Bell Tower, better known as Bevry Beach to students, is the place to hang out between classes, catch up with friends, and soak up the sun.

Temple University

PHILADELPHIA, PENNSYLVANIA
www.temple.edu/

Students who visit Temple University are quite impressed. Cutting-edge facilities and accomplished faculty members create a dynamic academic environment that draws students from around the world. But what can transform a student's life at Temple happens outside the classroom, too. Temple is located in Philadelphia, a world-class city with a thriving music and art scene. It is the perfect place to live and study. Two spectacular new academic buildings opened on Main Campus in January 2009—the Tyler School of Art and the Fox School of Business and Management's Alter Hall. Students who prefer not to attend college in the city should take a look at the Ambler campus, Temple's 187-acre suburban home. Just about all undergraduate programs can be started there, and eighteen can be fully completed there. Ambler's $17-million Learning Center includes smart classrooms; fully integrated technology (including wireless access throughout the building); five computer lab/classrooms; a math, science and writing center; a video editing lab; a cafe; and a 300-seat auditorium. Temple's other local campus is the Health Sciences Center, where the College of Health Professions, Temple University Hospital, Temple University School of Medicine and Temple Dental School are located. The on-campus activities calendar is crammed with theater, dance and music performances. The Liacouras Center, Temple's 10,200-seat entertainment complex, hosts the University's NCAA Division I basketball games (free tickets for students!) as well as concerts. Great performers like Kanye West, Green Day, Maroon 5, John Mayer, Rusted Root, Alicia Keys and Bob Dylan have performed at the Liacouras Center. Temple has every type of student doing every type of activity. Beyond sports, students can join one of 100 or so clubs and organizations and

Students enjoy a walk through Love Park in Philadelphia.

take advantage of the rich resources offered all around Philadelphia (which has a lot more than juicy sandwiches and cream cheese). With more than 100 museums, 700 Zagat-rated restaurants and the largest landscaped park in the country—Fairmount Park at 4,180 acres—Philly has a lot to offer. It is a walkable, manageable city that is just 1.5 miles from Temple's Main Campus. Just four stops on a quick subway ride and students are in Center City—or what most people call downtown. Shop, eat, play or just chill. In addition, students can find a variety of internships in all fields in the Philadelphia area and Temple has more than 100,000

alumni in the region who love to hire Temple students.

- **Enrollment:** *36,505*

- **Selectivity:** *moderately difficult*

- **Test scores:** *ACT—over 18, 92%; SAT—critical reading over 500, 74%; SAT—math over 500, 80%*

- **Application deadline:** *3/1 (freshmen), 6/1 (transfer)*

- **Expenses:** *Tuition $11,764; Room & Board $9198*

CONTACT INFORMATION

Ms. Karin Mormando, Director, Undergraduate Admissions

☎ 215-204-7200 or toll-free 888-340-2222

✉ tuadm@temple.edu

At Jefferson, future nurses, pharmacists, physicians, therapists, and technologists learn together in the same classrooms and simulated clinical settings.

THOMAS JEFFERSON UNIVERSITY

PHILADELPHIA, PENNSYLVANIA
www.jefferson.edu/

Thomas Jefferson University (TJU) is committed to educating health-care professionals and discovering ways to define the future of clinical care. The University is comprised of the Jefferson School of Health Professions, Jefferson School of Nursing, Jefferson School of Pharmacy, Jefferson School of Population Health, Jefferson Medical College and Jefferson College of Graduate Studies. The University shares its campus with Thomas Jefferson University Hospital, one of the nation's premier health-care facilities. In addition to its undergraduate degree programs, Jefferson offers numerous graduate degree programs, many of which students can enter in their third year of undergraduate school. The School of Health Professions offers master's degrees in bioscience technologies, couple and family therapy, occupational therapy and radiologic sciences as well as a Doctor of Physical Therapy (D.P.T.) degree. The School of Nursing offers master's degrees in nursing, post-master's certificates and a Doctor of Nursing Practice (D.N.P.). The School of Pharmacy offers the Doctor of Pharmacy degree. The School of Population Health offers master's degrees and certificates in health policy, public health and healthcare quality and safety. The Master's in Family Therapy (M.F.T.) program is a collaboration between Jefferson and the Council for Relationships, a pioneering institution in the field of couple and family therapy treatment and training. Jefferson is in Center City, Philadelphia. In this prime location, students can walk four blocks to Independence Hall and the Liberty Bell, three blocks to Chinatown, seven blocks to South Street's funky shops and restaurants and eight blocks to Rittenhouse Square's popular park and shopping area. Or

students can easily catch a bus (several lines run through campus) or subway (only two blocks away) to get across town. Living on campus means that classes, the hospital and the library are within easy walking distance. From studios to luxury three-bedroom apartments, Jefferson Housing offers something to match almost any budget. The on-campus community includes students from

CONTACT INFORMATION

Ms. Karen Jacobs, Director of Admissions

☎ 215-503-8890 or toll-free 877-533-3247

🖥 chpadmissions@mail.tju.edu

the four Jefferson schools, Jefferson Medical College and Jefferson College of Graduate Studies as well as postdoctoral fellows and medical residents.

The state-of-the-art Dorrance H. Hamilton Building on Thomas Jefferson University's center-city Philadelphia campus.

Pitt-Bradford's state-of-the-art Crime Scene Investigation House is part criminal justice lab, part real-life experience and part investigative work.

UNIVERSITY OF PITTSBURGH AT BRADFORD

BRADFORD, PENNSYLVANIA
www.upb.pitt.edu/

The University of Pittsburgh at Bradford (Pitt-Bradford) can take students beyond—beyond the classroom by offering internships and research opportunities; beyond the degree by providing a helpful Career Services Office and an informal alumni network; beyond 9 to 5 with its active student life and excellent athletic facilities; beyond place by exposing students to the world through study-abroad programs; and beyond students' expectations by giving them a college experience that changes them for the better. So it's no surprise that *The Princeton Review* has named the University of Pittsburgh at Bradford one of the Best Colleges in the Northeast every year since 2006. At Pitt-Bradford, students live and learn on a safe, intimate campus where they receive individual attention from committed professors who work at their side. In addition, students earn a degree from the

University of Pittsburgh, which commands respect around the world. Students here choose from forty-one majors and more than fifty minors, concentrations and pre-professional programs. Pitt-Bradford students can take a yoga class in the dance studio, play a game of pickup basketball in the McDowell Fieldhouse or swim in the six-lane swimming pool in the state-of-the-art Sport and Fitness Center. They can grab a bite in the recently renovated Frame-Westerberg Commons or head back to their comfortable townhouse or apartment to study—there are no cramped dorm rooms here. There are more than forty clubs and organizations, from the campus radio station and newspaper to academic clubs, honor societies and fraternities and sororities. Pitt-Bradford competes in Division III of the NCAA and fields seven men's teams in baseball, basketball, cross-country, golf, soccer, swimming and tennis and eight

The annual Cultural Festival is a time to sample global foods, music, dancing, fashion, and more from the Pitt-Bradford Community.

women's teams in basketball, cross-country, golf, soccer, softball, swimming, tennis and volleyball. Pitt-Bradford stretches across 317 acres in the foothills of the Allegheny Mountains, only steps from the Allegheny National Forest. The campus is a short drive from larger cities such as Buffalo, New York (80 miles north); Pittsburgh (160 miles southeast); and Erie, Pennsylvania (90 miles west). Pitt-Bradford students go off-campus to enjoy cross-country and downhill skiing, snowboarding, snowshoeing,

ice skating, biking, fishing, hiking and hunting.

- **Enrollment:** *1,652*
- **Selectivity:** *minimally difficult*
- **Test scores:** *ACT—over 18, 95%; SAT—critical reading over 500, 45.5%; SAT—math over 500, 48.41%*
- **Application deadline:** *Rolling (freshmen), rolling (transfer)*
- **Expenses:** *Tuition $11,722; Room & Board $7480*

CONTACT INFORMATION

Ms. Vicky Pingie, Associate Director of Admissions

☎ 814-362-7552 or toll-free 800-872-1787

monti@pitt.edu

VILLANOVA UNIVERSITY

St. Thomas of Villanova Church

VILLANOVA, PENNSYLVANIA
www.villanova.edu/

Villanova is the oldest and largest Catholic university in Pennsylvania, founded in 1842 by the Order of Saint Augustine. The Augustinian values of truth, unity and love guide the academic and social life at Villanova to this day. And *Bloomberg BusinessWeek* recently ranked Villanova #25 in the nation for value—drawing from pay reports of 1.4 million graduates of U.S. schools over a thirty-year period. Villanova University offers more than forty academic programs through four undergraduate colleges: the College of Liberal Arts and Sciences, the Villanova School of Business, the College of Engineering and the College of Nursing. There are more than 250 student organizations and thirty-two National Honor Societies at Villanova. Many students here choose to study abroad through the University's cutting-edge programs—students can explore everything from Irish politics in Galway to environmental protection in Geneva, Switzerland. On campus, incoming freshmen can opt to be part of a Villanova Learning Community. Through Learning Communities, students build friendships as they live together in specially-designated residence halls and learn together in courses and cocurricular programs. Villanova University has long attracted students who are interested in volunteerism. Each year, Villanovans provide more than 64,000 hours of service doing everything from throwing a yearly carnival for at-risk kids to adopting less-fortunate families at the holidays. Villanova is well-known for its competitive NCAA Division I athletics, too. The University's state-of-the-art facilities include eight USTA regulation tennis courts; a soccer complex with bleacher seating for 1,500 fans; a softball complex with press box and updated dugouts; the University's Pavilion with its four multipurpose courts, track, pole vault pit and batting cages; the

eco-friendly Davis Center for Athletics and Fitness with a weight room and sports medicine area; and the Villanova Ballpark (built in 2003) where the Wildcat baseball team plays. Villanova's 254-acre campus, located 12 miles west of Philadelphia, is completely high-tech. In fact, *PC Magazine* and *The Princeton Review* named Villanova #1 of the "Top 10 Wired Colleges and Universities." Whether it's going out for a world-famous Philly cheesesteak; visiting art, history and science museums; shopping; or cheering on professional

CONTACT INFORMATION

Mr. Michael Gaynor, Director of University Admission

☎ 610-519-4000
🖳 gotovu@villanova.edu

sports teams—there is something for everyone to enjoy in Philadelphia.

- **Enrollment:** *10,375*
- **Selectivity:** *very difficult*
- **Test scores:** *ACT—over 18, 100%; SAT—critical reading over 500, 96%; SAT—math over 500, 97%*
- **Application deadline:** *1/7 (freshmen), 6/1 (transfer)*
- **Expenses:** *Tuition $38,305; Room & Board $10,320*

Students on Mendel Field at Villanova University.

WEST CHESTER UNIVERSITY

WEST CHESTER, PENNSYLVANIA
www.wcupa.edu/

With a complete complement of traditional and innovative academic programs, you're certain to find one that's right for you.

West Chester University of Pennsylvania (WCU) is the second largest of the fourteen institutions in the Pennsylvania State System of Higher Education and the fourth-largest university in the Philadelphia metropolitan area. The University offers more than eighty undergraduate and seventy master's degree programs through its five colleges: Arts and Sciences, Business and Public Affairs, Education, Health Sciences, and Visual and Performing Arts. Education is the most popular major; but music has been taught here since the school's founding in 1871 and today West Chester is among only sixty-five schools worldwide with "all-Steinway" designation. West Chester's 402-acre campus includes two garden-style apartment complexes and a new performing arts center with an interior courtyard, an art gallery, a 375-seat auditorium and rehearsal hall. On the South campus lies a 100-acre preserved woodland, field and streamside habitat that serves as an outdoor classroom for the natural sciences and environmental studies students. The state-of-the-art Merion Science Center houses science labs, faculty research space, animal research space, multimedia lecture rooms and a greenhouse. In keeping with West Chester's rich heritage, the University's Quadrangle buildings, part of the original campus, are on the National Register of Historic Places. Each year, University students schedule programs with well-known musicians, authors and political figures. Students also jump into the more than 210 campus groups that include music, theater, fraternities, sororities, service organizations and honor societies. The University has twenty-three NCAA Division II teams and Division I field hockey. For more fun and less competition, undergrads can join club sports in everything from bowling to water polo. Hungry students can head to the many dining spots on campus, including a Starbucks and Einstein Bros. Bagels. The University is located in West Chester, a community in southeastern Pennsylvania that is strategically located at the center of the mid-Atlantic corridor. West Chester is just 25 miles west of Philadelphia and 17 miles north of Wilmington, Delaware, putting the libraries, restaurants, entertainment and historical sites of both cities within easy reach. The campus is also only 2 hours from New York City and 3 hours from Washington, D.C.

CONTACT INFORMATION

Ms. Marsha Haug, Vice President of Enrollment Services and Admissions

☎ 610-436-3414 or toll-free 877-315-2165

🖥 ugadmiss@wcupa.edu

- **Enrollment:** *14,211*
- **Selectivity:** *moderately difficult*
- **Test scores:** *SAT—critical reading over 500, 67.8%; SAT—math over 500, 73.4%*
- **Application deadline:** *Rolling (freshmen), rolling (transfer)*
- **Expenses:** *Tuition $7211; Room & Board $7032*

In addition to a sprawling suburban campus, West Chester University offers a full calendar of cultural, sporting, and other events.

Professors get to know you on a personal level to help you realize your capabilities. Then they challenge you to test-drive those skills beyond the classroom through real-world, hands-on experiences.

W WILKES
UNIVERSITY

WILKES-BARRE, PENNSYLVANIA
www.wilkes.edu/

Located at the foothills of the Pocono Mountains, along the shore of the Susquehanna River, Wilkes University is a private university structured into the College of Arts, Humanities, and Social Sciences; the College of Science and Engineering; the Nesbitt College of Pharmacy and Nursing; the Sidhu School of Business and Leadership;

the School of Education; and University College (for undecided students). In addition to its bachelors and master's degree programs, the University also offers doctoral degrees in the fields of Education (Ed.D.), Nursing (Doctor of Nursing Practice) and Pharmacy (Pharm.D.). Wilkes is the first school in Pennsylvania to offer a dual Doctor of Pharmacy and Master of Business Administration degree. The Wilkes campus features a parklike quad surrounded by modern classroom buildings and nineteenth-century mansions that have been restored as academic and residential buildings. Campus facilities include a sports and conference center, an outdoor athletic complex and field house, a state-of-the-art science building, a performing arts center, an indoor rec center and a student center with a food court, cafe, entertainment rooms and ballroom. Programs are designed to prepare students with a well-rounded liberal arts foundation that encourages independent thinking and gives students the necessary edge to enter graduate and professional schools and careers. In fact, more than 99 percent of students are employed or attending graduate/professional school within six months of graduation. The residence halls vary from modern, multifloor buildings to mansions listed on the National Register of Historic Places. At Wilkes University, student athletes play sixteen Division III sports; even more students join the active intramural program. Through the nearly seventy clubs and organizations on campus, students schedule and run movies and performances by comedians and musicians; they also throw a ton of dinner dances, block parties

and special events. The County seat, Wilkes-Barre is a medium-sized city with recreational facilities just minutes away. Students can head to the Lackawanna County Multi-Purpose Stadium (home of the Wilkes-Barre/Scranton Yankees Triple A baseball team); the Wachovia Arena, the home of the Wilkes-Barre/Scranton Penguins hockey team; Pocono Mountain ski resorts; numerous golf courses; state parks; outdoor tennis courts; and Pocono Downs harness racing. The entertainment district of Wilkes-Barre offers the Wilkes University/King's College Barnes and Noble bookstore and cafe, a fourteen-screen movie complex, a nightclub

At Wilkes University, we're all about being Colonel. That means stepping up to leadership, stretching beyond your comfort zone, and reaching out to help others.

CONTACT INFORMATION

Ms. Melanie Mickelson, Vice President of Enrollment Services

☎ 570-408-4400 or toll-free 800-945-5378 Ext. 4400
🖥 admissions@wilkes.edu

and numerous shops and restaurants. The city is about 2 hours from both New York City and Philadelphia.

- **Enrollment:** *6,239*
- **Selectivity:** *moderately difficult*
- **Test scores:** *SAT—critical reading over 500, 61%; SAT—math over 500, 69%*
- **Application deadline:** *Rolling (freshmen), rolling (transfer)*
- **Expenses:** *Tuition $26,010; Room & Board $11,100*

Classes in the C.V. Starr Financial Markets Center use real-time market data and Reuters 3000.

Bryant
UNIVERSITY

SMITHFIELD, RHODE ISLAND
www.bryant.edu/

Bryant University is the choice for students who want to blend business and liberal arts using state-of-the-art technology. Throughout its 147-year history, Bryant has encouraged students to achieve their personal best in life and in their professions. Bryant offers more than eighty majors, concentrations, minors and interest areas across disciplines and topics—and every student at Bryant receives a fully loaded laptop. The University's College of Business is accredited by AACSB International—The Association to Advance Collegiate Schools of Business—a distinction earned by only 5 percent of universities worldwide. The John H. Chafee Center for International Business, located on campus, links Bryant students directly to regional businesses that operate globally. The University's groundbreaking U.S.-China and Confucius Institutes forge academic, business and cultural partnerships between Bryant University and colleges, businesses and governmental offices in China. Sports and recreation play an important role at Bryant. The Elizabeth and Malcolm Chace Wellness and Athletic Center features a fully equipped fitness center, a six-lane swimming pool, circuit-training equipment and free weights, and a group exercise room with forty-four different fitness classes offered every week. Students participate in and root for Bryant's twenty-two intercollegiate varsity sports teams, which compete at the Division I level. Other students take part in club and intramural sports like flag football, field hockey and soccer. Teams compete on well-maintained athletic fields, and spectators can watch from the 4,000-seat Bulldog Stadium. Bryant has more than eighty student clubs and organizations, too: fraternities and sororities, the Student Programming Board, the Intercultural Center, the Running Club, the Marketing Association and the Outdoor Adventure Club to name a few. There are many places on and off campus for students to gather and enjoy music, comedy and sports. Bryant University sits on a beautiful 428-acre campus in Smithfield, only 15 minutes from the state capital of Providence. Bryant University is only 45 minutes from Boston and 3 hours from New York City. Many students take advantage of internship and employment opportunities at the Fortune 500 companies and not-for-profit organizations within driving distance of campus. Transportation includes buses (free for students) that travel to and from campus, a train station in Providence and airports near Providence and in Boston.

CONTACT INFORMATION

Ms. Michelle Beauregard, Director of Admission

☎ 401-232-6100 or toll-free 800-622-7001

🖳 admission@bryant.edu

- **Enrollment:** *3,632*
- **Selectivity:** *moderately difficult*
- **Test scores:** *ACT—over 18, 100%; SAT—critical reading over 500, 83.18%; SAT—math over 500, 92.73%*
- **Application deadline:** *2/1 (freshmen), rolling (transfer)*
- **Expenses:** *Tuition $32,106; Room & Board $11,757*

Bryant's safe suburban campus is only 15 minutes from Providence and an hour from Boston.

JOHNSON & WALES
UNIVERSITY
PROVIDENCE, RHODE ISLAND
www.jwu.edu/

At JWU you'll learn by doing with on-hands learning experiences.

Johnson & Wales University (JWU) is a recognized leader in career education. With a focus on degree programs in business, culinary arts, education, hospitality and technology, JWU lets students take major-related courses in their freshman year to see if they've chosen the right field. By integrating academics and professional skills, related work experiences, leadership opportunities and career services, JWU prepares students who are seeking a competitive advantage in the global economy. Most students who come to JWU are recent graduates of high school business, college-preparatory and vocational/technical programs. M.B.A. programs include global business leadership (with concentrations in accounting, financial management, international trade, organizational leadership or marketing) and hospitality and tourism global business leadership (with concentrations in finance and marketing). M.A. programs in teaching (with or without certification) include business, food service and special education. The Alan Shawn Feinstein Graduate School offers the Certificate of Advanced

Graduate Study (CAGS) in finance, human resources management and hospitality. The University also offers a doctoral program in educational leadership. Students are involved in a variety of extracurricular activities. Nearly 20 percent of JWU students are members of national student organizations such as Business Professionals of America; DECA (Delta Epsilon Chi), Future Business Leaders of America (Phi Beta Lambda); Family, Career, Community Leaders of America (FCCLA); SkillsUSA; and Technology Association of America. Sports and fitness programs include aerobics, baseball, basketball, golf, ice hockey, sailing, soccer, tennis, volleyball and wrestling. The University is committed to urban revitalization and thoughtful historic renovation in its campus communities in Providence, Rhode Island; North Miami, Florida; Denver, Colorado; and Charlotte, North Carolina. The location of each of the University's campuses enables students to take advantage

Johnson & Wales offers accredited degrees in business, hospitality, culinary arts, technology and education to more than 16,000 graduate and undergraduate students.

of internship and part-time work at many nearby businesses, community groups and government agencies. All of Johnson & Wales' city campuses retain a small-town feel and easy accessibility to students. The urban setting of the Providence campus provides students proximity to the city's many cultural and recreational facilities. The North Miami campus is a short trip from the sun and fun of Fort Lauderdale and the culture of Miami. The Denver campus invites students to come to the nation's sixth-leading tourist destination and *Fortune* magazine's "second best city in America to work and live." More than 300 Fortune 500 companies have offices in Charlotte,

which is known as the second-largest financial center in the United States.

- **Enrollment:** *10,709*
- **Selectivity:** *minimally difficult*
- **Test scores:** *SAT—critical reading over 500, 38.1%; SAT—math over 500, 42.7%*
- **Application deadline:** *Rolling (freshmen), rolling (transfer)*
- **Expenses:** *Tuition $24,141*

 http://bit.ly/collvid46

CONTACT INFORMATION

Ms. Maureen Dumas, Dean of Admissions

☎ 401-598-2310 or toll-free 800-598-1000 (in-state) 800-342-5598 (out-of-state)
✉ admissions.pvd@jwu.edu

Harkins Hall, which is the main administration building, also houses state-of-the-art classrooms.

PROVIDENCE
COLLEGE

PROVIDENCE, RHODE ISLAND
www.providence.edu/

Providence College (PC) invites students to be transformed—intellectually, socially and spiritually. This liberal arts college, the nation's only college or university operated by Dominican Friars, offers forty-nine majors and thirty-four minors. The most popular majors are in biology, management, psychology, special/elementary education, marketing, political science and accountancy. At the graduate level, Providence offers M.A., M.S., M.Ed., and M.B.A. degree programs and *U.S. News & World Report* has ranked Providence College one of the top two master's level colleges and universities in the North for twelve years in a row. The state-of-the-art campus has seen a number of upgrades and new construction. The newly renovated Slavin Center (September 2009) is open 24/7—it has lounges; McPhail's Entertainment Facility (with a stage, dance floor, cinema-like screen and pool tables); a late-night snack station; and studio space for WDOM radio and PCtv. The Concannon Fitness Center, a 23,000-square-foot, high-tech facility, opened in September 2007. The center offers cardio machines equipped with cable TV, strength machines and free weights—all overlooking the new artificial turf field. The Peterson Recreation Center is the site of intramural sports and Providence has one of the highest participation rates in the country. The center has five convertible basketball, tennis and volleyball courts; a 220-yard track; three racquetball courts; a 25-meter pool; and an aerobics room. Providence College hosts nineteen intercollegiate teams through the NCAA Division I, Hockey East Conference and the Big East Conference. PC students are also actively involved in community service. The alternative spring break program gives students the chance to spend a week on a sustainable farm or build a home for a family in Mexico. The College is situated on 105-acres in the city of Providence. The College has an established relationship with the Tony Award-winning Trinity Square Repertory Company, which is located downtown. The restored Providence Performing Arts Center, originally a movie palace, is the site of symphony concerts, opera, ballet and road shows of Broadway musicals. The Dunkin' Donuts Civic Center hosts concerts, trade shows and sports events and is the home court of the Friars (PC's basketball team). A Providence College ID lets students travel free on any RIPTA bus route throughout Rhode Island.

CONTACT INFORMATION

Mr. Christopher Lydon, Associate Vice President for Admission and Enrollment Planning

☎ 401-865-2535 or toll-free 800-721-6444

✉ pcadmiss@providence.edu

- **Enrollment:** *4,500*
- **Selectivity:** *very difficult*
- **Test scores:** *ACT—over 18, 98%; SAT—critical reading over 500, 86%; SAT—math over 500, 88%*
- **Application deadline:** *1/15 (freshmen), 4/1 (transfer)*
- **Expenses:** *Tuition $39,435; Room & Board $11,690*

http://bit.ly/collvid59

PC Perk, a café and snack-bar, is located in the newly renovated student union.

ROGER WILLIAMS UNIVERSITY

BRISTOL, RHODE ISLAND
www.rwu.edu/

Roger Williams University (RWU) is an independent liberal arts school that prepares students for life as twenty-first century citizen-scholars. In 2009, *U.S. News & World Report* named Roger Williams the seventh-ranked baccalaureate college in the North. Here, personal attention is a guarantee. Professors (not graduate assistants) teach all courses and the average class size is just 20. Students at Roger Williams are committed to community service. All entering freshmen participate in an annual Community Connections day of service; students, faculty and staff members team up to lend a helping hand at local organizations such as animal shelters and the food bank. The University encourages all students to study abroad, whether it's for a year, semester, summer session or even a mini-mester. Recently, students have studied marine biology in Bermuda and theatre in London. On campus, students enjoy cultural programs at the Intercultural Center, home to international student life, spiritual life and LGBT initiatives. In fall 2009, RWU opened Global Heritage Hall, an eco-friendly academic center with a three-story atrium, outdoor terrace for teaching and a high-tech center for learning. Students live on and off campus in RWU's University residence halls (shuttle service is available). A new residence hall (opened in fall of 2009) combines living space, classroom and study space, a café and retail shops to create a modern living and learning community. RWU students can choose from more than seventy clubs and organizations—everything from the Scuba Club to the radio station. Students can also join one of the University's eighteen NCAA Division III varsity teams or

an intramural team. At the modern Dining Commons, students eat locally grown, organic foods. They work out the state-of-the-art Campus Recreation Center, which has a swimming pool, basketball and squash courts, a weight lifting and cardio room, a Jacuzzi and a sauna. And the campus' waterfront location is perfect for sailing and kayaking. Roger Williams University is located in Bristol, a seaside town that is home to antique stores, gourmet restaurants, ice cream shops and spas. Providence, Rhode Island's

CONTACT INFORMATION

Mr. Didier Bouvet, Dean of Undergraduate Admission

☎ 401-254-3500 or toll-free 800-458-7144

✉ admit@rwu.edu

capital and largest city, is just a 30-minute bus ride away; it has museums, coffee shops, the Providence Place Mall, live music and more. Just 30 minutes in the other direction, students can visit Newport, home to famous beaches, shopping, festivals and open markets.

THE UNIVERSITY OF RHODE ISLAND

Scientific discoveries are not limited to the classroom. At least not here.

THINK BIG WE DO℠

KINGSTON, RHODE ISLAND
www.uri.edu

The University of Rhode Island (URI) welcomes students who are big thinkers, creative thinkers—people who want to transform the future in every area from architecture to music to engineering. The University encourages research and community involvement through a ton of extension and outreach programs. In fact, the University of Rhode Island receives more than $60 million annually in sponsored research funds and consistently ranks among the top schools in the nation receiving environmental research funds. Students here can

RHODE ISLAND

choose from more than eighty majors in the colleges of Arts and Sciences, Business Administration, Continuing Education, Engineering, Environment and Life Sciences, Human Science and Services, Nursing, Pharmacy, University College and Graduate School of Oceanography. The center of the country campus is a quad of old granite buildings surrounded by newer academic buildings, residence halls and fraternity and sorority houses. On the plain below Kingston Hill are a freshwater pond, agricultural fields, greenhouses and a large convocation center. URI athletes compete in eighteen NCAA Division I sports; students can also choose from another seventeen club sports (roller hockey, equestrian and Ultimate, to name a few). The Mackal Field House, Tootell Physical Education Center and the Keaney Gymnasium provide excellent facilities, including three pools, four gyms, weight-training rooms, a dance studio, an indoor track and an athletic training room. In addition to a football stadium, there are twelve tennis courts, two softball diamonds, a baseball field, a lighted lacrosse/soccer field, a hockey field, and numerous practice fields. The 8,000-seat Ryan Center houses the men's and women's basketball programs as well as concerts and other large events. The Boss Ice Arena is home to the club hockey teams and is also open for student skating. A sailing pavilion and rowing facility are located near campus. The Memorial Union Building has lounges, study rooms, a radio station, the campus newspaper, a game room, dining areas, a bookstore, a coffee shop, a restaurant and a ballroom. The University's 1,200-acre campus is located in the historic village of Kingston, 30 miles south of Providence. The Kingston Amtrak train station is 1 mile from campus, and the T. F. Green Airport in Warwick is only 25 miles from campus. For summer fun, URI is only 6 miles from the ocean. In winter, students often take weekend ski trips to the nearby mountains.

Intercollegiate, intramural, and club sports. Compete at any level you want.

- **Enrollment:** *16,392*
- **Selectivity:** *moderately difficult*
- **Test scores:** *ACT—over 18, 95.67%; SAT—critical reading over 500, 67.95%; SAT—math over 500, 73.11%*
- **Application deadline:** *2/1 (freshmen), 6/1 (transfer)*
- **Expenses:** *Tuition $9528; Room & Board $9892*

CONTACT INFORMATION

Ms. Joanne Lynch, Assistant Dean of Admissions

☎ 401-874-7110

✉ lynch@uri.edu

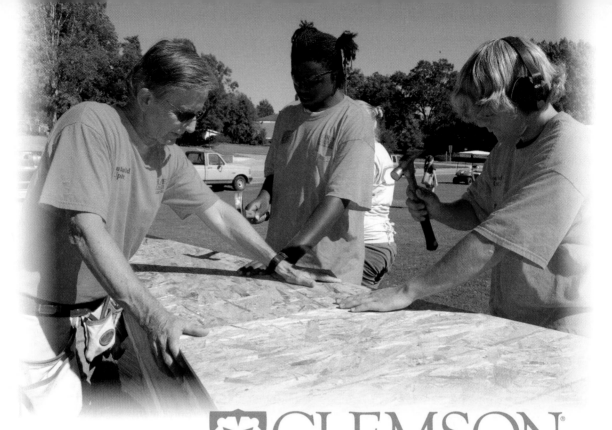

Habitat for Humanity build on Bowman Field

CLEMSON UNIVERSITY
1889

CLEMSON, SOUTH CAROLINA
www.clemson.edu/

One of the country's most selective public universities, Clemson is dedicated to teaching, research and service. Today, these three concepts remain at the heart of the University. At Clemson, professors take the time to get to know students and to explore innovative ways of teaching. Exceptional teaching is one reason Clemson's retention and graduation rates rank among the highest in the country among public universities. Exceptional teaching is also why Clemson continues to attract an increasingly talented student body. In 2009, roughly half of the entering freshmen were ranked in the top 10 percent of their high school classes. Clemson is committed to world-class research, too. With over $140 million in sponsored research support each year, Clemson is one of the National Science Foundation's top-100 research universities. Clemson encourages faculty members to engage their classes through service-learning as well. One example of this is the Clemson Elementary Outdoors project, in which more than 750 Clemson students from all majors helped research and design outdoor learning areas for the city's elementary school. Clemson has received national recognition for its innovative Communication-Across-the-Curriculum (CAC) program, in which students are presented with real-life challenges that require them to think and communicate effectively. At Clemson, CAC has become a standard teaching method used in nearly every department. From cheering on the Tigers at a football game to socializing at the Hendrix Student Center, Clemson students participate in many activities outside the classroom. The more than 300 campus clubs and organizations range from the professional to the performing arts. Some students come together for the Air Rifle Club while others gather for laughs in the Clemson Improv group—there is a place for everyone at Clemson. With 19 intercollegiate sports, Clemson offers exciting

spectator sports all year long. Clemson is a charter member of the Atlantic Coast Conference (ACC) and is an NCAA Division I school. Admission to regular-season events played at Clemson is included in University fees for full-time students. Clemson University awards bachelor's, master's, specialist and doctoral degrees. About midway between Charlotte, North Carolina, and Atlanta, Georgia, Clemson's campus is located on 1,400 acres of beautiful rolling hills within the foothills of the Blue Ridge Mountains and along the shores of Lake Hartwell. Great weather and proximity to natural wonders and large

CONTACT INFORMATION

Ms. Audrey R. Bodell, Associate Director of Admissions

☎ 864-656-2287
✉ cuadmissions@clemson.edu

cities offer year-round recreational opportunities.

- **Enrollment:** *18,317*
- **Selectivity:** *moderately difficult*
- **Test scores:** *ACT—over 18, 99%; SAT—critical reading over 500, 92%; SAT—math over 500, 96%*
- **Application deadline:** *5/1 (freshmen), 7/1 (transfer)*
- **Expenses:** *Tuition $11,609; Room & Board $6774*

 http://bit.ly/collvid34

Fans cheer on their Tigers during the traditional "running down the hill" before a football game.

Founded in 1845, Limestone College is an accredited, independent, coeducational, four-year liberal arts institution chartered by the state of South Carolina.

Limestone College

GAFFNEY, SOUTH CAROLINA
www.limestone.edu/

Limestone is a private, liberal arts college that intentionally maintains a small student body so that each student develops intellectually, physically and socially. Limestone offers programs that lead to a Bachelor of Arts, Bachelor of Science, Bachelor of Social Work, Associate of Arts or Associate of Science degree. In addition to its programs on campus, Limestone offers several of its academic majors in an accelerated format for working adults called The Block Program. The College also has an impressive Virtual Campus Program via the Internet with many majors offered. The two programs were combined in 2005 to be the Extended Campus. Extracurricular activities play a vital role at Limestone College. There are intercollegiate athletics in men's baseball, basketball, cross-country, golf, lacrosse, soccer, swimming, tennis, track and field, volleyball and wrestling and in women's basketball, cross-country, golf, field hockey, lacrosse, soccer, softball, swimming, tennis, track and field and volleyball. Students who are interested in music can join several instrumental and choral ensembles. A theater program is also popular. Limestone's 115-acre campus is well laid out and it blends the old (nine buildings are included on the National Register of Historic Places) with the new (Winnie Davis Hall reopened in spring 2010 with six wireless, multimedia classrooms and three museums and galleries). The Timken LYFE Center is a physical education complex that houses the gymnasium, an AAU-size swimming pool and athletic training facilities. The Walt Griffin Physical Education Center, named for the current Limestone College president, has classrooms and offices, locker rooms,

athletic training facilities, a state-of-the-art fitness center and a wrestling practice facility. The College also has eight lighted tennis courts, a baseball field, a softball field, a soccer/lacrosse field, field hockey field and several practice fields. Gaffney, a small city with a population of 25,000, provides an ideal setting for a college campus. Students don't have the daily distractions of a large city, but they are only 50 miles from the cities of Charlotte, North Carolina and Greenville, South Carolina. Other students head off campus for weekend trips to the Blue Ridge Mountains, the Great Smoky Mountains and the beaches of the Atlantic Coast. Minutes from campus are water sports, horseback riding, golf, tennis and skiing.

At Limestone College, the Athletics Department helps to develop students' minds, bodies, and spirits. Limestone sponsors 22 varsity sports and all the sports compete at the NCAA Division II level.

- **Enrollment:** *808*

- **Selectivity:** *minimally difficult*

- **Test scores:** *ACT—over 18, 66%; SAT—critical reading over 500, 23%; SAT—math over 500, 41%*

- **Application deadline:** *Rolling (freshmen), rolling (transfer)*

- **Expenses:** *Tuition $19,200; Room & Board $7000*

CONTACT INFORMATION

Ms. Sharon Chery, Admissions Office Manager

☎ 864-488-4554 or toll-free 800-795-7151 Ext. 554

✉ cphenicie@limestone.edu

Steps for a successful Apple Day @ Marlboro: (1) harvest October crop from campus orchards; (2) add cider press, live music, and student-organized activities; (3) allow hilarity to ensue.

Marlboro College

Marlboro, Vermont

www.marlboro.edu/

Students come to Marlboro College with a passion for learning and a desire to create their own course of study. Tucked away in the foothills of Vermont's Green Mountains, Marlboro offers a liberal arts curriculum that is taught in small classes and advanced one-to-one instruction, called tutorials. Marlboro's goal is to teach students to think clearly and learn independently, develop concise and correct writing and aspire to academic excellence. The College's 8:1 student-faculty ratio sparks dynamic exchanges between students and faculty members both in and out of the classroom and creates a close-knit community in which asking the right questions is more important than knowing the right answers. Two thirds of all Marlboro students go on to graduate study. When Marlboro first opened in the fall 1947, the campus was a cluster of barns and other farm buildings that the first students converted into classrooms and dorms. Today, the Marlboro campus has modern facilities and technology (a DNA lab, a digital photography lab, a digital film/video lab) while still maintaining its relaxed, outdoorsy feel. The fields and woodlands that make up its rural 350-acre campus are ideal for cross-country skiing and other outdoor activities. The Outdoor Program offers instruction and equipment for canoeing, kayaking, rock climbing, backpacking and other sports that bring students in touch with the surrounding environment. The soccer team competes with other colleges, and more impromptu volleyball, basketball, softball and Ultimate Frisbee teams compete intramurally. In addition, Marlboro's broomball (a game similar to hockey) tournament takes place each winter,

*Who says liberal arts students aren't rugged? *Everyone* from Marlboro's president on down takes part in Work Day each semester to complete manual labor projects that beautify the campus.*

with prizes for the winning teams and those with the best costumes. Campus committees organize many events both on and off campus, including concerts, lectures, poetry and fiction readings, art shows and trips to Boston, Montreal and New York for museum visits, shopping and baseball games. Other popular activities on campus include parties, dances, plays and film screenings. Marlboro is—and intends to remain—one of the nation's smallest liberal arts colleges. Most students live in campus housing that includes dorms, four-bedroom cottages and a renovated country inn. During the summer, the village of Marlboro swells to accommodate the famous Marlboro

Music Festival. The College is 2 hours by car from Boston and 4 hours from New York City and Montreal.

- **Enrollment:** *313*
- **Selectivity:** *moderately difficult*
- **Test scores:** *ACT—over 18, 100%; SAT—critical reading over 500, 96%; SAT—math over 500, 77%*
- **Application deadline:** *3/1 (freshmen), 4/1 (transfer)*
- **Expenses:** *Tuition $33,660; Room & Board $9220*

CONTACT INFORMATION

Mr. Mark Crowther, Associate Director of Admission

☎ 800-343-0049 toll-free
✉ admissions@marlboro.edu

Saint Michael's stunning 440 acre campus is just minutes from downtown Burlington and beautiful Lake Champlain.

SAINT MICHAEL'S COLLEGE

COLCHESTER, VERMONT
www.smcvt.edu/

Saint Michael's College students get involved, take risks and think differently. They come to Saint Michael's to learn how to make the world a better place—and they leave prepared to do just that. Saint Michael's is among the 270 colleges and universities nationwide allowed to host a prestigious Phi Beta Kappa chapter on campus. This liberal arts college offers twenty-nine major fields of study with an emphasis on honors, independent study, independent research, study abroad and internships. The superb faculty members are committed first and foremost to teaching and are known for challenging students to reach higher than they ever thought possible. With a student-faculty ratio of just 12:1, students receive personal attention from their professors both in class (lively First-Year Seminars set the interactive tone) and out of class. The Saint Michael's campus is just a little bit different, too—and that's how students like it. Recently, a zen-like Word Garden was installed. Students, faculty and visitors can leave messages, poetry, birthday shout-outs and more in the 60 foot circle using concrete stones with words on them. Service to the community is an important part of student life. More than 70 percent of students actively pursue community service projects through the College's Mobilization of Volunteer Efforts (MOVE) program; some volunteer with humane societies while others entertain children at local shelters. With nearly 100 percent of the students living on campus (with guaranteed housing for four years), the 24/7 living and learning environment means that teaching goes beyond the classroom. Saint Michael's lies less than 3 miles from Burlington, Vermont's largest city and a vibrant college town that is home to five local colleges and universities. In addition to the shops, restaurants and cafés of the Church Street Marketplace and a hot local music scene, Burlington offers great opportunities for hands-on learning through internships. Vermont, known for its natural beauty, environmentalism and year-round recreational activities, inspires many students to take advantage of some of the best skiing in the East through a relationship with Smugglers' Notch ski resort—a program that provides an all-access season pass to any Saint Michael's student in good academic standing—and through the College's own Wilderness Program.

CONTACT INFORMATION

Ms. Jacqueline Murphy, Director of Admission

☎ 802-654-3000 or toll-free 800-762-8000

✉ admission@smcvt.edu

- **Enrollment:** *2,466*
- **Selectivity:** *moderately difficult*
- **Test scores:** *SAT—critical reading over 500, 84%; SAT—math over 500, 84%*
- **Application deadline:** *2/1 (freshmen), 3/15 (transfer)*
- **Expenses:** *Tuition $34,845; Room & Board $8685*

EMORY & HENRY COLLEGE

EMORY, VIRGINIA
www.ehc.edu/

With an emphasis on service, excellence and action, Emory & Henry encourages students to envision the world in which they would like to live and then challenges them to create it. Founded in 1836, the College is named for two men who symbolize this dual emphasis on thought and action—Bishop John Emory, a Methodist church leader at the time the College was founded, and Patrick Henry, a famous orator of the American Revolution and Virginia's first governor. Emory & Henry graduates find tremendous personal success, which they use to improve the world around them. Through its comprehensive liberal arts programs, Emory & Henry has produced leading scientific researchers, NASA engineers, well-known writers, and successful physicians, ministers, lawyers, educators

Wiley Hall

and businesspeople. Emory & Henry provides innovative programs in public policy and community service as well as in international studies and environmental science. Students get involved in a ton of campus activities: service clubs, fraternities, sororities, sports clubs, honor groups, religious life and multicultural groups. Student staffs produce a yearbook, an online magazine and a literary magazine; others operate an educational FM radio station. The prestigious Concert Choir has toured throughout the United States and in parts of Europe. The Barter Theatre, the nation's oldest professional theater in nearby Abingdon, works with Emory & Henry College to provide a theater education program that integrates college-level drama study with the benefits of experience on a professional stage. The Appalachian Center for Community Service is available for students committed to community service and integrates service learning into many classes. The King Health and Physical

Emory & Henry College, Emory, Virginia

Education Center includes a state-of-the-art fitness center, racquetball courts, a gym with seating for 1,350 fans and a dance studio. Varsity sports for men are baseball, basketball, cross-country, football, golf, soccer and tennis; women compete in basketball, cross-country, soccer, softball, swimming, tennis and volleyball. Within an hour's drive of campus are slopes for skiing, lakes for waterskiing, the Appalachian Trail for hiking and spots for horseback riding and canoeing. Seven miles away in Abingdon, students head to movie theatres, restaurants and museums. The town also hosts the annual Virginia

Highlands Festival, bringing together musicians, artists and craftsmen for exhibitions and competition.

- **Enrollment:** *1,002*
- **Selectivity:** *moderately difficult*
- **Test scores:** *ACT—over 18, 82%; SAT—critical reading over 500, 58.14%; SAT—math over 500, 63.26%*
- **Application deadline:** *Rolling (freshmen), rolling (transfer)*
- **Expenses:** *Tuition $24,880; Room & Board $8300*

CONTACT INFORMATION

Mr. David Hawsey, Vice President of Enrollment Management

☎ 276-944-6133 or toll-free 800-848-5493

✉ ehadmiss@ehc.edu

Students chat on Hollins University's Front Quadrangle, which features buildings on the National Historic Register. The campus has beautiful mountain views, but is close to Roanoke, a city of 250,000.

HOLLINS
U N I V E R S I T Y

ROANOKE, VIRGINIA
www.hollins.edu/

Hollins University is an independent arts and sciences university that enrolls women in its undergraduate programs and has coed graduate programs. In addition to the Bachelor of Arts degree in twenty-seven major fields, Hollins awards a Bachelor of Science degree in four fields; a B.A./B.F.A. degree in dance; a Master of Arts degree in children's literature, liberal studies, screenwriting and film studies, and teaching; and a Master of Fine Arts degree in creative writing, children's literature, dance, playwriting and screenwriting. Hollins' coed graduate creative writing program has long been acknowledged as one of the best of its size in the country—graduates of the program have published some 200 books in the last ten years. Hollins gives students the month of January to focus on an internship, senior thesis, independent study or travel/study abroad. Students have interned at the New York Stock Exchange, UBS Financial Services, Centers for

Disease Control, ABC News, Lincoln Center, the *London Times*, *Vanity Fair* magazine, and the Metropolitan Museum of Art, to name a few. Through Hollins' innovative Batten Leadership Institute, undergrads earn a Certificate in Leadership Studies through a 20-hour program of classes, skill-building groups, seminars and student-designed leadership projects. Situated on a 475-acre campus in the Shenandoah Valley of the Blue Ridge Mountains, Hollins is a quiet campus for the serious student. The Wyndham Robertson Library features state-of-the-art technology, is a National Literary Landmark, and won the 2009 Excellence in Academic Libraries Award. The well-equipped athletic complex is where Hollins athletes train for NCAA Division III competition in basketball, golf, lacrosse, riding, soccer, swimming, tennis and volleyball. Hollins has been named the "Hottest Riding School" by *Kaplan/ Newsweek*. There are twenty-eight clubs and organizations, including a multicultural club, Black Student Alliance,

literary societies, and political and environmental organizations. Each year, students volunteer their time locally and internationally. Through the Hollins-directed Jamaica service project, undergrads teach in a Jamaican school or work in an infirmary. The Hollins Outdoor Program (HOP) sets up adventure activities such as canoeing, hiking, rock climbing and caving. Hollins is located on the outskirts of Roanoke. The campus is a 3½-hour drive from both Washington, D.C., and Richmond; 5 hours from Virginia Beach; and within easy driving distance of more than a dozen other colleges. The Blue Ridge Mountains

CONTACT INFORMATION

Ms. Rebecca Eckstein, Dean of Admissions

☎ 540-362-6401 or toll-free 800-456-9595

🖥 huadm@hollins.edu

are minutes from campus and ideal for hiking the Appalachian Trail, camping and skiing.

- **Enrollment:** *1,057*
- **Selectivity:** *moderately difficult*
- **Test scores:** *ACT—over 18, 100%; SAT—critical reading over 500, 80.4%; SAT—math over 500, 57.5%*
- **Application deadline:** *Rolling (freshmen)*
- **Expenses:** *Tuition $28,115; Room & Board $10,040*

Comfortable dorms, a lively and engaged Student Government Association, and many clubs and traditions make Hollins a place where lifelong friendships begin.

Want to have lunch with your Dean of Students? Happens at Lynchburg College all the time!

LYNCHBURG COLLEGE EST. 1903

LYNCHBURG, VIRGINIA
www.lynchburg.edu/

Lynchburg College—included in *Princeton Review*'s "The Best 371 Colleges: 2010 Edition"—offers thirty-eight majors and forty-five minors in the liberal arts, sciences and professional disciplines and graduate programs in art, business, education and nursing. A Doctorate of Physical Therapy program will begin in the fall of 2010. The 214-acre campus has long been considered one of the most beautiful in the South with the majestic Blue Ridge Mountains as a backdrop. The Claytor Nature Study Center, a 470-acre farm in nearby Bedford County, is used as an environmental and educational learning laboratory and is home to the Belk Astronomical Observatory, a 700-square-foot facility with an RC Optical Systems 20-inch (0.51 meter) Truss Ritchey-Chretien telescope. There is also a 384-square-foot observation deck equipped with twelve piers for mounting smaller telescopes. An observatory control room has instrumentation

VIRGINIA

that allows LC to conduct research in conjunction with other colleges and universities. Many activities are open to the Lynchburg College community: service and honor groups; more than 100 clubs and organizations; fraternities and sororities; student publications and musical groups. Community service is an important part of the Lynchburg experience—students, staff and faculty contribute more than 48,000 hours to the community each year through projects like Habitat for Humanity, Camp Jaycees and Special Olympics. The varsity athletic program (NCAA Division III) includes baseball, basketball, cheerleading, cross-country, equestrian sports, golf, indoor/outdoor track and field, lacrosse, soccer and tennis for men and basketball, cheerleading, cross-country, equestrian sports, field hockey, lacrosse, soccer, softball, tennis, indoor/outdoor track and field and volleyball for women. Other students join club sports, including cycling, skiing, snowboarding and

karate. The Turner Athletic Facility includes state-of-the-art exercise and fitness areas, a dance studio and one of the top exercise physiology labs in Virginia. Shellenberger Field boasts a brand new artificial turf field, an eight-lane track, 3,000-spectator capacity including chair and bleacher seating and night lighting. Also included are Moon Field upgrades—a permanent softball outfield fence and new areas for track and field events. The baseball field, Fox Field, was updated recently to include seating for up to 1,000 fans, batting cages and a press box. Lynchburg College is located in central Virginia, 100 miles from Richmond,

CONTACT INFORMATION

Ms. Sharon Walters-Bower, Director of Admissions

☎ 434-544-8300 or toll-free 800-426-8101

✉ admissions@lynchburg.edu

180 miles southwest of Washington, D.C., and 50 miles east of Roanoke. The city of Lynchburg is noted for its climate, culture and historic landmarks.

- **Enrollment:** *2,589*
- **Selectivity:** *moderately difficult*
- **Test scores:** *ACT—over 18, 84%; SAT—critical reading over 500, 59%; SAT—math over 500, 54%*
- **Application deadline:** *Rolling (freshmen), rolling (transfer)*
- **Expenses:** *Tuition $28,925; Room & Board $6970*

Have a group project to work on or want to take a break from studying? The Westover Room patio is a great place!

Sweet Briar College is a campus of 3,200 acres of wide open space to learn and grow.

SWEET BRIAR
COLLEGE

SWEET BRIAR, VIRGINIA
www.sbc.edu/

Sweet Briar College is consistently ranked as one of the top liberal arts and sciences colleges in the country. Its excellent academic reputation and beautiful campus attract ambitious, self-confident women who want to excel. Small classes (averaging 12 students per class) ensure personal attention and academic interaction. Most students are enrolled at Sweet Briar's Virginia campus; about 120 students are enrolled in Sweet Briar's coed Junior Year in France and Junior Year in Spain programs. The College offers more than forty majors, minors and certificate programs and in 2004, Sweet Briar launched two graduate degree programs: the Master of Arts in Teaching and the Master of Education. Sweet Briar also introduced a degree program in engineering, only the second such undergrad program at a women's college. More than fifty campus organizations are open to students, including honor societies, community service groups, political groups, drama and dance clubs, a radio station and singing groups. Recent speakers on campus include author Salman Rushdie, environmental attorney Robert F. Kennedy Jr., Olympic swimmer Maddy Crippen, *USA Today* sports columnist Christine Brennan, and civil rights pioneer Elaine Jones. In 2006, Sweet Briar opened a beautiful new studio arts building. Sweet Briar is the only college in the United States with a residential artists' colony on campus. Known as the Virginia Center for the Creative Arts, the colony is a working retreat for international writers, visual artists and composers. The new 53,000 square foot fitness and athletic center has a three-lane elevated track, a field house, an aerobics/spinning room and racquetball and squash courts. The on-campus equestrian center, one of the largest and best college facilities in the country, attracts competitive and recreational riders. The 100-acre Rogers Riding Center has a 120-foot by 300-foot indoor arena with Perma-Flex footing, stables for about 90 horses, outdoor rings, paddocks and miles of hacking trails—all within walking distance of the main campus. Many of the academic buildings and common spaces are equipped for wireless connection to the campus network. Varsity athletes compete in NCAA Division III field hockey, lacrosse, soccer, softball, swimming, tennis and volleyball. Club sports include cross-country, fencing and riding. Sweet Briar's 3,250-acre campus in the foothills of the Blue Ridge Mountains includes hiking, biking, riding trails and two lakes. The College is centrally located on the outskirts of Lynchburg, southwest of Washington, D.C., and Charlottesville.

At Sweet Briar, young women graduate with the charge to re-shape business, science, engineering and the arts.

CONTACT INFORMATION

Mr. Ken Huus, Director of Admissions

☎ 434-381-6142 or toll-free 800-381-6142

✉ admissions@sbc.edu

- **Enrollment:** *756*
- **Selectivity:** *moderately difficult*
- **Test scores:** *ACT—over 18, 94.23%; SAT—critical reading over 500, 70.92%; SAT—math over 500, 58.87%*
- **Application deadline:** *2/1 (freshmen), 5/1 (transfer)*
- **Expenses:** *Tuition $30,195; Room & Board $10,780*

MOUNTAIN STATE UNIVERSITY™

BECKLEY, WEST VIRGINIA
www.mountainstate.edu/

Mountain State University (MSU) provides students with an outstanding career-oriented education in a relaxed environment. With six campuses, dozens of educational sites and many distance learning options, MSU is full of choices. Students here earn associate to doctoral degrees through MSU's four undergraduate schools and three graduate schools. Selected degree programs and courses are available through MSU's branch campuses, located in Center Township, Pennsylvania; Martinsburg, West Virginia; Mooresville, North Carolina; Orlando, Florida; and Washington, D.C. Mountain State recently partnered with nearby Pinecrest Hospital to open a $1 million tuberculosis unit and library; here, MSU students abandon the classroom for real-world experience through practicum field placements. In intercollegiate competition, the men's basketball team regularly appears in NAIA Division I tournament play and won the 2004 national championship. MSU's other intercollegiate teams—men's and women's soccer, track and field, and cross-country, as well as women's volleyball—compete in NAIA Division II. Updated Hogan

The Lewin Family Bell Tower, a Holocaust memorial donated by a local resident, is a focal point of Mountain State University's primary campus, in Beckley, West Virginia.

Hall provides two-bedroom suites and apartment-style living in a central campus. Here, students enjoy high-speed Internet connections, lounges, study rooms and laundry facilities. A new hall—so new it doesn't even have a name yet—is being built on the south end of campus. It will have wifi, group study areas and balconies over-looking common areas. For fun and fitness, Mountain State students head to the Beckley–Raleigh County YMCA, where they have free memberships. Located within easy walking distance of the campus, the YMCA has an indoor pool and track, racquetball and basketball courts, a newly renovated fitness center and a variety of classes like spinning and Pilates. Mountain State University's main campus is located in Beckley, in the heart of the southern West Virginia highlands. Beckley is about an hour away by car from the state capital of Charleston. City, state and national parks provide

breathtaking views as well as perfect settings for outdoor activities like mountain biking, rock climbing, hiking, pic-nicking and swimming. In season, outdoor enthusiasts enjoy white-water rafting on the Gauley and New Rivers or hit the slopes of nearby ski areas. All are within a 20-minute drive of the campus.

- **Enrollment:** *5,951*

- **Selectivity:** *noncompetitive*

CONTACT INFORMATION

Ms. Darlene Brown, Enrollment Coordinator

☎ 304-929-1433 or toll-free 800-766-6067 Ext. 1433

✉ gomsu@mountainstate.edu

- **Test scores:** *ACT—over 18, 52%*

- **Application deadline:** *Rolling (freshmen), rolling (transfer)*

- **Expenses:** *Tuition $8700; Room & Board $6116*

http://bit.ly/collvid56

Mountain State University is the home of the National Institute for the Culinary Arts, accredited by the American Culinary Federation.

WEST VIRGINIA UNIVERSITY INSTITUTE OF TECHNOLOGY

MONTGOMERY, WEST VIRGINIA
www.wvutech.edu/

West Virginia University Institute of Technology (WVU Tech) offers more than forty programs in engineering, sciences, mathematics, health care, business, humanities and social sciences that provide a high value for their investment. The University has experienced a number of significant changes since it began as a preparatory school extension of West Virginia University in 1895. And more changes are in store. In fact, WVU Tech just summed up a strategic plan for 2015. Among the goals outlined are creating a sustainable campus, increasing study abroad and undergrad research opportunities and widening the University's communications through online event newsletters and an interactive web site. There are a number of social,

WEST VIRGINIA

athletic and cultural activities on campus from fraternities/sororities to intramural sports such as bowling and flag football. WVU Tech's Student Recreation Center is one of the best in the country. It has a 50-foot indoor climbing wall with more than 1,000 interchangeable hand-holds; six-lane pools; an elevated jogging track; a whirlpool that seats twenty people; courts for basketball, volleyball, squash, racquetball and badminton; and an outdoor area where students can rent ski and camp equipment. Living on the WVU Tech campus may make students forget about their bedrooms back home. Furnished suites have cable TV and Internet, lounges have 54-inch TVs, fitness rooms have new exercise equipment and there are even sundecks off the buildings. Montgomery, West Virginia, is just 28 miles southeast of Charleston, the state capital. A major asset to WVU Tech is the Amtrak service located across from the campus. With stops to Chicago, Cincinnati, New York City and Washington, D.C., the railway provides convenient transportation for many students living in the continental United States. WVU Tech's campus is also convenient to a ton of tourist attractions and thrill-seekers' adventures. Hawks Nest State Park, with its aerial tram to the bottom of the New River canyon, is only 30 miles from the campus. The New River, considered by many geologists to be the second-oldest river in the world, is perfect for white-water rafting. WVU Tech is also close to popular skiing areas, including Snowshoe Mountain, Silver Creek and Winter Place Ski Lodge.

CONTACT INFORMATION

**Reeta Piirala-Skoglund,
Director of Admissions and
Recruitment**

☎ 304-981-6240 or toll-free
888-554-8324

🖥 Reeta.Piirala-Skoglund@
mail.wvu.edu

THE MIDWESTERN REGION
OF THE UNITED STATES

Alabama

Illinois

Indiana

Iowa

Kentucky

Louisiana

Michigan

Minnesota

Missouri

Ohio

Oklahoma

Tennessee

Wisconsin

The BSC Fountain Plaza

BIRMINGHAM–SOUTHERN COLLEGE

BIRMINGHAM, ALABAMA
www.bsc.edu/

Birmingham-Southern College (BSC) knows that students learn best by doing. That's why much of the teaching here takes place in labs, in the campus wetlands and gardens and through study abroad. The new Urban Environmental Park at BSC is just one of BSC's "outdoor classrooms." This relaxing place to meet friends is also where the Urban Environmental Studies students get hands-on instruction. The 22-acre site has a lake, an amphitheatre, walkways, a fountain and rain gardens for storm water management; it was selected as one of 150 landscapes across the country to participate in a program testing the nation's first rating system for green landscape design. The brand-new Stephens Science Center brings new meaning to learning, too, with its greenhouse, teaching and research labs, zoological

     ALABAMA

museum/herbarium and radioisotope lab—all with the latest high-tech equipment. Birmingham-Southern is one of only six liberal arts colleges or universities in the nation to have both an accreditation by AACSB International and a Phi Beta Kappa chapter. And each year, Birmingham-Southern ranks first in Alabama and among the nation's best in percentage of all graduates accepted to medical, dental or health career programs. BSC students dominate athletically, too. The Birmingham-Southern Panthers compete at the NCAA Division III level with twenty-one varsity sports. Men's teams are baseball, basketball, cross country, football, golf, lacrosse (the fastest growing sport in the United States), soccer, tennis and track and field. Women's teams include basketball, cross country, golf, lacrosse, rifle, soccer, softball, tennis, track and field and volleyball. The state-of-the-art Striplin Center has basketball/volleyball courts, strength training and cardio rooms, an indoor pool, an aerobics/martial

BSC Saturday in the fall

arts studio and even a golf simulator. The College has more than eighty clubs and organizations and intramural sports. Fun events happen throughout the year including Homecoming, E-fest Fall Festival and Sound Check, the spring music festival that has attracted Grammy-award winning bands like Nickel Creek. Located on a 197-acre hilltop campus, the College is about 3 miles from the downtown business district of Birmingham, which is Alabama's largest city. Birmingham has restaurants, museums, a 17,000-seat Civic Center, city and state parks as well as four other colleges and has been

called the "Most Livable City in America" by the U.S. Conference of Mayors.

- **Enrollment:** *1,549*
- **Selectivity:** *moderately difficult*
- **Test scores:** *ACT—over 18, 99.97%; SAT—critical reading over 500, 85.18%; SAT—math over 500, 82.54%*
- **Application deadline:** *Rolling (freshmen), rolling (transfer)*

http://bit.ly/collvid30

CONTACT INFORMATION

Ms. Sheri E. Salmon, Dean of Enrollment Management

☎ 205-226-4696 or toll-free 800-523-5793

✉ admitme@bsc.edu

Small class sizes allow professors to form connections with students, on a campus with luscious trees and grass.

AURORA UNIVERSITY

347 S. Gladstone Ave., Aurora, IL 60506-4892
www.aurora.edu

AURORA, ILLINOIS
www.aurora.edu/

Aurora University (AU) knows it's all about you—where you want to go, what you want to do and who you want to be. An Aurora education guides and prepares students for life after graduation. This private university has two separate campuses and an educational center.

The main campus is in Aurora, just 40 miles west of Chicago; the George Williams College campus sits on the shores of Geneva Lake in Williams Bay, Wisconsin. In addition to the College of Arts and Sciences, the University comprises the College of Education and the College of Professional Studies. AU students can choose from more than forty undergraduate programs and eleven graduate degree programs including the B.S. in communication, business leadership and recreation administration; the RN to B.S.N.; the

Master of Arts in Teaching; the M.A. in reading instruction; the M.A. in special education; the M.S. in recreation administration; the M.B.A.; a weekend M.S.W. program; and an Ed.D. degree. Outside the classroom, Aurora has more than sixty clubs and organizations—everything from the Scrapbooking Club to Colleges Against Cancer. On a typical day, students are seen playing a round of golf on the George Williams campus course or listening to bands on the grassy quad of the main campus. The University is a member of the NCAA Division III and fields intercollegiate teams in baseball, basketball, cross-country, football, golf, indoor track, lacrosse, soccer, softball, tennis, track and volleyball. And Aurora athletes have a winning spirit—forty-four recent conference titles and twenty-five appearances in national tournaments prove that much. At AU, even more students join the extensive intramural program that offers 3-on-3 basketball, 6-on-6 volleyball, Texas Hold'em, and a ton more. Aurora University is located in a residential neighborhood on the southwest side of Aurora, which is the state's second-largest city. Students live on campus in completely updated air-conditioned suites with cable TV. The 32-acre main campus is located only minutes from the Illinois Research and Development Corridor, the site of dozens of nationally and internationally based businesses and industries. Located within an hour's drive or train ride is Chicago, one of the most exciting cities in the world.

CONTACT INFORMATION

Mr. James Lancaster, Director, Freshman Admission

☎ 630-844-5533 or toll-free 800-742-5281

✉ admission@aurora.edu

- **Enrollment:** *4,355*
- **Selectivity:** *moderately difficult*
- **Test scores:** *ACT—over 18, 98%; SAT—critical reading over 500, 68%; SAT—math over 500, 59%*
- **Application deadline:** *5/1 (freshmen), rolling (transfer)*
- **Expenses:** *Tuition $18,700; Room & Board $8800*

Small, private, yet full of opportunities. AU offers over 40 undergraduate majors, music and theatre programs, and an honors program. Students have many choices and opportunities.

DE PAUL UNIVERSITY

CHICAGO, ILLINOIS
www.depaul.edu/

DePaul University's more than 150 undergraduate degree programs combine practical expertise with broad-based liberal studies to prepare students for immediate and long-term success. The nation's largest Catholic university and the only one of the nation's ten largest private universities to make teaching its primary focus, DePaul provides an interactive learning environment through expert instruction and small class sizes. With a wide range of backgrounds and perspectives, students learn from each other through DePaul's discussion- and project-oriented approach. In addition to its bachelor's degree programs, DePaul offers more than 130 graduate programs, including master's degrees in accountancy, business, computer science, education, liberal arts and sciences, and music; the Master of Fine Arts (M.F.A.) in theater;

the Juris Doctor (J.D.); the Master of Law in health law, intellectual property and taxation; and doctoral programs in computer science, education, philosophy and psychology. Recognized by *U.S. News & World Report* for its service-learning program, DePaul takes full advantage of its Chicago location. Professors have long-standing professional relationships with corporations, government agencies, cultural and civic organizations and a ton of nonprofits. Students tap into these connections for internships, mentors, class projects, professional contacts and more. DePaul has nearly 140,000 alumni, with more than 90,000 residing in the metropolitan area, providing students with a local and global network. Competitive on the field as well as in the classroom and workplace, students love to cheer on the DePaul Blue Demons who participate in NCAA Division I sports. Women's sports include basketball, cross-country, soccer, softball, tennis, track and field and volleyball.

Men's sports include basketball, cross-country, golf, soccer, tennis and track and field. DePaul has six campuses in the Chicago metropolitan area. The Loop Campus is just blocks from Chicago's business district, the Art Institute, Orchestra Hall, Millennium Park and Lake Michigan. The 40-acre Lincoln Park Campus, just 5 miles north of the Loop Campus, is a classic residential campus surrounded by stores, theaters, restaurants and music clubs. From either campus, a short walk or ride on public transit lets students browse unique shops or visit museums, the zoo, ethnic neighborhoods and professional sports arenas, such as Wrigley Field and the United Center. DePaul undergrads can get a CTA U-Pass for free rides on CTA-operated bus and rail lines 24/7. DePaul's four suburban campuses (Naperville, Oak Forest, Rolling Meadows and O'Hare) provide convenient locations for adult and graduate students to earn a degree.

CONTACT INFORMATION

Carlene Klaas-Kennelly, Dean of Undergraduate Admissions

☎ 312-362-8300
✉ admission@depaul.edu

- **Enrollment:** *25,072*
- **Selectivity:** *moderately difficult*
- **Test scores:** *ACT—over 18, 98.4%; SAT—critical reading over 500, 85.2%; SAT—math over 500, 82%*
- **Application deadline:** *2/1 (freshmen), rolling (transfer)*
- **Expenses:** *Tuition $27,342; Room & Board $10,617*

Elmhurst students enjoy the benefit of small classes, which helps them tests their interests and find their passions. Internships and research opportunities help them set a professional path.

Elmhurst College

ELMHURST, ILLINOIS
www.elmhurst.edu/

A friendly campus, challenging classes and a faculty who cares— these are just some of the reasons students choose Elmhurst College. The College offers more than fifty majors, four accelerated majors for adults, fifteen pre-professional programs and nine graduate programs. In fact, Elmhurst ranks in the top tier of Midwest colleges and universities with master's programs, according to *U.S. News & World Report*'s "America's Best Colleges" issue. *The Princeton Review* also lists Elmhurst among the region's premier institutions of higher learning. And Elmhurst's internship program is a key factor to success after graduation. Recent interns have worked for companies such as ABC-TV, the House of Blues, IBM, Kraft, Loyola University Medical Center and the Sierra Club. Back on campus, students can take their pick of more than 100 clubs, including theater, the Jazz Band, the radio station, the Gamers Association and student government. More than half of Elmhurst students play intramurals or participate in one of eighteen NCAA Division III varsity teams. The Blue Jays field intercollegiate teams in men's and women's basketball, cross country, golf, soccer, tennis and track and field. Men also compete in baseball, football and wrestling and women have bowling, softball and volleyball teams. Elmhurst students live on campus in comfortable halls, apartments and houses with Internet, cable TV and individualized phones and voicemail. Elmhurst, a quiet suburb of Chicago, is filled with family-owned stores and restaurants, as well as theater, clubs and art museums. In *Chicago* magazine's 2003 study of the "best places to live" among 192 Chicago suburbs, the city of Elmhurst ranked number 1.The beautiful 38-acre campus looks like a college

The college's recognizable gate opens onto a 48-acre Arboretum campus in suburban Elmhurst, Illinois, about a half-hour west of Chicago.

should look: big trees, wide lawns and twenty-four stately redbrick buildings. With more than 600 varieties of trees and shrubs, the Elmhurst campus is an arboretum. Just 16 miles away (30 minutes by train), Chicago has something for everyone. Sports fans can watch the Bears, Bulls, Cubs or White Sox in action, or play touch football or Frisbee in Millennium Park or along the waterfront. Students who are interested in art or culture can visit the Museum of Contemporary Art, the Art Institute of Chicago or the 57-acre Museum Campus, featuring the Adler Planetarium and

Astronomy Museum. Chicago is also known for its world-class shopping, dining and nightlife.

- **Enrollment:** *3,363*

- **Selectivity:** *moderately difficult*

- **Test scores:** *ACT—over 18, 97%; SAT—critical reading over 500, 61%; SAT—math over 500, 66%*

- **Application deadline:** *Rolling (freshmen), rolling (transfer)*

- **Expenses:** *Tuition $28,660; Room & Board $8216*

CONTACT INFORMATION

Mrs. Stephanie Levenson, Director of Admission

☎ 630-617-3400 or toll-free 800-697-1871
✉ admit@elmhurst.edu

Kendall College
RIVERWORKS CAMPUS • CHICAGO

CHICAGO, ILLINOIS
www.kendall.edu/

Kendall College, located near the heart of downtown Chicago, prepares its graduates for leading-edge opportunities in the culinary, hospitality and business industries. Whether choosing Kendall's acclaimed School of Culinary Arts, distinctive School of Hospitality Management, innovative School of Business or well-established School of Education, students are encouraged to explore their talents and passions. Kendall's bachelor's and associate degree programs in the culinary arts are intensive and hands-on; students learn and prepare food in twelve commercial-grade kitchens, an exclusive onsite fine-dining restaurant and an equally well-regarded cafeteria. Students also intern locally, nationally and internationally at top-notch hospitality and culinary venues. Instructors here have strong credentials, formal culinary training and at least ten years of professional experience. Kendall's School of Hospitality Management combines European customer-focused expertise with American management skills. The B.A. program offers several concentrations: asset management, casino management, club management, events management, hotel and lodging management, restaurant and foodservice management and sports and leisure management. Kendall's School of Business offers a Bachelor of Arts in Business with five concentration options: baking and pastry, food service management, management, personal chef and catering and professional cookery. The curriculum is taught by an accomplished faculty of industry experts and uses situation-based challenges, actual case studies, management simulations and integrative projects to produce employment-ready graduates. The School of Business also offers a B.A. in psychology with three concentrations—advanced studies in psychology, organizational psychology and human resources management. Kendall's School of Education is designed specifically for working adults. Courses are offered on campus and

online; students have the flexibility of working full-time while also getting to interact with classmates and faculty in small-class environments. For students looking to earn a bachelor's degree in early childhood education, Kendall provides two concentration options: special education and infants and toddlers. Kendall College is a member of the Laureate International Universities, a global network of more than fifty colleges and universities with more than 100 campuses in twenty countries. Through this partnership, students have access to study-abroad programs, internships and professional opportunities in Asia, Australia, Europe and Latin America. The school is minutes from some of the country's best restaurants, hotels and companies, providing students prime access to internships and work experiences. The campus also has amazing views of the Chicago skyline, access to newly developed areas on the Chicago River, and all benefits of being in the

CONTACT INFORMATION

Lisa Marrello, Director of Admissions

☎ 312-752-2020 or toll-free
866-667-3344 (in-state)
877-588-8860 (out-of-state)
🖳 admissions@kendall.edu

third-largest city in the United States.

- **Enrollment:** *2,389*
- **Selectivity:** *moderately difficult*
- **Application deadline:** *Rolling (freshmen), rolling (transfer)*
- **Expenses:** *Room & Board $13,200*

The entrance to Lewis University's main campus in Romeoville, Illinois.

LEWIS UNIVERSITY

A Catholic and Lasallian University

ROMEOVILLE, ILLINOIS
www.lewisu.edu/

Lewis University is a comprehensive Catholic and Lasallian school that provides students with a practical, relevant and focused education. Here, coursework is tied to a student's goals and the learning experience is all about the student. Lewis offers almost eighty undergraduate majors and programs, twenty-two graduate programs and certificates of advanced study. Lewis stands out from the crowd in so many ways. Not only does Lewis have the largest bachelor's degree program in Nursing in Illinois, it also has the largest graduate program in School Counseling and Guidance in Illinois. And this is the only university in the state with an aviation program and an on-campus airport. The campus itself is beautiful. In fact, Lewis was recently named a Tree Campus USA University for its dedication to the environment and forestry—more than 60 different deciduous trees grow on its Romeoville campus. The campus residence halls offer newer apartments and suites; the buildings have full kitchens, game rooms and rec rooms with projection TVs. Eighteen intercollegiate sports include men's and women's basketball, cross-country, golf, soccer, swimming, track, tennis and volleyball plus men's baseball and women's softball. All teams compete in NCAA Division II. Lewis teams have captured the Great Lakes Valley Conference (GLVC) All-Sports Trophy twelve times—more than any other conference member. Lewis student-athletes also dominate in the classroom. The University produced another Academic All-American in 2008–09 (nine recipients altogether in the past seven years), and was second in GLVC in the number of Academic All-GLVC honorees (113). The JFK Student Recreation Center is open

A Division II volleyball game at Lewis University's Neil Carey arena in Romeoville, Illinois.

to all students. It has a pool; a 45,000-square-foot field house with playing courts surrounded by a running track; a fitness center with upgraded equipment; an aerobics studio with suspended wood floor that offers yoga, martial arts and kickboxing classes; and a state-of-the-art weight room with $45,000 worth of equipment. Outside are tennis courts, an outside track, a sand volleyball court and a nine-hole Frisbee golf course. Located in Romeoville, Lewis is only 30 minutes southwest of Chicago. Students can take advantage of the resources of one of the nation's largest

cities while enjoying the beautiful suburban campus.

- **Enrollment:** *5,847*
- **Selectivity:** *moderately difficult*
- **Test scores:** *ACT—over 18, 95.22%; SAT—critical reading over 500, 47.37%; SAT—math over 500, 73.68%*
- **Application deadline:** *8/1 (freshmen), rolling (transfer)*
- **Expenses:** *Tuition $22,990; Room & Board $8350*

http://bit.ly/collvid49

CONTACT INFORMATION

Mr. Ryan Cockerill, Director of Freshman Admission

☎ 815-838-0500 Ext. 5237 or toll-free 800-897-9000

✉ admissions@lewisu.edu

Olivet's 250-acre park-like campus is nestled in the historic Village of Bourbonnais, Illinois, just 50 miles south of Chicago.

OLIVET NAZARENE UNIVERSITY

BOURBONNAIS, ILLINOIS
www.olivet.edu/

Olivet Nazarene University (ONU) is a private, Christian university that offers one of the finest liberal arts educations in the Midwest, world-class facilities for learning and entertainment and a fun atmosphere where students make lifelong friends. Olivet's high retention, graduation and employment/placement rates show the University's commitment to student success. The campus offers a champion athletics department (eighteen intercollegiate men's and women's sports in all) and a large intramural sports program. Music and drama groups involve hundreds of students, and students join a ton of other clubs from the Film Club to the Equestrian Club. Olivet students are also heavily involved in dozens of ministry groups and volunteer efforts, small-group Bible studies and weekly student-led services. The

University recently made a number of campus improvements, including renovating the lower level of Ludwig Center student union to include a glass-enclosed gaming room with plasma TVs, a convenience store and new student leadership offices. And the Department of Communication moved to a new, technologically advanced facility in Benner Library, which also houses Jazzman's Café where students can sip a latte while studying. A new 3,059-seat chapel is under construction. The University is home to the Chicago Bears' summer training camp and Shine.FM, a 35,000-watt station ranked among the top stations in the nation and staffed by the broadcasting students. In addition to its traditional undergraduate programs, Olivet offers six degree-completion and continuing-studies programs, more than twenty master's degrees and a Doctor of Education in ethical leadership. Aside from the classes held on the main campus, the School of Graduate and Continuing

Studies offers courses for students throughout the Chicago area. Students gather for classes with other working adults in churches, schools, hospitals and other convenient locations near their home or workplace. The main University campus is located just 50 miles south of Chicago's Loop in the historic village of Bourbonnais. The area has malls, restaurants, entertainment and the Kankakee River State Park system. Students also find many job and internship opportunities in the area—which is ranked as one of the top locations in the nation for small businesses.

CONTACT INFORMATION

Susan Wolfe, Director of Admissions

☎ 815-939-5203 or toll-free 800-648-1463

✉ swolfe@olivet.edu

Students, faculty members and staff also find themselves working side by side in local and regional ministry projects. Olivet students are recognized professionally and ministerially as a valuable commodity by area businesses, churches and parachurch organizations.

- **Enrollment:** *4,636*
- **Selectivity:** *minimally difficult*
- **Application deadline:** *Rolling (freshmen), rolling (transfer)*

Besides 18 intercollege athletic teams (11 went to NAIA nationals in 2009–10), Olivet boasts an active intramurals program.

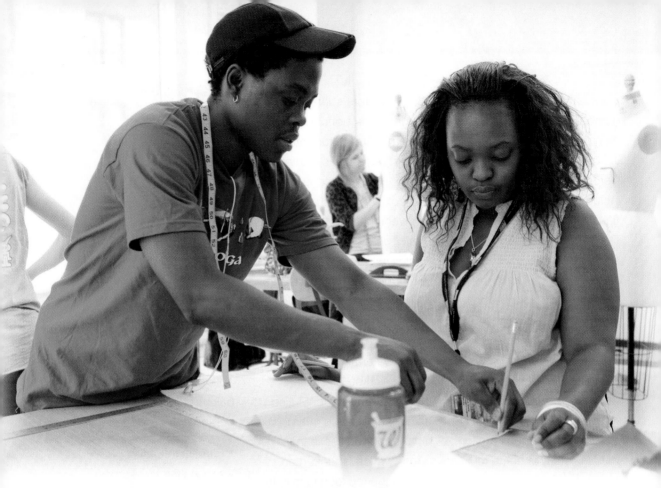

SAIC's diverse faculty are practicing artists, designers and scholars who will help you acquire and refine your technical and conceptual abilities.

School of the Art Institute of Chicago

CHICAGO, ILLINOIS
www.artic.edu/saic/

The School of the Art Institute of Chicago (SAIC) is the most influential art school in the United States according to a Columbia University poll of art critics. SAIC educates artists and designers in a highly professional, studio-oriented environment. And *U.S. News & World Report* has consistently ranked SAIC's Master of Fine Arts program as number one of the top three in the nation. SAIC stands apart from other art and design schools in its comprehensive curriculum, with more than 900 courses offered each semester. Instead of declaring a major, students are free to design a path of study that suits their creative needs. A student may choose to do all their course work in one area of study or among multiple department areas. Liberal arts and art history are central to the life of SAIC; the Institute has one of the largest art history departments in the nation and is the only college in the country that offers courses on the history, theory and philosophical bases of art criticism. SAIC students live in loft-style rooms with individual bathrooms, kitchens, voice mail and Internet. The residence halls have 24-hour security, well-lit studios, lounge rooms with big screen TVs and computer labs. Students have access to SAIC's sister institution—the Art Institute of Chicago— with its new Modern Wing and its Ryerson & Burnham Libraries, the largest art and architecture research libraries in the country. The Gene Siskel Film Center screens about 1,500 cutting-edge independent and international films every year and hosts guest appearances (Robert Downey, Jr., recently stopped by). SAIC's Video Data Bank houses more than 1,600 titles and is the leading resource in the United States for video-tapes by and about contemporary artists. SAIC is located in the heart of downtown Chicago, home to the nation's second-largest art scene with its world-class museums, galleries, alternative spaces and organizations that support the arts. Students have plenty of places to go: ballet, opera, theater, libraries, blues and jazz clubs, parks, ethnic restaurants, professional sports venues and street festivals. SAIC is located across the street from an extraordinary space. Millennium Park is a twenty-first-century mix of art, architecture and nature, and SAIC, its faculty and students played a key role in its realization. One of the signature pieces of public art at the park, the Crown Fountain has 1,000 video portraits that are screened continuously on the fountain's twin video towers.

CONTACT INFORMATION

Mr. Scott Ramon, Director, Undergraduate Admissions

☎ 312-629-6100 or toll-free 800-232-SAIC

✉ ugadmiss@saic.edu

- **Enrollment:** *3,170*
- **Selectivity:** *very difficult*
- **Application deadline:** *6/1 (freshmen), 8/15 (transfer)*
- **Expenses:** *Tuition $35,950; Room only $9800*

SAIC puts the latest tools at your fingertips from the first day of classes, and it surrounds you with a vast array of modern and traditional resources in state-of-the-art facilities.

At SIUC, opportunities for research, creative and academic projects begin the first semester. More than 80% of classes have fewer than 30 people, so individualized, hands-on learning is standard.

Southern
Illinois University
Carbondale

CARBONDALE, ILLINOIS
www.siuc.edu

For outstanding academics, a competitive sports program and a fun campus with lots to do, it doesn't get any better than Southern Illinois University Carbondale (SIUC). This university is nationally and internationally recognized for its research (top 5 percent of all U.S. universities) and service programs. SIUC offers two associate degree programs; more than 100 bachelor's degree programs; seventy-four master's degree programs; thirty-two doctoral programs; and professional degrees in law and medicine. SIUC is a multicampus university and includes the Carbondale campus as well as the SIUC School of Medicine at Springfield. Students who are ready to start college but not ready to pick a specific major can enroll in SIUC's Pre-Major Program. Premajor advisers and counselors help these students plan their education and careers. SIUC faculty members, staff members and alumni also help students arrange internships, cooperative education programs and work-study programs. SIUC students enjoy the many dining options (late-night, vegetarian, display cooking) and modern, Internet and cable-ready residence halls and apartments. Student athletes play intercollegiate sports at the NCAA Division I level (football is Division I-FCS). Men and women compete in basketball, cross-country, diving, golf, swimming, tennis and track and field. Men also compete in baseball and football and women also compete in softball and volleyball. The campus has a ton of fields, several tennis courts and even a campus lake with a beach and boat dock. SIUC's Student Recreation Center has an Olympic-size pool; indoor tracks; handball/racquetball and squash courts; a climbing wall; weight rooms; basketball, volleyball and tennis courts; outdoor equipment rental; an aerobic area; walleyball; martial arts; and dance and cardio studios. The Student Center is one of the largest in the United States without a hotel. It holds a bookstore, several restaurants, a craft shop, a bakery, bowling and billiards, headquarters for 400 active student organizations, four ballrooms and an auditorium. On-campus events throughout the year include concerts, plays, festivals, guest speakers and musicals. Carbondale is 6 hours south of Chicago, 2 hours southeast of St. Louis and 3 hours north of Nashville. Four large recreational lakes, the two great rivers (the Mississippi and the Ohio), and the spectacular 270,000-acre Shawnee National Forest are within minutes of the campus. The mid-South climate is ideal for year-round outdoor activities. Carbondale is a city of 26,000 people that supports one large enclosed mall, several mini-malls, theaters and restaurants.

CONTACT INFORMATION

Patsy Reynolds, Director, Undergraduate Admissions

☎ 618-536-4405

✉ pradmit@siu.edu

- **Enrollment:** *20,350*
- **Selectivity:** *moderately difficult*
- **Test scores:** *ACT—over 18, 85%; SAT—math over 500, 40%*
- **Application deadline:** *Rolling (freshmen), 7/1 (transfer)*
- **Expenses:** *Tuition $10,411; Room & Board $7673*

Many students fall in love with SIUC from their first visit. It's not just the beautiful campus and collegiate atmosphere; it's also our tradition of academic excellence, accessibility and diversity.

Don't fit the mold? Don't worry, just "B U"—with 55 undergraduate, one first professional and 17 master's degrees, plus over 140 recognized student organizations, Butler has something for everyone.

BUTLER UNIVERSITY

INDIANAPOLIS, INDIANA
www.butler.edu/

Butler University has a proud tradition of excellence and innovation. Butler is a comprehensive university that offers more than sixty-five majors and graduate degrees in business administration, creative writing, education administration (EPPSP), effective teaching and leadership, English, history, music conducting, music composition, music education, music history, music theory, music performance, piano pedagogy, pharmaceutical science, physician assistant, public accounting and school counseling. In addition, Butler offers a doctor of pharmacy (Pharm.D.) program. On campus, the state-of-the-art health and recreation complex is equipped with recreation courts, an indoor jogging track, an aquatics area, a weight and fitness space, a lounge and a juice bar. Since opening in 2006, the complex has also won two national awards, including one for innovative architecture and design and one for its outstanding indoor sports facilities. There are more than 140 official student organizations, fourteen Greek organizations and nineteen Division I varsity athletic teams.

Students take advantage of Broadway shows at Butler's Clowes Memorial Hall, the city's premier performing arts center. Basketball fans cheer on the Bulldogs at the 10,000-seat historic Hinkle Fieldhouse, where the final game in the movie *Hoosiers* was filmed. Located near the center of campus, Atherton Union is as a natural gathering spot for students. Atherton Union has e-mail stations, wireless capabilities, a 24-hour computer lab, Starbucks coffee shop, bookstore, food court, dining hall and convenience store. The 290-acre campus (just six miles from downtown Indianapolis) maintains its heritage with centuries-old trees; open, landscaped malls; curving sidewalks; and fountains. The University's students enjoy a nature preserve, prairie, historical canal, botanical garden, observatory and jogging paths—all on campus. Indianapolis, Indiana's state capital and the thirteenth-largest city in the nation, boasts a variety of cultural activities, including the Indianapolis

Symphony Orchestra, the Indiana Repertory Theatre, the Indianapolis Museum of Art (just two blocks from campus), the Eiteljorg Museum, the Indiana State Museum and the world's largest children's museum. The Indianapolis Motor Speedway is the anchor of Indianapolis' professional sports, while basketball, football, hockey and baseball have homes in three major sports arenas. Indianapolis is home to the NCAA headquarters, its Hall of Champions and the men's and women's Big Ten basketball championships. In 2012, Indianapolis will host the Super Bowl.

CONTACT INFORMATION

Mr. Scott Ham, Director of Admissions

☎ 317-940-8100 or toll-free 888-940-8100

✉ admission@butler.edu

- **Enrollment:** *4,505*
- **Selectivity:** *moderately difficult*
- **Test scores:** *ACT—over 18, 100%; SAT—critical reading over 500, 85.2%; SAT—math over 500, 88.4%*
- **Application deadline:** *Rolling (freshmen), 8/15 (transfer)*
- **Expenses:** *Tuition $29,246; Room & Board $9740*

 http://bit.ly/collvid32

Butler's administration takes pride in being accessible to students—even the president takes time to let loose. High-fiving with students? Just another day at the office.

FC freshmen doing a community service project during FOCUS day.

FRANKLIN, INDIANA
www.franklincollege.edu/

As an innovative scientist, diplomat, thinker, writer and leader, Benjamin Franklin's remarkable life and accomplishments left a mark on not only a young nation, but also on the world. Named in the spirit of this American icon, Franklin College continues his legacy of exploration and knowledge. Since its founding in 1834, Franklin College has had a long history of preparing students for lives committed to excellence, leadership and service. Franklin offers thirty-six majors—including biology, business, education and journalism—as well as thirty-five minors and nine pre-professional programs. In fact, Franklin College combines liberal arts training with professional development like no other college. The innovative Professional Development

Program (PDP) gives students opportunities to dine with corporate executives, network with national and community leaders, learn the finer points of corporate communication and develop a level of polish and sophistication that sets them apart from other college graduates. And when students are ready to kick back and relax, they can come home to air-conditioned residence halls with fireplaces and big-screen TVs. Many students join one of the more than sixty clubs—from Habitat for Humanity to fraternities and sororities, there's a group for every interest. Other students head over to Faught Stadium or Spurlock Center to cheer on Franklin's NCAA Division III teams. A new athletics facility is under construction; Grizzly Park will have a new softball field, new tennis courts, an area for track and field events and new fitness trails for walkers and runners. Located in the heart of the Midwest, Franklin College offers students the best of both a small community and a big city's excitement. The campus has its own 31-acre biology woodland where students step outside the class to learn. Franklin College is only 20 miles south of Indiana's capital city of Indianapolis—the thirteenth largest city in the United States.

CONTACT INFORMATION

Ms. Jacqueline Acosta, Director of Admissions

☎ 317-738-8062 or toll-free 800-852-0232

📧 jacosta@franklincollege.edu

- **Enrollment:** *1,153*
- **Selectivity:** *moderately difficult*
- **Test scores:** *ACT—over 18, 91%; SAT—critical reading over 500, 50%; SAT—math over 500, 60%*
- **Application deadline:** *Rolling (freshmen)*
- **Expenses:** *Tuition $23,275; Room & Board $6885*

Captains taking the field for the coin toss at Red Faught Stadium.

Saint Mary's provides a rigorous liberal arts education.

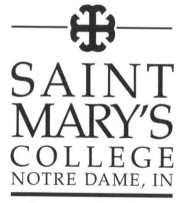

SAINT MARY'S COLLEGE
NOTRE DAME, IN

NOTRE DAME, INDIANA
www.saintmarys.edu/

She's a staff nurse in a Chicago neurology intensive care unit or a Peace Corps volunteer in Uganda. She's studied abroad in Rome or been a student teacher at Marquette School in South Bend. She's received a first place award in the North Central Sociological Association's National Student Competition or danced the entire night to help raise over $90,000 to benefit Riley's Children's Hospital. She's a woman using her talents to make a difference in our world— she's a Saint Mary's woman. A Saint Mary's education challenges students to reach beyond the ordinary. St. Mary's offers professional programs such as accounting, education, nursing, social work and communicative disorders. Nearly half of the students complete a semester-long study abroad experience in one of over thirty locations worldwide from Italy to Argentina. Saint Mary's has a unique co-exchange program with the University of Notre Dame. Saint Mary's and Notre Dame's students can take courses and be part of the study-abroad programs at both schools. Saint Mary's students can try out for Notre Dame's legendary marching band (10 percent of its members are Saint Mary's students); work for *The Observer*, the daily newspaper published jointly; or gain broadcast experience on WVFI, the Notre Dame/Saint Mary's radio station. And Saint Mary's has an active campus life. There are over sixty clubs and organizations, eight varsity athletic teams and over twenty community service organizations. The modern residence halls offer a full calendar of activities—from twice-yearly dances to coffee nights with the College President to intramural sports. The College has a new student center, a dining hall and a clubhouse for extracurricular activities. All residence halls have chapels, and the Church of Loretto, the main chapel, offers mass on a daily basis. As an NCAA Division III school, Saint Mary's sponsors varsity teams in basketball, cross-country, golf, soccer, softball, swimming and diving, tennis and volleyball. Club sports, cosponsored with Notre Dame, include equestrian, gymnastics, lacrosse and figure ice skating. The College's Angela Athletic Facility has multipurpose courts for tennis, volleyball and basketball; a training and fitness center; and racquetball courts. Saint Mary's 75-acre campus, set alongside the Saint Joseph River, has great natural beauty. The College is located just across the street from the University of Notre Dame, minutes north of the city of South Bend (with a population of more than 200,000) and only 90 miles from Chicago.

CONTACT INFORMATION

Mona Bowe, Director of Admission

☎ 574-284-4587 or toll-free 800-551-7621

✉ admission@saintmarys.edu

- **Enrollment:** *1,664*
- **Selectivity:** *moderately difficult*
- **Test scores:** *ACT—over 18, 98.73%; SAT—critical reading over 500, 81.65%; SAT—math over 500, 80.16%*
- **Application deadline:** *2/15 (freshmen), 4/15 (transfer)*
- **Expenses:** *Tuition $29,616; Room & Board $9206*

Tradition intersects innovation: Students study in the state-of-the-art Cushwa-Leighton Library, with a view of Saint Mary's iconic Le Mans Hall bell tower.

Laugh up a Storm at Thunder athletic events, as mascot "Storm" makes the scene. The Marching Thunder plays and performs on the football field to add to the excitement of the game.

Trine University

ANGOLA, INDIANA
www.trine.edu/

Trine University has always provided an affordable, career-oriented, hands-on education. With a worldwide reputation for being "job-ready," Trine graduates are in demand. That is why each year more than 94 percent of Trine graduates are employed in major-related positions within six months of graduation. Trine offers associate and bachelor's degrees in more than thirty-five programs in engineering, mathematics, science, computer science, business administration, teacher education, communications and criminal justice. In 2002, Trine became a graduate-degree-granting school and now offers five-year Bachelor of Science/Master of Engineering dual-degree programs. In fall 2006, Trine introduced an interdisciplinary major in entrepreneurship. Majors in informatics and hospitality and tourism management have since been added. The University's 400-acre campus includes an eighteen-hole championship golf course. In 2009,

Trine's Golf Course Village, four student apartment buildings, opened on Zollner Golf Course. In August 2007, Trine opened its new $15.5-million University Center and Center for Technology and Online Resources, which houses a new dining hall, deli, bakery, bookstore, climbing wall, sports and wellness center, movie theater, post office, radio station and library. Trine is a member of NCAA Division III and the Michigan Intercollegiate Athletic Association (MIAA), the nation's oldest athletic conference. Men's sports include baseball, basketball, cross-country, football, golf, lacrosse, soccer, tennis, track and wrestling. Women's sports include basketball, cross-country, golf, lacrosse, soccer, softball, tennis, track and volleyball. Women's field hockey is slated to be added in fall 2010. Intramural sports are also a big part of life at Trine. The Athletic and Recreation Center (ARC), which has a 200-meter indoor track and training and practice facilities for other sports, opened in 2009. Artificial turf was installed on the main athletic field and the Fred Zollner Athletic Stadium is scheduled to be completed in summer 2010. Student organizations include the student senate, honor societies, professional organizations, the campus newspaper, the FM radio station, the drama club, music ensembles, pep and marching band and fraternities and sororities. Trine is located in Angola, in the heart of northeast Indiana's scenic lake resort region and about halfway between Chicago, Illinois, and Cleveland, Ohio. Just a 45-minute drive from Fort Wayne, Indiana, Trine offers the safety and ease of a small-town environment, located near some of the nation's most exciting cities. Pokagon State Park provides year-round recreation and is just 5 miles north of campus.

CONTACT INFORMATION

Mr. Scott Goplin, Dean of Admission

☎ 260-665-4365 or toll-free 800-347-4TSU
✉ admit@trine.edu

- **Enrollment:** *1,616*
- **Selectivity:** *moderately difficult*
- **Test scores:** *ACT—over 18, 92%; SAT—critical reading over 500, 45%; SAT—math over 500, 72%*
- **Application deadline:** *8/1 (freshmen), 8/1 (transfer)*
- **Expenses:** *Tuition $25,400; Room & Board $8500*

Join friends in the University Center, the campus nerve center. Where you can grab a snack at Express Cafe, work out in the fitness room, study in the library or catch a free film.

Graceland Chemistry Professor Brad Mercer leads students through an experiment in the new Resch Science and Technology Hall: state-of-the-art facilities and industry-standard equipment await students.

GRACELAND
UNIVERSITY

LAMONI, IOWA
www.graceland.edu/

Graceland University (GU) offers a strong liberal arts education with a focus on career preparation. Students can choose from sixty degree programs through its two campuses—one in Lamoni and another in Independence, Missouri. Graduate programs include the Master of Arts in Christian Ministries, Master of Arts in Religion, Master of Education and Master of Science in Nursing. In addition to its traditional programs, Graceland offers many options for distance learners. One highlight of the campus is the University's Center for the Study of the Korean War. With a number of documents, photographs and other items related to the Korean War and its time period, this building is home to the largest archival collection of its kind in the United States. The University members believe that a big part of a student's learning happens in the residence halls. Here, students live in men's and women's "houses." Members of each house elect a house council to plan social, athletic, religious and academic support activities. Residence halls are equipped with voice mail, e-mail, Internet connections and cable TV. Graceland is a member of the NAIA and its athletes compete in nineteen varsity sports. Men's and women's teams are basketball, cross country, golf, soccer, tennis, track and volleyball. Men also compete in baseball and football and women also compete in cheer squad, dance team and softball. Facilities include The Bruce Jenner Sports Complex, where the football players draw in large crowds and runners enjoy the

state-of-the-art all-weather track; eight lighted tennis courts; and the Razz soccer field, which is getting resodded for the 2010 season. Lamoni, in south-central Iowa, is about 3 miles north of the Missouri border, 1 hour from Des Moines, 2 hours from Kansas City and 3 hours from Omaha. Lamoni is the home of Liberty Hall Historic Center, a 6-mile bike trail, an annual Civil War Days Re-Enactment and Living History Event, numerous hometown restaurants and unique shops. A county lake, Slip Bluff County

CONTACT INFORMATION

Mr. Greg Sutherland, Vice President of Enrollment and Dean of Admissions

☎ 641-784-5110 or toll-free 866-GRACELAND

✉ sutherla@graceland.edu

Park, and Nine Eagles State Park are within 10 miles.

- **Enrollment:** *2,355*
- **Selectivity:** *moderately difficult*
- **Test scores:** *ACT—over 18, 79%; SAT—critical reading over 500, 40%; SAT—math over 500, 39%*
- **Application deadline:** *Rolling (freshmen), rolling (transfer)*
- **Expenses:** *Tuition $20,980; Room & Board $7040*

Graceland is famous for its strong sense of community. And how! Students pile on for a moment of fun out in front of our 1895 Higdon Administration Building.

GRAND VIEW UNIVERSITY

DES MOINES, IOWA
www.grandview.edu/

Grand View offers 38 majors that lead to bachelor's degrees. You'll be challenged in small classes, participating in academic competitions, researching with faculty, and learning from fellow students.

At Grand View University, students find a winning combination of high-quality programs, experienced professors and caring individuals. Learning is an interactive process at Grand View—students engage in lively discussions, work on real-world projects and participate in career-related work experiences. Grand View University stands out from other colleges because of its partnerships with leading businesses and organizations in Des Moines, which has led to challenging internships and to nearly 100 percent of students finding jobs right after graduation or continuing their education. Grand View is known for its ability to connect students with exciting and challenging career opportunities. Students get involved in many campus organizations including intramural sports, speech and theater groups, departmental clubs, student government and musical ensembles. Student athletes compete in men's baseball, basketball, bowling, cross-country, football, golf, soccer, track and field and wrestling and women's basketball, bowling, competitive dance, cross-country, golf, soccer, softball, track and field and volleyball. Grand View participates in the Midwest Collegiate Conference of the NAIA. Two locations offer Grand View students convenient scheduling options. Weekend and evening classes are offered at the main campus in Des Moines and at Grand View's campus in Johnston, Iowa. For motivated students looking to complete their degree quickly, accelerated schedules are available for several of the fifteen evening majors. Grand View is located in Des Moines, a metropolitan area of more than half a million people in central Iowa. Des Moines is the state capital and serves as the communications hub for Iowa. Grand View's campus is Des Moines—and as part of the Grand View community, students are not limited by a small school or small town. In a given day, students can catch an Iowa Cubs professional baseball doubleheader, head down to the Court Avenue district for great food and nightlife or take in a rock concert at Wells Fargo Arena. A thriving arts program in Des Moines features the Des Moines Metro Opera, Ballet Iowa, the Des Moines Symphony, the Des Moines Art Center and the Des Moines Playhouse. The summer Des Moines Art Festival is ranked third in the nation. Except for a month or so of bundle-up, see-your-breath weather, the climate is ideal for outdoor activities. Grand View students can access several golf courses, Saylorville Lake and many city parks and state forests. Grand View is 4 hours from Minneapolis, 6 hours from

CONTACT INFORMATION

Ms. Diane Schaefer, Director of Admissions

☎ 515-263-2810 or toll-free 800-444-6083 Ext. 2810

✉ admissions@grandview.edu

Chicago and 3 hours from Kansas City.

- **Enrollment:** *2,039*
- **Selectivity:** *minimally difficult*
- **Test scores:** *ACT—over 18, 89%; SAT—critical reading over 500, 29%; SAT—math over 500, 25%*
- **Application deadline:** *8/15 (freshmen), 8/15 (transfer)*
- **Expenses:** *Tuition $19,324; Room & Board $6442*

Grand View offers 10 sports each for men and women. Scholarships are available for qualifying athletes. Scholar-athletes have access to first-class facilities and interact with top-notch coaches.

LUTHER COLLEGE

DECORAH, IOWA
www.luther.edu/

Where prairie, woodland, and river meet, Luther's hilly green campus is home to more than 2,500 students. It is truly a beautiful place to spend four years.

Luther College, which was founded by Norwegian immigrants, is an academic community of faith and learning where students from all beliefs and backgrounds are free to learn, to express themselves, to perform, to compete and to grow. This liberal arts college welcomes over 125 international students to its campus every year. Learning at Luther is about engagement: faculty members who are passionate about teaching, students who are active and involved and a College community known for hands-on experiences. Luther has a year-long course for first-year students called Paideia. This course, unique in its approach, develops students' research and writing skills as they explore human cultures and history. In addition, Luther offers a Phi Beta Kappa chapter and several departmental honor societies, proof of the quality of teaching and learning on campus. At Luther, students are encouraged to seek out connections between their lives in the classroom and their lives outside the classroom.

The College has an exciting atmosphere and a full calendar of events. The College sponsors seven choirs, three orchestras, three bands, two jazz bands and a full theater and dance program. As a community of faith, students can participate in daily chapel, weekly Sunday worship, outreach teams and midweek Eucharist. Nineteen intercollegiate sports are offered. Men compete in baseball, basketball, cross-country, football, golf, soccer, swimming, tennis, track and field and wrestling. Women compete in basketball, cross-country, golf, soccer, softball, swimming, tennis, track and field and volleyball. Club sports include Ultimate Frisbee, rugby and men's volleyball. Most of the student body is involved in intramural and recreational sports and all students can access the twelve outdoor tennis courts, an eight-lane polyurethane 400-meter track and the numerous cross-country running and ski trails. The well-equipped field house contains a 25-yard indoor pool, three racquetball courts, four hardwood basketball courts, a wrestling complex and a 3,000-seat gymnasium. A sports forum houses a six-lane, 200-meter indoor track; six indoor tennis courts; and athletic training facilities. The Legends Fitness for Life Center provides the latest fitness equipment and a 30-foot-high rock-climbing wall. The College is located in Decorah, in the scenic bluff country of northeast Iowa. The Upper Iowa River, which runs through the campus, is designated as a National Scenic and Recreational River. Many students head off campus to go canoeing, fishing, hunting, cross-country skiing, camping, hiking, cycling and spelunking.

CONTACT INFORMATION

Kirk Neubauer, Director of Recruiting Services

☎ 563-387-1287 or toll-free 800-458-8437

✉ admissions@luther.edu

- **Enrollment:** *2,519*

- **Selectivity:** *moderately difficult*

- **Test scores:** *ACT—over 18, 98.9%; SAT—critical reading over 500, 75.2%; SAT—math over 500, 85.4%*

- **Expenses:** *Tuition $33,480; Room & Board $5800*

Luther's faculty maintain a hands-on approach to teaching, remaining accessible to students in and out of the classroom.

Small class sizes and a low student-to-faculty ratio give Morningside College students an opportunity to work closely with their instructors.

Morningside College

SIOUX CITY, IOWA
www.morningside.edu/

Morningside College's primary goal is to provide students with a high-quality education. Rooted in a strong liberal arts tradition, Morningside's faculty challenges students to be flexible in thought, open in attitude and confident in themselves. So it's no surprise that The Princeton Review has named Morningside College a "Best Midwestern College" since 2003. This private college affiliated with the United Methodist Church offers a number of undergraduate degrees as well as a Master of Arts in Teaching with professional educator or special education tracks. Morningside College's undergrads take part in a wide variety of activities, including departmental, professional and religious organizations; honor societies; and sororities and fraternities.

A newspaper, literary magazine and campus radio station are all student run. A ton of concerts, theater productions and lectures series take place throughout the year. The Morningside Mustangs participate and win in NAIA Division II sports. Men's varsity sports are baseball, basketball, cross-country, football, golf, soccer, swimming, tennis, track and field and wrestling. Women compete in basketball, cross-country, golf, soccer, softball, swimming, tennis, track and volleyball. For fun, many Morningside students play intramurals—everything from dodgeball to tennis to 5-on-5 basketball. The state-of-the-art Hindman-Hobbs Center has a pool, saunas, racquetball courts, a weight room, basketball courts, a wrestling room and a jogging track. Students live in traditional halls, apartments and in themed housing (Wellness Floor, Greek Floor and so on). Students enjoy large game rooms, free computer printing spots and kitchens.

Morningside College is located on a 68-acre campus in Sioux City, the fourth-largest city in Iowa. The campus sits next to a city park, swimming pool and tennis courts and within 5 minutes of a major regional shopping mall and a new shopping center. The Sioux City area offers a mix of urban shopping and recreation in a scenic setting. Students find Morningside's Sioux City location to be an ideal place to find internships; recently, students have interned for New York Life, Big Brothers/Big Sisters,

CONTACT INFORMATION

Ms. Amy Williams,
Co-Director of Admissions

☎ 712-274-5111 or toll-free
800-831-0806 Ext. 5111
💻 mscadm@morningside.edu

KCAU-TV Channel 9 and the Siouxland Community Bloodbank.

- **Enrollment:** *2,036*
- **Selectivity:** *moderately difficult*
- **Test scores:** *ACT—over 18, 96%*
- **Application deadline:** *Rolling (freshmen), rolling (transfer)*
- **Expenses:** *Tuition $22,980; Room & Board $7040*

All full-time students at Morningside College receive a laptop computer that gives them access to the college's wireless network from anywhere on campus.

Simpson offers more than 50 academic programs. With research opportunities, study abroad and service projects, Simpson students have optimal career and graduate school preparation!

SIMPSON COLLEGE

INDIANOLA, IOWA
www.simpson.edu/

Simpson College combines the best of a liberal arts education with outstanding career preparation and extracurricular programs. Simpson professors are as dedicated to their fields of study as they are to teaching—and it shows in the classroom. When this type of passion is combined with well-prepared and motivated students, the potential for success is unlimited. The 4-4-1 academic calendar includes a May Term that provides students with unique learning opportunities in the classroom, through internships or while studying abroad in Tahiti, Argentina or London. Extracurricular activities at Simpson range from an award-winning music program to nationally recognized NCAA Division III teams. Students here participate in student government, campus publications, fraternities and sororities, religious life, music, theater, residence hall organizations and departmental clubs. Simpson athletes compete in nineteen intercollegiate sports: baseball, basketball, cheer squad, cross country, dance team, football, golf, soccer, softball, swimming, tennis, track and field, volleyball and wrestling. Even more students join the extensive intramural program that includes late-night coed softball, mud volleyball, floor hockey and ladder golf, just to name a few. Campus facilities are continually enhanced and updated, including the state-of-the-art Carver Science Hall, named after Simpson's most distinguished alumnus, George Washington Carver. Simpson's beautiful 85-acre, tree-lined campus is alive with creativity, energy and productivity. All college housing is air conditioned and comfortable, equipped with wireless access. Hungry undergrads head to Pfeiffer Dining Hall for all-you-care-to-eat homemade soups, healthy salads and freshly

baked desserts. Simpson is located in Indianola, just 12 miles south of Des Moines, Iowa's capital city. The Des Moines International Airport is 20 minutes from campus. Indianola is host to nationally known events including the Des Moines Metropolitan Opera and the National Balloon Classic. The area offers Lake Ahquabi State Park, Summerset Trail and unique restaurants and shops within walking distance of campus. Indianola's proximity to Des Moines gives students plenty of advantages. Within minutes, students are right in the heart of some of the best entertainment and employment options Iowa and the Midwest have to offer.

At Simpson, student-athletes receive a great education while having the opportunity to compete at the NCAA Division III level. Simpson's 19 varsity teams compete for championship titles each year.

CONTACT INFORMATION

Deborah Tierney, Vice President for Enrollment

☎ 515-961-1624 or toll-free 800-362-2454 (in-state) 800-362-2454 Ext. 1624 (out-of-state)

🖥 admiss@simpson.edu

- **Enrollment:** *2,023*
- **Selectivity:** *moderately difficult*
- **Test scores:** *ACT—over 18, 99.2%*
- **Application deadline:** *8/15 (freshmen), 8/15 (transfer)*
- **Expenses:** *Tuition $25,733; Room & Board $7261*

UNIVERSITY of DUBUQUE

DUBUQUE, IOWA
www.dbq.edu/

The University of Dubuque (UD) is a private liberal arts university with a theological seminary located in Iowa's first city— Dubuque. The Key City is on the Mississippi River at the point where the borders of Wisconsin, Illinois and Iowa meet. The University offers a number of degree programs through its four schools: School of Business, School of Liberal Arts, School of Professional Programs and School of Theology. Throughout its history, the University has been known as a place of educational opportunity. Even today, a large portion of its students are from first-generation or underrepresented populations. The University of Dubuque's welcoming interfaith community comes from across the country and around the globe. The school is convinced that students living in today's world are better prepared for life if they have a global perspective. The UD Spartans compete in varsity sports at the NCAA Division III level. All students (not just the athletes) have access to the Chlapaty Recreation and Wellness Center that opened in 2008. This state-of-the-art building has a two-level fitness center with the latest in cardio equipment and weights; a 200-meter, six-lane track with synthetic flooring; four multi-use courts; and a 16-foot concourse running the length of the building. The University of Dubuque, located in eastern Iowa, is in the heart of the Midwest. Dubuque is a city for all seasons. From bluffs blazing with autumn oranges and reds to the river sparkling with summer's blues and greens, the area scenery is spectacular year-round. Dubuque is a dynamic community built along the majestic Mississippi River and surrounded by dramatic bluffs. The setting is ideal for outdoor enthusiasts, with four seasons to go hiking, biking, boating, skiing, camping, golfing, climbing and caving. A lively cultural scene includes the Grand Opera House, the Dubuque Symphony Orchestra and the Dubuque Museum of Art. The National Farm Toy Museum and the National Mississippi River Museum provide glimpses of the area's past. The city's theater productions, shops and restaurants are wonderful ways to take a study break. Nearby are some of the Midwest's most interesting cities, an easy drive for a weekend road trip. Historic Galena offers quaint shops and period architecture, while Chicago is famous for its museums and night life. Madison, Milwaukee and Minneapolis–St. Paul are only hours away.

CONTACT INFORMATION

Mr. Jesse James, Director of Admissions

☎ 563-589-3214 or toll-free 800-722-5583

✉ admissns@dbq.edu

- **Enrollment:** *1,718*
- **Selectivity:** *moderately difficult*
- **Test scores:** *ACT—over 18, 78%; SAT—critical reading over 500, 40%; SAT—math over 500, 45%*
- **Application deadline:** *Rolling (freshmen), rolling (transfer)*
- **Expenses:** *Tuition $21,590; Room & Board $7370*

Engage in lively, interactive learning with an option to conduct undergraduate research! Our average class size is small—about 24 students, and the student faculty ratio is 14:1.

NKU NORTHERN KENTUCKY UNIVERSITY

HIGHLAND HEIGHTS, KENTUCKY
www.nku.edu/

Northern Kentucky University (NKU), founded in 1968, is the newest of Kentucky's eight state universities. Students can choose from seventy bachelor's degrees, six associate degrees, twenty graduate programs, one Juris Doctor and a Doctor of Education in Educational Leadership. The most popular bachelor's programs are in teacher education, nursing, human resources management and services, psychology and marketing. The atmosphere of the campus is futuristic, emphasizing a high-quality education by supporting the liberal arts. Campus buildings are of modern, contemporary design and are set on 300 acres of rolling countryside. NKU opened its $37 million student union building in 2008; it houses a mulitpurpose room for concerts and comedians, a fully-equipped game room, seven dining spots (including a Starbucks) and outdoor areas for lounging and studying. The state-of-the-art, $60 million Bank of Kentucky Center also opened in 2008. This arena is the home of the NKU basketball teams; it seats 9,400 fans and also has a study lab, media room and top-of-the-line workout and physical therapy rooms. There are more than 200 student organizations to pick from at NKU—everything from the Wiffle Ball Club to the Students for 9/11 Truth. Student athletes compete in the NCAA Division II Great Lakes Valley Conference. Men and women play intercollegiate sports in basketball, cheerleading, cross-country, golf, soccer and tennis. Men also compete in baseball and women also compete in fastpitch softball and volleyball. Intramurals include basketball, dodgeball, field hockey, flag football, ice hockey, racquetball, soccer, softball, Tae Kwan Do and volleyball. NKU is located in the largest metropolitan area of any state university in Kentucky. It is located 8 miles southeast of Cincinnati, Ohio and only 60 miles from Dayton, 79 miles from Lexington,

93 miles from Louisville and 114 miles from Indianapolis. While the immediate area is suburban, NKU is part of the metropolitan area of greater Cincinnati—where many students find internships through the United Way, the Kentucky Symphony Orchestra, the U.S. Secret Service and so many other organizations.

- **Enrollment:** *15,372*
- **Selectivity:** *minimally difficult*

CONTACT INFORMATION

Ms. Melissa Gorbandt, Director of Admissions and Outreach

☎ 859-572-5220 Ext. 5744 or toll-free 800-637-9948

✉ admitnku@nku.edu

- **Test scores:** *ACT—over 18, 88.03%; SAT—critical reading over 500, 46.66%; SAT—math over 500, 42.66%*
- **Application deadline:** *8/1 (freshmen), 8/1 (transfer)*
- **Expenses:** *Tuition $6792*

 http://bit.ly/collvid57

Go beyond the brochures and experience NKU for yourself—visit campus. Learn more about upcoming visits online at http://visit.nku.edu.

Close interaction with faculty (16:1) offers students the individual attention that true intellectual inquiry requires.

THOMAS MORE
COLLEGE
TOGETHER IN PURSUIT OF TRUTH

CRESTVIEW HILLS, KENTUCKY
www.thomasmore.edu/

Thomas More College boasts a strong academic reputation, small class sizes and an ongoing dedication to a Catholic liberal arts curriculum. With a faculty committed to teaching, the academic experience is one of personal attention and a hands-on approach to learning that forms the basis of a Thomas More education. In addition to its undergraduate programs, Thomas More College offers graduate programs in business administration (M.B.A.) and teaching (M.A.T.). Students can live on campus in suite-style or townhouse-style residence halls. All residence halls offer comfortable, air-conditioned rooms; Internet and cable TV access; and free laundry facilities. The 27,000-square-foot Holbrook

Student Center has a bookstore, computer and study lounges, a cafe and a dance rehearsal studio. Thomas More College competes at the NCAA Division III level in men's baseball, basketball, cross-country, football, golf, soccer and tennis and in women's basketball, cross-country, fast-pitch softball, golf, soccer, tennis and volleyball. Track and field was added as a club sport in 2009 and will become competitive in 2011. Intramural sports include coed flag football, basketball, cornhole, dodgeball, softball and volleyball. Thomas More opened an on-campus athletic complex in fall 2008 for football and soccer, in addition to the Connor Convocation Center which houses basketball and volleyball facilities and the College's baseball and softball fields. Students also enjoy swimming, tennis, racquetball and basketball and a complete fitness area at the Five Seasons Sports Club, next to the campus. Thomas More College is located in northern Kentucky, 10 minutes south of Cincinnati, Ohio. The Greater Cincinnati/Northern Kentucky International Airport is just 10 minutes from the College. Thomas More's suburban setting provides a safe environment for students as well as a ton of opportunities for employment and internships. Local attractions include the Broadway Series, the Cincinnati Pops, the Cincinnati Zoo, the Newport Aquarium, the Riverbend Music Center and the Cincinnati Reds and Bengals. Shopping and restaurants are also nearby, including the new Crestview Hills Town

CONTACT INFORMATION

Mr. Billy Sarge, Associate Director of Admissions

☎ 859-344-3332 or toll-free 800-825-4557

✉ admissions@thomasmore.edu

Center, located across the street from the College.

- **Enrollment:** *1,858*
- **Selectivity:** *moderately difficult*
- **Test scores:** *ACT—over 18, 99%; SAT—critical reading over 500, 46%; SAT—math over 500, 49%*
- **Application deadline:** *8/1 (freshmen), 8/1 (transfer)*
- **Expenses:** *Tuition $24,720; Room & Board $6530*

Ninety percent of Thomas More graduates are employed or in graduate/professional schools within 6 months of graduation.

TRANSYLVANIA UNIVERSITY

LEXINGTON, KENTUCKY
www.transy.edu/

Transy has an incredible record for graduate school acceptance rates. More than 90% of students recommended by our faculty are accepted to medical school and virtually 100% are accepted to law school.

Transylvania University, a private liberal arts school, is consistently ranked among the best small colleges in the nation. The name, from the Latin meaning "across the woods", refers to the heavily forested Transylvania settlement in which the University was founded in 1780. Transylvania was the first college west of the Allegheny Mountains and the sixteenth in the nation. The University established the first schools of medicine and law in what was then the West and educated the doctors, lawyers, ministers and political leaders who helped shape our young nation. Transylvania also founded the first college literary magazine in the West, *The Transylvanian*, still published by students today. Transylvania continues as a pioneer in higher education, preparing leaders in business, government, education, the sciences and the arts. While professors engage in research, they never lose sight of their primary role—being great teachers. With their dedication to students, it is not surprising that Transylvania faculty members have dominated Kentucky Professor of the Year awards, winning six times in the last nine years. Students work closely with professors in small classes, many with fewer than 10 students. Transylvania students are an active and involved group, and they benefit from a ton of opportunities for learning outside the classroom and off-campus. Transylvania has over sixty active student organizations—ranging from the Karate Club to the Anthropology Club, there is something for everyone here. Over two thirds of students study abroad and many participate in internships, research projects and volunteer activities. Transylvania is located in Lexington, a city of 270,000 and a growing center of business, culture, research and education. Known as the horse capital of the world, Lexington is surrounded by the rolling green pastures of the famous Bluegrass region of central Kentucky. Transylvania's parklike campus is just a 5-minute walk from downtown, with easy access to restaurants, shops and entertainment. Being so close to the downtown area makes it easy for students to take on part-time jobs and internship opportunities in law offices, financial firms, hospitals, non-profits and other organizations. Transylvania offers its students a shuttle service between the Transylvania library and the University of Kentucky libraries, and the main branch of the Lexington Public Library is only a few blocks from campus. Lexington is only 80 miles

CONTACT INFORMATION

Mr. Bradley Goan, Director of Admissions

☎ 859-233-4242 or toll-free 800-872-6798

✉ admissions@transy.edu

away from both Louisville and Cincinnati.

- **Enrollment:** *1,092*
- **Selectivity:** *very difficult*
- **Test scores:** *ACT—over 18, 100%; SAT—critical reading over 500, 83%; SAT—math over 500, 86%*
- **Application deadline:** *2/1 (freshmen), rolling (transfer)*
- **Expenses:** *Tuition $25,280; Room & Board $7770*

The average class size at Transylvania is 17 and many courses are taught in a discussion based format. This relaxed dialogue allows for many classes to meet in comfortable, non-traditional settings.

LOYOLA
UNIVERSITY
NEW ORLEANS

NEW ORLEANS, LOUISIANA

www.loyno.edu/

Students in between classes outside the new William H. Hannon Library.

Founded by the Jesuits in 1912, Loyola University's more than 35,000 graduates have excelled in professional fields for over ninety years. Loyola undergrads enjoy the individual attention of a caring faculty in a university dedicated to creating community and encouraging individualism while educating the whole person intellectually, spiritually, socially and athletically. Loyola's 20-acre main campus and 4-acre Broadway campus are located in the historic area of New Orleans. The University's modern residence halls are equipped with computer labs, kitchen, laundry and study facilities. The Joseph A. Danna Center houses six food venues, including the Orleans Room, Flambeaux's, Fresh Market, Smoothie King and Satchmo's, Loyola's own jazz hall. Nationally affiliated fraternities and sororities are among Loyola's more than 120 student organizations. During the fall's Organizational Fair, students can join the 2006 Pacemaker Award–winning newspaper, the Loyola University Community Action Program (a volunteer community service organization, the largest

LOUISIANA

organization on campus) or one of the many special interest groups. Students can also sign up for one of Loyola's club sports such as cheerleading, crew, cycling, dance, golf, swimming volleyball, lacrosse, rugby and soccer. Loyola participates in the National Association of Intercollegiate Athletics (NAIA) in men's baseball, basketball, cross-country and track and in women's basketball, cross-country and volleyball. The University Sports Complex offers six multipurpose courts, an elevated running track, an Olympic-size swimming pool, weight rooms, and aerobics and combat-sports facilities. The Career Development Center offers career counseling and testing, assistance with choosing a course of study, recommendations about graduate and professional school and help in landing internships and jobs. The College of Music and Fine Arts hosts the Thelonious Monk Institute

The world is our blackboard.

of Jazz Performance. The College of Social Sciences houses a School of Mass Communication that offers award winning programs in advertising, journalism and public relations. Loyola's main campus fronts St. Charles Avenue in uptown New Orleans. Its red-brick buildings overlook Audubon Park, home of the famous Audubon Zoo. The downtown area is a 20-minute streetcar ride away, where students take advantage of the city's cultural and artistic environment. Considering that New Orleans enjoys an average temperature of 70 degrees, students can enjoy year-round outdoor activities in a city famous for

its food, music and festivals. Lake Pontchartrain is within the city limits and provides facilities for water sports.

- **Enrollment:** *4,714*
- **Selectivity:** *moderately difficult*
- **Test scores:** *ACT—over 18, 100%; SAT—critical reading over 500, 97.9%; SAT—math over 500, 94.5%*
- **Application deadline:** *Rolling (freshmen), rolling (transfer)*
- **Expenses:** *Tuition $31,504; Room & Board $10,388*

http://bit.ly/collvid52

CONTACT INFORMATION

Mr. Keith E Gramling, Director, Admissions

☎ 504-865-3240 or toll-free 800-4-LOYOLA

✉ admit@loyno.edu

Activities like Chaos Day create strong communities in residence halls.

CALVIN
College

GRAND RAPIDS, MICHIGAN
www.calvin.edu/

Calvin College values both intellect and faith and this is seen in every area of campus life, from the classroom to service-learning opportunities to life in the residence halls. Calvin is one of the nation's largest and most respected Christian colleges. Calvin maintains a strong affiliation with the Christian Reformed Church, and students from more than fifty other church denominations across North America and around the world choose Calvin for its unique curriculum and faith-based mission. At Calvin, students are challenged not only to prepare for a career but also to live lives of commitment and service. Calvin's Service-Learning Center encourages students to get involved in programs such as big brothers/big sisters, services for the elderly and school tutoring. Career Development guides students from their first year through their last, helping them prep for interviews, land internships and search for full-time employment after graduation. A wide variety of clubs and events keep students busy including music, theater, athletics, art, culture, service and campus ministries. Calvin is an NCAA Division III school and participates in the Michigan Intercollegiate Athletic Association. The men's basketball team won the national championship in 2000; the women's cross-country team took second place honors in 2008. In 2000, 2003, 2004 and 2007, the men's cross-country team won the national championship. And the men's ice-hockey club won the 2004 ACHA DIII national championship. The 400-acre campus is a modern, well-planned community. High-speed computing is available throughout the campus and wireless service is offered in the residence halls. Calvin's new $55-million athletic complex features a 5,000-seat arena, an indoor track and tennis center, a health center and an aquatics center with a 50-meter by 25-yard pool. Calvin's outdoor sites include baseball and softball diamonds, a premier soccer field with seating for 1,500 and two practice fields, an eight-lane track, a six-court tennis facility, a paved jogging path and two sand volleyball courts. Calvin's wooded campus, which includes a 100-acre ecosystem preserve, is located in the suburbs of Grand Rapids. Hundreds of restaurants, dozens of theaters, seven shopping malls and a bunch of museums and parks are within a short drive. Lake Michigan beaches, ski areas, parks and trails are just a 40-minute drive away. Cultural and community activities take place weekly on the Calvin campus, on the campuses of six other local colleges and at DeVos Hall and VanAndel Arena in downtown Grand Rapids.

CONTACT INFORMATION

Mr. Dale Kuiper, Director of Admissions and Financial Aid

☎ 616-526-6106 or toll-free 800-688-0122

✉ admissions@calvin.edu

- **Enrollment:** *4,092*

- **Selectivity:** *moderately difficult*

- **Test scores:** *ACT—over 18, 98.9%; SAT—critical reading over 500, 82.6%; SAT—math over 500, 89%*

- **Application deadline:** *8/15 (freshmen), rolling (transfer)*

- **Expenses:** *Tuition $24,035; Room & Board $8275*

Students do research with professors in the sciences and the humanities each summer.

HILLSDALE COLLEGE

PURSUING TRUTH · DEFENDING LIBERTY SINCE 1844

HILLSDALE, MICHIGAN

www.hillsdale.edu/

Founded in 1844, Hillsdale College is a liberal arts institution of approximately 1,350 that operates independently of government aid and is located on a picturesque campus in southern Michigan.

Hillsdale College is a private college that values its academic excellence and its independence. In fact, Hillsdale does not accept any federal or state taxpayer subsidies. Students here can pick from a number of majors leading to a Bachelor of Arts or Bachelor of Science degree and an impressive 98 percent of Hillsdale students are employed or attending graduate school with six months of graduation. Hillsdale students live in dorms, fraternity and sorority houses and in off-campus apartments. Recent campus upgrades include a new music hall, a new dorm, the newly built Grewcock Student

Union and renovations to the Strosacker Science Center. Hillsdale's Charger athletes compete in eleven intercollegiate NCAA Division II varsity sports as part of the Great Lakes Intercollegiate Athletic Conference (GLIAC). In the past 20 years, the College has produced 180 athletic and academic All-Americans, 24 conference champions and seventeen teams that have finished tenth or better nationally. Men's teams are baseball, basketball, cross country, football and track. Women's teams are basketball, cross country, softball, swimming, track and volleyball. An active intramural program is also available. Four national fraternities, three national sororities and more than seventy other social, academic, spiritual and service organizations provide Hillsdale students with a ton of cocurricular opportunities. A resident drama troupe and dance company, a bagpipe and drum corps, a concert choir, and chamber chorale, a jazz program with big band and combos, instrumental

chamber ensembles from string quartets to percussion ensemble and a College-community orchestra and band round out the College's performing arts organizations. Special student services provided by the College include career planning and placement counseling, academic advising and tutoring and a health service staffed by a physician and a resident nurse. Hillsdale College is surrounded by the hills, dales and lakes of south-central Michigan. The College is close to Detroit, Chicago, Cleveland, Toledo, Ft. Wayne and Indianapolis.

CONTACT INFORMATION

Mr. Jeffrey S. Lantis, Director of Admissions

☎ 517-607-2327
📠 admissions@hillsdale.edu

Stores, churches, restaurants and movie theaters are all within walking distance of the campus.

- **Enrollment:** *1,316*
- **Selectivity:** *very difficult*
- **Test scores:** *ACT—over 18, 100%; SAT—critical reading over 500, 100%; SAT—math over 500, 96%*
- **Application deadline:** *2/15 (freshmen), 2/15 (transfer)*
- **Expenses:** *Tuition $20,500; Room & Board $7990*

Bright, ambitious Hillsdale College students benefit from a vibrant student life with activities that are the catalyst to lasting friendships and proud achievements.

Hope
College

HOLLAND, MICHIGAN
www.hope.edu/

Hope College's challenging academic program is supported by an accepting campus community. Students from all walks of life are welcomed, respected and given freedom to grow in this exciting environment. Preparation for a career and for life in general involves both classroom and extracurricular activities. Hope offers eighty different majors leading to the Bachelor of Arts, Bachelor of Music, Bachelor of Science or Bachelor of Science in Nursing degree. Activities include student publications, musical groups and political organizations. Students manage an FM radio station, and their cable TV shows are broadcast weekly to the Holland community. There are four major theater productions each year as well as a film series, a Great Performance Series and lectures by well-known speakers.

With over 80 student organizations, strong winning division three athletic programs, a fun variety of intramural sports, and downtown Holland just blocks away, there is a lot going on at Hope!

f www.facebook.com/find.colleges

Many Christian groups come together on campus, including the Crossroads Project, Fellowship of Christian Athletes and Intervarsity Christian Fellowship. Chapel services are offered Monday, Wednesday and Friday (plus an extended service on Sunday evening)—although voluntary, all services are well attended. The Hope College Flying Dutchmen participate in NCAA Division III sports. Varsity teams for men include baseball, basketball, cross-country, football, golf, soccer, swimming, tennis and track and varsity teams for women include basketball, cross-country, golf, soccer, softball, swimming, tennis, track and volleyball. Club sports offered are lacrosse, ice hockey, sailing, men's volleyball and Ultimate Frisbee. Most students live on campus in corridor, cluster, suite, coed and single-sex residence halls. In addition, upperclass students can opt to live in one of fifteen apartment buildings or sixty-two cottages on or near the campus. Students and alumni both head to the Career Services Center for help with everything from assessing interests to arranging job interviews. Hope College's 77-acre wooded campus sits in a residential area two blocks from the central business district of Holland, Michigan. The town is only a 30-minute drive from Grand Rapids and a 2-hour drive from Chicago and Detroit. An 85-acre biological field station is located on the shores of Lake Michigan, 5 miles from the campus. Holland has long been known as a summer resort area, but it is also a fine spot for winter sports.

CONTACT INFORMATION

Hope College Admissions

☎ 616-395-7850 or toll-free 800-968-7850

✉ admissions@hope.edu

- **Enrollment:** *3,230*
- **Selectivity:** *moderately difficult*
- **Test scores:** *ACT—over 18, 99.6%; SAT—critical reading over 500, 83.1%; SAT—math over 500, 85.9%*
- **Application deadline:** *Rolling (freshmen), rolling (transfer)*
- **Expenses:** *Tuition $26,510; Room & Board $8110*

Faculty members teach all courses, and Hope's professors are genuinely interested in supporting their students to succeed.

Kettering University students working in our state-of-the-art Crash Safety Center with mechanical engineering Professor Janet Brelin-Fornari.

KETTERING UNIVERSITY

FLINT, MICHIGAN
www.kettering.edu/

Kettering University is a private university specializing in technical degrees. Most classes have fewer than 20 students and are taught by Ph.D.-level professors, not teaching assistants. This combination of small class size and highly qualified teaching staff guarantees a much more personalized learning experience. Kettering is a highly acclaimed university with the one of the country's most modern cooperative education programs. During study terms, students learn material in small, intense classes taught by University professors. During co-op terms, students work as paid professionals at businesses and organizations related to their major. Kettering co-op students have done everything from testing ballistic systems for the U.S.

government to reengineering crowd management at Disney World. Kettering has the only co-op program of its kind where students begin working as early as their freshman year. By graduation from Kettering, students have up to 2½ years of professional experience and an impressive resume. Kettering students usually graduate with job offers or graduate school acceptances in hand. Kettering also offers Master of Science degree programs in engineering, engineering management, information technology, manufacturing management, manufacturing operations, and operations management, in addition to an M.B.A. program. Kettering students also bring a wide range of hobbies and interests to campus. Kettering offers more than fifty student organizations, including fraternities and sororities, student government and competitive intramural sports. Recreation facilities include athletic fields, tennis courts, and a recreation center with an Olympic-size, six-lane pool; aerobics rooms; a full

Kettering University students hard at work at their co-op positions for Plex Systems, Inc.

line of Nautilus equipment; and basketball, tennis and racquetball courts. A public golf course sits next to the campus. Kettering University is located in Flint, which is 60 miles west of Lake Huron and 60 miles north of Detroit. Flint's Cultural Center, which is only 10 minutes from campus, includes the Alfred P. Sloan Museum, the Whiting Auditorium (home of the Flint Symphony and host to leading shows and entertainers), the Robert T. Longway Planetarium (Michigan's largest and best-equipped sky show facility), the Flint Institute of Arts, the F. A. Bower Theater, the Dort Institute of Music, Mott Community College and the Flint Public Library. Nearby is the University of

Michigan–Flint campus. Within a few minutes' drive of campus are skiing spots, lakes, public golf courses, indoor and outdoor skating rinks and a ton of shops and restaurants.

- **Enrollment:** *2,410*

- **Selectivity:** *very difficult*

- **Test scores:** *ACT—over 18, 99.74%; SAT—critical reading over 500, 85.49%; SAT—math over 500, 96.77%*

- **Application deadline:** *Rolling (freshmen), rolling (transfer)*

- **Expenses:** *Tuition $29,120; Room & Board $6390*

CONTACT INFORMATION

Mrs. Shari Luck, Director of Admissions

☎ 810-762-7865 or toll-free 800-955-4464 Ext. 7865 (in-state)
800-955-4464 (out-of-state)
✉ admissions@kettering.edu

Lawrence Technological University's A. Alfred Taubman Student Services Center is an innovative 42,000-square-foot "living laboratory."

LAWRENCE TECHNOLOGICAL UNIVERSITY

SOUTHFIELD, MICHIGAN
www.ltu.edu/

Lawrence Technological University is a premier private university offering over 100 undergraduate and graduate degrees in architecture and design, arts and sciences, engineering and management. The University's Leadership Program, integrated into all the bachelor's degree programs, helps students gain critical thinking, teamwork and communication skills. An honors program is available to highly qualified students, as well as Quest, which encourages students to explore their interests on a deeper level. Lawrence Tech is known for cutting-edge technology, small class sizes and a commitment to theory and practice. The 102-acre campus features state-of-the-art learning facilities including the Technology and Learning Center (opened in 2001) as well as the Student Services Center and the Center for Innovative Materials Research (both opened in 2006). And always at the forefront, Lawrence Tech was Michigan's first college or university to go completely wireless. Outside of class, a number of fraternities, sororities and social and professional organizations sponsor a variety of activities during the year. Recreational facilities include the Don Ridler Field House, which features a fitness track, gym, racquetball courts, game room, saunas and a weight and conditioning room. Intramural and club sports in badminton, basketball, billiards, curling, flag football, golf, hockey, racquetball, soccer, softball, table tennis, tennis, volleyball, and wallyball are active throughout the academic year. Southfield is a dynamic suburb that provides a nice balance between big-city entertainment opportunities and a quiet residential atmosphere. Lawrence Tech's campus is about a 30-minute drive north of downtown Detroit. Within a few miles of the campus, students can head to restaurants, parks, shopping areas and recreational facilities. Research, manufacturing, scientific and business industries are also nearby, making it easy for students to land co-ops and internships. More than 200 Fortune 500 companies have headquarters or business operations in the Detroit metropolitan area.

CONTACT INFORMATION

Jane Rohrback, Director of Admissions

☎ 248-204-3160 or toll-free 800-225-5588
🖳 admissions@ltu.edu

- **Enrollment:** *4,518*
- **Selectivity:** *moderately difficult*
- **Test scores:** *ACT—over 18, 92%*
- **Application deadline:** *8/15 (freshmen), 8/15 (transfer)*
- **Expenses:** *Tuition $23,008; Room & Board $9353*

Lawrence Technological University's small class sizes ensure individual attention, and all classes, lectures, and labs are taught by faculty with current industry experience.

WESTERN MICHIGAN UNIVERSITY

KALAMAZOO, MICHIGAN
www.wmich.edu/

Feeling of community—
With 230 degree programs, WMU attracts students from across the United States and 90 other nations who come to live and study together in the classic college town setting of the University's Kalamazoo campus.

Western Michigan University (WMU) is one of the country's top public universities and is recognized for its outstanding programs in aviation, fine arts, communications and business marketing. WMU is also home to Lee Honors College, which has been in continuous operation longer than almost any other honors program in the country.

WMU is one of only 101 public universities in the United States to have a chapter of Phi Beta Kappa, the nation's premier honor society. In addition, *U.S. News & World Report* has ranked WMU among America's top 100 public universities for the past eleven years. WMU is a large university with a broad range of programs at both the undergraduate and graduate levels. But at the same time, WMU is one of the most affordable of Michigan's fifteen public universities—ranking tenth from the

MICHIGAN

top in tuition and fees. WMU has seven degree-granting colleges: Arts and Sciences, Aviation, the Haworth College of Business, Education and Human Development, Engineering and Applied Sciences, Fine Arts and Health and Human Services. Students choose from 237 academic programs, 140 of them at the undergraduate level. WMU also offers twenty-nine doctoral programs. The Haenicke Institute for Global Education has study-abroad programs all over the world. There are nearly 300 student organizations, including Greek, academic and professional organizations. The University fields sixteen varsity teams at the NCAA Division I level. Kalamazoo is an ideal college town, where business leaders recognize Western as their second-largest employer and where students and employees contribute more than $500 million annually to the local economy. Located just 40 miles from the eastern shoreline of Lake Michigan, the area has cool, sunny summers and moderate winters. Outdoor recreation is unlimited, from skiing in winter to water sports in spring. Fall is a great time to hike or bike on the Kal-Haven trail that connects Kalamazoo to the Lake Michigan resort town of South Haven. And Kalamazoo always has something going on. On a typical Saturday afternoon, faculty members rub elbows with students at the Art Hop, Blues Festival or Taste of Kalamazoo. Kalamazoo also offers professional baseball, hockey, and soccer; music, from jazz to heavy metal; coffee houses and comedy clubs; and dining, from fast food to international cuisine. West Michigan is home to businesses and Fortune 500 companies including Haworth Inc., the Whirlpool Corporation and the Kellogg Company where many WMU students intern.

CONTACT INFORMATION

Mrs. Penny Bundy, Director, Office of Admissions and Orientation

☎ 269-387-2000
✉ ask-wmu@wmich.edu

- **Enrollment:** *24,576*

- **Selectivity:** *moderately difficult*

- **Test scores:** *ACT—over 18, 90.51%*

- **Application deadline:** *Rolling (freshmen), 8/1 (transfer)*

- **Expenses:** *Tuition $8382; Room & Board $7784*

A good fit—*WMU's campus continues to nurture its "just right" feel by blending a century of traditional architecture with new state-of-the art instructional facilities like this health and human services classroom building.*

Carleton College

NORTHFIELD, MINNESOTA
www.carleton.edu/

Students hang out, study, and toss Frisbees on the Bald Spot. In the winter, Carleton provides two ice rinks on the Bald Spot for ice skating, hockey, and broomball.

Take charge of your education and your life at Carleton College. Here, it's all about choice. Students choose from thirty-seven different majors and fifteen concentrations or they can work with an adviser to design their own major. Most first-year students opt to take a first-year seminar and most upperclass students do at least some independent study in their major. Still more students take advantage of internship and work experience. Carleton students also take part in over 100 organizations, clubs and other activities, ranging from the Quiz Bowl team (which won the nationals in 2007) and the improvisational comedy troupe (Cujokra) to Ultimate Frisbee (Carleton's women's team won the national intercollegiate championship in 2000, and the men's team won in 2001) and one of the top Model United Nations teams in the country. Musicians can play in the orchestra or smaller ensembles or sing in the choir, the Carleton Singers, or join one of six a cappella groups. Athletes participate in ten NCAA Division III varsity sports for men or eleven for women, eighteen competitive club teams or any of fifteen intramural sports. In the classroom and on the campus, Carleton students remain active and engaged—which explains the 96 percent of freshmen who choose to return for their sophomore year. And the campus is ever-changing and growing. Construction is underway on a new Arts Union building (opening in 2011-2012) that will feature high-tech classrooms and teaching and learning spaces for students of cinema and media studies, theatre and dance. The town of Northfield is about 35 miles from the Minneapolis–St. Paul International Airport and

40 miles from the downtown Twin Cities. Once a small, rural community, Northfield is also the home of St. Olaf College and several multi-national businesses and a number of its residents now commute to the Twin Cities. Most of the buildings in down-town Northfield look much as they did at the turn of the century. Carleton College students head off campus to take a walk along the revital-ized riverbank and hit the downtown businesses and shops.

CONTACT INFORMATION

Paul Thiboutot, Vice President and Dean of Admissions and Financial Aid

☎ 507-222-4190 or toll-free 800-995-2275

✉ admissions@carleton.edu

- **Enrollment:** *2,009*
- **Selectivity:** *very difficult*
- **Test scores:** *ACT—over 18, 100%; SAT—critical reading over 500, 99.73%; SAT—math over 500, 99.46%*
- **Application deadline:** *1/15 (freshmen), 3/31 (transfer)*
- **Expenses:** *Tuition $41,304; Room & Board $10,806*

Carleton boasts a 9:1 student-faculty ratio. In fact, 66 percent of Carleton class sections have fewer than 20 students.

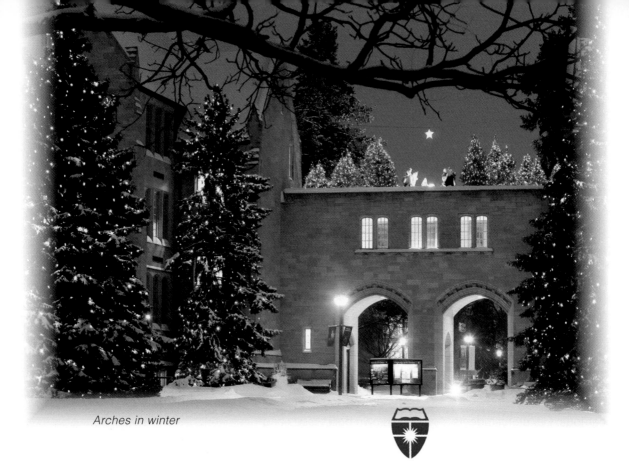

Arches in winter

UNIVERSITY *of* ST. THOMAS

MINNESOTA

ST. PAUL, MINNESOTA
www.stthomas.edu/

The University of St. Thomas is a Catholic, liberal arts school that provides a career-oriented education. As Minnesota's largest independent college or university, St. Thomas offers a number of degrees through its seven academic divisions. St. Thomas has undergraduate and graduate seminaries and its Center for Catholic Studies is home to the nation's oldest and largest undergrad program in Catholic studies. St. Thomas offers ninety-six majors and five bachelor's degrees. At the graduate level, St. Thomas has forty-three master's degree programs, two education specialist programs, one Juris Doctor and four doctorates. And the entrepreneurship programs at St. Thomas' Opus College of Business are ranked among the top 50 in the nation, according to *Entrepreneur* magazine. Murray-Herrick

Campus Center, the center of student life, has a bookstore, several comfy lounges and Scooter's—a popular spot to eat a slice, shoot some pool or watch the news on flat-screen TVs. More than 100 clubs and groups come alive on campus. Students produce a multimedia news portal, tommiemedia.com; the *Aquinas* yearbook; a literary magazine, *Summit Avenue Review*; and on-campus television and radio programs. St. Thomas has an extensive intramural sports program, too, and is home to eleven men's and eleven women's varsity teams that compete at the NCAA Division III level. The brand-new (fall 2010) Anderson Athletic and Recreation Complex will feature a 2,000-seat basketball and volleyball arena; an aquatic center with an eight-lane, 25-meter swimming pool and diving area; and a field house with a 200-meter track. The west wing will include a fitness center, weight room and aerobic rooms. The historic Chapel of St. Thomas Aquinas houses the magnificent 2,787-pipe

Gabriel Kney organ. St. Thomas' main campus is located in St. Paul along the Mississippi River. The 78-acre campus is only minutes from Minnesota's Twin Cities— St. Paul and Minneapolis. Its three-block downtown Minneapolis campus is home to the University's business law, psychology and education divisions. The Bernardi Campus in Rome, Italy, is located on the Tiber River. St. Paul has been called a "Most Livable City" and is the home of the acclaimed Ordway Music Center for the Performing Arts and the Science Museum of Minnesota. Minneapolis, the "City of Lakes," has the renowned Guthrie Theater, Walker Art Center and Nicollet Mall. The cities also have a ton of lakes, professional sports teams and top companies such as 3M, Best Buy, General Mills and Medtronic.

- **Enrollment:** *10,851*
- **Selectivity:** *moderately difficult*

Tommie Pride

- **Test scores:** *ACT—over 18, 100%; SAT—critical reading over 500, 84%; SAT—math over 500, 84%*
- **Application deadline:** *Rolling (freshmen), rolling (transfer)*
- **Expenses:** *Tuition $29,467; Room & Board $8042*

http://bit.ly/collvid71

CONTACT INFORMATION
Ms. Marla Friederichs,
Associate Vice President of
Enrollment Management

☎ 651-962-6150 or toll-free
800-328-6819 Ext. 26150
✉ admissions@stthomas.edu

LINDENWOOD

Lindenwood University's thriving main campus in historic St. Charles, Missouri, is home away from home to nearly 4,000 residential students each year.

LINDENWOOD UNIVERSITY

ST. CHARLES, MISSOURI
www.lindenwood.edu/

An independent teaching university founded in 1827, Lindenwood University (LU) is the oldest university west of the Missouri River. Lindenwood is a dynamic liberal arts school that offers more than eighty undergraduate programs as well as master's programs and Education Specialist and Doctor of Education degrees. The University's athletic teams compete in the Heart of America Athletic Conference and the National Association of Intercollegiate Athletics (NAIA). Over the last eight years, the Lindenwood Lions have won forty national championships. All students have access to the Robert F. Hyland Performance Arena, Harlen C. Hunter Stadium, baseball and softball fields and a new eight-lane all-weather track. Students looking for a little less competition and a little more fun join in a number of intramural sports at the University's Fitness Center—wiffleball, powderpuff football and volleyball to name a few. The University radio station, 35,000-watt KCLC-FM, and LUTV, Lindenwood's new television station, are both staffed by students. Students living on campus choose from residence halls, houses and apartment-style living. Six new residence halls have opened since 2000. In fact, expansion is taking place all across the campus. Harmon Hall will reopen in 2010–11 to offer state-of-the-art facilities to students in the School of Business and Entrepreneurship. And the University broke ground in May 2010 for a new student center. This building will have a dining hall, three basketball courts, a suspended jogging track, rec rooms, comfortable lounge areas to study and relax and a workout facility. The 500-acre campus is located in St. Charles, a city of about 55,000 people, about 20 miles from downtown St. Louis. Resting on the banks of the Missouri River,

just south of the Mississippi, St. Charles is the site of Missouri's first state capital. Lindenwood's proximity to a major city means that students only have to drive a short distance to enjoy theme parks, a zoo, professional sporting events, Broadway plays and theater, state parks and lakes. St. Louis–Lambert International Airport is located just 5 miles from Lindenwood University.

- **Enrollment:** *10,413*
- **Selectivity:** *moderately difficult*
- **Test scores:** *ACT—over 18, 98%; SAT—critical reading over 500, 56%; SAT—math over 500, 57%*
- **Application deadline:** *Rolling (freshmen), rolling (transfer)*
- **Expenses:** *Tuition $13,600; Room & Board $7210*

CONTACT INFORMATION

Mr. Joseph Parisi, Dean of Undergraduate Day Admissions

☎ 636-949-4949
✉ jparisi@lindenwood.edu

http://bit.ly/collvid50

Stephens College students become career-ready women of distinction connected through a supportive network of alumnae.

STEPHENS COLLEGE

COLUMBIA, MISSOURI
www.stephens.edu/

Students from around the world come to Stephens College to share their talents, interests and backgrounds. Founded in 1833, Stephens is the nation's second-oldest women's college and repeatedly appears on The *Princeton Review's* list of the best colleges in the country (listed one of the Best in the Midwest, 2009, and seventh on the list of best college theater programs in the nation). Stephens students can choose from more than fifty majors and minors—or design their own major. They can also opt for cooperative programs or pre-professional study in law, medicine and veterinary medicine. Graduate programs include the master of Business Administration, Master in Strategic Leadership and Master of Education (in Counseling and in Curriculum & Instruction) as well as post-graduate studies in counseling. The study abroad program at Stephens is nothing short of amazing—students can live and learn in places like Korea, Ecuador, Sweden and Ireland. Student athletes participate in intercollegiate sports in the American Midwest Conference (AMC) and NAIA. They compete in basketball, cross country, softball, tennis and volleyball. Many students gain leadership experience through the many clubs and organizations on campus—everything from the Seven Star Film Club to the College Democrats. Stephens' residence halls are a focal point of campus activity. The Honors House Plan offers a living/learning environment in the humanities to a select group of freshmen each year. Some buildings have hardwood floors and elevators, others have balconies and cozy lounges—and they all host a ton of events each semester. Stephens College is located in Columbia, Missouri. Situated halfway between Kansas City and St. Louis, Columbia is the cultural, medical and business center of mid-Missouri. Often called "College Town, USA," Columbia is also the home of Columbia College and the University of Missouri. Stephens students have easy access to Columbia's shopping, dining and entertainment areas. And *Money* magazine has consistently named Columbia one of the country's best cities in which to live.

CONTACT INFORMATION

Mr. Chris Collier, Interim Dean of Enrollment Management

☎ 573-876-7207 or toll-free 800-876-7207

🖥 apply@stephens.edu

- **Enrollment:** *1,238*
- **Selectivity:** *moderately difficult*
- **Test scores:** *SAT—critical reading over 500, 81%; SAT— math over 500, 53%*
- **Expenses:** *Tuition $25,400; Room & Board $7170*

One of Stephens' residence halls is a pet-friendly community where students live with their furry, feathery and scaly companions.

Truman's 16:1 student to faculty ratio allows students to get to know their professors and peers.

TRUMAN
STATE UNIVERSITY

KIRKSVILLE, MISSOURI
www.truman.edu/

Truman has gained a national reputation for offering a high-quality undergraduate education at a competitive price. For the thirteenth consecutive year, *U.S. News & World Report* has ranked Truman as the number one public institution in the Midwest offering bachelor's and master's degrees. In addition, Truman is ranked in the top fifty best values in higher education by The Princeton Review's 2010 edition of *America's Best Value Colleges*. A commitment to student achievement and learning is at the core of everything Truman does—and Truman students achieve at remarkable levels. The 2009 freshman class had an average GPA of 3.75 on a 4.0 scale. Undergraduate research is another important part of the Truman experience. Each year, about 1,200 students work side by side with

MISSOURI

professors on University research projects and these students then present the results of their research at the annual Student Research Conference. Selected students can travel to the National Undergraduate Research Symposium to present their research findings. With more than 250 clubs and organizations open to students—service, Greek, honorary, professional, religious, social, political and recreational—Truman students have unlimited opportunities to get involved. Truman's Student Activities Board schedules special events; comedians such as Demetri Martin and Jen Kober and musicians such as Cake, Dashboard Confessional and Regina Spektor have all made recent appearances on campus. Truman is located in Kirksville in the northeast corner of Missouri. The town square, located within walking distance of the Truman campus, provides a connection to Kirksville's past. A multiplex movie theater is located on the town square as are gift,

Purple Pride is evident at one of the many home football games.

book and clothing stores. Several restaurants offer a wide selection of American and international cuisine. The Kirksville Aquatic Center is a great place to have fun and stay in shape. It houses a six-lane indoor swimming pool that is perfect for swimming, relaxing or playing a game of water-basketball. The outdoor pool is designed with a zero-depth entry, a 1-meter diving board and four 25-yard outdoor lap lanes as well as a 20-foot water slide. The northeast region of Missouri is also home to Thousand Hills State Park. A 3,252-acre state park and 573-acre lake for camping, hiking, biking, fishing, swimming, boating and waterskiing is located

within 10 minutes of the Truman campus.

- **Enrollment:** *5,747*
- **Selectivity:** *moderately difficult*
- **Test scores:** *ACT—over 18, 99.85%; SAT—critical reading over 500, 87.86%; SAT—math over 500, 87.86%*
- **Application deadline:** *Rolling (freshmen), rolling (transfer)*
- **Expenses:** *Tuition $6692; Room & Board $6854*

http://bit.ly/collvid64

CONTACT INFORMATION

Melody Chambers, Director of Admissions

☎ 660-785-4114 or toll-free 800-892-7792

✉ admissions@truman.edu

BEREA, OHIO
www.bw.edu/

Baldwin-Wallace College is committed to the success of its students. In addition to their liberal arts classes, students jump into internships, faculty-directed research and service-learning programs. Undergrads can choose from fifty different majors and graduate students can take programs in business and education. And Baldwin-Wallace has helped working adults for more than fifty years to develop skills, change careers and better their lives through convenient evening and weekend classes. In all, Baldwin-Wallace College provides a unique place to study and prepare for future success. In fact, more than 90 percent of Baldwin-Wallace graduates find employment or enter graduate or professional school within nine months of graduation. Recent Baldwin-Wallace graduates have been accepted at some of the best graduate schools in the world, including Carnegie Mellon, Case Western

Involvement in campus life and co-curricular activities is just as important to your education as classes, papers and field experiences. B-W is a friendly, active social community.

Reserve, Cornell, Eastman School of Music, Harvard, Johns Hopkins, Rice, William and Mary and the Universities of Michigan and Virginia. Baldwin-Wallace students work hard and play even harder. Athletes participate in twenty-one varsity sports at the NCAA Division III level. Men and women compete in basketball, cross country, golf, indoor/outdoor track and field, soccer, swimming and diving and tennis. Men also have baseball, football and wrestling teams and women also have softball and volleyball teams. All students have access to the newly renovated Lou Higgins Center, which has multipurpose courts, a track, a six-lane pool with diving board and moveable pool bottom, updated workout spaces and a state-of-the-art athletic training facility. Or students can join one of more than 100 clubs and organizations on campus—from BuzzTV (a half-hour TV show students produce and air on local cable) to the Hepcat Society of Swing Dance, there is really something for everyone here. B-W students do enjoy the best of both worlds. Berea, Ohio, is a quiet and classic college town but students are only 20 minutes from the heart of Cleveland, which is home to Fortune 500 companies as well as out-standing museums and galleries, professional sporting events, a world-class orchestra, an exciting nightlife and an extensive park system.

CONTACT INFORMATION

Patricia Skrha, Director of Undergraduate Admission

☎ 440-826-2222 or toll-free 877-BWAPPLY

✉ admission@bw.edu

- **Enrollment:** *4,397*
- **Selectivity:** *moderately difficult*
- **Test scores:** *ACT—over 18, 93.96%; SAT—critical reading over 500, 71.07%; SAT—math over 500, 71.19%*
- **Application deadline:** *3/1 (freshmen), 8/1 (transfer)*
- **Expenses:** *Tuition $24,230; Room & Board $7960*

B-W has a great location—a suburban, tree-lined campus that is located just minutes away from downtown Cleveland and the cultural, recreational and entertainment opportunities of a major metropolitan area.

In additional to classes in their major and professional programs, undergraduate students at Capital receive a strong foundation in the liberal arts.

Capital University
Ask. Think. Lead.

COLUMBUS, OHIO
www.capital.edu/

Students at Capital University are part of the "CAP Family," a family that cares about the growth and well-being of each of its members. Five schools make up The College at Capital University: the Conservatory of Music and School of Communication; the School of Humanities; the School of Management and Leadership; the School of Natural Sciences, Nursing, and Health; and the School of Social Sciences and Education. In addition to the sixty majors and forty minors for undergrads, graduate students can earn master's degrees in business, music education and nursing, as well as the Juris Doctor and four other advanced degrees from Capital University Law School. The university also offers working adults an opportunity to balance their lives and their goals as they complete undergraduate degrees through the Center for Lifelong Learning. Students live on campus in comfortable suite-style housing and apartments. Students enjoy wireless Internet access and cable TV in their rooms and Saylor-Ackermann Hall even has its own café where students can grab a Starbucks or snack. There are more than seventy student organizations for students to join and lead: musical groups, pre-professional groups, theater, the student newspaper, fraternities/sororities and the debate team to name a few. There is an active and powerful student government on the Capital campus, too. Capital's sports teams are members of the NCAA Division III. Men compete in baseball, basketball, cross-country, football, golf, soccer, tennis and track. Women's varsity sports are basketball, cross-country, golf, soccer, softball, tennis, track, and volleyball. Intramural sports are also a big part of campus

life. From bowling to sand volleyball and cornhole to co-ed dodgeball, Capital students know how to have fun. As the fifteenth-largest city in the country and part of a major metropolitan area, Columbus offers a lot to do and see. Students can enjoy performances by BalletMet, Opera Columbus or the Columbus Jazz Orchestra, or they can visit the more than fifty art galleries in the area. They can watch a game, too: the Columbus Crew (Major League Soccer), the Columbus Blue Jackets (National Hockey League) and the Columbus Clippers (AAA franchise of the Cleveland Indians) all play in nearby stadiums. For outdoor buffs, there are a ton of parks and recreation facilities, bike trails and the Columbus Zoo. And Columbus is the home of many national and international companies that offer Capital students unlimited opportunities for internships and employment after graduation.

CONTACT INFORMATION

Ms. Amanda Steiner, Director of Admission

☎ 614-236-6574 or toll-free 800-289-6289

✉ asteiner@capital.edu

- **Enrollment:** *3,540*
- **Selectivity:** *moderately difficult*
- **Test scores:** *ACT—over 18, 96%; SAT—critical reading over 500, 72%; SAT—math over 500, 70%*
- **Application deadline:** *5/1 (freshmen), rolling (transfer)*
- **Expenses:** *Tuition $28,480; Room & Board $7510*

Crusader spirit is a team effort at Capital, whether you're a varsity athlete or a cheering fan.

Class at the Cleveland Museum of Art

CASE WESTERN RESERVE
U N I V E R S I T Y ___ EST. 1826

CLEVELAND, OHIO
www.case.edu/

Ranking consistently among the top private universities in the United States, Case Western Reserve University offers unlimited opportunities for motivated students. Its faculty members challenge and support students, and its partnerships with world-class cultural, educational and scientific institutions guarantee that undergraduate education goes beyond the classroom. Co-ops, internships and study abroad bring theory to life in amazing settings, and nearly every student completes some research or independent study. Although Case Western Reserve was formed in 1967 by the merger of Western Reserve University and Case Institute of Technology, it traces its roots back to the 1826 founding of Western Reserve College—this makes Case both a young university and one of the oldest private colleges in the nation. Undergrads are enrolled in programs in engineering, science, management, nursing, the arts, the humanities and the social and behavioral sciences. Students attend Case's graduate and professional schools in applied social sciences, dental medicine, graduate studies, law, management, medicine and nursing. Several undergraduate programs and majors combine undergraduate and graduate and professional degrees and resources. Examples are five-year B.A./M.A. or B.S./M.S. degrees, including a five-year B.S./M.S. degree in engineering and management, and dual admission to undergraduate and professional school. And collaborations with neighboring cultural and healthcare institutions enable the University to provide special opportunities in other fields—for example, a student can learn art history both in the classroom and in the world-renowned Cleveland Museum of Art. Greek life (sixteen national fraternities and seven sororities) is big here; about 30 percent of undergrads join. Through its NCAA Division III sports, Case has won championships in cross-country, football, softball, track and field and wrestling. Twenty percent of undergraduates wear the blue-and-white varsity uniform, and an amazing 70 percent join an intramural team. Club sports include fencing, golf, ice hockey, skiing and Ultimate (Frisbee). Case is located in University Circle, a unique cultural district with 550 acres of parks, gardens, museums, schools, hospitals, churches and human service institutions. The Cleveland Museum of Art, the Cleveland Museum of Natural History, and Severance Hall (home of the Cleveland Orchestra) are within walking distance; downtown Cleveland is 10 minutes away by car or public transportation. Students get free access to many local attractions, including the Rock and Roll Hall of Fame and Museum.

Campus walk

- **Enrollment:** *9,738*

- **Selectivity:** *very difficult*

- **Test scores:** *ACT—over 18, 100%; SAT—critical reading over 500, 95.1%; SAT—math over 500, 98.8%*

- **Application deadline:** *1/15 (freshmen), 5/15 (transfer)*

- **Expenses:** *Tuition $36,238; Room & Board $10,890*

CONTACT INFORMATION

Mr. Robert McCullough, Director of Undergraduate Admission

☎ 216-368-4450
✉ admission@case.edu

For over 80 years, the Cleveland Institute of Music has been a magnet for talented young musicians who want to study with celebrated professionals, hone their skills, and prepare to take their place on stage.

Cleveland Institute of Music

CLEVELAND, OHIO
www.cim.edu/

The mission of the Cleveland Institute of Music (CIM) is to provide talented students from around the world an outstanding, professional education in the art of music performance and related musical disciplines. The Institute also provides training for gifted precollege musicians and serves as a resource for the community by offering training for people of all ages and abilities. And CIM is committed to continually bringing in new technologies and new methods into the classroom from world-class computer technology to state-of-the-art recording equipment. CIM maintains small class sizes, too. In admitting the optimum number of students to each performance area rather than an unlimited number, CIM maximizes the performance experiences of its students so that they are well prepared to meet the challenges of professional life. The achievements of the Cleveland Institute of Music's alumni throughout the world really show the Institute's commitment to high quality and professionalism. The distinguished-artist faculty includes the principals and other section players of The Cleveland Orchestra. And all college courses are taught by members of the CIM faculty—not by teaching assistants. CIM students live in Cutter House, the Institute's residence hall, which is located to the school's main building. Each room is connected to the computer network operated by Case Western Reserve University (CWRU), whose campus borders CIM. Aside from its undergrad majors and minors, the Cleveland Institute of Music offers the following graduate degrees and diplomas: Master of Music, Doctor of Musical Arts, Artist Diploma and Professional Studies. CIM is located in University Circle, a cultural, educational, and scientific center about 4 miles east of downtown Cleveland. The 500-acre complex includes museums, libraries, concert halls, colleges and universities, hospitals, gardens, churches and temples. Located within easy walking distance of CIM are Case Western Reserve University, with which CIM cooperates in the Joint Music Program, and Severance Hall, the restored home of The Cleveland Orchestra, whose rehearsals are open to CIM students by special arrangement. Students can also visit the Cleveland Museum of Art, the Cleveland Institute of Art, the Cleveland Play House, the Cleveland Museum of Natural History, the Western Reserve Historical Society, the Crawford Auto-Aviation Museum and the Cleveland Botanical Garden.

CONTACT INFORMATION

Mr. William Fay, Director of Admission

☎ 216-795-3107

🖳 cimadmission@po.cwru.edu

Vocal students at CIM receive intensive training in art song and opera. Private lessons are augmented by weekly classes in which students perform and develop their presentation skills.

Nestled in the hills of western Cincinnati, Ohio, the beauty of the Mount's campus is enjoyed from several vantage points. The Mater Dei Chapel is a focal point of the center of campus, known as the Quad.

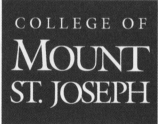

COLLEGE OF
MOUNT
ST. JOSEPH

CINCINNATI, OHIO
www.msj.edu/

The College of Mount St. Joseph offers more than fifty academic programs, a faculty known for high standards of excellence and innovation and an active campus life. Small class sizes and individual attention, as well as opportunities for leadership and service learning, contribute to a positive college experience and student success. The Mount is a private, Catholic college that emphasizes values, integrity and social responsibility. Specialized services are also part of a Mount education. These include renewable scholarships, financial aid, cooperative education, multicultural programs, a state-of-the-art Wellness Center and child care services for students with children. A new Success Coaching program provides first-year students with guidance from a staff member trained to help them address first-year challenges and achieve their goals. A wireless network enables students to e-mail faculty members, check grades, complete research and register for classes anytime, from anywhere. Comfortable, open rooms are available in the newly renovated Seton Center Residence Hall, with some offering private bedrooms, private bathrooms and a shared living area for studying and hanging out. The close-knit campus community is part of a living and learning environment that encourages and nurtures the personal and academic growth of each student. There are more than thirty clubs and organizations at the College including student government, the student newspaper, academic honor societies, environmental clubs, social clubs, symphonic and community concert bands, jazz and percussion ensembles, chorale groups, theater/drama clubs, political clubs and intramural sports. Events and activities include Homecoming, spring break service trips, Exam Jam and Little Sibs

Weekend. The Mount Lions compete in twenty-two varsity sports at the NCAA Division III level as a member of the Heartland Collegiate Athletic Conference. Women's teams are basketball, cheerleading, cross-country, dance, golf, lacrosse, soccer, softball, tennis, track and field and volleyball. Men's teams are baseball, basketball, cross-country, football, golf, lacrosse, soccer, tennis, track and field, volleyball and wrestling. Students at the Mount ranked the College higher than their peers at similar institutions did, according to the nationwide 2008 Noel Levitz Student Satisfaction Inventory. And the College is consistently ranked among the top Midwest regional universities for quality and value by *U.S. News & World Report* in its guide to *America's Best Colleges*. Located 15 minutes from downtown Cincinnati, the College sits on a 92-acre suburban campus overlooking the Ohio River. Greater Cincinnati has a number of parks, museums, theaters, professional sports

CONTACT INFORMATION

Peggy Minnich, Director of Admission

☎ 513-244-4531 or toll-free 800-654-9314

✉ admissions@mail.msj.edu

arenas, shopping areas and restaurants.

- **Enrollment:** *2,324*
- **Selectivity:** *moderately difficult*
- **Test scores:** *ACT—over 18, 90%; SAT—critical reading over 500, 44%; SAT—math over 500, 43%*
- **Application deadline:** *8/15 (freshmen), 8/1 (transfer)*
- **Expenses:** *Tuition $22,800; Room & Board $7000*

A student-to-faculty ratio of 12:1 is a great environment for learning, interacting with classmates and receiving extra support from the professor.

Music is big at Denison—from bluegrass to classical. A standing ovation greeted the concert choir and orchestra after their performance of Handel's Messiah. Those rehearsals in Swasey Chapel paid off.

DENISON

DENISON UNIVERSITY

GRANVILLE, OHIO
www.denison.edu/

Denison University (DU) is a private, liberal arts college that provides a top-notch education while preparing students for lives of leadership and service. About 40 percent of Denison students take part in at least one of the University's summer internship programs by the time they graduate. And more than half of Denison's graduates enroll in graduate or professional schools within ten years of graduation. Denison students are consistent finalists for a number of postgraduate awards, including the Rhodes and Marshal scholarships. The University has had 11 National Science Foundation Fellows, 11 Goldwater Science scholars, 2 Truman Scholars, 1 Udall Fellow, 1 Charles B. Rangel International Affairs Fellowship and 49 Fulbright Scholarship winners in the last seventeen years. Historic Cleveland Hall, built in 1904, has been completely renovated and renamed Bryant Arts Center. It houses the studio art and art history departments and offers state-of-the-art facilities for ceramics, painting, printmaking, photography and digital media. The Burton D. Morgan Center, completed in 2003, houses high-tech classrooms and seminar spaces as well as the Career Development Center and it links to the new underground parking garage beneath the Campus Common. Other newer buildings are the F. W. Olin Science Hall, Mitchell Recreation and Athletics Center, McPhail Center for Environmental Studies and eight suite-style residence halls. Denison has twenty-three varsity sports teams that participate at the NCAA Division III level. The Mitchell Recreation and Athletics Center and the Physical Education Center has a six-lane, 200-meter indoor track; four state-of-the-art indoor tennis courts; a strength room; a modern fitness room with top-of-the-line equipment; a large multipurpose and aerobics room; and international squash courts. The Physical Education Center is home to the Alumni Memorial Field House with its recreational track and three hardwood basketball/volleyball courts; Livingston Gym,

home of varsity basketball and volleyball with seating for 3,000; Gregory Pool, a six-lane, 25-yard competition and recreation facility; and five racquetball/handball courts. DU's varsity teams have won a record eleven North Coast Athletic Conference All-Sports titles and captured 104 conference championships since 1984, the founding year of the Conference. The 900-acre Denison campus is located on a ridge overlooking the village of Granville, in central Ohio. Students provide about 18,000 hours of volunteer work in the area each year. Columbus, the state capital and sixteenth largest U.S. city, is just 27 miles west. State parks, lakes, bike trails and ski areas are all nearby.

Hot soup from Slayter Snack Bar. Football on the quad. A stroll down Chapel Walk to East Quad. It's all part of fall at Denison. Stop by and see us. You'll find a great place to learn—and have fun.

CONTACT INFORMATION

Mr. Perry Robinson, Director of Admissions

☎ 740-587-6276 or toll-free 800-DENISON

✉ admissions@denison.edu

- **Enrollment:** *2,267*

- **Selectivity:** *very difficult*

- **Test scores:** *ACT—over 18, 100%; SAT—critical reading over 500, 99%; SAT—math over 500, 100%*

- **Application deadline:** *1/15 (freshmen), 6/1 (transfer)*

- **Expenses:** *Tuition $36,560; Room & Board $8930*

JCU's 4-year graduation rates are among the best in Ohio and the United States.

John Carroll
UNIVERSITY

UNIVERSITY HEIGHTS, OHIO
www.jcu.edu/

John Carroll University wants its graduates to make a difference in their careers and in their communities. One of twenty-eight Jesuit colleges and universities in the United States, John Carroll offers degree programs at the undergraduate and graduate levels in fifty-four arts and sciences, business and pre-professional fields. The Graduate School at John Carroll offers Master of Science degree programs in accountancy, biology and mathematics; Master of Arts degree programs in biology, communications management, community counseling, education, English, history, humanities, integrated science, mathematics, nonprofit administration and religious studies; the Master of Education; and Master of Business Administration degree programs. In addition, Economics America (the Cleveland Center for Economic Education), a nonprofit educational organization located on John Carroll's campus, provides advanced course work in economics for educators. The University also owns Thorne Acres, a 30-acre recreational facility near the campus used for fishing, canoeing, retreats and student-group meetings. The campus has seen two major additions since 2003—The Dolan Center for Science and Technology (with an atrium, a 250-seat auditorium and high-tech classrooms) and the Don Shula stadium (home to the Blue Streak football, soccer and track teams). John Carroll offers more than 100 student organizations and clubs including the newspaper, radio station, yearbook, Student Union, fraternities and sororities and Late Night at Carroll. A natatorium, racquetball and tennis courts, two gymnasiums and weight-training and fitness facilities are located in the Student Center. The University's Center for Career Services offers resources for students looking to choose a major or trying to land their first job. Students at John Carroll, in the Jesuit spirit of "making a difference," take advantage of the many opportunities and programs

offered to help improve the local community as well as communities across the country and around the globe. Just 20 minutes from downtown Cleveland, John Carroll is located in the quiet Heights neighborhood; it is surrounded by Shaker Heights, University Heights and Cleveland Heights. Three shopping centers are within walking distance, so restaurants, theaters, banks, department stores, grocery stores and specialty shops are all nearby. Downtown Cleveland offers comedy clubs, world-class shopping, theater at the Cleveland Play House, the Rock and Roll Hall of Fame, the Great Lakes Science Center, Progressive Field (home to the Cleveland Indians), Quicken Loans

CONTACT INFORMATION

Mr. Steven P. Vitatoe, Executive Director of Enrollment

☎ 216-397-4294

✉ svitatoe@jcu.edu

Arena (home to the Cleveland Cavaliers), and Cleveland Browns Stadium.

- **Enrollment:** *3,714*

- **Selectivity:** *moderately difficult*

- **Test scores:** *ACT—over 18, 95.4%; SAT—critical reading over 500, 69.9%; SAT—math over 500, 64.6%*

- **Application deadline:** *2/1 (freshmen), rolling (transfer)*

- **Expenses:** *Tuition $30,250; Room & Board $8750*

http://bit.ly/collvid45

Our campus is beautiful, our culture is high energy.

At Notre Dame College students receive the personal attention they need to succeed.

EST. 1922

NOTRE DAME
C O L L E G E

SOUTH EUCLID, OHIO
www.notredamecollege.edu/

Notre Dame College, a Catholic liberal arts school, welcomes students who want to succeed personally and professionally. The College offers associate, bachelor's and master's degrees in nearly thirty different areas. Outside of class, students join a number of clubs and organizations. The Campus Ministry program promotes the spiritual growth of the Notre Dame College community and helps students who want to get involved in community service, retreats, liturgy and more. The Masquers Drama Club provides performing arts entertainment for the College community and general public. Campus publications include the *Notre Dame News* and *PIVOT*, the literary magazine. Faculty members and students schedule lectures, plays, performances and concerts. Most on-campus events are free, and students may purchase tickets at reduced rates for off-campus performances of the world-famous Cleveland Orchestra, the Cleveland Opera and road shows of Broadway productions at the Palace Theatre, State Theatre and Ohio Theatre at Playhouse Square. Notre Dame College is a member of the National Association of Intercollegiate Athletics (NAIA) and competes in the American Mideast Conference. The College fields twenty-one scholarship athletic teams, including men's and women's varsity basketball, bowling, cross-country, golf, soccer, swimming and diving and track

Peer tutors work with fellow students to improve their course work at Notre Dame College.

and field; men's baseball, football, tennis and wrestling; and women's lacrosse, softball and volleyball. In July 2009, NDC announced that a membership application for NCAA Division II had been approved. Notre Dame began the 2009–10 academic year as a candidacy-year-one institution in the NCAA Division II membership process. The 53-acre campus is located in South Euclid, 25 minutes from downtown Cleveland and only 5 minutes from Legacy Village, Cleveland's lifestyle retail center. The area combines the excitement of a major urban and educational center with the relaxed atmosphere of a suburban setting.

University Circle in Cleveland, a 500-acre complex with a mix of cultural, educational, medical, religious and social service institutions, is easily accessible from the College. Situated on the shores of Lake Erie, Cleveland is the home of the Rock and Roll Hall of Fame and several professional sports teams. Snowy winters give students plenty of opportunities for skiing and tobogganing, and popular ski areas are just a short distance from the city.

CONTACT INFORMATION

Mr. David Armstrong, Dean of Admissions

☎ 216-373-5214 or toll-free 800-632-1680

✉ admissinos@ndc.edu

The Adam Joseph Lewis Center for Environmental Studies is a solar powered building that has earned national acclaim as a showcase for green building technologies and operating systems.

OBERLIN

COLLEGE OF ARTS *&* SCIENCES
CONSERVATORY OF MUSIC

OBERLIN, OHIO
www.oberlin.edu/

Oberlin College is an independent, liberal arts school with two divisions: the College of Arts and Sciences and the Conservatory of Music. Students in both divisions share one campus; they also share residence and dining halls as part of one academic community. Many students take courses in both divisions. Oberlin awards the Bachelor of Arts (B.A.) and the Bachelor of Music (B.Mus.) degrees. In Oberlin's double-degree program, students earn the B.A. and the B.Mus. degrees in a five-year program. Selected master's degrees are offered in the Conservatory. Oberlin made interracial education central to its mission in 1835; by 1900, nearly half of all the black college graduates in the country—128 to be exact—had graduated from Oberlin. This core of Oberlin-educated men and women formed the first black professional class in the country. In 1837, Oberlin became the first consistently coed school in the United States. This legacy continues today in a strong sense of community—one that celebrates differences and recognizes them as opportunities for learning. Today, Oberlin is a community of thinkers, scholars, scientists, musicians, athletes, activists and artists—all looking to make the world a better place. As *The New York Times* noted in an article marking Oberlin's 150th anniversary, "In its century and a half, while Harvard worried about the classics and Yale about God, Oberlin worried about the state of America and the world beyond." More Oberlin graduates have gone on to earn Ph.D.'s than at any other American college. Its alumni, who include 3 Nobel laureates and 7 MacArthur "Genius" award recipients, are leaders in law, scientific research, medicine, the arts, theology, communications, business and government. Oberlin offers a small-town atmosphere and is located

35 miles from Cleveland. Students are never bored here. More than 500 concerts and recitals take place on campus every year, from ticketed events like the Cleveland Orchestra to free student and faculty recitals. Each year, the Conservatory stages two operas, and the theater and dance programs present more than fifty productions. Numerous lectures and readings feature famous guests. Over 140 student organizations are active, from the Bike Co-op to the Forensic Team. The College is located in the center of town, close to the business district, and virtually everything a student needs is within walking or biking distance.

CONTACT INFORMATION

Ms. Debra Chermonte, Dean of Admissions and Financial Aid

☎ 440-775-8411 or toll-free 800-622-OBIE

✉ college.admissions@oberlin .edu

- **Enrollment:** *2,919*
- **Selectivity:** *very difficult*
- **Test scores:** *ACT—over 18, 100%; SAT—critical reading over 500, 98%; SAT—math over 500, 98%*
- **Application deadline:** *1/15 (freshmen), 3/15 (transfer)*
- **Expenses:** *Tuition $40,004; Room & Board $10,480*

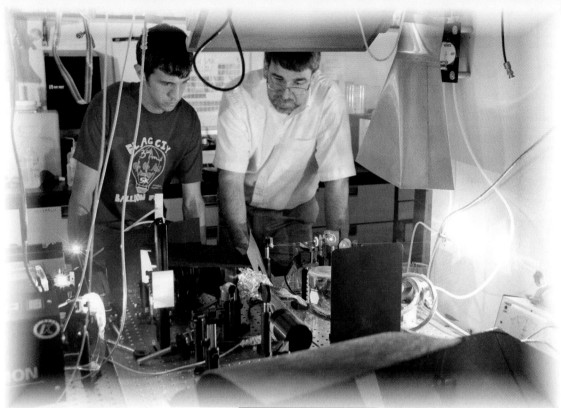

Faculty and students participate in research in state-of-the-art facilities.

OHIO NORTHERN UNIVERSITY

ADA, OHIO

www.onu.edu/

Ohio Northern University (ONU) is a selective, comprehensive school and one of the few private universities to offer nationally ranked liberal arts and professional programs in its five colleges: Arts & Sciences, Business Administration, Engineering, Pharmacy and Law. The University's motto—*Ex diversitate* vires, which means "out of diversity, strength"—illustrates ONU's mission to provide experiences and programs that prepare graduates to live in a world that embraces difference. Ohio Northern is a student-centered, service-oriented, values-based university. Education is a collaborative process at Ohio Northern. Students work side-by-side with faculty members. The result is serious research and meaningful learning experiences that extend to both sides of the classroom. Students can choose from a variety of campus activities including nearly 200 student organizations, four national sororities and six national fraternities, music and theatre and intramural and club sports. There are ten residence halls on campus as well as seven campus apartment complexes and an Affinity Housing complex, which usually houses juniors and seniors. The University participates in NCAA Division III athletics and is a member of the Ohio Athletic Conference. The eleven men's teams are baseball, basketball, cross-country, football, golf, soccer, swimming and diving, tennis, indoor/outdoor track and wrestling. Women compete in basketball, cross-country, fast-pitch softball, golf, soccer, swimming and diving,

tennis, indoor/outdoor track and volleyball. Ohio Northern is strongly committed to creating an environmentally friendly campus. The use of geothermal technology to heat and cool recently built or renovated buildings is the most recent example of this commitment. The campus of Ohio Northern University is located on 342 beautiful acres in the friendly, rural village of Ada. Located in northwestern Ohio, ONU is not far from Columbus, Dayton, Toledo and Fort Wayne, Indiana. And family and visitors can stay at Ohio Northern University's own hotel right on campus. The Inn at Ohio Northern University offers seventy deluxe guest rooms, a beautiful courtyard area, a

CONTACT INFORMATION

Ms. Deborah Miller, Director of Admission

☎ 419-772-2260 Ext. 2464 or toll-free 888-408-4ONU

⌨ admissions-ug@onu.edu

comfortable pub and large meeting spaces—all within walking distance to the Freed Center (performing arts), Presser Recital Hall, Elzay Gallery of Art and the ONU Dial-Roberson Stadium (home of ONU football).

- **Enrollment:** *3,651*
- **Selectivity:** *moderately difficult*
- **Test scores:** *ACT—over 18, 99%; SAT—critical reading over 500, 78%; SAT—math over 500, 92%*
- **Application deadline:** *8/15 (freshmen), 9/1 (transfer)*
- **Expenses:** *Tuition $31,866; Room & Board $8280*

Ohio Northern is a private, comprehensive University that blends nationally-ranked arts, sciences and professional programs.

Students celebrate the end of a successful academic year at OWU's annual Day on the JAY activities.

Ohio Wesleyan University

DELAWARE, OHIO

www.owu.edu/

A unique blend of liberal arts learning, pre-professional preparation, internships, research opportunities, study-travel and study abroad sets Ohio Wesleyan University (OWU) apart. The University is committed to educating for leadership and service, to combining theory and practice and to prepping students to succeed in a global community. Housing options include modern residence halls; small living units (SLUs), such as the Creative Arts House, the Modern Foreign Languages House, and the Peace and Justice House; and fraternity houses. Ohio Wesleyan has long been committed to education for a global society. In fact, OWU has the highest percentage of international students among undergraduate, bachelor's degree-granting colleges in the state of Ohio and the fourteenth-highest percentage among similar colleges in the United States. And OWU stands out when it comes to service. The University sends as many as ten mission teams throughout the world each year. Students here publish the nation's oldest independent student newspaper. They also participate in cultural- and ethnic-interest groups such as the Student Union on Black Awareness (SUBA), the College Republicans and College Democrats and prelaw and premed clubs. Every year, the University puts on more than 100 concerts, plays, dance programs, films, exhibits and speakers. The Department of Theatre & Dance stages four major productions each year, while the Music Department sponsors four large performance groups. OWU is home to twenty-two Division III varsity athletic teams—eleven for men and eleven for women. In 2009, the University won the North Coast Athletic Conference (NACA) All-Sports Trophy for the third consecutive year and the ninth time overall. In fall 2010, Ohio Wesleyan is scheduled to open the Meek Aquatics and Recreation Center, which will feature a ten-lane pool, 1- and 3-meter diving boards and a 13-foot-deep diving well. The entire building and pool

is to be heated and cooled by ninety geothermal wells. Intramural and club sports programs are extensive, and all students have access to racquet sports and weight-lifting facilities in the Branch Rickey Physical Education Center. Fitness equipment and health services are housed in the 7,000-square-foot Health and Wellness Center. Off-campus, students go backpacking, boating, camping, golfing, skiing and swimming. Delaware combines the small-town pace and maple-lined streets of the county seat with easy access to Columbus, the sixteenth-largest city in America. Thirty minutes south of the campus,

CONTACT INFORMATION

Ms. Carol DelPropost, Assistant Vice President of Admission and Financial Aid

☎ 740-368-3059 or toll-free 800-922-8953

✉ cjdelpro@owu.edu

Columbus provides rich internship opportunities, international research centers, fine dining and shopping, and an exciting nightlife.

- **Enrollment:** *1,893*
- **Selectivity:** *very difficult*
- **Test scores:** *ACT—over 18, 98.2%; SAT—critical reading over 500, 85.66%; SAT—math over 500, 83.03%*
- **Application deadline:** *3/1 (freshmen), 6/1 (transfer)*
- **Expenses:** *Tuition $35,030; Room & Board $9224*

THE UNIVERSITY OF FINDLAY

FINDLAY, OHIO
www.findlay.edu/

Findlay ranks in the top tier of U.S. News & World Report's "America's Best Colleges in the Midwest" and has been named a "Best Midwesten College" by the Princeton Review *for the past four years.*

The University of Findlay (UF) is a private university that focuses on liberal arts and career education. Bachelor's degree programs are available in nearly sixty different majors. Master's degrees are offered in athletic training; business administration; education; environmental, safety, and health management; occupational therapy; physician assistant studies; teaching English to speakers of other languages (TESOL) and bilingual education. A Doctor of Pharmacy (Pharm.D.) degree program graduated its first class in 2010 and a Doctor of Physical Therapy program will graduate its first students in 2011. Majors in the sciences and health professions include athletic training, chemistry, computer science, equestrian studies (English, Western and equine management), nuclear medicine, occupational therapy, physical therapy, premedicine and animal science/pre-veterinary medicine. Opportunities for internships and work-related experiences are available in most major fields. Social life at Findlay centers on a variety of clubs and organizations: fraternities and sororities, the newspaper, musical groups, a radio and TV station and Circle K. The varsity teams at UF are affiliated with NCAA Division II and the Great Lakes Intercollegiate Athletic Conference, with the exception of the equestrian teams, which have won national championships in the Intercollegiate Horse Show Association. Findlay offers twelve intercollegiate sports for men: baseball, basketball, cross-country, equestrian, football, golf, indoor track and field, outdoor track and field, soccer, swimming and diving, tennis and wrestling. Women compete in basketball, cross-country, equestrian, golf, indoor track and field, outdoor track and field, soccer, softball, swimming and diving, tennis and volleyball. The Koehler Recreation and Fitness Complex has a six-lane, NCAA-regulation track; sand pits for long jump; state-of-the-art timing system; wrestling room; and four multipurpose courts. Also under the same roof are a cardio center, and as of

Be active! Findlay offers 60 student organizations and intercollegiate, club and intramural sports, allowing you to learn leadership and interpersonal skills outside the classroom.

August 2010, a student rec center with basketball, volleyball and tennis courts; a rock climbing wall; and a game room. Findlay was voted the most livable micropolitan city in Ohio and scored among the top twelve in the United States. It is within easy driving distance of Toledo, Columbus and Detroit. The Findlay campus consists of more than 385 acres on several sites. A campus-owned farm houses the pre-veterinary medicine and Western equestrian studies programs, including a 31,000-square-foot animal science center dedicated in 2009 with 50-seat classrooms, a laboratory, a pharmacy, a student lounge, demonstration areas and holding pens.

A second facility houses the English riding program. Approximately 450 horses are stabled and trained at the equestrian facilities, which offer barns and indoor and outdoor riding arenas.

- **Enrollment:** *4,278*
- **Selectivity:** *moderately difficult*
- **Test scores:** *SAT—critical reading over 500, 67.9%; SAT—math over 500, 65.7%*
- **Application deadline:** *Rolling (freshmen), rolling (transfer)*
- **Expenses:** *Tuition $25,774; Room & Board $8554*

CONTACT INFORMATION

Mr. Donna Gruber, Director of Undergraduate Admissions

☎ 419-434-4540 or toll-free 800-548-0932

🖵 admissions@findlay.edu

THE UNIVERSITY of TULSA

TULSA, OKLAHOMA
www.utulsa.edu/

The University of Tulsa (TU) is a private, liberal arts university that gives students highly personalized study in engineering, natural sciences, business, health professions, the humanities and fine and performing arts. TU has three undergraduate colleges: the Henry Kendall College of Arts and Sciences, the Collins College

Bayless Plaza on the University of Tulsa Campus

of Business and the College of Engineering and Natural Sciences. Students can customize their combination of majors, minors, concentrations within majors and certificate programs—or even design their own major. Long regarded for programs that include accounting; petroleum, mechanical and chemical engineering; English; environmental law; MIS; and psychology, TU is also emerging as a leader in computer science and information security. TU was the first institution selected by the National Science Foundation for the Federal Cyber Service Initiative (Cyber Corps). And based on academic reputation and other factors, *U.S. News & World Report* ranks TU 83rd among doctoral/research universities in the United States. The University participates in NCAA Division I sports. The Tulsa Hurricanes compete in men's and women's basketball, cross country, golf, soccer, tennis and track and field. Men also play football and women have teams in rowing, softball and volleyball. The 34-acre sports and recreation complex features a student fitness facility, competition-grade tennis

 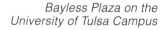

complex, NCAA soccer and softball fields, multiuse recreational fields and an NCAA track and field. TU offers 160 campus-based organizations, including intramural sports, special interest clubs, pre-professional organizations, fraternities and sororities and campus ministry groups. Students can choose to live in traditional residence halls, suite-style halls, premium student apartments and special living communities. The University of Tulsa features a residential campus in midtown Tulsa. Tulsa's main industries include energy, telecommunications and data, finance, medicine, aerospace, transportation and education—all of which open the door to internship and work opportunities for TU students and graduates. *Newsweek* has named Tulsa one of ten "New Frontier" technology cities, and the *New York Times* called Tulsa "a new economy hotbed." Tulsa is known for hosting a ton of cultural festivals such as Jazzfest, Mayfest and Oktoberfest. Professional sports in Tulsa include baseball, basketball, golf, hockey, arena football and horse racing. The extensive River Parks development, 3 miles from campus, is where students go to jog and bike and it even has an outdoor floating amphitheater.

- **Enrollment:** *4,192*
- **Selectivity:** *very difficult*
- **Test scores:** *ACT—over 18, 100%; SAT—critical reading over 500, 89%; SAT—math over 500, 90%*

CONTACT INFORMATION

Mr. Earl Johnson, Dean of Admission

☎ 918-631-2307 or toll-free 800-331-3050

✉ admission@utulsa.edu

- **Application deadline:** *Rolling (freshmen), rolling (transfer)*
- **Expenses:** *Tuition $25,144; Room & Board $8544*

H.A. Chapman Stadium on the campus of the University of Tulsa

Music in the Quad

NASHVILLE, TENNESSEE
www.belmont.edu/

Nationally recognized liberal arts programs come alive on the Belmont University campus, which is located in the state capital of Nashville, known as Music City, U.S.A. and the Athens of the South (for its many colleges and universities). Belmont is the second-largest of Tennessee's private colleges and universities and its goal is to be a leader among teaching universities. Working to make that happen are faculty members who believe that premier teaching is interactive, technology-supported, motivational, creative and exciting. And these efforts have not gone unnoticed—in fact, Belmont was recently named one of two "Schools to Watch" in the nation by *U.S. News & World Report*. In addition to a number of bachelor's degrees, Belmont University offers twelve graduate degrees: the Master of Accountancy, the Master of Arts in Teaching, the Master of Business Administration, the Master of Sport Administration, the Master of English, the Master of Music, the Master of Education, the Master of Science in Nursing, the Master of Science in Occupational Therapy, the Doctor of Occupational Therapy, the

Doctor of Pharmacy and the Doctor of Physical Therapy. The Belmont Bruins participate in varsity sports at the NCAA Division I level. Men and women compete in basketball, cross country, golf, soccer, tennis and track and field. Men also compete in baseball and women also have softball and volleyball teams. And Belmont has top-notch facilities to go with their top-ranked sports. The Curb Event Center, which opened in 2003, has 5,000 seats in an oval configuration, three full-size basketball courts with maple hardwood floors and three suites. The Center has played host to the CMT Video Music Awards since 2006. Belmont's beautiful campus reflects a long, rich history that dates back to the nineteenth century, when the grounds were Adelicia Acklen's Belle Monte estate. University buildings that were erected over the past 110 years surround the Italianate mansion, which is still used by the campus. On the way to classes that prep them for the twenty-first century, students walk by historic Victorian gardens, statuary and gazebos. With a metropolitan area of roughly a million residents, Nashville is a cultural, educational, healthcare, commercial and financial center in the mid-South. The city's location halfway between the northern and southern United States makes it accessible to students from across the country.

CONTACT INFORMATION

Dean of Enrollment Services

☎ 615-460-6785 or toll-free 800-56E-NROL

✉ buadmission@belmont.edu

- **Enrollment:** *5,424*
- **Selectivity:** *moderately difficult*
- **Test scores:** *ACT—over 18, 100%; SAT—critical reading over 500, 92%; SAT—math over 500, 88%*
- **Application deadline:** *8/1 (freshmen), 8/1 (transfer)*
- **Expenses:** *Tuition $22,360; Room & Board $10,000*

http://bit.ly/collvid29

In the Belmont recording studio

Carson-Newman: A Christ-centered liberal arts college focused on Academic Excellence and Christian Commitment.

CARSON-NEWMAN
COLLEGE

JEFFERSON CITY, TENNESSEE
www.cn.edu/

Founded in 1851, Carson-Newman (C-N) is the oldest coed college in Tennessee. The College offers sixty-two majors (including a new Film major) leading to four undergraduate degrees: Bachelor of Arts, Bachelor of Music, Bachelor of Science and Bachelor of Science in Nursing. Students can also earn graduate degrees in teaching, education, nursing and counseling. And new in 2010 is Carson-Newman's MBA program. Outside of class, C-N students join any of the fifty clubs and organizations on campus including music and drama groups, an award-winning forensics team, ROTC and the Martial Arts Club. The Carson-Newman Eagles compete in sixteen different NCAA Division II varsity sports. Men and women have teams in basketball, cross country, golf, soccer, tennis and track and field. Men also play baseball and football and women also field teams in softball and volleyball. Even more students get involved in the College's extensive intramurals program—everything from ping pong and flag football to badminton and "Family Feud." The intramural "champion t-shirt" is one of the most prized possessions on campus. Most students meet friends over at the amazing 96,000-square-foot Maddox Student Activities Center. It has three full gyms, two racquetball courts, an indoor track, two game rooms, a weight room, a gymnastics room, swimming pool, snack bar, Internet lounge and TV lounge. C-N students live in comfortable residence halls or apartments—most built or renovated since 2001—and all with Internet connections and cable TV. And dining on campus just may make students forget about food from back home. Students

can head to Stokely Dining Hall for chocolate chip pecan streusel muffins or throw back wings in the Eagle's Nest Snack Bar. When studying in the library, students grab a hand-roasted coffee or salad in Java City. There is something for every taste on campus. C-N is conveniently located in eastern Tennessee, just 30 miles from Knoxville and 45 miles from Gatlinburg, the gateway to the Great Smoky Mountains. And C-N just added 18.2 acres of land to its campus along Mossy Creek through a generous donation from alumnus

CONTACT INFORMATION

Melanie Redding, Director of Admissions

☎ 865-471-3223 or toll-free 800-678-9061
✉ cnadmiss@cn.edu

Sharon Hayes and her husband David. Shopping, dining and entertainment are all near the College campus.

- **Enrollment:** *2,148*
- **Selectivity:** *moderately difficult*
- **Test scores:** *ACT—over 18, 96%*
- **Application deadline:** *8/1 (freshmen), 8/1 (transfer)*
- **Expenses:** *Tuition $20,562; Room & Board $5918*

Students cheering our football team on to victory. Go Eagles!

As a Christian community, Milligan offers a nurturing environment where students are strengthened and encouraged in their spiritual growth.

MILLIGAN COLLEGE, TENNESSEE
www.milligan.edu/

Milligan College is a private, liberal arts college in northeast Tennessee. From its beginning in 1866, Milligan College has combined academic excellence with a Christian worldview. Students receive specialized training in more than twenty-five majors and in master's degrees in education, occupational therapy and business administration. More than forty clubs and organizations are open to students—everything from Buffalo Ramblers (students who gather to explore the gorges, waterfalls and caves surrounding the campus) to the Photography

Club, from the Jazz Ensemble to the radio station. The campus is high-tech (all campus buildings are networked with fiber optics) and eco-friendly (Milligan's brand-new Wellness Center is LEED-certified). Most students live on campus in modern residence halls and apartments that feature a high-speed data connection to the campus network and the Internet as well as telephone service, voice mail and cable TV. Milligan is well recognized as an NAIA athletic powerhouse with a highly competitive athletic program in twenty varsity sports. In the past ten years, Milligan has won more than fifty conference titles and has made over fifty-seven national tournament appearances. Men's varsity teams include baseball, basketball, cross-country, golf, mountain biking, soccer, swimming, tennis and track and field. Women's varsity teams include basketball, cheerleading, cross-country, golf, mountain biking,

soccer, softball, swimming, tennis, track and field and volleyball. Milligan continues to be named among the top Southern colleges and universities in *U.S. News & World Report*'s *America's Best Colleges* issue. And more than 90 percent of its graduates are employed full-time, attending graduate school or in voluntary service within six months after graduation. Milligan's beautiful 181-acre campus, with its more than twenty buildings of Colonial architecture, is located in the mountains of northeast Tennessee just minutes from the dynamic Tri-Cities region. Students enjoy historical locations, theaters, parks, restaurants and shops; explore the breathtaking Appalachian Mountains by hiking or camping in state parks near the campus; visit local lakes and rivers for swimming and fishing; or ski the nearby North Carolina slopes.

A low student-faculty ratio offers personal attention and class sizes that typically range from 10-15 students.

- **Enrollment:** *1,100*

- **Selectivity:** *moderately difficult*

- **Test scores:** *ACT—over 18, 94%; SAT—critical reading over 500, 66%; SAT—math over 500, 61%*

- **Application deadline:** *8/1 (freshmen), rolling (transfer)*

- **Expenses:** *Tuition $23,460; Room & Board $5650*

CONTACT INFORMATION

Ms. Tracy Brinn, Director of Enrollment Management

☎ 423-461-8730 or toll-free 800-262-8337

✉ admissions@milligan.edu

Union University faculty members excel as leaders in their fields, yet they are committed to teaching, mentoring and the highest levels of Christian scholarship.

UNION UNIVERSITY

JACKSON, TENNESSEE
www.uu.edu/

Union University believes that today's world is in need of great thinkers ready to do great things. That's why this private, liberal arts-based university is committed to prepping a new generation of change agents. Union is proud of its four core values of being excellence driven, Christ centered, people focused and future directed. The University consistently receives national recognition; independent research by *America's 100 Best College Buys* ranks Union among the nation's best for combining academic quality and affordable price. Union University offers a number of bachelor's, master's and doctoral degrees through its six schools and colleges. Union graduates enjoy a high acceptance rate at top graduate and law schools, too.

Nearly 100 percent of faculty-recommended health science students have been accepted to medical school or professional graduate study. On its Jackson campus, the University provides each student with a private bedroom within apartment-style complexes, most of which were built in 2008. The new units have four bedrooms with Internet connection, a kitchen, living room, washer/dryer unit and two bathrooms. A new student commons building has two fireplaces, TV and multipurpose rooms, piano and band practice rooms, two kitchens, a gymnasium, a walking track and outdoor grills and patios. The University coffeehouse is another favorite student hangout for concerts, conversation and study. In all, the campus has seen more than $120 million in new construction in the last ten years. For fun and relaxation, the University has seventy campus clubs, societies, fraternities, sororities and intramural sports such as sand volleyball and team tennis. In addition, students and faculty set aside one day a year to serve the local community though more than fifty different volunteer projects. Union participates in NAIA athletics in men's and women's basketball, cross country and soccer. Mean also compete in baseball and golf and women also compete in cheerleading, softball and volleyball. The 290-acre campus is located in suburban Jackson. Jackson is located 80 miles east of Memphis and 120 miles west of Nashville—and *Forbes* magazine recently named Jackson one of America's top 150 cities for business and careers.

CONTACT INFORMATION

Mr. Robbie Graves, Director of Enrollment Services

☎ 731-661-5590 or toll-free 800-33-UNION

✉ rgraves@uu.edu

- **Enrollment:** *3,922*

- **Selectivity:** *moderately difficult*

- **Test scores:** *ACT—over 18, 98%; SAT—critical reading over 500, 80%; SAT—math over 500, 80%*

- **Application deadline:** *Rolling (freshmen), rolling (transfer)*

- **Expenses:** *Tuition $20,940; Room & Board $6930*

Most of Union University's residence life buildings have been built since 2008 and were designed with student input.

The University Center is the place to be at the University of Memphis. Opened in March 2010, the UC is where our students gather for dining, socializing, studying and organizing student activities.

THE UNIVERSITY OF MEMPHIS.

MEMPHIS, TENNESSEE
www.memphis.edu/

Located on a beautifully landscaped campus in the heart of one of the South's largest and most progressive cities, the University of Memphis (U of M) is the flagship institution of the Tennessee Board of Regents System. The University of Memphis is recognized regionally and nationally for its academic, research and athletic programs. The University offers more than 254 areas of study from which to choose and is spread across a total of 1,160 acres at eight sites. In addition to the main campus, the Park Avenue campus has modern living accommodations for married students, a research park and outstanding varsity athletic training facilities. The University of Memphis also owns the Meeman Biological Field Station, a 623-acre tract used for biological and ecological studies. The Chucalissa Archaeological

Museum in southwest Memphis is often used as a research and training facility for archaeology and anthropology students. The Memphis Tigers participate and win in NCAA Division I sports. Men and women compete in basketball, cross country, golf, rifle, soccer, tennis and track and field. Men also play baseball and football and women also play softball and volleyball. The outstanding facilities include the $3.2 million Larry O. Finch Center with $50,000 worth of weight and cardio equipment and a fully-equipped training room. The Liberty Bowl Memorial Stadium is one of the finest football stadiums in the nation. And the amazing FedExForum, home to the basketball teams, is a $250 million, state-of-the-art arena. It has a 35,000-square-foot outdoor plaza, four full-service restaurants, a massive center hung scoreboard with live video and instant replays and luxury suites. The greater Memphis area has a population of approximately 1.1 million, making it the eighteenth largest in the country. Centrally located on the Mississippi River, Memphis is an active hub for business, agriculture and transportation industries. The city has the Mid-South's largest medical center. Major museum exhibits, sporting events, concerts, art shows, lectures and even barbecue contests take place throughout the year. The AAA baseball team, the Redbirds, and the NBA team, the Grizzlies, both make their homes in Memphis. Memphis provides students with employment and internship opportunities in a variety of fields.

CONTACT INFORMATION

Dr. Brian Meredith, Director of Admissions

☎ 901-678-2111 or toll-free 800-669-2678

✉ bmeredith@memphis.edu

- **Enrollment:** *21,424*
- **Selectivity:** *moderately difficult*
- **Test scores:** *ACT—over 18, 84.5%*
- **Application deadline:** *7/1 (freshmen), 7/1 (transfer)*
- **Expenses:** *Tuition $7058; Room & Board $5950*

More than 21,000 students attend the University of Memphis from 49 states and 99 countries. With more than 160 active student organizations, there is something for everyone.

The Commodore spirit can be seen and felt throughout Vanderbilt's campus—from the seven principals of the Community Creed to deafening "Go 'Dores" chants heard in Memorial Gym.

VANDERBILT
UNIVERSITY

NASHVILLE, TENNESSEE
www.vanderbilt.edu/

In 1873, on the heels of the Civil War, Commodore Cornelius Vanderbilt gave a million dollars to the university that now bears his name, with the hope that it would "contribute to strengthening the ties which should exist between all sections of our common country." Today, Vanderbilt enrolls America's most talented students and challenges them daily to expand their intellectual horizons and to free their imaginations. Vanderbilt's interdisciplinary approach to education lets students take a variety of courses outside of their main focus of study. Vanderbilt is a medium-sized university that includes four undergraduate schools and six graduate and professional schools. Known for its gorgeous 330-acre, national arboretum campus, Vanderbilt provides a

TENNESSEE

variety of housing options for students—traditional dorms, apartments, suites and even the McTyeire International House, designed for students who are interested in foreign languages such as Chinese, French, German, Japanese and Spanish. Vanderbilt students can take their pick of the more than 300 clubs and organizations on campus. From the Momentum Dance Group to the Running Club and from fraternities/sororities to the Culinary Society, Vanderbilt students are never bored. Student athletes compete in the Southeastern Conference. Men and women have varsity teams in basketball, cross country, golf and tennis. Men also have baseball and football teams and women also have bowling, lacrosse, soccer, swimming and track and field teams. Memorial Gymnasium received $25 million in upgrades in 2002—a new practice gym, private suites, a new lighting and sound system and new court design. The Commons

Center includes a new dining area with study space, a post office and an exercise facility. The Sarratt Student Center houses a cinema, pub, art gallery, craft and darkroom facilities, an FM radio station and plenty of meeting space. Facilities at the Student Recreation Center include gymnasiums, an indoor swimming pool, squash and racquetball courts, a rock climbing wall, an indoor suspended track and a weight room. Other recreational facilities include indoor and outdoor tennis courts, baseball and softball diamonds and a sand volleyball court. Vanderbilt University is located in Nashville, the capital of Tennessee. Known as Music City, USA, Nashville has more than 1 million residents. The greater Nashville area is home to two major-league professional sports teams, eighty-one parks and more than 30,000 acres of lakes.

• **Enrollment:** *12,506*

• **Selectivity:** *very difficult*

Vanderbilt's 330-acre campus is known for both its natural beauty and its proximity to Nashville's urban center.

• **Test scores:** *ACT—over 18, 100%; SAT—critical reading over 500, 98.9%; SAT—math over 500, 99.8%*

• **Application deadline:** *1/3 (freshmen), 3/1 (transfer)*

• **Expenses:** *Tuition $38,578; Room & Board $12,650*

http://bit.ly/collvid73

CONTACT INFORMATION

John O. Gaines, Director of Admissions

☎ 615-936-2811 or toll-free 800-288-0432

✉ admissions@vanderbilt.edu

Beloit
College

BELOIT, WISCONSIN
www.beloit.edu/

Beloit College is an independent college of liberal arts and sciences that engages the intelligence, imagination and curiosity of its students. Beloit is Wisconsin's first college, founded in 1846 to serve a frontier society. Today, Beloit students can choose from more than fifty majors, more than thirty minors and a number of dual-degree and preprofessional programs. The range of student activities reflects the students' varied interests. Beloit students manage an annual music festival, host their own radio and cable TV shows and organize movie screenings. In any given week, students attend (or plan) a lecture series, music performances, poetry

In 2008, the National Science Foundation ranked Beloit College 31st among U.S. colleges in producing alumni with science and math Ph.D.'s. Beloit faculty are national leaders in science education.

readings or an environmental debate. Seventy percent of Beloit's students participate in club, intramural or varsity athletics. The Beloit Buccaneers participate in nineteen varsity sports at the NCAA Division III level. Those who live on campus (and most do) choose to live in residence halls, on quiet floors or substance-free floors, in one of three fraternity houses or three sorority houses, or in one of the special-interest houses (for example, languages, gay and lesbian, anthropology, the arts, black student issues, faith and spirituality, music, the environment, peace and justice, science fiction and fantasy, Latino issues and women's issues). Two new townhouse complexes have been constructed in the past five years and they offer roomy, apartment-style living for juniors and seniors. The College's two dining halls serve up food for all tastes—including organic, vegetarian and vegan meals. New students quickly become part of this active environment through First-Year Initiatives (FYI), an innovative program that places new students in interdisciplinary seminars that begin the first day students arrive on campus. Students in this program meet with advisers who assist them in their adjustment to Beloit and encourage them to get involved on campus. Beloit's 40-acre campus is located on the border between Wisconsin and Illinois, 90 miles northwest of Chicago, 50 miles south of Madison and 70 miles southwest of Milwaukee. Students may take advantage of the resources of the three major metropolitan areas, and Beloit's hospital, clinics, manufacturers and service organizations provide a ton of internship, job shadowing and community outreach opportunities. The academic buildings of Beloit College cluster around lawns dotted with ancient North American Indian mounds. A 25-acre athletic field and Strong Memorial Stadium are located a few blocks east of the main campus.

CONTACT INFORMATION

Mr. James S. Zielinski, Director of Admissions

☎ 608-363-2500 or toll-free 800-9-BELOIT

⌨ admiss@beloit.edu

- **Enrollment:** *1,407*
- **Selectivity:** *very difficult*
- **Test scores:** *ACT—over 18, 99.55%; SAT—critical reading over 500, 87.42%; SAT—math over 500, 88.08%*
- **Application deadline:** *1/15 (freshmen), rolling (transfer)*
- **Expenses:** *Tuition $33,368; Room & Board $6830*

International students carry their home country flags in a ceremony that opens the school year. Students from 40 countries give Beloit College's campus an international flavor.

MILWAUKEE SCHOOL OF ENGINEERING

MILWAUKEE, WISCONSIN
www.msoe.edu/

Ambitious students who want personal and professional success find a home at Milwaukee School of Engineering (MSOE). In addition to its undergraduate degree programs in the fields of engineering, architectural engineering and building construction, engineering technology, computers, business, nursing and health-related areas, MSOE offers nine Master of Science degree programs: cardiovascular studies, engineering, engineering management, environmental engineering, marketing and export management, medical informatics (jointly offered with the Medical College of Wisconsin), new product management, perfusion and structural engineering. Graduates begin their careers as work-ready problem solvers and develop into leaders: creating new products, starting or heading companies and working to better their communities. For the past five years, MSOE's average graduate placement rate has been 95 percent. The average starting salary for graduates is more than $53,300. Representatives from hundreds of firms from throughout the country, including Fortune 500 companies, visit MSOE during the year to interview graduating students and

MSOE has long been known for implementing technology into the classroom, as well as for its strong ties with industry and high job-placement rates.

WISCONSIN

discuss career opportunities. Free on-campus tutoring is provided by the Learning Resource Center and Tau Omega Mu, an honorary fraternity. The Student Life and Campus Center houses student activity rooms, a TV viewing area, a market-place eatery and a game room. The Kern Center is a 210,000-square-foot health, wellness, fitness and recreation facility that houses a 1,600-seat ice arena, a fitness center, a 1,200-seat basketball arena, a field house, a running track and a wrestling area. More than seventy professional societies, fraternities, and other special-interest groups welcome new students. MSOE's students also participate in intramural sports—everything from kickball to floor hockey. MSOE is a member of the NCAA Division III and the Northern Athletics Conference (NAC). Men's varsity teams are baseball, basketball, cross-country, golf, ice hockey, indoor/outdoor track and field, lacrosse, rowing, soccer, tennis, volleyball and wrestling. Women compete

MSOE has 22 men's and women's NCAA Division III athletic teams. The Raider intercollegiate programs consistently produce successful teams and quality athletes.

in basketball, cross-country, golf, indoor/outdoor track and field, soccer, softball, tennis and volleyball. MSOE's (and one of Milwaukee's) newest attraction and home to the world's most comprehensive art collection dedicated to the evolution of human work opened in October 2007. The MSOE campus is located in downtown Milwaukee. Nearby are the Bradley Center sports arena, the Midwest Airlines Center, the Marcus Center for the Performing Arts, the theater district, many churches, major hotels, restaurants and department stores. The metropolitan area has more than 15,000 acres

of parks and river parkways and miles of bike trails. A few blocks east of the MSOE campus is Lake Michigan.

- **Enrollment:** *2,648*
- **Selectivity:** *moderately difficult*
- **Test scores:** *ACT—over 18, 100%; SAT—critical reading over 500, 87%*
- **Application deadline:** *Rolling (freshmen), rolling (transfer)*
- **Expenses:** *Tuition $29,520; Room & Board $7431*

CONTACT INFORMATION

Dana-Marie Grennier, Director of Admissions

☎ 414-277-6761 or toll-free 800-332-6763
✉ grennier@msoe.edu

Located on the northwest side of Milwaukee, Mount Mary is home to over 1900 students and sits on 80 gorgeous acres.

Mount Mary College

MILWAUKEE, WISCONSIN
www.mtmary.edu/

Mount Mary College, one of only 65 women's colleges in the nation, is located on a beautiful 80-acre wooded campus only 15 minutes from downtown Milwaukee. Students at Mount Mary are fully engaged in and outside of the classroom, learning not just the subject matter but also how to express opinions and develop leadership skills. Through exciting internships, club activities, community service and campus ministry programs, students explore their interests and discover their skills. Students here choose from more than sixty undergraduate and graduate majors. Caroline Hall, the student residence hall, offers private rooms and suites. Over 90 percent of the rooms feature walk in closets and over two thirds have private bathrooms. Every floor in Caroline Hall has a kitchen, lounge area and a mini-computer lab. All residence hall rooms have wireless computer access and are wired for cable television and telephone service. Mount Mary College encourages students to take advantage of the many on-campus events including performances by comedians, holiday dances and picnics. Mount Mary College is a provisional member of the NCAA Division III. The Blue Angels compete in basketball, cross-country, soccer, softball, tennis and volleyball. Facilities on campus and in the Bloechl Recreation Center, which opened in 2006, include a gymnasium, an indoor swimming pool, outdoor soccer fields and a fitness center. Bordering the campus is the Menomonee River Parkway, ideal for biking, jogging, cross-country skiing and much more. Academic and professional student services are available to all Mount Mary students, including free tutoring and assistance with tests through the Academic Resource Center; advising, resume writing and career planning through the Advising and Career Development Center; and personal counseling through the Counseling Center. Mount Mary College is located in a residential area in northwestern Milwaukee, just 20 minutes from downtown and less than 5 minutes from a major shopping mall. Students can hop on public transportation right in front of the campus. Several other private and public universities call Milwaukee home, making it easy to meet and hang with students from other colleges.

CONTACT INFORMATION

**Mary Ellen Strieter,
Admission Counselor
Assistant/Receptionist**

☎ 414-258-4810 Ext. 219

✉ admiss@mtmary.edu

- **Enrollment:** *1,925*
- **Selectivity:** *moderately difficult*
- **Test scores:** *ACT—over 18, 58%*
- **Application deadline:** *Rolling (freshmen), rolling (transfer)*
- **Expenses:** *Tuition $22,118; Room & Board $7498*

Mount Mary College offers over 60 academic programs including Art Therapy, Art, Interior Design, Fashion, Graphic Design, and many professional fields.

Rowing past St. Norbert College's campus center, the crew team enjoys the quiet of sunrise on the Fox River.

ST. NORBERT COLLEGE

DE PERE, WISCONSIN
www.snc.edu/

High national rankings, a new state-of-the-art library, a new apartment-style residence hall, a brand-new athletics facility and plans for newly remodeled science facilities—these are just a few of the exciting things happening at St. Norbert College. The riverfront campus is part of the thriving corporate, entertainment, educational, arts and cultural environment of northeastern Wisconsin. Learning takes place in residence halls and classrooms, on campus, and, literally, around the world. The St. Norbert learning community helps students becomes critical thinkers, strong writers and effective communicators in a setting that encourages student-faculty research. The graduate-level work done by St. Norbert undergrads, even as freshmen, is surprising and puts them ahead of their peers when heading to graduate school or the workforce. St. Norbert College offers more than forty programs of study, including several preprofessional programs. Students can also design their own major. The study abroad program is a highlight of the St. Norbert experience—with seventy-five program sites in thirty-seven countries on six continents. There are also numerous service opportunities for students locally, nationally and internationally. Each St. Norbert student is paired with an adviser who helps ensure that the student stays on track with classes and graduates in four years. Typically, 95 percent of St. Norbert graduates are employed or attending graduate school within nine months of graduation. With more than sixty-five clubs and organizations on campus—from the boxing club to the improv group—there's no shortage of ways to get involved. Student athletes participate in twenty intercollegiate sports at the NCAA Division III level. The state-of-the-art athletic facilities include the $4.1 million Resch Olympic

Pavilion (completed in 2009), the Schuldes Sports Center with basketball and tennis courts and an indoor track, and the much anticipated Donald J. Schneider Stadium (opening to students and fans for fall 2010). The St. Norbert campus, approximately 93 acres, is located on the banks of the Fox River in De Pere, just minutes south of Green Bay—home to the world-famous Green Bay Packers football team. Located near the gateway to Door County, one of Wisconsin's favorite vacation spots, the campus

CONTACT INFORMATION

Ms. Bridget O'Connor, Vice President for Enrollment Management and Communications

☎ 920-403-3005 or toll-free 800-236-4878

✉ admit@snc.edu

is part of a eighteen-county region of 1.2 million people.

- **Enrollment:** *2,175*
- **Selectivity:** *moderately difficult*
- **Test scores:** *ACT—over 18, 98%*
- **Application deadline:** *Rolling (freshmen), rolling (transfer)*
- **Expenses:** *Tuition $26,972; Room & Board $7052*

Whether they're gathering for bands or movies, to play volleyball or just to socialize, St. Norbert students take some time to relax and have fun at the campus center's riverfront marina.

THE WESTERN REGION OF THE UNITED STATES

Arizona
California
Colorado
Hawaii

Montana
Oregon
Texas

Utah
Washington
Wyoming

GRAND CANYON
UNIVERSITY™

PHOENIX, ARIZONA
www.gcu.edu/

Students looking to earn their degree at a top 10 Christian college often choose Grand Canyon University (GCU). The University offers bachelor's, master's and doctoral degree programs through the Ken Blanchard College of Business, College of Education, College of Nursing and Health Sciences, College of Liberal Arts and College of Fine Arts and Production. GCU's two newest degrees are the Bachelor of Science in Sports Management and the Master of Science in Accounting. With twenty-two NCAA sports and a 5,000-seat events center opening in 2012, the sports management degree is already a popular choice. More than just a four-year education, a degree from

 　　　　ARIZONA

GCU represents a well-rounded education gained through learning hands-on in classes; participating in GCU's "Adopt-a-Block" outreach; becoming mentors; taking part in intercollegiate and intramural sports; and enjoying campuswide social events. For GCU students, their future starts the day they move onto campus. Dorm suites include a furnished living room, a private bathroom and two bedrooms—each equipped with telephone, cable and high-speed wireless Internet. Outside of class, students head to the student center that houses a fitness center, a full-service cafeteria and a gourmet coffee shop (Latte Dah). Students here kick back in big cushy chairs and watch their favorite shows on large-screen plasma TVs. They also enjoy student movie nights on "The Slab," an outdoor area where students soak up Arizona's wonderful weather. From intramural sports to pickup games of Ultimate Frisbee on Mariposa Lawn, GCU students love to stay active. The

GCU Antelopes—"Lopes"—compete in Division II intercollegiate sports in men's and women's basketball, cross country, golf, soccer, swimming and diving, tennis, track and field and volleyball. Men also have baseball, lacrosse and wrestling teams and women also play softball. Beyond the fun, there's faith. GCU students come together at the Gathering (a contemporary evening chapel), at the Grand Celebration (a weekly worship assembly), through GCU's campus and community ministries and on mission trips. Grand Canyon University is located just minutes from downtown

CONTACT INFORMATION

Enrollment

☎ 800-486-7085 or toll-free 800-800-9776

🖥 admissionsonline@gcu.edu

Phoenix, Arizona's state capital and one of the fastest-growing regions in the nation. The greater Phoenix area, known as the "Valley of the Sun" for its more than 300 days of sunshine each year, has a ton of things to do and see including golfing, hiking, biking, horseback riding and water sports. Within a 2-hour drive of GCU's campus is some of the best snow skiing in the Western United States.

UAT's Computer Commons is pictured above. With three research centers and a suite of technology-centered undergraduate and graduate degrees, UAT is a recognized leader in technology education.

TEMPE, ARIZONA
www.uat.edu/

The beginning of the twenty-first century is an exciting time to be in the technology community, and the University of Advancing Technology (UAT) is serious about technology. Students who are looking for a strictly career-oriented technical college experience will not find it here. Because of UAT's dedication to both scholastic excellence and technological innovation, it stands apart as an ideal destination for the geeks of the world who feel disenfranchised by conventional colleges and universities. As technologists, UAT students see that there will always be newer and newer tools created to address mankind's emerging needs and desires. Current subjects of ongoing research at UAT include robotics and embedded systems, artificial life programming, network security and game development. UAT has always devoted its resources to creating an environment where students are challenged to achieve, explore new and traditional concepts and practice what they learn in real-world situations. This combination of research and application creates technically adept graduates who are equally at home in the academic and working worlds and valued by both. UAT graduates land jobs with associate and bachelor's degrees, and many return to pursue a master's degree in the Graduate College of Applied Technology. UAT's students still find plenty of time to time to join clubs and other activities such as ancient games, anime, Yu-Gi-Oh, game developers, Web development, biking, C++ and photography. Special on-campus events include live-action games, Oktoberfest, LAN parties, Guitar Hero tournaments and Thanksgiving dinner. At any time, day or night, there are groups of students pounding

coffee while working on projects, looking to create the next big thing. Students pull all-nighters, exchanging ideas and searching for solutions to perfect their innovations. There are also gatherings of students and instructors engaged in discussions of the latest technology developments and how they can make them better. Located in sunny Tempe, near the heart of downtown Phoenix, the University of Advancing Technology is 4 hours from Mexico and 2 hours from snowboarding. Tempe is located in the "Valley of the Sun", which is surrounded by beautiful mountain ranges. Within a

CONTACT INFORMATION

Admissions Office

☎ 602-383-8228 or toll-free 800-658-5744

✉ admissions@uat.edu

short drive are attractions like the Grand Canyon (4½ hours), a variety of lakes and rivers (30–90 minutes), the red rocks of Sedona (2 hours) and the Sonoran Desert, just outside of town. UAT is close to every desert sport imaginable—golf, mountain biking, hiking, swimming, rollerblading and skateboarding.

- **Enrollment:** *1,142*
- **Application deadline:** *Rolling (freshmen)*
- **Expenses:** *Tuition $18,900; Room & Board $11,034*

A small, private college designed for technophiles and dedicated to a well-rounded education, UAT's average classroom size is 15 students, with a student-to-faculty ratio of 14:1.

For your first year you will be based at CCA's Oakland Campus, a traditional college setting complete with residence halls and well-equipped studios.

CCa

CALIFORNIA COLLEGE OF THE ARTS

SAN FRANCISCO, CALIFORNIA
www.cca.edu/

Students from all over the world come to California College of the Arts (CCA) to push the boundaries of art. This internationally respected college offers degrees in twenty undergraduate and seven graduate majors in fine arts, architecture, design and writing. The College has world-class, eco-friendly facilities at its two campuses in San Francisco and Oakland. In fact, the San Francisco campus has one of the largest solar-heated buildings in Northern California—designated one of the top-10 green buildings nationwide by AIA COTE (American Institute of Architects, Committee on the Environment). CCA alumni have been at the forefront of nearly every major art movement of the past century and its students begin making their mark well before graduation. Students from just about every CCA program participated in the high-profile 2009 Solar Decathlon, winning several awards. A CCA animation student was one of only 12 selected (out of 2,500 applicants) for a Pixar internship in 2008. Alex Beckman (M.F.A. 2010) was nominated for a Primetime Emmy in interactive media for his work on the TV show *Glee*. And one of the College's industrial design students recently signed a contract with Universal Toys to manufacture a toy he first conceived as a class project. For these reasons and more, *BusinessWeek* magazine recently named CCA one of the world's best design schools. Outside the class or design studios, students join or start up professional organizations such as the Industrial Designers Society of America (IDSA) or social groups such as the Basketball Club. From glass studios to student galleries and 4D classrooms to photography studios, the state-of-the-art facilities on both campuses are

unmatched anywhere else. The San Francisco Bay Area is known for creative and technological innovation, environmental leadership and its thriving art and design communities. Napa Valley, Mendocino, Monterey, Lake Tahoe and Yosemite National Park are all close by. CCA's San Francisco campus spans a city block in the Potrero Hill neighborhood, near the design district. The Oakland campus occupies 4 acres in the Rockridge neighborhood, 3 miles from the University of California, Berkeley. A free

CONTACT INFORMATION

Ms. Robynne Royster, Director of Admissions

☎ 415-703-9523 Ext. 9532 or toll-free 800-447-1ART

✉ enroll@cca.edu

shuttle connects the campuses and residence halls.

- **Enrollment:** *1,831*
- **Selectivity:** *moderately difficult*
- **Test scores:** *ACT—over 18, 100%; SAT—critical reading over 500, 67%; SAT—math over 500, 70%*
- **Application deadline:** *2/1 (freshmen), rolling (transfer)*
- **Expenses:** *Tuition $33,264; Room only $6600*

At CCA no single discipline, philosophy, or medium confines you. You can feel safe taking risks. While you major in one subject, you'll explore many.

ORANGE, CALIFORNIA
www.chapman.edu/

Chapman is a comprehensive liberal arts and sciences university that is distinguished for its nationally recognized programs in film and television production, business and economics, theater, dance, music, education and the natural and applied sciences. Chapman's ivy-covered, tree-lined campus blends historic buildings with the newest in state-of-the-art Internet and satellite-connected learning environments. Located in the center of the campus is Liberty Plaza, featuring a raised replica of a Lincoln chair that views a 5-ton section of the Berlin Wall. Chapman University is comprised of seven schools and colleges: the Wilkinson College of Humanities and Social Sciences, the Dodge College of Film and Media Arts, the Argyros School of Business and Economics, the School of Education, the School of Law, the Schmid College of Science and the College of Performing Arts, which includes the Conservatory of Music and Department of Dance. In addition to traditional undergraduate, graduate and professional school students enrolled on the campus in Orange, Chapman also enrolls a number of working adults in evening and weekend classes through its Chapman University College and network of thirty University College corporate campus centers located in California and Washington. The University environment is electric,

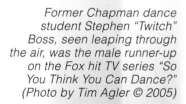

Former Chapman dance student Stephen "Twitch" Boss, seen leaping through the air, was the male runner-up on the Fox hit TV series "So You Think You Can Dance?" (Photo by Tim Agler © 2005)

involving and outdoor-oriented. Over the past five years, Chapman students have been named Truman Scholars, Coro Fellows, *USA Today* All-USA College Academic Team members, NCAA All-Americans and NCAA Academic All-Americans. Chapman competes as an independent in the NCAA Division III level and fields teams in baseball, basketball (m/w), crew (m/w), cross-country (m/w), football, golf, lacrosse, soccer (m/w), softball, swimming (w), tennis (m/w), track and field (m/w), volleyball (w) and water polo (m/w). In 2007–08, 4 student-athletes were named as NCAA All-Americans and 8 as NCAA Academic All-Americans. More than seventy clubs and organizations are open to students including fraternities and sororities, intramural sports (everything from billiards to touch football) and academic groups such as the Ad Club. Orange County, California, has been rated by *Places Rated Almanac* as "the #1 place to live in North America," because of its climate as well as its cultural, recreational, educational and career opportunities. Los Angeles is 35 miles to the north, and San Diego is 80 miles to the south. Nearby attractions include Disneyland, Knott's Berry Farm, the Orange County Performing Arts Center, major-league baseball and hockey. West Coast beaches are less than 10 miles from the campus, and ski spots are 90 minutes away.

CONTACT INFORMATION

Ms. Marcela Mejia-Martinez, Assistant Vice Chancellor and Chief Admission Officer

☎ 714-997-6711 or toll-free 888-CUAPPLY

✉ admit@chapman.edu

- **Enrollment:** *6,398*
- **Selectivity:** *very difficult*
- **Test scores:** *ACT—over 18, 100%; SAT—critical reading over 500, 97%; SAT—math over 500, 96%*
- **Application deadline:** *1/15 (freshmen), 3/1 (transfer)*
- **Expenses:** *Tuition $38,524; Room & Board $12,957*

http://bit.ly/collvid33

Chapman students produce and perform in the University's annual live song-and-dance revue, American Celebration, which raises millions for student scholarships.

DOMINICAN UNIVERSITY OF CALIFORNIA

SAN RAFAEL, CALIFORNIA
www.dominican.edu/

Imagine yourself at Dominican University of California—an independent, learner-centered university of Dominican heritage. Students here achieve success, give back to the community and learn inside and outside the classroom. Dominican undergrads can choose from sixty different programs—everything from Art to Women and Gender Studies. Students can also earn graduate degrees in biological sciences, counseling psychology, education, global management, humanities, nursing, occupational therapy, strategic leadership and sustainable enterprise. Dominican recently established a mentoring program with Kaiser Permanente where premed students get to shadow mentors/physicians and observe emergency room procedures during four-hour shifts during their first semester. And all eyes will be on campus in October 2010 when Dominican University of California will host the California gubernatorial debates. Dominican students are a powerful force on the playing field, too. Dominican has twelve intercollegiate teams that compete in the NCAA's Pacific Western Conference (with NCAA Division II status in the works): men's and women's basketball, golf, cross-country and soccer; men's lacrosse; and women's softball, tennis and volleyball. Forest Meadows, which sits on about 25 acres, is the site of the Conlan Recreation Center, a soccer field, tennis courts and an outdoor amphitheater. The Recreation Center has regulation basketball and volleyball courts, two cross-courts for volleyball and basketball and 1,285 spectator seats. It also features a weight-training and fitness room, a multipurpose room, an outdoor, six-lane swimming pool and grassy patio area. Students also join the chorus, drama group, literary magazine, campus newspaper, campus ministry activities or special interest clubs—there's a club or activity for every interest. Catholic liturgies, ecumenical activities for students of all faiths and community service projects run throughout the year. The University is located on 80 wooded acres in scenic Marin County, which is 12 miles north of San Francisco and within a half hour's drive of Pacific Ocean beaches.

- **Enrollment:** *2,094*
- **Selectivity:** *moderately difficult*

Meadowlands Residence Hall is pictured above. Dominican has dorms, meeting spaces, classrooms, and beautiful blue skies.

- **Test scores:** *ACT—over 18, 90.3%; SAT—critical reading over 500, 53.9%*
- **Application deadline:** *2/1 (freshmen), 2/1 (transfer)*
- **Expenses:** *Tuition $35,587; Room & Board $13,560*

http://bit.ly/collvid36

CONTACT INFORMATION

Ms. Rebecca Finn Kenney, Director of Undergraduate Admissions

☎ 415-485-3204 or toll-free 888-323-6763

✉ enroll@dominican.edu

Students in between classes outside the new William H. Hannon Library.

LMU|LA

Loyola Marymount University

LOS ANGELES, CALIFORNIA
www.lmu.edu/

Loyola Marymount University (LMU) offers competitive students a high-quality education in a friendly and relaxed atmosphere. LMU offers more than fifty-three majors, fifty-seven minors, thirty-one master's degrees, one doctoral degree and fifteen credential programs—students can choose an endless number of course combinations. The School of Law, located at a separate campus, has both day and evening divisions. Undergrads live on campus in one of nineteen residential halls and apartments. Theme housing is popular here—first-year students enjoy the LAX (Los Angeles Experience) and ROAR (Recreation Outdoor Adventure in Rosecrans) communities where they get out and get acquainted with the L.A.

area. Loyola Marymount turns everything students hear about campus food upside down. Here, students can grab a smoothie at Jamba Juice, order a cookie and coffee in Jazzman's Café in the new Hannon Library or head to Iggy's Diner for 1950's comfort food while listening to the jukebox. Loyola Marymount students also have access to a sports pavilion, a swimming pool, baseball and soccer fields, tennis and volleyball courts and four indoor racquetball courts. A new recreation center includes three additional courts and a fitness center. LMU fields teams in thirteen intercollegiate sports (baseball, basketball, cheer, crew, cross-country, golf, soccer, softball, swimming, tennis, track, women's volleyball and water polo) and has club teams in lacrosse, rugby, men's volleyball and more. Student organizations include the AM/FM radio station (KXLU), Chemistry Society, Black Students Union, Han

Tao Chinese Cultural Club, MEChA, Business Law Society, Student-Athlete Advisory Committee, University choruses, fraternities and sororities and a number of honor and service groups. LMU's Debate Team and Air Force ROTC detachment have received national recognition. LMU is ideally located on a 152-acre mesa that overlooks the southwest section of Los Angeles and the Pacific Ocean from Malibu to Santa Monica. The campus is close to the beach, and Los Angeles International Airport is only 10 minutes away.

CONTACT INFORMATION

Mr. Matthew Fissinger, Director of Admissions

☎ 310-338-2750 or toll-free 800-LMU-INFO

✉ admissions@lmu.edu

- **Enrollment:** *9,010*
- **Selectivity:** *very difficult*
- **Test scores:** *ACT—over 18, 99.4%; SAT—critical reading over 500, 89.1%; SAT—math over 500, 90.5%*
- **Application deadline:** *1/15 (freshmen), 3/15 (transfer)*
- **Expenses:** *Tuition $35,419; Room & Board $12,025*

http://bit.ly/collvid51

Between classes on Alumni Mall

Forty percent of Menlo College students participate in NAIA sports. The Department of Athletics complements the Menlo College experience by developing leaders who take initiative in their teams.

MENLO
C O L L E G E
Silicon Valley's Business School

ATHERTON, CALIFORNIA
www.menlo.edu/

Menlo College stands out among colleges and universities in five exciting ways: programs, location, small size, sports and alumni. Rather than offer a traditional set of majors as many schools do, Menlo provides excellent programs in business management with a strong foundation in the liberal arts. The College is small enough to be a real community but large enough to support a ton of intercollegiate sports, student organizations and internship opportunities. Menlo's distinguished alumni provide a strong base of support for graduates, which helps students make the transition from college to career with great success. A Menlo education is a process that trains and cultivates leaders. This process begins with a broad-based liberal arts education in the humanities, mathematics, sciences and social sciences. Next, students take on major programs with faculty who are experts in their respective fields. The advantage is a cutting-edge curriculum that equips students to succeed. Menlo's superior business program is renowned throughout the world and has produced generations of dynamic and successful business, industrial and civic leaders. The learning process does not end in the classroom. Students are encouraged to participate in internships and study abroad programs that bridge the gap between theory and practice. These opportunities range from Fortune 500 companies to innovative start-up enterprises, from San Francisco to South America, Asia and Europe. Students join a variety of clubs or organizations, ranging from the Alpha Chi National Honor Society and the Poetry, Art, and Music Society to the newspaper and the Outdoor Club. Menlo offers NCAA Division III sports in men's baseball, basketball, cross-country, football, golf, soccer and wrestling, and in women's basketball, cross-country, soccer, softball, volleyball

and wrestling. Menlo College is located on the San Francisco peninsula, near the cities of Menlo Park and Palo Alto. The area ranks among the most attractive and exciting in the world, with a load of outdoor activities to do in a mild climate. The campus is in the heart of Silicon Valley, where high-tech companies in the electronics, computer, aerospace, biotechnology and pharmaceutical industries are literally transforming the world in which we live and work. Surrounding the San Francisco Bay Area is the great natural beauty of northern California, extending from the spectacular California coast to the majestic Sierra Nevada Mountains. Favorite

CONTACT INFORMATION

Cindy McGrew, Director, Enrollment Management Operations

☎ 650-543-3940 or toll-free 800-556-3656

✉ admissions@menlo.edu

spots such as Big Sur, Monterey Bay, Lake Tahoe, Napa Valley and Yosemite National Park are just a few hours' drive from Menlo.

- **Enrollment:** *594*
- **Selectivity:** *moderately difficult*
- **Test scores:** *ACT—over 18, 75.5%; SAT—critical reading over 500, 38.6%; SAT—math over 500, 46.4%*
- **Application deadline:** *Rolling (freshmen), rolling (transfer)*
- **Expenses:** *Tuition $33,550; Room & Board $11,330*

Menlo College provides students with the knowledge, skills and abilities that ensure graduates an effective leading edge in a global business environment where the only constant is change.

Mills is an independent liberal arts college for women with graduate programs for women and men located in Oakland, California.

MILLS

MILLS COLLEGE

OAKLAND, CALIFORNIA
www.mills.edu/

For more than 150 years, Mills College has shaped women's lives. Offering a progressive liberal arts curriculum taught by nationally renowned faculty, Mills gives students the personal attention that leads to extraordinary learning. At Mills, students gain the ability to make their voices heard, the strength to risk bold visions, the eagerness to experiment and the desire to change the world. Located in the heart of the San Francisco Bay Area, Mills College is a hidden gem. This ideal setting, combined with the College's community of forward-thinking individuals, makes Mills home to one of the most dynamic, creative liberal arts educations available to women today. Historically a college for women only, Mills continues that proud tradition today at the undergraduate level. The graduate programs here are open to both women and men, though. Ranked one of the top colleges in the West by *U.S. News & World Report,* Mills has also been named one of the greenest colleges in the nation by *The Princeton Review.* The hallmark of a Mills education is the collaboration between students and faculty members that goes beyond the classroom and into innovative research. Mills students compete in seven intercollegiate sports—cross-country, rowing, soccer, swimming, tennis, track and field and volleyball—as members of the NCAA Division III. Mills students live on campus in unique halls with hardwood floors, courtyards and California sleeping porches (with high-speed and wireless Internet and satellite TV). Amid the rolling hills and the century-old eucalyptus trees of the Mills campus, students find a welcoming place to live and learn with new friends and new ideas at every turn. The campus is heavily accented with Mediterranean-style

buildings, many designed by architectural innovator Julia Morgan. Paths and streams wind their way through groves and meadows throughout the 135-acre wooded campus. Outside the campus gates, students can enjoy all the Bay Area has to offer—Berkeley, San Francisco, Napa and Silicon Valley are all easy driving distance away. The close proximity allows Mills students to connect with centers of learning, business and technology and pursue research and internship opportunities.

CONTACT INFORMATION

Ms. Giulietta Aquino, Vice President of Enrollment Management

☎ 510-430-2135 or toll-free 800-87-MILLS

🖳 admission@mills.edu

- **Enrollment:** *1,501*
- **Selectivity:** *moderately difficult*
- **Test scores:** *ACT—over 18, 100%; SAT—critical reading over 500, 89.3%; SAT—math over 500, 76.4%*
- **Application deadline:** *2/1 (freshmen), 3/1 (transfer)*
- **Expenses:** *Tuition $37,605; Room & Board $11,644*

Mills College students enjoy classes on a lush 135-acre oasis in the San Francisco Bay Area. With a full calendar of activities available on campus, there's never a shortage of engaging opportunities.

Residential halls at Pitzer

CLAREMONT, CALIFORNIA
www.pitzer.edu/

Pitzer College's focus on interdisciplinary studies, intercultural understanding and social responsibility sets it apart from most other colleges in the country. Because there are fewer required general education courses, Pitzer gives its students more freedom to choose the courses they want to take. Pitzer offers the best of both worlds: membership in a small, close-knit academic community and access to the resources of a midsize university through Pitzer's partnership with The Claremont Colleges. The Claremont Colleges are a consortium of five undergraduate colleges (Pitzer, Claremont McKenna, Harvey Mudd, Pomona and Scripps) and two graduate schools (Claremont Graduate University and the Keck Institute for Applied Biological Sciences). Each college has its own personality, but all share major facilities, such as the library, bookstore, campus security, health services, counseling center, ethnic study centers and chaplains' offices. Students at Pitzer may enroll in courses offered by the other colleges and can rub elbows with professors on all of the campuses. Pitzer offers forty-three majors in the arts, humanities, sciences and social sciences. The most popular majors are anthropology, art, biology, economics, English, environmental studies, history, organizational studies, political studies, psychology and sociology. All residence hall rooms are wired for Internet access, television and phone service; three new Gold LEED Certified residence halls opened in fall 2007.

Pitzer students can join a wide variety of sports, clubs (more than 150!), community service programs and social activities. Pitzer partners with Pomona College to field NCAA Division III teams in baseball, basketball, cross-country, football, golf, soccer, softball, swimming and diving, tennis, track and field, volleyball and water polo. Club sports for men include crew, cycling, lacrosse, rugby, Ultimate Frisbee and volleyball. Club sports for women include crew, cycling, lacrosse, rugby and Ultimate Frisbee. Pitzer is located in the city of Claremont at the base of the San Gabriel Mountains, about 35 miles east of Los Angeles and 78 miles west of Palm Springs.

Pitzer is a short drive from rock climbing at Joshua Tree National Park, a number of ski resorts and the beautiful beaches of southern California.

- **Enrollment:** *1,043*
- **Selectivity:** *moderately difficult*
- **Test scores:** *ACT—over 18, 100%; SAT—critical reading over 500, 97%; SAT—math over 500, 98%*
- **Application deadline:** *1/1 (freshmen), 4/15 (transfer)*
- **Expenses:** *Tuition $39,330; Room & Board $11,440*

CONTACT INFORMATION

Angel Perez, Director of Admission

☎ 909-621-8129 or toll-free 800-748-9371
✉ admission@pitzer.edu

UWest's Investment Lab is where business students manage a real securities portfolio in real time.

University of the West

ROSEMEAD, CALIFORNIA
www.uwest.edu/

University of the West (UWest) is a Buddhist-founded campus open to students of all beliefs and backgrounds who are interested in gaining cultural awareness as well as a solid education in religious studies, business administration, psychology or languages. Founded in 1991 by Buddhist Venerable Master Hsing Yun, who is one of the earliest promoters of Humanistic Buddhism, University of the West's goals are to deliver an education informed by Buddhist wisdom and values and to serve as a bridge between East and West. Outside the well-known Buddhist studies programs, Buddhist knowledge is available to students of all programs on a voluntary basis through workshops and other campus activities. Students and faculty members come together to participate in an ongoing dialogue to advance knowledge, address societal and cultural issues and promote education and understanding across cultures. At UWest, creativity, adaptability and leadership are fostered together with tolerance, ethical commitment and social consciousness. Outside the classroom, students talk about and take part in yoga, martial arts, music, meditation and travel. The Student Recreation Center is equipped with fitness and weight-training equipment, table tennis, billiards and a student lounge with a kitchen. The two residential halls each have a 24-hour study room and a multipurpose lounge on each floor. Rooms are all furnished and have air-conditioning, private bathrooms, telephone and high-speed Internet access. Recreational facilities include a swimming pool, a spa, and exercise and game rooms. UWest is located in the city of Rosemead in Los Angeles County. It has 10 acres of beautifully landscaped grounds as well as modern, well-equipped facilities. The campus sits on a hillside overlooking the Whittier Narrows nature preserve with an unobstructed view of the San Gabriel Mountain range and the Puente Hills range.

UWest is about 10 minutes from downtown Los Angeles, which a Harvard scholar called "the most complex Buddhist city in the world."

- **Enrollment:** *255*
- **Application deadline:** *6/1 (freshmen)*
- **Expenses:** *Tuition $8140; Room & Board $6182*

CONTACT INFORMATION

Ms. Grace Hsiao, Admissions Officer

☎ 626-571-8811 Ext. 120
✉ graceh@uwest.edu

University of the West is Los Angeles County's only Buddhist-founded university with accreditation. Students from diverse backgrounds and faiths attend UWest for a quality education.

Many graduates consider graduation day the most memorable day of their life. It is certainly a day to remember, and it signifies the beginning of your new journey as a member of the Air Force officer corps.

U.S. AIR FORCE
ACADEMY

COLORADO SPRINGS, COLORADO
www.usafa.edu/

The United States Air Force Academy prepares and motivates cadets for careers as Air Force officers. The Academy stresses character development, military training and physical fitness as well as academics. Students can choose fom thirty-two majors in technical fields such as aeronautical engineering, computer science, space operations and system engineering management. The common bond among the student body is the desire to be military officers. All cadets must live in on-campus dorms and wear uniforms. All cadets must participate in intramural, club or intercollegiate athletics every semester. Intramural sports include basketball, boxing (men's), cross-country, flag football, flickerball, mountain biking, racquetball, rugby (men's and women's), soccer, softball, team handball, tennis, Ultimate Frisbee, volleyball and wallyball. The intercollegiate teams compete in Division I of the NCAA. Men's teams include baseball, basketball, boxing, cheerleading, cross-country, diving, fencing, football, golf, gymnastics, hockey, indoor and outdoor track, lacrosse, rifle, soccer, swimming, tennis, water polo and wrestling. Women's teams include basketball, cross-country, cheerleading, diving, fencing, gymnastics, indoor and outdoor track, rifle, soccer, swimming, tennis and volleyball. Cadets may also choose from more than eighty extracurricular activities, which include professional organizations, mission support, competitive and recreational clubs, sports groups and hobby clubs. Qualified Academy graduates may enter flight training upon graduation, and approximately 75 percent of the students in each graduating class pursue graduate education at other schools

This challenging environment fosters a sense of accomplishment you will share with friends and classmates. Through your trials, you will develop unbreakable bonds that will last the rest of your life.

within ten years of graduation. Each year, numerous Academy graduates receive graduate scholarships and fellowships, such as the Marshall, Rhodes, National Science Foundation, National Collegiate Athletic Association and Guggenheim awards. The Academy campus sits in the foothills of the Rampart Range of the Rocky Mountains in a setting of natural beauty. Built on a mesa at 7,000 feet, it is one of Colorado's top tourist attractions. The Cadet Chapel, with its seventeen aluminum spires towering 150 feet into the air, highlights the contemporary architecture of the buildings in the cadet area. The space-age effect reflects the Academy's mission of preparing cadets to become officers and leaders in the Air Force of the future. The Academy borders the

northern edge of Colorado Springs, which lies at the foot of the famous 14,100-foot Pikes Peak. Denver, the state's capital, is located 55 miles north. Cadets enjoy skiing, hunting, horseback riding, white-water rafting and other activities in the Colorado Rocky Mountains and nearby resorts.

- **Enrollment:** *4,620*
- **Selectivity:** *most difficult*
- **Test scores:** *SAT—critical reading over 500, 99%; SAT—math over 500, 100%*
- **Application deadline:** *1/31 (freshmen), 1/31 (transfer)*
- **Expenses:** *Tuition $0*

http://bit.ly/collvid65

With a student to faculty ratio of 8:1 and an average class size of just 20 students, our professors play a dynamic role in our students' learning and growth.

UNIVERSITY OF DENVER
START FROM A HIGHER PLACE

DENVER, COLORADO
www.du.edu/

The University of Denver (DU) has grown into one of the West's premier universities. As the oldest private university in the Rocky Mountain region, DU is home not only to a top-ranked undergraduate program but also to a number of world-renowned research centers and professional programs, including the Josef Korbel School of International Studies, the Sturm College of Law and the Graduate School of Professional Psychology. DU offers more than 200 bachelor's, master's and doctoral degrees as well as dual degrees and convenient online degrees and certificates for working students. The 125-acre campus is an environment that prizes innovation, cross-disciplinary exploration and adventurous learning partnerships between students and faculty. And the campus is ever-changing and evolving

COLORADO

to meet student needs—in fact, nineteen new buildings have opened on campus since 1997 including a state-of-the-art soccer stadium and the Sie Cheou-Kang Center for Security and Diplomacy. Whatever their backgrounds and majors, DU students are engaged and active, taking advantage of the area's many recreational and cultural opportunities—everything from world-class skiing and white-water rafting to award-winning professional theater and alternative music. On campus, students attend performances at the three-venue Newman Center for the Performing Arts and cheer for the seventeen varsity teams that compete in NCAA Division I at the Ritchie Center for Sports & Wellness. Even more students get geared up for intramural and club sports in indoor soccer, flag football, dodgeball and more. The residence halls have dining areas with made-to-order food, huge game rooms with ping pong and big-screen

TVs, 24/7 help desks where students can borrow DVDs and board games and comfortable rooms with fridges and microwaves. Located just 8 miles from downtown Denver and mere minutes from the Rocky Mountain foothills, the University of Denver's tree-shaded campus is surrounded by urban neighborhoods loaded with coffee shops, retail stores and ethnic restaurants. DU students can ride all public transportation for free, using their University-supplied Eco-passes.

CONTACT INFORMATION

Mr. Todd R. Rinehart, Assistant Vice Chancellor for Enrollment

☎ 303-871-3125 or toll-free 800-525-9495

✉ admission@du.edu

- **Enrollment:** *11,644*

- **Selectivity:** *moderately difficult*

- **Test scores:** *ACT—over 18, 99.89%; SAT—critical reading over 500, 89.85%; SAT—math over 500, 90.57%*

- **Application deadline:** *1/15 (freshmen), rolling (transfer)*

- **Expenses:** *Tuition $36,501; Room & Board $10,224*

 http://bit.ly/collvid67

Pioneer Pride is alive and well at the University of Denver! Our students are very active in Division I club, and intramural sports, and have a strong tradition of success.

HONOLULU, HAWAII
www.hpu.edu/

Hawaii Pacific University (HPU) is a private university with an international student population. In fact, HPU is one of the most culturally diverse universities in America with students from all 50 U.S. states and more than 100 countries. HPU offers more than fifty undergrad programs and twelve graduate programs and is recognized as a Best in the West college by The Princeton Review and a Best Buy by *Barron's* business magazine. The diversity of the HPU student body stimulates learning about other cultures firsthand, both inside and outside the classroom. There is no majority population at HPU. Students are encouraged to examine the values, customs, traditions and principles of others. What results are graduates prepared for the

Dr. Christopher Winn and students explore a tidepool near the Oceanic Institute.

global workplace. The HPU Sea Warriors participate in NCAA Division II intercollegiate sports. Men's teams are in baseball, basketball, cross-country, golf, soccer and tennis. Women's teams are in basketball, cross-country, soccer, softball, tennis and volleyball. HPU's Cheerleading Team and Dance Team have both won national championship titles, too. Hawaii Pacific University's main campus in downtown Honolulu provides a fast-paced, exciting urban environment in the heart of the business community. The downtown campus is home to the College of Business Administration and the College of Humanities and Social Sciences. This campus location makes it easy for students to find and maintain internship opportunities at neighboring businesses. Eight miles away, the 135-acre windward Hawaii Loa campus, which is set in the lush foothills of the Koolau Mountains, is home to the College of Nursing and Health Sciences and the College of Natural and

Computational Sciences. The Hawaii Loa campus includes residence halls, the Educational Technology Center, a student center and outdoor facilities (a soccer field, tennis courts, a softball field and an exercise room). HPU is also affiliated with the Oceanic Institute, a 56-acre aquaculture research facility located at Makapuu Point on the southeastern coast of Oahu, Hawaii. At this facility, undergraduate and graduate students are able to get hands-on experience in marine science. All three sites are conveniently linked by a free shuttle.

CONTACT INFORMATION

Mr. Scott Stensrud, Vice President Enrollment Management

☎ 808-544-0238 or toll-free 866-225-5478

✉ admissions@hpu.edu

- **Enrollment:** *8,113*
- **Selectivity:** *moderately difficult*
- **Test scores:** *ACT—over 18, 81.2%; SAT—critical reading over 500, 48%; SAT—math over 500, 52.2%*
- **Application deadline:** *Rolling (freshmen), rolling (transfer)*
- **Expenses:** *Tuition $14,960; Room & Board $11,094*

 http://bit.ly/collvid42

Students discuss research with Professor Brian Metcalf in the Psychology Lab.

To really learn, lose the desk. Intern for business, media, government, nonprofits, engineering firms. Do hospital clinicals and scientific field research. Join Carroll Outreach Team or Engineers Without Borders to change the world. Study abroad on six continents.

Carroll
MONTANA

HELENA, MONTANA
www.carroll.edu/

Student centered and affordable, Carroll College is a private, Catholic college located in Montana's state capital. Carroll's faculty is results-oriented, assisting students in classwork, research, job searches and graduate school admissions. This personal touch is also reflected by Carroll's award-winning financial aid staff who offers generous grants and scholarships—available to 95 percent of all students. And Carroll makes sure students can enroll in the courses needed to complete their majors in four years. One course, the College's Human-Animal Bond minor (the first of its kind in the nation) educates students to train dogs and horses as service and therapy animals with a foundation in psychology. Carroll's Fighting Saints football team has won five NAIA national championships, all while maintaining a record number of scholar-athletes. In the 2009–10 season, all nine of Carroll's athletic teams were honored as NAIA Scholar Teams, earning at least a 3.0 team GPA. Carroll's soccer team led the nation in 2007–08 for the highest GPA in the NAIA. The Carroll Talking Saints forensics team, a training ground for future attorneys, politicians and business professionals, is ranked in the top five of all colleges and universities (of all sizes) nationwide and has reigned as the Northwest regional champion for the past twenty years. Eighty-four percent of Carroll premed students applying to medical school are accepted, while the national average hovers near 50 percent. Students discover Carroll's dedication to service learning and social justice right from the first semester of freshman year. Projects take students into the community, where they offer volunteer hours and research expertise to organizations and schools. Through service abroad, Carroll's student chapter of Engineers Without Borders built an integrated sewer, farm irrigation and fish hatchery system at a Mexican orphanage. And for four years now, students have held a fundraiser to raise more

than $100,000 for St. Jude Children's Research Hospital. Helena lies in the heart of southwestern Montana's Rocky Mountains. It is a wonderland for hikers, mountain bikers, climbers, skiers and boarders, kayakers and enthusiasts of every outdoor sport. Carroll's Adventures and Mountaineering Program guides hundreds of students on backpacking, camping and rock-climbing trips in addition to sponsoring outdoor survival clinics and extreme sport film screenings. The Great Divide Ski Area is a 45-minute trek from Carroll. Two world-class ski

CONTACT INFORMATION

Ms. Cynthia Thornquist, Director of Admissions and Enrollment Operations

☎ toll-free 800-992-3648

resorts are easy day trips and four other ski hills are about 2½ hours from campus.

- **Enrollment:** *1,409*
- **Selectivity:** *moderately difficult*
- **Test scores:** *ACT—over 18, 97%; SAT—critical reading over 500, 74%; SAT—math over 500, 76%*
- **Application deadline:** *6/1 (freshmen), 6/1 (transfer)*
- **Expenses:** *Tuition $22,592; Room & Board $7118*

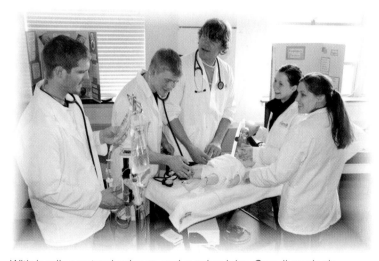

With leading natural science and nursing labs, Carroll grads do groundbreaking research on global warming, illnesses like West Nile Virus, Mad Cow Disease, and environmental contamination. Eighty-five percent of Carroll premeds are accepted to medical school.

University of Great Falls

GREAT FALLS, MONTANA
www.ugf.edu/

Life takes courage. An extraordinary life takes uncommon courage.

The University of Great Falls (UGF) students prepare for living and making a living. Courage is a meaningful word here—from the courageous early settlers of Montana to the courage today's students earn through exploring new majors and research. This private, Catholic university offers forty undergraduate degrees, eight graduate degrees and four distance learning degrees. UGF also has a signature program for first-year students—the Corps of Discovery. This in- and out-of-classroom program helps students develop their leadership and team abilities through physical challenges like rafting, trips and retreats and volunteer service. The campus has more than a dozen buildings including the state-of-the-art E.L. Wiegand Science Center (opened in 2009), the Wellness Center (with over 6,000-square feet of workout space, a juice bar and wireless Internet), Galerie Trinitas (an art gallery) and the library (which doubled in size in 1999). The University participates in the Frontier Conference and varsity teams include men's and women's basketball, cross-country, golf, soccer and track; men's wrestling; and women's softball, volleyball, cheer and dance. UGF recently formed a rodeo team, which joins twelve other college rodeo teams in the Big Sky Region. Life on campus is relaxed and fun. On a winter day, it's common to see students snowboarding on the large hill next to Emilie Hall. On fall and spring days, students are known to start up a game of flag football or Ultimate Frisbee or even break out a Slip 'N' Slide. The city of Great Falls is located in north-central Montana. Situated next to the five waterfalls of the Missouri River, the city lies between the Rocky Mountains and Great Plains. The river, explored by the Lewis and Clark Expedition, provides a ton of recreational opportunities like boating, canoeing and fishing its blue-ribbon trout waters. The Little Belt Mountains,

The Corps of Discovery: Explore Montana, your values and inner courage.

an hour south of Great Falls, offer excellent downhill skiing at Showdown Ski Area and miles of cross-country trails at Silver Crest. The surrounding area is also ideal for biking, hiking, camping, technical rock climbing, white-water rafting, archaeological exploration and hunting. About an hour west of the city lies the Rocky Mountain Front Range extending north to Glacier National Park. The majestic peaks of this area provide outdoor buffs with hundreds of miles of trails and lakes and streams. Four hours to the south of Great Falls is Yellowstone National Park, where herds of bison and elk roam free. Many other species of wildlife call Yellowstone home, including the reintroduced wolf.

CONTACT INFORMATION

April Clutter, Director of Admissions

☎ 406-791-5200 or toll-free 800-856-9544

✉ enroll@ugf.edu

At 193 acres, our park-like campus is spacious for a small school. Driving from McMinnville, students are 60 minutes to Portland, 45 minutes to the Oregon Coast and 2 hours to Mt. Hood.

LINFIELD COLLEGE

MCMINNVILLE, OREGON
www.linfield.edu/

Linfield College helps students find their calling through its mix of liberal arts and professional programs. In 1998, Linfield more than doubled the size of its McMinnville campus when it bought 115 acres and four buildings from Hewlett-Packard. As a result, the James F. Miller Fine Arts Center opened in 2001, the Kenneth W. Ford Hall and a new library opened in 2003 and 2006 saw construction of a new music building. Linfield students live in comfortable residence halls, houses, apartments and fraternity houses. Social clubs, professional organizations, sororities/fraternities, service clubs and almost forty other organizations play an important role in the daily life of a Linfield student. Linfield athletes also participate in nineteen intercollegiate sports at the NCAA Division III level. Women compete in basketball, cross-country, golf, lacrosse, soccer, softball, swimming, tennis, track and field and volleyball. Men

OREGON

compete in intercollegiate baseball, basketball, cross-country, football, golf, soccer, swimming, tennis and track and field. Water polo, Ultimate Frisbee and men's lacrosse are popular club sports here. Linfield hosts the Oregon Nobel Laureate Symposium. (There are only five such symposiums worldwide.) At these symposiums, Nobel laureates share their backgrounds and expertise within the context of a basic theme. The Linfield–Good Samaritan School of Nursing, an academic unit of the College at its Portland campus, prepares transfer students for the BSN or a degree in health science or environmental studies. This campus, at the Good Samaritan Hospital and Medical Center, has modern suites for students as well as an active student life in clubs and activities like the Running Club and the Wildcatheters (members aim to reduce stress while organizing sports and activities). Located in McMinnville, 40 miles southwest of Portland, Linfield College is a leader in the cultural, educational and recreational events of its fast-growing community. Movie theatres, a community theater, bowling alleys, coffeehouses and a variety of restaurants welcome Linfield students. Shopping is within walking distance. The central Oregon coast is an hour to the west, and the Oregon Cascade Range (with its year-round skiing at Mt. Hood) is 2 hours east. Salem, the state capital of Oregon, is 25 miles southeast of campus.

CONTACT INFORMATION

Ms. Lisa Knodle-Bragiel, Director of Admission

☎ 503-883-2213 or toll-free 800-640-2287

✉ admission@linfield.edu

- **Enrollment:** *1,677*
- **Selectivity:** *moderately difficult*
- **Test scores:** *ACT—over 18, 93%; SAT—critical reading over 500, 70%; SAT—math over 500, 71%*
- **Application deadline:** *2/15 (freshmen), 4/15 (transfer)*
- **Expenses:** *Tuition $29,034; Room & Board $8280*

Linfield faculty strive to connect academics to the real world—and with a 12:1 student-to-faculty ratio, they also establish genuine, caring relationships that guide students through all four years.

Multnomah University—Main Campus Sign and Historic Sutcliffe Hall

MULTNOMAH UNIVERSITY

PORTLAND, OREGON
www.multnomah.edu/

Multnomah Bible College and Biblical Seminary—together Multnomah University—has been devoted to teaching the Bible to men and women since the 1930s. The mission of Multnomah University is to produce biblically competent servants of Jesus Christ, whose love for God, His Word and people shapes their lives into a transforming force in the church and world. Multnomah's education is more than time in the classroom—it's learning through hands-on ministry, late-night talks with friends in the coffee shop and discovering the heart of God through prayer. At Multnomah, the Bible is central to everything students learn. Whether majoring in journalism or pastoral ministry, students are challenged at the end of the day to think and live biblically. Multnomah offers one of the most comprehensive Bible programs in the nation, requiring each student to complete a Bible and theology major. Multnomah also offers a Master of Arts in Teaching and a Master of Arts in Teaching English to Speakers of Other Languages (TESOL). Effective education teaches the whole person and the University continually seeks ways to train students to have the greatest possible impact on the world today. Outside the classroom, students learn through internships or service in the community. Students work side-by-side with instructors as they share the gospel in the community or minister in a home for abused women. Something is always happening on campus. Students can join student government, intramural sports, the Ambassador Choir or chapel worship bands. Programs at the Biblical Seminary include the graduate certificate, the Master of Arts in biblical studies or in pastoral studies (emphases in family ministry, intercultural studies, ministry management, spiritual formation and

women's ministry), the Master of Divinity and the Master of Theology. The city of Portland offers an endless supply of adventure and excitement. The campus is only 15 minutes from downtown. On weekends, the Saturday Market offers a huge collection of handmade crafts, art and ethnic food. Waterfront Park hosts the Rose Festival in late May, and many shops and restaurants overlook the Willamette River. The eclectic Hawthorne, Hollywood, Pearl and northwest Portland districts have shopping, arts and restaurants—all within 5 miles of campus. Portland is home to museums, concert venues and the Trail Blazer basketball team. Less than 2 hours from Multnomah are Oregon's sandy beaches. The slopes of Mt. Hood, a favorite for skiers and snowboarders

CONTACT INFORMATION

Ms. Nancy Gerecz, Admissions Assistant

☎ 503-255-0332 Ext. 5373 or toll-free 800-275-4672

🖳 admiss@multnomah.edu

throughout the world, are just an hour east.

- **Enrollment:** *841*
- **Selectivity:** *moderately difficult*
- **Test scores:** *ACT—over 18, 93.4%; SAT—critical reading over 500, 85.8%; SAT—math over 500, 57.2%*
- **Application deadline:** *7/15 (freshmen), 7/15 (transfer)*

Faculty spend a lot of 1-on1 time with students. Dr. Kutz, Biblical Languages Professor.

Men's soccer, one of 21 NCAA Division III sports.

Pacific University Oregon

FOREST GROVE, OREGON
www.pacificu.edu/

Founded in 1849 by Congregational pioneers, Pacific University is still a frontier school, proud of its tradition in liberal arts and sciences and innovative in its programs. This private university includes the undergraduate College of Arts and Sciences and nine graduate programs—seven in the health professions, an MFA in writing and one in teacher education. The College of Arts and Sciences offers programs in the natural sciences, education, business, psychology, world languages and the humanities. Pacific's graduate health profession programs include the Pacific Northwest's only College of Optometry, as well as the School of Professional Psychology, School of Occupational Therapy, School of Physical Therapy, School of Dental

Health Sciences, School of Pharmacy and School of Physician's Assistant Studies. Students live on campus in suites or in the Vandervelden Apartments. Two eco-friendly halls opened in 2006 and 2008; they are completely wireless and have large-screen TVs, fireplaces and BBQ areas. The University Center houses Boxer Dining (everything from Starbucks to salads), the new Fireside Lounge, Macintosh and PC labs and the campus radio station. Students can choose to join more than sixty groups, ranging from the Outback program to the Politics and Law Forum. Outback schedules a ton of activities like kayaking, hiking, skiing trips, camping and outings to Portland-area events. Pacific University is a member of the NCAA Division III. Men's intercollegiate sports are baseball, basketball, cross-country, golf, soccer, swimming, tennis, track and field and wrestling. Women compete in basketball, cross-country, golf, lacrosse, soccer, softball, swimming, tennis, track and

field, volleyball and wrestling. All students can use the Pacific Athletic Center, which houses a gymnasium (with three basketball courts), a state-of-the-art fitness center, a field house, three handball/racquetball courts, a dance studio, a wrestling room and a sports medicine training facility. The brand-new Lincoln Park Athletic Complex features a 1,100-seat stadium with a nine-lane, 400-meter track and a FieldTurf soccer and lacrosse field; a Bond baseball field with a permanent grandstand; and a varsity softball field with permanent grandstand seating. In addition to the Forest Grove campus, the University has a campus in Eugene and another in Hillsboro. Forest Grove is about 35 minutes from Portland. The campus is surrounded by green countryside and the foothills of the Coast Range Mountains, beyond which is the 300-mile stretch of Oregon coast. The area is ideal for hiking, skiing, camping, fishing, beachcombing and bicycling.

CONTACT INFORMATION

Ms. Karen Dunston, Executive Director

☎ 503-352-2218 or toll-free 877-722-8648
📧 admissions@pacificu.edu

- **Enrollment:** *3,167*
- **Selectivity:** *moderately difficult*
- **Test scores:** *ACT—over 18, 96%; SAT—critical reading over 500, 71%; SAT—math over 500, 74%*
- **Application deadline:** *8/15 (freshmen), rolling (transfer)*
- **Expenses:** *Tuition $29,966; Room & Board $8118*

Physical Therapy is one of 13 graduate/professional programs at Pacific University.

Reedies are an independent-minded, creative, passionate group of students who truly love to learn. They discuss Durkheim for fun, play the ukulele in the sunshine, and later earn Ph.D.'s in many fields.

Reed College

PORTLAND, OREGON
www.reed.edu/

Reed College attracts students with a high degree of self-discipline and an enthusiasm for intellectual challenge. Students here choose from twenty-two departmental and twelve interdisciplinary majors in the arts, sciences, humanities and social sciences. Reed students know success. Undergrads and graduate students regularly win Fulbright, Watson, National Science Foundation and other scholarships and a higher percentage of Reed graduates go on to earn Ph.D.'s across fields than do graduates of all but three other U.S. colleges and universities. Recent campus improvements include a new, 30,000-square-foot technology building; expanded physics labs with VideoPoint technology; and additions to the library, biology building, studio arts building, sports center and psychology building. The Watzek Sports Center has basketball courts; squash, racquetball and handball courts; a dance studio; a weight room; and a lap pool. Community life is full of activity and variety with more than seventy student organizations and competitive club sports such as rugby, soccer and Ultimate Frisbee. Reed's Outdoor Club sponsors rock-climbing trips around the state, cross-country trips to the Reed ski cabin and hiking trips. Students also head over to Paradox in the Student Union for coffee or to the Pool Hall, another favorite hangout. And the twenty-six residence halls offer more than just a place to hang your clothes; they have everything from hardwood floors and fireplaces to full kitchens and indoor bike storage. Reed's 119-acre wooded campus is located in southeast Portland. The campus has a lake and canyon with abundant wildlife and native plants. Downtown Portland is about 15 minutes away and the campus is only 90 minutes from the Pacific coast.

- **Enrollment:** *1,481*

- **Selectivity:** *most difficult*

CONTACT INFORMATION

Mr. Keith Todd, Dean of Admission

☎ 503-777-7511 or toll-free 800-547-4750

✉ admission@reed.edu

- **Test scores:** *ACT—over 18, 100%; SAT—critical reading over 500, 100%; SAT—math over 500, 100%*

- **Application deadline:** *1/15 (freshmen), 3/1 (transfer)*

- **Expenses:** *Tuition $39,700; Room & Board $10,250*

Reed is located in the city of Portland, Oregon. Surrounded by lush greenery, mountain peaks, and flowing waters, Reed has a 28-acre watershed in the center of campus, complete with a fish ladder.

The best way to decide if the UO is right for you is to visit us here in clean, green Eugene.

O

UNIVERSITY OF OREGON

EUGENE, OREGON
www.uoregon.edu/

At the University of Oregon (UO), students are part of a community dedicated to making a difference in the world. Whether changing a community, a law or someone else's mindset, the UO can give students the inspiration and resources needed to succeed. The University offers 271 comprehensive academic programs (including new programs in African studies, cinema studies, Latin American studies and queer studies) and more than 250 student organizations. The architecture, biochemistry, chemistry, economics, English, entrepreneurship, molecular biology, neuroscience, physics, psychology, special education, sports business and sustainable design programs all rank among the top 10 in the United States. Programs in comparative literature, finance, historic preservation, and mathematics rank in the top 20 in the nation. Global degree options include twenty-eight languages, as well as international, ethnic, religious, Asian, Judaic, and Russian and East European studies. The UO offers 165 study programs and internships in ninety-five countries. Campus buildings date from 1876, when Deady Hall opened, to 2010, when the Jacqua Center for Student Athletes was completed. Students can join cultural organizations, fraternities and sororities, student government, campus ministries, political groups, performing arts groups, international student clubs and honor societies. The University is among the top universities in the U.S. for Peace Corps volunteers, student voter registration and the number of graduates who hold high-ranking military offices. The University of Oregon fields nineteen NCAA Division I teams, as well as forty-four club sports. In the fall, students root for the Ducks' football team at Autzen Stadium. In the winter,

the men's and women's basketball teams thrill the crowds at the state-of-the-art Matthew Knight Arena. In the spring, UO track stars compete at the world-famous Hayward Field. The UO is located in the center of Eugene, a classic college town small enough to bike across but large enough to offer many art, music and social scenes. The Oregon Bach Festival and numerous music venues lure a variety of nationally acclaimed musical acts; in fact, *Rolling Stone* magazine included Eugene in its list of top 10 College Towns that Rock. The city of Eugene offers more than 100 city parks, 250 miles of

CONTACT INFORMATION

Brian Henley, Director of Admissions

☎ 541-346-3201 or toll-free 800-232-3825

✉ uoadmit@uoregon.edu

bicycle trails, rock climbing areas, and beautiful public gardens—all within the city limits.

- **Enrollment:** *22,335*
- **Selectivity:** *moderately difficult*
- **Test scores:** *SAT—critical reading over 500, 75%; SAT—math over 500, 75%*
- **Application deadline:** *1/15 (freshmen), 5/15 (transfer)*
- **Expenses:** *Tuition $7428; Room & Board $8620*

The engaged student body loves to cheer on the UO's nineteen Oregon Ducks NCAA Division 1 teams.

Warner Pacific College's personalized internships, independent study courses and interdisciplinary approach to learning help prepare students to pursue successful careers.

WARNER PACIFIC COLLEGE

PORTLAND, OREGON
www.warnerpacific.edu/

Located in the heart of Portland, Warner Pacific College prepares the next generation of leaders by providing a liberal arts education taught with a Christian worldview. The city of Portland draws people from around the globe. It's one of the best places to experience new perspectives, art forms, foods and cultures—and to prepare for life in today's increasingly metropolitan world. The school has an extensive network of connections around Portland and a reputation for providing excellent internship opportunities. Nationally recognized for its commitment to community service, the College was named to the 2009 President's Higher Education Community Service Honor Roll. Through various outreach projects and class projects, Warner Pacific students regularly read to school children, paint murals at local elementary schools, serve hot chocolate to the homeless and landscape at shelters for women and children. Beyond Portland, Warner Pacific's Missions program offers at least two major service trips a year to countries along the Pacific Rim, as well as to U.S. cities like San Francisco and New Orleans. Additionally, students can spend a semester studying abroad through the Best Semester program offered by the Coalition for Christian Colleges and Universities. The campus is alive with activity: intramurals, drama, music, multicultural events and even an ethics-bowl competition. Warner Pacific is a member of the National Association of Intercollegiate Athletics (NAIA Division II) and the Cascade Collegiate Conference. Women's sports include basketball, cross-country, golf, soccer, track and field and volleyball. Men compete in basketball, cross-country, golf, soccer, and track and field. The College recently opened a new dining hall, coffee shop and book-store. All student residences have been remodeled since 2006; rooms, apartments and houses have high-speed Internet connections, kitchens and lounges with cable TV. Warner Pacific is an urban campus adjacent to 195-acre Mount Tabor Park and just 10 minutes from downtown Portland. Situated in the beautiful Pacific Northwest, the city of Portland was named one of the best places to live in the United States by *CNN*, *Money*, and *Outside* magazines and the green-est city in the United States according to SustainLane.com. It is consistently listed in the top 10 for walking, biking and other fitness activities. In fact, Portland was named "FitTown, USA" by *Fit* maga-zine. Snow-capped moun-tains, rugged coastlines and the Columbia Gorge are all an hour away, where students

CONTACT INFORMATION

Mrs. Shannon Mackey, Executive Director of Enrollment Management

☎ 503-517-1020 or toll-free 800-804-1510

✉ admiss@warnerpacific.edu

enjoy skiing, hiking, kayaking, windsurfing and exploring nature.

- **Enrollment:** *1,333*
- **Selectivity:** *moderately difficult*
- **Test scores:** *ACT—over 18, 76.9%; SAT—critical reading over 500, 61.4%; SAT—math over 500, 62.7%*
- **Application deadline:** *Rolling (freshmen), rolling (transfer)*
- **Expenses:** *Tuition $17,110; Room & Board $6646*

Because of Warner Pacific's urban campus, students enjoy a wide range of cultural, internship, service, and employment opportunities.

Colleges that change lives don't just teach students. They inspire them to learn more, dream big, make a difference. and to inquire within.

AUSTIN COLLEGE

SHERMAN, TEXAS
www.austincollege.edu/

One of the leading liberal arts and sciences colleges in the nation, Austin College is nationally recognized for excellence in international education, pre-professional training and leadership studies. The Austin College environment is perfect for students who want to be known and challenged by faculty members and peers alike. Affiliated with the Presbyterian Church (U.S.A.), Austin College nurtures the whole person through academic, cocurricular and social involvement. More than 70 percent of Austin College graduates spend at least one month in international study during their college experience. On campus, students can join one of more than sixty student organizations, ranging from environmental clubs to local fraternities and sororities. Austin fields intercollegiate sports through membership in the Southern Collegiate Athletic Conference. Men compete in baseball, basketball, football, soccer, tennis and swimming and diving; women compete in basketball, soccer, softball, tennis, swimming and diving and volleyball. The College maintains a 29-acre recreational area on Lake Texoma, about 20 minutes from the campus, for retreats, meetings and outdoor learning. Austin College offers guidance to students through Career Services, the Academic Skills Center and Health Services. At Austin, students don't miss mom and dad's cooking. Here they sink their teeth into made-to-order hoagies, burritos and sautéed pasta—all in an "unlimited seconds" program. The fully-furnished and modern rooms, apartments and suites have kitchens with microwaves, lounges and computer labs. Students of German, French, Japanese, Chinese and

Spanish may choose to live in the language hall, where the target languages are spoken in common areas. Austin College is located in Sherman, Texas, just about 30 minutes north of the greater Dallas metroplex. Sherman is a small city that *Money* magazine includes among the top 15 percent of the 300 "most livable small cities" in the United States. Sherman has a ton of shopping and restaurants, and nearby Lake Texoma has even more for outdoor buffs to do (including overnight camping). For those seeking "big-city" excitement, the Dallas–Fort Worth metroplex is a short drive south.

There are no faces in the crowd. We look you in the eye, call you by name and challenge you to excel. If you dream of exploring the world and connecting with others then you belong at Austin College.

CONTACT INFORMATION

Ms. Nan Davis, Vice President for Institutional Enrollment

☎ 903-813-3000 or toll-free 800-442-5363

✉ admission@austincollege.edu

- **Enrollment:** *1,364*
- **Selectivity:** *very difficult*
- **Test scores:** *ACT—over 18, 99.5%; SAT—critical reading over 500, 90.1%; SAT—math over 500, 94.38%*
- **Application deadline:** *5/1 (freshmen), 5/1 (transfer)*
- **Expenses:** *Tuition $29,235; Room & Board $9549*

ST. EDWARD'S UNIVERSITY

AUSTIN

AUSTIN, TEXAS
www.gotostedwards.com/

St. Edward's University offers students the best of both worlds—small classes and a supportive community in the middle of one of the most exciting cities in the country. Located 10 minutes from downtown Austin, the 160-acre campus features hills, trees and historic architecture—and one of the best views of the Austin skyline. But it is the University's vision, more than the view, which sets it apart. A St. Edward's University education combines the critical-thinking skills of a liberal arts curriculum with hands-on experience in internships, service learning and study abroad. It is an exciting time to be at St. Edward's. The University has built nine new buildings since 2000, including a 65,000-square-foot science building with state-of-the-art labs and a rooftop greenhouse. Three new residence halls opened in 2009; they showcase urban living with suite-style rooms above a dining area, coffeehouse and wellness center. St. Edward's has also added eleven new majors, including forensic science, graphic design and entrepreneurship. The most popular majors at St. Edward's are psychology, communication, biology and business. The unique theater arts program allows students to earn points toward their Actors' Equity membership card while working with professional mentors. The Academic Exploration Program guides students who have not chosen a major; freshmen take a course designed to find their strengths and interests. Outside of class, students join the more than ninety student organizations including intramural sports, Student Government Association, political groups, honor societies, spirit groups and cultural organizations. Campus Ministry offers retreats, volunteer projects and support for the campus Hillel group and the Muslim student organization. Athletic events, theater productions, concerts and campus traditions give students a chance to relax and have fun. St. Edward's is a member of the NCAA Division II Heartland Conference; in the past three years, its teams have won nineteen conference championships. Men compete in baseball, basketball, golf, soccer and tennis. Women compete in basketball, golf, soccer, softball, tennis and volleyball. St. Edward's University is located in Austin. Along with its internationally known film festival and music scene, Austin also offers local theaters, galleries and museums. Students at St. Edward's enjoy year-round use of Austin's three major lakes and nearly 200 parks, such as nearby Zilker Park with its natural, spring-fed swimming pool, canoe rentals for use on Lady Bird Lake, a hike-and-bike trail, a botanical garden and playing fields.

CONTACT INFORMATION

Ms. Karen Gregg, Inquiry Coordinator

☎ 512-448-8580 or toll-free 800-555-0164

🖥 seu.admit@stedwards.edu

- **Enrollment:** *5,293*
- **Selectivity:** *moderately difficult*
- **Test scores:** *ACT—over 18, 99%; SAT—critical reading over 500, 83%; SAT—math over 500, 83%*
- **Application deadline:** *5/1 (freshmen), 7/1 (transfer)*
- **Expenses:** *Tuition $26,484; Room & Board $9036*

http://bit.ly/collvid62

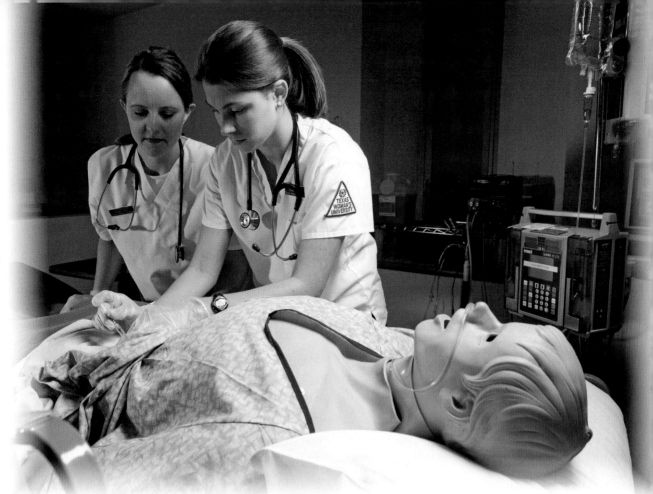

TWU is one of the state's leading providers of new healthcare professionals.

TWU
TEXAS WOMAN'S UNIVERSITY

DENTON   DALLAS   HOUSTON

DENTON, TEXAS
www.twu.edu/

Texas Woman's University (TWU) is a leading teaching and research university—and the nation's largest university primarily for women. TWU offers bachelor's, master's and doctoral degree programs that focus on the health sciences, education and the liberal arts through its three major academic divisions: the University General Divisions, the Institute of Health Sciences and the Graduate School. Included in the University General Divisions are the College of Arts and Sciences, College of Professional Education and School of Library and Information Studies. The Institute of Health Sciences includes the College of Health Sciences, College of Nursing, School of Occupational Therapy and School of Physical Therapy (TWU has the only Ph.D. in Physical Therapy in Texas). And TWU graduates more new nurses and health care professionals than any other college or university in Texas. Old Main, the University's first building, still stands amid high-rise buildings and other modern facilities on the beautiful 270-acre wooded campus. Other campus landmarks include the statue of the Pioneer Woman and the historic Little Chapel in the Woods. The 19,000-square-foot Redbud Theater (built in 2007) is home to the drama program. This state-of-the-art building has practice and rehearsal rooms, a green room, scene and costume shops and student lounges. The foundation was just poured in July 2010 for a brand-new fitness center. This facility will have three group exercise rooms, a climbing wall, a full size gym with basketball and volleyball courts, a fitness area with weights and cardio equipment and an outdoor adventure center. The TWU Pioneers compete in NCAA Division II sports in basketball, gymnastics, softball, tennis and volleyball. TWU's main campus is in Denton, just 35 miles north of Dallas and Fort Worth—the nation's ninth-largest urban center. Clinical centers, offering upper-level and graduate studies in the health sciences, are located in Dallas near the Parkland and Presbyterian hospitals and in Houston in the Texas Medical Center.

CONTACT INFORMATION

Ms. Erma Nieto-Brecht, Director of Admissions

☎ 940-898-3188 or toll-free 888-948-9984
💻 admissions@twu.edu

- **Enrollment:** *13,237*
- **Selectivity:** *minimally difficult*
- **Test scores:** *ACT—over 18, 81%; SAT—critical reading over 500, 51%; SAT—math over 500, 53%*
- **Application deadline:** *7/1 (freshmen), 7/15 (transfer)*
- **Expenses:** *Tuition $6660; Room & Board $5967*

TWU has one of the most diverse student bodies in Texas.

A tradition since 2002, the annual Oozeball tournament pits UT Dallas students, faculty and staff against each other in a muddy competition for the trophy.

THE UNIVERSITY OF TEXAS AT DALLAS

RICHARDSON, TEXAS
www.utdallas.edu/

Students looking for the close-knit community of a liberal arts college and the reputation and resources of a research university find the perfect balance at the University of Texas at Dallas (UT Dallas). Here, students enjoy easy access to a first-rate faculty and research team that has included Nobel laureates and members of the National Academies of Sciences and Engineering. The UT Dallas chess team is ranked among the top intercollegiate chess teams in the nation, and its debate team has qualified for the National Debate Tournament for the past three years. UT Dallas ranks among the top 100 colleges and universities in the United States in number of freshmen National Merit Scholars and is ranked one of the Top 100 best values among public universities by *Kiplinger's*. UT Dallas has more than 125 degree programs in such areas as audiology, telecommunications, arts and technology, brain health, digital forensics and cybercrime prevention, sickle-cell disease research and space science. UT Dallas launched the first accredited telecommunications engineering degree in the United States. Exciting research in next-generation technology and biotechnology is at the crux of many collaborative efforts at such UT Dallas centers as NanoTech Institute, Digital Forensics and Emergency Preparedness Institute and the Callier Center for Communications Disorders. Students live in four-bedroom apartments and suites with balconies, washer/dryers and full kitchens, a swimming pool, outdoor grills, study centers and a clubhouse with billiards and Ping-Pong tables. The campus Activities Center houses basketball courts, a 25-meter pool, a fitness/weight room, racquetball and squash courts and a gym for indoor soccer. The more than 160 organizations on campus are a mix of professional organizations; student government; ethnic and honor societies; fraternities and sororities; political, religious and service groups; music; and theater. The Comets participate in NCAA Division III intercollegiate sports. Men and women compete in basketball,

The new 28,000-square-foot dining hall at UT Dallas is open seven days a week, with space for mingling, relaxing and dining.

cross-country, golf, soccer and tennis; men also play baseball and women have softball and volleyball teams. Located in the Dallas suburb of Richardson, UT Dallas is next door to one of the largest concentrations of corporate headquarters in the nation. Many alumni work in the area, and the University actively maintains relationships with corporate partners to provide internships and co-op programs for students. The Dallas-Fort Worth Metroplex is one of the nation's largest urban areas and offers five major sports teams, live bands, museums and theme

parks. An on-campus bus— the Comet Cruiser—provides free transportation to local shopping centers and DART rail lines.

- **Enrollment:** *15,783*
- **Selectivity:** *very difficult*
- **Test scores:** *ACT—over 18, 98%; SAT—critical reading over 500, 83%; SAT—math over 500, 92%*
- **Application deadline:** *7/1 (freshmen)*
- **Expenses:** *Tuition $10,340; Room & Board $7733*

CONTACT INFORMATION

Enrollment Services

☎ 972-883-2270 or toll-free 800-889-2443

🖥 interest@utdallas.edu

Students showcase their rail-riding skills in Westminster's rail jam!

WESTMINSTER COLLEGE

SALT LAKE CITY, UTAH
www.westminstercollege.edu/

Westminster College offers students a unique environment for learning. Traditionally, colleges measure student success by the time they spend in classes and the grades they earn. Westminster focuses on outcomes—what students actually learn and what they can do with that knowledge. Students actively participate in their own learning; faculty members directly mentor and guide their development through experiences that are experiential, collaborative and cross-disciplinary. Westminster knows that learning takes place out of the classroom too so it offers a full range of activities on campus: fifty clubs, health and wellness programming, plays, concerts and lectures. And Westminster's location near the Rocky Mountains means students can be at ski resorts, forests or national parks within 20 minutes. After graduation, Westminster students have gone to work at General Electric, American Express and Hewlett-Packard; others have gone on to graduate school at Columbia, Georgetown, Berkeley and the University of London. Westminster sits in the eclectic Sugar House neighborhood of Salt Lake City marked by old-growth trees, a small creek and a blend of old and new architecture. The College's on-campus housing includes new apartment-style suites with entertainment systems and wireless Internet. Westminster College offers intercollegiate basketball, cross-country, golf, lacrosse, and soccer for men, and basketball, cross-country, golf, soccer and volleyball for women, as well as men's and women's ski and snowboard teams. In 2007, *Outside* magazine described Salt Lake as "a near-perfect location for avid outdoor adventures," and in 2008 *Forbes* magazine ranked SLC first for job growth. Downtown Salt Lake is 10 minutes away from campus by bus, car or bicycle. The city offers internship and employment opportunities, clubs and restaurants, professional sports and great shopping. Salt Lake has been rated as one of the ten most fun places to live, was home of the 2002 Winter Olympics and offers easy access to the Sundance Film Festival. The Wasatch Mountains that border the Salt Lake Valley on the east are

famous for the "greatest snow on earth." With about 500 inches of annual snowfall, these mountains are ideal for winter sports enthusiasts as well as for those who enjoy summer hiking, biking and camping. Ten excellent ski and snowboard resorts lie within an hour's drive of the campus, and sixteen national parks and recreational areas are within a day's drive or less. Golf, backpacking, mountain biking, kayaking, wakeboarding, mountain climbing, canyoneering, spelunking and rafting are

CONTACT INFORMATION

Louis Levy, Interim Director of Undergraduate Admissions

☎ 801-832-2200 or toll-free 800-748-4753

🖥 admission@ westminstercollege.edu

all within easy reach of the campus.

- **Enrollment:** *3,037*
- **Selectivity:** *moderately difficult*
- **Test scores:** *ACT—over 18, 97%; SAT—critical reading over 500, 80%; SAT—math over 500, 76%*
- **Application deadline:** *Rolling (freshmen), rolling (transfer)*
- **Expenses:** *Tuition $24,996; Room & Board $7006*

At Westminster College your academic experience goes far beyond textbooks and classrooms. Every course you take is lively, interactive, and engaging.

Students in the Herbal Sciences and Naturopathic Medicine programs make good use of the medicinal herb garden on campus, which includes more than 350 species of herbs and vegetables.

BASTYR
UNIVERSITY

KENMORE, WASHINGTON
www.bastyr.edu/

An undergraduate education at Bastyr University is the first step on a path leading to a rewarding future in the field of science-based natural health. Bastyr's programs are based on a mind-body-spirit approach to wellness, with a curriculum that challenges students to further their goals in scientific, medical and wellness-related fields. Expertise in natural and holistic healing is increasingly in demand, so graduates with degrees in the natural health sciences fulfill an important role in the marketplace. Founded as a naturopathic medical college in 1978, Bastyr has since expanded its offerings to become a multidisciplinary university with a wide range of graduate and undergraduate degrees. The foundation of Bastyr University's entire curriculum rests on the integration of modern science with traditional healing methods.

Bastyr's small size means students can enjoy a relaxed relationship with graduate students as well as with faculty and staff members. Bastyr undergrads are goal-oriented individuals who bring a passionate interest and intense focus to their areas of study. They thrive on diversity and individual expression, and they continually seek out opportunities to grow both intellectually and personally. As part of its mission to improve the well-being of the human community, Bastyr University conducts research studies at its research institute and delivers premier care at its natural health care clinic. The Bastyr University Research Institute is devoted to the evaluation of natural medicine practices and the exploration of natural therapies for serious chronic diseases. Participation in research projects is available to a select number of students. The University's teaching clinic in Seattle, Bastyr Center for Natural Health, is the largest natural health clinic in the Northwest and provides

the main venue for graduate students' clinical training. In 1989, Bastyr University became the first naturopathic school to achieve accreditation and is accredited by the Northwest Commission on Colleges and Universities. The Bastyr University campus is located in Kenmore, just north of Seattle. Bastyr's inviting campus environment attracts many students who think it's the perfect place for studying healing practices. Next to the University's fields and gardens are miles of wooded trails winding through the St. Edward State Park on the shore of Lake Washington. The park also

CONTACT INFORMATION

Mr. Ted Olsen, Director of Admissions

☎ 425-602-3101
🖳 admissions@bastyr.edu

has a swimming pool, volleyball courts, tennis courts and playfields—all open to Bastyr students. Seattle has easy access to mountains, ocean beaches, lakes, as well as national, state and city parks. Several ski areas are within an hour's drive.

- **Enrollment:** *928*
- **Application deadline:** *3/15 (transfer)*
- **Expenses:** *Tuition $19,050*

Bastyr offers several undergraduate and graduate nutrition degrees, including Nutrition and Culinary Arts, Nutrition and Clinical Health Psychology, and a Dietetics option.

Seattle Pacific
UNIVERSITY

Engaging the culture, changing the world®

SEATTLE, WASHINGTON
www.spu.edu/

With a long and distinguished history, Seattle Pacific University (SPU) provides students with a high-quality education grounded on the gospel of Jesus Christ. This combination of scholarship and faith is a powerful one that brings about lasting change in the lives of graduates and in the people and communities they serve. SPU has been designated one of "America's Best Colleges" by *U.S. News & World Report* and has been touted as one of the country's character-building institutions. In addition to its bachelor's degrees, SPU awards M.A., M.B.A., M.Ed., M.F.A., M.S., M.A. (TESOL), M.S.N., Ed.D. and Ph.D. degrees. Located just minutes from Seattle, SPU engages and serves its students and communities, cultivates a global consciousness, supports

WASHINGTON

the church and addresses the crisis of meaning in modern culture. More than half of Seattle Pacific's undergraduate students live on campus in residence halls and apartment complexes that are wired for e-mail, Internet and the campus computer network. Seattle Pacific University celebrates diversity and learning to live together in Christian community. In 2004, civil rights leader John Perkins and SPU President Philip Eaton founded the John Perkins Center on campus. The first of its kind in the nation, the Perkins Center helps SPU become a more diverse campus, practice reconciliation, build new relationships in the city and bring about positive change in the world. The Ames Minority Leadership Scholarships support high school graduates who come from minority groups and have leadership potential. Prospective students from urban areas and diverse backgrounds visit the campus each year for Urban Youth Preview. Seattle Pacific's intercollegiate athletic program fields

NCAA Division II teams in men's and women's basketball, crew, cross-country, soccer, and track and field and women's gymnastics and volleyball. Students can also join thirty-two intramural sports as well as extramurals, special events and health and fitness activities. Seattle Pacific's beautiful, 43-acre city campus lies in a residential area just 10 minutes from downtown Seattle, the business and cultural heart of the Pacific Northwest. A gateway to Canada and the Pacific Rim, Seattle offers easy access to a wide variety of outdoor recreation such as sailing, skiing, hiking and camping. The city also offers world-class opera, theater, symphony and ballet. Seattle

CONTACT INFORMATION

Mr. Jobe Korb-Nice, Director of Admissions

☎ 206-281-2021 or toll-free 800-366-3344

✉ admissions@spu.edu

Pacific takes advantage of its urban setting by providing hundreds of internship and service experiences in the city's hospitals, schools, businesses and churches.

- **Enrollment:** *4,000*
- **Selectivity:** *moderately difficult*
- **Test scores:** *ACT—over 18, 95.08%; SAT—critical reading over 500, 78.77%; SAT—math over 500, 72.29%*
- **Application deadline:** *2/1 (freshmen), 8/1 (transfer)*
- **Expenses:** *Tuition $27,810; Room & Board $8544*

BELLINGHAM, WASHINGTON
www.wwu.edu/

Fisher Fountain in Red Square is the central hub of student activity at Western, and is a "free speech zone".

Since the first class of 88 students entered New Whatcom Normal School in 1899, Western Washington University (WWU) has grown into the third-largest institution of higher education in the state. For twelve consecutive years, *U.S. News & World Report* has ranked WWU as the best regional public university in the Pacific Northwest and second in the western United States. In addition, *Kiplinger's Personal Finance* magazine has ranked WWU thirty-eighth on its list of 100 Best Values in Public Colleges in the United States. Western Washington University is comprised of the Graduate School and seven undergraduate units—the College of Business and Economics, the College of Fine and Performing Arts, Fairhaven College of Interdisciplinary Studies, the College of Humanities and Social Sciences, Huxley College of the Environment, the College of Sciences and Technology and Woodring College of Education. Undergrads take advantage of unique opportunities to engage in research and showcase their work regionally and nationally— experiences usually reserved for graduate students at bigger schools. And sustainability is key here. From applying pesticide-free products on its landscaping to using 100 percent alternative energy to power the campus, WVU is a national leader in campus sustainability. Students can choose from more than 200 student clubs: arts and music, cultural, departmental, political, recreational, religious, service and special interest. The WWU Vikings compete in NCAA Division II basketball, crew, cross-country, golf, soccer, softball, track and field and volleyball. All residence halls and apartments are coed by floor, wing or suite. They have a ton of cool features such as fireplaces, lounges with pianos and game rooms. A coastal city of 75,000, Bellingham lies 90 miles north of Seattle and 55 miles south of Vancouver, British Columbia, Canada. The University's proximity to two major cities provides easy access for national and international visiting artists, scholars and touring groups. Puget Sound and the San Juan Islands lie directly to the west; Mt. Baker and the North Cascades Mountain Range are an hour to the east. Bellingham is both an urban community and a natural setting, providing outstanding entertainment and recreation opportunities. With mountains, glaciers, rivers and saltwater nearby, Western's location is ideal for fieldwork and outdoor research.

- **Enrollment:** *14,575*

- **Selectivity:** *moderately difficult*

CONTACT INFORMATION

Ms. Karen Copetas, Director of Admissions

☎ 360-650-3440
✉ admit@wwu.edu

- **Test scores:** *ACT—over 18, 95.85%; SAT—critical reading over 500, 78.38%; SAT—math over 500, 79.42%*

- **Application deadline:** *3/1 (freshmen), 4/1 (transfer)*

- **Expenses:** *Tuition $6159; Room & Board $8393*

 http://bit.ly/collvid74

Western Washington University's campus is nestled between the peak of nearby Mt. Baker and the waters of Bellingham Bay.

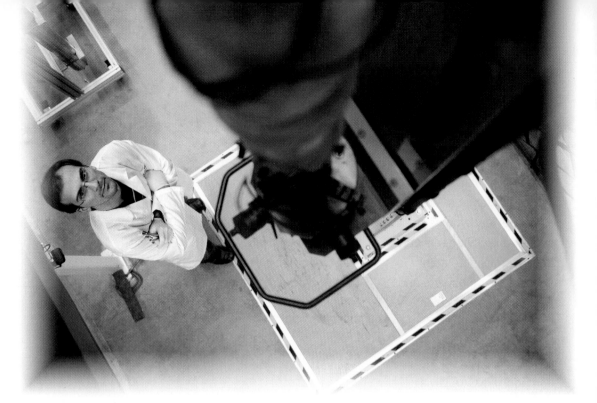

University of Wyoming's Petroleum Engineering lab.

UNIVERSITY OF WYOMING

LARAMIE, WYOMING
www.uwyo.edu/

Being a student at the University of Wyoming (UW) means more than just a first-rate education, it also gives you the opportunity for adventure and challenge. The University of Wyoming has the feel of a small school with all the benefits of a larger university—awesome research opportunities, state-of-the-art technology and NCAA Division I athletics. The range of academic programs offered at UW inspires the development of new thinking and promotes fulfilling careers in this rapidly evolving world. The research done by the professors and students of the University of Wyoming pushes the boundaries of modern science and technology and has resulted in UW's classification as a Carnegie Doctoral/Research University–Extensive. Wyoming, unique among the fifty states, has only one university. UW enjoys tremendous support from within its state as well as from an alumni network that spans the globe. UW offers bachelor's degree programs in six undergraduate colleges: the Colleges of Agriculture, Arts and Sciences, Business, Education, Engineering and Applied Science, and Health Sciences. UW also offers graduate and professional programs, including the Doctor of Pharmacy and the Juris Doctor. There are more than 200 campus clubs and organizations including fraternities and sororities, honor and professional societies, political and religious organizations and special interest groups. Students can also participate in more than sixty different intramural and club sports. UW is a Division I member of the NCAA and competes in seventeen men's and women's sports. On-campus facilities are nothing short of amazing. Students have complete access to Half Acre Gym, an indoor climbing wall, an eighteen-hole golf course, tennis and racquetball courts, weight rooms, two swimming pools, rifle and archery ranges, indoor and outdoor tracks, softball and baseball fields and a hockey rink. UW houses students

University of Wyoming Division 1-A women's tennis invitational September 2009.

in six residence halls with a number of unique living environments such as quiet/study floors, special interest floors, honors floors and single-sex floors. UW's 785-acre campus is located at the foot of the Rocky Mountains in Laramie, a scenic town in southeastern Wyoming. Many UW students enjoy the easy access to Alpine and Nordic skiing, snowboarding, snowmobiling, hiking, backpacking, camping, hunting, fishing, rock climbing and mountain biking. Laramie—with its blue skies, clean air and 320 days of sunshine a year—is a friendly and supportive university town, conveniently located 45 miles west of Wyoming's capital,

Cheyenne, and only 130 miles northwest of Denver, Colorado.

- **Enrollment:** *12,427*

- **Selectivity:** *moderately difficult*

- **Test scores:** *ACT—over 18, 95.8%; SAT—critical reading over 500, 69.9%; SAT—math over 500, 74.8%*

- **Application deadline:** *8/10 (freshmen), 8/10 (transfer)*

- **Expenses:** *Tuition $3927; Room & Board $8360*

http://bit.ly/collvid72

CONTACT INFORMATION

Aaron Appelhans, Assistant Director of Admissions

☎ 307-766-5160 or toll-free 800-342-5996

🖳 why-wyo@uwyo.edu

INTERNATIONAL

Field work at Bishop's University. Bishop's provides a truly hands-on education and some of the smallest class sizes in Canada.

BISHOP'S UNIVERSITY

SHERBROOKE, CANADA

www.ubishops.ca/

Bishop's offers undergraduate degrees in business, education, humanities, natural sciences, and social sciences to students from every Canadian province, twenty U.S. states and sixty-five countries around the world. Although it is located in Quebec, Bishop's is an English-language university in a bilingual setting. The mission of Bishop's University is to educate students to realize their full potential intellectually, spiritually, socially and physically. To this end, Bishop's emphasizes excellence in teaching enriched by scholarship and research. In fact, Bishop's created its own Research Office in 2001 to manage research grants, network with agencies and other universities and support researchers in protecting their inventions. More than fifty clubs and organizations offer a variety of student activities at Bishop's, including the Student Representative Council, a student-run newspaper, the yearbook, the debating team and the Big Buddies Association. The seven residence halls on campus are all wired for Internet access and have comfortable lounges and laundry on-site. Athletics plays a major role at Bishop's. Varsity sports include football and golf for men, soccer for women, and alpine skiing, basketball and rugby for both men and women. Club sports include men's lacrosse and women's ice hockey. Bishop University's excellent facilities include two gyms, two weight rooms, an indoor pool, an indoor running track, six squash courts, an aerobics studio, a multi-sport stadium with a state-of-the-art turf field and ten outdoor tennis courts (including six lighted courts). The sports and wellness complex is about to receive a $30-million in expansion and renovations—when completed in 2012, the building will have a modern 800-seat arena, a double gymnasium, changing rooms and conference rooms. Bishop's also has a nine-hole golf course on campus and 124 kilometers (77 miles) of bike trails and cross-country ski paths

that begin on the campus. The region is surrounded by excellent skiing and snowboarding mountains. Bishop's peaceful campus is located in the borough of Lennoxville, just minutes away from downtown Sherbrooke, one of the largest cities in Quebec. The Eastern Townships of Quebec are less than a day's drive from Ottawa, Toronto, Boston and New York City. Nearby are Montreal, Quebec City and the American-border states of Vermont, New Hampshire and Maine. Sherbrooke topped the *Canadian Business'* sixth annual ranking of the best places to set up a business.

CONTACT INFORMATION

Mrs. Jacqueline Belleau, Coordinator of Student Recruitment

☎ 819-822-9600 Ext. 2691 or toll-free 877-822-8200
🖳 recruitment@ubishops.ca

- **Enrollment:** *2,291*
- **Selectivity:** *moderately difficult*
- **Test scores:** *ACT—over 18, 100%*
- **Application deadline:** *3/1 (freshmen), 3/1 (transfer)*
- **Expenses:** *Tuition $2883; Room & Board $6900*

An outdoor playground with seven major ski hills within an hour's drive. Bishop is ideally located for outdoor fun in all four seasons.

Everyone Makes a Mark

TORONTO, CANADA
www.ryerson.ca/

Ryerson University is Canada's leader in providing a high standard of professionally relevant education that combines theory with practice and application. Ryerson offers close to 100 undergraduate, master's and Ph.D. programs. Undergraduate degree programs are offered through the University's five faculties:

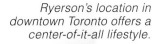

Ryerson's location in downtown Toronto offers a center-of-it-all lifestyle.

the Faculty of Arts; the Faculty of Engineering, Architecture, and Science; the Faculty of Community Services; the Ted Rogers School of Management; and the Faculty of Communications and Design. Known for attracting people with motivation, direction and drive, Ryerson offers professionally targeted programs (Business Management, Early Childhood Education) as well as contemporary arts and science degrees. Ryerson's three residences—Pitman Hall, O'Keefe House and the International Living Learning Centre—offer a unique, comfortable place for students to live and learn. The ILC has private bedrooms with queen-size beds. O'Keefe offers a sun deck, barbeque and garden. Pitman has private bedrooms, lounges and a music room with piano. Ryerson has fourteen men's and women's varsity teams that often make it to postseason playoffs. Ryerson student athletes travel throughout Ontario, across Canada and south to the United States to represent the University. Ryerson's intramural program is open to all students; more than twenty-five different leagues, from badminton to hockey, run throughout the academic year. The Recreation and Athletics Centre (RAC) at Ryerson boasts an extensive fitness centre with free weights and weight machines; a large cardio room with treadmills, elliptical trainers, station-ary bikes, recumbent bikes and rowing machines; a three-lane, 160-yard, banked indoor running track; two sprung hardwood-floor dance studios; four international squash courts; six gyms; a pool; locker rooms with saunas; and helpful staff members. Ryerson University is located right in the heart of downtown Toronto. Recognized internationally for its high quality of life, Toronto is Canada's hub for busi-ness and finance providing students with exciting learn-ing opportunities. Ryerson's campus lies within walking distance of music, movies, theaters and great food and shopping, and it is a short distance from professional sports complexes. One of North America's cleanest, safest and most ethnically diverse cities, Toronto offers many neighborhoods to explore—Chinatown, the Beaches and the Danforth. Other nearby attractions include Ontario Place, the Canadian National Exhibition (CNE), the Ontario Science Centre and the Royal Ontario Museum (ROM).

CONTACT INFORMATION

Michelle Beaton, Manager of International Student Recruitment

☎ 416-979-5080
✉ inquire@ryerson.ca

- **Enrollment:** *25,181*
- **Selectivity:** *moderately difficult*
- **Application deadline:** *2/1 (freshmen)*
- **Expenses:** *Tuition $4983*

Ryerson students are a short walk or subway ride from everything Toronto has to offer.

UNIVERSITY OF GUELPH

GUELPH, CANADA
www.uoguelph.ca/

Built in 1932 as a student residence and administrative office, Johnston Hall is one of the University's most recognized buildings.

The University of Guelph is a high quality, student-focused college that offers a wide range of undergraduate and graduate programs in the arts, humanities, social sciences, engineering and natural sciences. Guelph has a strong commitment to interdisciplinary programs, to professional and applied programs and to agriculture and veterinary medicine as areas of special responsibility. The success of the Center for New Students, which assists incoming students with the transition from secondary school to university, is reflected in Guelph's 90.5 percent student retention rate and a 96.6 percent graduate employment rate—both well above the Canadian national average. The University of Guelph offers a Doctor of Veterinary Medicine degree as well as several diploma programs and more than eighty master's and doctoral degree programs. Established in 1964 when three century-old founding colleges joined with a new college of arts and science, the University of Guelph is a campus of historical and modern buildings and redbrick walkways.

Guelph's 408-acre Arboretum has thirty-eight species of mammals, 188 species of birds, thirty-nine species of butterflies, eighteen different reptiles and amphibians and 1,700 types of trees and shrubs. It's a great place for a stroll, and an amazing real-world classroom for Biology students. Guelph features state-of-the-art athletic facilities that include a double arena with an Olympic-size ice surface, two pools, a field house and indoor track, aerobic and weight-training gyms, six squash courts and a climbing wall. Guelph offers thirty varsity sports teams and has recently fielded national and provincial championship football, hockey, track and field and rugby teams. The University of Guelph's main campus is located in the southwestern Ontario region *The New York Times* calls "Canada's Technology Triangle," an area known for its top-tier colleges and innovative companies. This city features internationally recognized folk, jazz and writers'

festivals as well as a multipurpose performing arts center and a sports and entertainment center. Within an hour's drive of Toronto, Canada's largest city, Guelph offers the comfort of small-community living with the excitement of an international metropolis at its doorstep. In addition to the main campus, the University of Guelph offers degrees in Toronto at the University of Guelph–Humber and regional campuses throughout Ontario

Ms. Mary Haggarty, Admissions Coordinator

☎ 519-824-4120 Ext. 58711
✉ usainfo@registrar
.uoguelph.ca

in Alfred, Kemptville and Ridgetown.

- **Enrollment:** *19,530*
- **Selectivity:** *moderately difficult*
- **Application deadline:** *3/1 (freshmen), 5/1 (transfer)*
- **Expenses:** *Room & Board $9310*

We've got school spirit! Each September our energetic group of Orientation Volunteers help students start the year off right with a high-energy Pep Rally on the famous Johnston Green.

University of Windsor

WINDSOR, CANADA
www.uwindsor.ca/

Historic Dillon Hall is the centrepiece of campus architecture.

The University of Windsor offers a broad range of programs—its students are enrolled in some 150 bachelor's, master's and doctoral degree programs. Academic tracks vary from humanities and liberal arts to science. Professional studies are offered in business, engineering, education, law, computer science, creative writing, kinesiology, nursing, social work, clinical psychology, music, dramatic art and visual arts. The University has an impressive commitment to research (even at the undergrad level), with a special focus on automotive-, environmental- and social justice-oriented interdisciplinary research. Community and business partnerships have helped to establish research institutions at the University of Windsor that are unmatched in Canada. The University's Great Lakes Institute for Environmental Research is the world's leading institution in large lakes research, attracting top students from around the world. The University of Windsor is also Canada's most international campus—10 percent of its population comes from eighty countries outside of Canada. This sharing of international experiences helps prepare Windsor graduates for the global workforce. In fact, the University has an impressive placement rate—more than 95 percent of graduates find employment within six months. In recent years, the University has spent millions of dollars in new buildings, classroom upgrades and lab renovations, including a new residence hall and facilities for health education, dramatic arts and a medical education building. The $112 million Centre for Engineering Innovation is also in the process of being built. The University offers everything from traditional residence rooms to suites. Each residence hall includes wireless Internet, laundry rooms, common lounge areas for watching TV or relaxing, vending machines and kitchens. Through the flexible meal plans, students can eat at one of the University's cafes,

Campus beautification has been a priority. Students can now enjoy these benches courtesy of our alumni, staff and donors.

restaurants or coffee shops or off campus at partnering restaurants such as Harvey's or Pizza Pizza. The tree-lined campus of the University of Windsor is located in Windsor, Ontario. Windsor is Canada's southernmost city and is located just across the river from Detroit. The city is bordered by Lake Erie, Lake St. Clair and the Detroit River. Its temperate climate makes it ideal for biking, golfing, hiking and swimming. Many students head to nearby attractions like Dieppe Gardens, Jackson Park and the Odette

Sculpture Park. Windsor also offers restaurants, shopping venues, museums and galleries as well as performances in dance, music, and theatre.

- **Enrollment:** *15,999*
- **Selectivity:** *moderately difficult*
- **Application deadline:** *Rolling (freshmen), rolling (transfer)*
- **Expenses:** *Tuition $5662; Room & Board $8185*

CONTACT INFORMATION

Ms. Charlene Yates, Manager of Undergraduate Admissions

☎ 519-253-3000 Ext. 3315 or toll-free 800-864-2860
✉ registr@uwindsor.ca

RICHMOND
THE AMERICAN INTERNATIONAL
UNIVERSITY
IN LONDON

LONDON, ENGLAND
www.richmond.ac.uk/

Located in one of the great world capitals, Richmond distinguishes itself as a truly international university by enrolling students from over 100 countries.

Richmond, The American International University in London, is a comprehensive American liberal arts and professional university. Richmond offers a strong academic program with many fields of study, an exceptional faculty, a fun campus life and fellow students from all over the world. In addition to its undergrad programs, Richmond offers Master of Arts degrees in art history and international relations. Freshmen and sophomores study and live at the Richmond campus, 7 miles from central London. Junior and senior years are spent at the Kensington campus in one of London's most beautiful residential and historic districts. As part of their four-year B.A. degree program,

                ENGLAND

students may spend a semester or a year studying at one of the University's two international study centers in Florence and Rome, Italy. Approximately 21 percent of the degree students are from Europe and the United Kingdom, 13 percent are from Asia and 18 percent are from the Middle East. Fifteen percent of the student body represents the continent of Africa, and 3 percent are from South America. The remaining students are from North America. About 350 study-abroad students from various universities are enrolled for a semester or a year at Richmond. Outside the classroom, many Richmond students get involved in extracurricular activities such as student government, the Green Project (an environmental group), Model United Nations, Gay Straight Alliance, RTV (Richmond Television) and sports and business clubs. The Richmond Hill campus has a ton of nearby entertainment, shopping, cultural and recreational opportunities. Only yards from the University campus is Richmond Park, more than 2,200 acres of rolling hills and woodland, where students can ride horses, play tennis, jog or simply relax. The trip from Richmond into Central London takes about 30 minutes. The Kensington campus has fine museums, libraries, theatres, concert halls and historic buildings. The University takes full advantage of London's resources through selected academic courses, work experience placements with multinational corporations, and special visits to museums, art galleries, theatres and concert halls.

CONTACT INFORMATION

Mr. Nick Atkinson, Director of United States Admissions

☎ 617-450-5617
🖳 us_admissions@richmond.ac.uk

- **Enrollment:** *1,043*
- **Selectivity:** *moderately difficult*
- **Test scores:** *ACT—over 18, 100%; SAT—critical reading over 500, 78.94%; SAT—math over 500, 82.56%*
- **Application deadline:** *Rolling (freshmen), rolling (transfer)*
- **Expenses:** *Tuition $27,000; Room & Board $12,900*

Richmond degrees are accredited in the United States and validated in the United Kingdom—the world's two most highly regarded higher education systems—and are thereby acknowledged worldwide.

Students studying in the courtyard of the Louvre and enjoying the beautiful Parisian summer.

THE AMERICAN UNIVERSITY OF PARIS

PARIS, FRANCE
www.aup.edu/

The American University of Paris (AUP) is an urban, independent, international university located in one of the world's greatest cities. The University aims to provide the finest American programs to students from all backgrounds, and to take its place as a global center for innovative interdisciplinary research. AUP offers seventeen majors and thirty-three minors in everything from Film to Finance. Its nine graduate programs are cutting edge; students can earn a master's degree in Cross-Cultural and Sustainable Business Management; Cultural Translation; Global Communications; Global Communications and Civil Society; International Affairs, Conflict Resolution, and Civil Society Development; Middle East and Islamic Studies; Middle

FRANCE

East & Islamic Studies and International Affairs; Public Policy and International Affairs; and Public Policy and International Law. Many AUP students go on to the finest graduate schools and careers in the United States, Europe and elsewhere around the world. AUP educates its graduates to communicate well in a world of many languages; to think critically about history, culture, the arts, science, politics and business; to develop creative approaches to important contemporary challenges; to be both technologically and culturally literate in a fast-changing world; and to take responsibility for their communities around the globe. Americans represent about one third of the student body, Europeans from Moscow to London (more than twenty-five countries) another third and the final third come from the Middle East, Africa, Asia and Latin America. Students make friends through a large number of clubs and organizations. Some popular ones include WhiteMask Theatre club, AUP's award-winning debate club, Model United Nations, the Photo Club and the A'Cappella Choir. AUP students also manage several student-run publications, including the biweekly student newspaper, *The Planet*; *Core*, AUP's humanities journal; *Scripta Politica et Economica;* and *Paris/ Atlantic*, a literary journal. AUP students live off campus, many in the beautiful Parisian neighborhoods near the University. The Housing Office helps AUP students find lodging in chambres de bonne (small private rooms usually on the top floor of French apartment buildings), with French hosts or in apartments. AUP's campus

CONTACT INFORMATION

International Admissions Office

☎ +33 1 40 62 07 20
✉ admissions@aup.edu

is centrally located in the seventh arrondissement of Paris, on the Left Bank, near the Eiffel Tower and the Seine. Students can easily reach all of the landmarks of this historic city by foot or public transportation.

- **Enrollment:** *614*
- **Selectivity:** *moderately difficult*
- **Application deadline:** *3/15 (freshmen), 3/15 (transfer)*
- **Expenses:** *Tuition 25,175; Room & Board 9500*

AUP's small class sizes and interactive teaching style encourage discussions between professors and students.

JOHN CABOT UNIVERSITY

ROME, ITALY
www.johncabot.edu/

John Cabot University (JCU) is the first overseas American university in Italy with regional accreditation by the Middle States Commission of Higher Education. This four-year liberal arts college follows the American system of education with a distinctive European character. JCU's international setting in Rome and its unique relationship with leading multinational corporations, media and other organizations, provides students the academic training and opportunities to participate in internships and enter directly into demanding careers or graduate schools. JCU graduates are accepted into top graduate programs in the United States, United Kingdom and Italy such as Columbia University, Johns Hopkins University, London School of Economics, and l'Universita Bocconi. Since 2000, the University has had a validation agreement with the University of Wales allowing students to simultaneously earn both the American B.A. and the British B.A. Honors degree for JCU majors in business administration, international affairs, marketing and political science. John Cabot University is located in the Trastevere neighborhood of Rome, just down the river from St. Peter's Basilica and the Vatican and a short walk from the Roman Forum. John Cabot has two campuses within a 5-minute walk of each other. The Frank J. Guarini Campus, a former convent, has a central, three-story building and an adjacent wing connected by terraces and courtyards. The original separate chapel now serves as the student lounge. The property offers students a quiet environment in which to study and live, while bustling Rome is just a few steps away. Surrounded by the green gardens of the Accademia dei Lincei (the National Academy of Sciences, of which Galileo was an early member) and next door to the Villa Farnesina of Raphael's famous frescoes, the Guarini Campus is supported by the Aurelian Wall of the Roman Empire. John Cabot also has the Tiber Campus, along the banks of the famous Tiber River. Both campuses are equipped with Wi-Fi and state-of-the-art multimedia equipment and JCU's Frohing Library is one of the most impressive English language libraries in Rome. JCU's fine arts and art history classes often meet at famous monuments such as the Colosseum and the Forum, which are within easy reach of campus. In effect, all of Rome is John Cabot University's campus—students regularly meet with friends and faculty at local cafes and trattorias as well as in many of the piazzas that are hidden within the small streets of Rome's historic center.

CONTACT INFORMATION

Ms. Jill Peacock, Director of Admissions

☎ 39 06 681 9121 or toll-free 866-227-0112

✉ admissions@johncabot.edu

- **Enrollment:** *750*
- **Selectivity:** *moderately difficult*
- **Application deadline:** *7/15 (freshmen), 7/15 (transfer)*
- **Expenses:** *Tuition $18,600; Room & Board $13,200*

Students at SLU–Madrid

Madrid
SAINT LOUIS UNIVERSITY

MADRID, SPAIN
www.spain.slu.edu/

Saint Louis University is consistently ranked by *U.S. News & World Report* among the top 100 teaching and research institutions in the United States. The University's Madrid campus (SLU–Madrid), originally established in the 1960s as a study-abroad destination, is the first free-standing campus in Europe operated by a U.S.-based university. Today, students from more than sixty-five countries earn either U.S. four-year undergraduate degrees, graduate degrees or, in the case of study-abroad students, credits towards their degrees from their home campuses. About 25 percent of the University's students come from Spain, 40 percent from the

United States (all fifty states) and 35 percent from over sixty-five countries around the world. Major courses (Business Administration/International Business, Political Science/International Relations, Spanish Language and Literature, Communication, English and Economics) are typically taught in English, with a few classes taught in Spanish. The University hosts several day trips at the beginning of each term in order to give new students the opportunity to make friends and settle into life in Spain before the start of classes. Students here can participate in nineteen different sports, join local gyms or take a scuba diving course. Basketball, football, volleyball, lacrosse, soccer, Ultimate (Frisbee), squash, American football and field hockey are just some of the sports offered at SLU–Madrid. *La Voz*, the student-led newspaper, and the Campus Ambassador group are two popular activities on campus. Through the Campus Ministry, many student volunteers help out in soup kitchens or organize retreats to Loyola in the Basque country to learn about the founder of the Jesuits, Saint Ignatius of Loyola. SLU–Madrid strongly encourages students to take advantage of the host family option through which students who wish to experience Spanish society to the fullest can be part of a Spanish household. Through this program, students learn and experience day-to-day life in urban Madrid. Spain's capital, Madrid, with a population of more than 4 million, is politically, culturally and geographically the heart of Spain. From the Prado Museum to

CONTACT INFORMATION

Ms. Maria-Jose Morell, Director of Enrollment Management

☎ 34 91-554-5858
🖥 mmorell@slu.edu

the Royal Palace, the city's spectacular cultural offerings are eclipsed only by its vibrant nightlife. SLU–Madrid is located in the city, near many other public and private universities.

- **Selectivity:** *moderately difficult*
- **Application deadline:** *5/31 (freshmen), 5/31 (transfer)*
- **Expenses:** *Tuition $15,660; Room only $5880*

The SLU–Madrid campus

Getting Into College

EXPLORING POSSIBLE CAREER PATHS IN HIGH SCHOOL

The word "career" has a scary sound to it when you're still in high school. Careers are for college graduates or those who have been in the workplace for years. But unless you grew up knowing for sure that you wanted to fly airplanes or be a botanist, what will you do? You'll be happy to know that interests you have now can very possibly lead to a college major or career. A job at a clothing store, for instance, could lead to a career designing clothes. Perhaps those hours you spend on your Xbox will lead to a career creating video games! Maybe you babysit and love being around kids, so teaching becomes an obvious choice. Perhaps cars fascinate you, and you find out you want to fix them for a living.

This chapter will show you how you can begin exploring your interests—sort of like getting into a swimming pool starting with your big toe, rather than plunging in. Vocational/career and tech-prep programs, summer jobs, and volunteering are all ways you can test various career paths to decide if you like them.

The Vocational/Career Education Path

If you're looking for a more real-world education, add yourself to the nearly 11 million youths and adults who are getting a taste of the workplace through vocational and career education programs offered in high schools across the nation. These programs are designed to help you develop competency in the skills you'll need in the workplace as well as in school.

What makes this kind of program different is that you learn in the classroom and in the "real world" of the workplace. Not only do you learn the academics in school, but you also get hands-on training by job shadowing, working under a mentor, and actually performing a job outside of school. Your interests and talents are usually taken into consideration, and you can choose from a variety of traditional, high-tech, and service industry training programs. Take a look at the following categories and see what piques your interest.

Agricultural education. These programs prepare students for careers in agricultural production, animal production and care, agribusiness, agricultural and industrial mechanics, environmental management, farming, horticulture and landscaping, food processing, and natural resource management.

Business education. Students prepare for careers in accounting and finance and computer and data processing as well as administrative/secretarial and management/supervisory positions in professional environments (banking, insurance, law, public service).

Family and consumer sciences. These programs prepare students for careers in child care, food management and production, clothing and interiors, and hospitality and facility care. Core elements include personal development, family life and planning, resource management, and nutrition and wellness.

Trade and industrial and health occupations. Students prepare for careers in auto mechanics, the construction trades, cosmetology, electronics, graphics, public safety, and welding. Health occupation programs offer vocational training for careers in dental and medical assisting, practical nursing, home health care, and medical office assisting.

Marketing education. These programs prepare students for careers in sales, retail, advertising, food and restaurant marketing, and hotel management.

There are many vocational/career education programs available; the kinds just listed represent only a few of the possibilities. To get more information about vocational education programs, call 202-245-7700 or visit the U.S. Department of Education, Office of Vocational and Adult Education Web site, www.ed.gov/about/offices/list/ovae/index.html.

The Tech-Prep Path

An even more advanced preparation for the workplace and/or an associate degree from a college is called tech-prep. It's an educational path that combines college-prep and vocational/technical courses of study.

During the sequence of courses, the focus is on blending academic and vocational/technical competencies. When you graduate from high school, you'll be able to jump right into the workforce or get an associate degree. But if you want to follow this path, you've got to plan for it starting in the ninth grade. Ask your guidance counselor for more information.

Using the Summer to Your Advantage

When you're sitting in class, a summer with nothing to do might seem appealing. But after you've listened to all of your CDs, aced all of your video games, hung out at the same old mall, and talked to your friends on the phone about being bored, what's left? How about windsurfing on a cool, clear New England lake? Horseback riding along breathtaking mountain trails? Parlez français in Paris? Trekking through spectacular canyon lands or living with a family in Costa Rica, Spain, Switzerland, or Japan? Exploring college majors or possible careers? Helping out on an archeological dig or community-service project? Along the way, you'll meet some wonderful people and maybe even make a couple of lifelong friends.

Interested? Get ready to pack your bags and join the 1 million kids and teens who will be having the summer of a lifetime at thousands of terrific camps, academic programs, sports clinics, arts workshops, internships, volunteer opportunities, and travel adventures throughout North America and abroad.

Oh, you don't have the money, you say? Not to worry. There are programs to meet every budget, from $50 workshops to $5000 world treks and sessions that vary in length from just a couple of hours to a couple of months.

Flip Burgers and Learn about Life

A lot of teenagers who are anxious to earn extra cash spend their summers in retail or food service since those jobs are plentiful. If you're flipping burgers or helping customers find a special outfit, you might think the only thing you're getting out of the job is a paycheck. Think again. You will be amazed to discover that you have gained far more.

Being employed in these fields will teach you how to get along with demanding (and sometimes downright unpleasant) customers, how to work on a team, and how to handle money and order supplies. Not only do summer jobs teach you life skills, but they also offer ways to explore potential careers. What's more, when you apply to college or for a full-time job after high school graduation, the experience will look good on your application.

Sometimes, summer jobs become the very thing you want to do later in life. Before committing to a college major, summer jobs give you the opportunity to try out many directions. Students who think they want to be engineers, lawyers, or doctors might spend the summer shadowing an engineer, being a gofer in a legal firm, or volunteering in a hospital.

However, rather than grab the first job that comes along, find out where your interests are and build on what is natural for you. Activities you take for granted provide clues to what you are good at. What about that bookcase you built? Or those kids you love to baby-sit? Same thing with that big party you arranged. The environments you prefer provide other hints, too. Perhaps you feel best in the middle of a cluttered garage instead of surrounded by people. That suggests certain types of jobs.

Getting a summer job while in high school is the first step in a long line of work experiences to come. And the more experience you have, the better you'll be at getting jobs all your life.

FROM THE GUIDANCE OFFICE

Q: What options are open to students who take high school career/technology classes and who feel they can't go to college?

A: Students have the opportunity to develop many skills through classes, student organizations, and career/technology classes during high school. These skills form an essential core that they can use to continue on to college, enter the job market, or participate in additional training after graduation. When students can identify those skills and make the connection by applying and expanding their skills as lifelong learners, then the possibilities are endless.

Linda S. Sanchez
Career and Technology
Counselor
South San Antonio I.S.D.
Career Education Center
San Antonio, Texas

Try Your Hand at an Internship

Each year, thousands of interns work in a wide variety of places, including corporations, law firms, government agencies, media organizations, interest groups, clinics, labs, museums, and historical sites. How popular are internships? Consider the recent trends. In the early 1980s, only 1 in 36 students completed an internship or other experiential learning program. Compare this to 2006, where one study found that 62 percent of college students had planned for a summer internship. And an increasing number of high school students are signing up for internships now, too.

THE EMPLOYER'S PERSPECTIVE

Employers consider internships a good option in both healthy and ailing economies. In healthy economies, managers often struggle to fill their positions with eager workers who can adapt to changing technologies. Internships offer a low-cost way to get good workers "into the pipeline" without offering them a full-time position up front. In struggling economies, on the other hand, downsizing often requires employers to lay off workers without thinking about who will cover their responsibilities. Internships offer an inexpensive way to offset position losses resulting from disruptive layoffs.

THE INTERN'S PERSPECTIVE

If you are looking to begin a career or supplement your education with practical training, internships are a good bet for several reasons.

1. **Internships offer a relatively quick way to gain work experience and develop job skills.** Try this exercise. Scan the Sunday want ads of your newspaper. Choose a range of interesting advertisements for professional positions that you would consider taking. List the desired or required job skills and work experiences specified in the ads. How many of these skills and experiences do you have? Chances are, if you are still in school, you don't have most of the skills and experience that employers require of their new hires. What do you do?

   The growing reality is that many entry-level positions require skills and experiences that schools and part-time jobs don't provide.

Sure, you know your way around a computer. You have some customer service experience. You may even have edited your school's newspaper or organized your junior prom. But you still lack the relevant skills and on-the-job experiences that many hiring managers require. A well-chosen internship can offer a way out of this common dilemma by providing you job training in an actual career field. Internships help you take your existing knowledge and skills and apply them in ways that will help you compete for good jobs.

2. **Internships offer a relatively risk-free way to explore a possible career path.** Believe it or not, the best internship may tell you what you *don't* want to do for the next ten or twenty years. Think about it. If you put all your eggs in one basket, what happens if your dream job turns out to be the exact opposite of what you want or who you are? Internships offer a relatively low-cost opportunity to "try out" a career field to see if it's right for *you.*

3. **Internships offer real opportunities to do career networking and can significantly increase your chances of landing a good full-time position.** Have you heard the saying: "It's not what you know, but who you know"? The reality is that who you know (or who knows you) can make a big difference in your job search. Studies show that fewer than 20 percent of job placements occur through traditional application methods, including newspaper and trade journal advertisements, employment agencies, and career fairs. Instead, 60 to 90 percent of jobs are found through personal contacts and direct application.

Career networking is the exchange of information with others for mutual benefit. Your career network can tell you where the jobs are and help you compete for them. Isn't it better to develop your networking skills now, when the stakes aren't as high, than later when you are competing with everyone else for full-time jobs? The internship hiring process and the weeks you actually spend on the job provide excellent opportunities to talk with various people about careers, your skills, and ways to succeed.

Volunteering in Your Community

You've probably heard the saying that money isn't everything. Well, it's true, especially when it comes to volunteering and community service. There are a number of benefits you'll get that don't add up in dollars and cents but do add up to open doors in your future.

Community service looks good on a college application. Admissions staff members look for applicants who have volunteered and done community service in addition to earning good grades. You could have gotten top grades, but if that's all that's on your application, you won't come across as a well-rounded person.

Community service lets you try out careers. How will you know you'll like a certain type of work if you haven't experienced it? For instance, you might think you want to work in the health-care field. Volunteering in a hospital will let you know if this is really what you want to do.

Community service is an American tradition. You'll be able to meet some of your own community's needs and join with all of the people who have contributed their talents to our country. No matter what your talents, there are unlimited ways for you to serve your community. Take a look at your interests, and then see how they can be applied to help others.

Here are some ideas to get you started:

- ❏ **Do you like kids?** Volunteer at your local parks and recreation department, for a Little League team, or as a big brother or sister.

- ❏ **Planning a career in health care?** Volunteer at a blood bank, clinic, hospital, retirement home, or hospice. There are also several organizations that raise money for disease research.

- ❑ **Interested in the environment?** Volunteer to assist in a recycling program. Create a beautification program for your school or community. Plant trees and flowers or design a community garden.

- ❑ **Just say no.** Help others stay off drugs and alcohol by volunteering at a crisis center, hotline, or prevention program. Help educate younger kids about the dangers of drug abuse.

- ❑ **Lend a hand.** Collect money, food, or clothing for the homeless. Food banks, homeless shelters, and charitable organizations need your help.

- ❑ **Is art your talent?** Share your knowledge and skills with youngsters, the elderly, or local arts organizations that depend on volunteers to help present their plays, recitals, and exhibitions.

- ❑ **Help fight crime.** Form a neighborhood watch or organize a group to clean up graffiti.

- ❑ **Your church or synagogue may have projects that need youth volunteers.** The United Way, your local politician's office, civic groups, and special interest organizations also provide exceptional opportunities to serve your community. Ask your principal, teachers, or counselors for additional ideas.

For more information on joining in the spirit of youth volunteerism, write to the Federal Citizen Information Center (FCIC), Pueblo, Colorado 81009, and request the *Catch the Spirit* booklet. Also check out the FCIC's Web site at www.pueblo. gsa.gov.

PLANNING YOUR EDUCATION

Non-planners see the words "plan" and "future" and say, "Yeah, yeah, I know." Meanwhile, they're running out the door for an appointment they were supposed to be at 5 minutes ago.

Unfortunately, when it comes time to really do something about those goals and future hopes, the non-planners often discover that much of what should have been done wasn't done—which is not good when they're planning their future after high school. What about those classes they should have taken? What about those jobs they should have volunteered for? What about that scholarship they could have had if only they'd found out about it sooner?

But there is hope for poor planners. Now that you've thought about the direction you might want to go after graduating, you can use this chapter to help you plan what you should be doing and when you should be doing it, while still in high school.

Regardless of what type of education you're pursuing after high school, here's a plan to help you get there.

Your Education Timeline

Use this timeline to help you make sure you're accomplishing everything you need to accomplish on time.

NINTH GRADE

- As soon as you can, meet with your guidance counselor to begin talking about colleges and careers.

- Make sure you are enrolled in the appropriate college-preparatory or tech-prep courses.

- Get off to a good start with your grades. The grades you earn in ninth grade may be included in your final high school GPA and class rank.

- College might seem a long way off now, but grades really do count toward college admission and scholarships.

- Explore your interests and possible careers. Take advantage of Career Day opportunities.

- Get involved in extracurricular activities (both school and non-school-sponsored).

- Talk to your parents about planning for college expenses. Continue or begin a savings plan for college.

- Look at the college information available in your counselor's office and school and public libraries. Use the Internet to check out college Web sites.

- Tour a nearby college, if possible. Visit relatives or friends who live on or near a college campus. Check out the dorms, go to the library or student center, and get a feel for college life.

- Investigate summer enrichment programs.

TENTH GRADE

Fall

- In October, take the Preliminary SAT/National Merit Scholarship Qualifying Test (PSAT/NMSQT) for practice. When you fill out your test sheet, check the box that releases your name to colleges so you can start receiving brochures from them.

- Ask your guidance counselor about the American College Testing program's PLAN® (Pre-ACT) assessment program, which helps determine your study habits and academic progress and interests. This test will prepare you for the ACT next year.

- Take geometry if you have not already done so. Take biology and a second year of a foreign language.

- Become familiar with general college entrance requirements.
- Participate in your school's or state's career development activities.

Winter

- Discuss your PSAT score with your counselor.
- The people who read college applications aren't just looking for grades. Get involved in activities outside the classroom. Work toward leadership positions in the activities that you like best. Become involved in community service and other volunteer activities.
- Read, read, read. Read as many books as possible from a comprehensive reading list.
- Read the newspaper every day to learn about current affairs.
- Work on your writing skills—you'll need them no matter what you do.
- Find a teacher or another adult who will advise and encourage you to write well.

Spring

- Keep your grades up so you can have the highest GPA and class rank possible.
- Ask your counselor about postsecondary enrollment options and Advanced Placement (AP) courses.
- Continue to explore your interests and careers that you think you might like.
- Begin zeroing in on the type of college you would prefer (two-year or four-year, small or large, rural or urban).
- If you are interested in attending a military academy, such as West Point or Annapolis, now is the time to start planning and getting information.
- Write to colleges and ask for their academic requirements for admission.

f www.facebook.com/find.colleges

- Visit college campuses. Read all of the mail you receive from colleges. You may see something you like.

- Attend college fairs.

- Keep putting money away for college. Get a summer job.

- Consider taking SAT Subject Tests in the courses you took this year while the material is still fresh in your mind. These tests are offered in May and June.

ELEVENTH GRADE

Fall

- Meet with your counselor to review the courses you've taken, and see what you still need to take.

- Check your class rank. Even if your grades haven't been that good so far, it's never too late to improve. Colleges like to see an upward trend.

- If you didn't do so in tenth grade, sign up for and take the PSAT/NMSQT. In addition to National Merit Scholarships, this is the qualifying test for the National Hispanic Recognition Program.

- Make sure that you have a social security number.

- Take a long, hard look at why you want to continue your education after high school so you will be able to choose the best college or university for your needs.

- Make a list of colleges that meet your most important criteria (size, location, distance from home, majors, academic rigor, housing, and cost). Weigh each of the factors according to their importance to you.

- Continue visiting college fairs. You may be able to narrow your choices or add a college to your list.

- Speak to college representatives who visit your high school.

- If you want to participate in Division I or Division II sports in college, start the certification process. Check with your counselor to make sure you are taking a core curriculum that meets NCAA requirements.

- If you are interested in one of the military academies, talk to your guidance counselor about starting the application process now.

Winter

- Collect information about college application procedures, entrance requirements, tuition and fees, room and board costs, student activities, course offerings, faculty composition, accreditation, and financial aid. The Internet is a good way to visit colleges and obtain this information. Begin comparing the schools by the factors that you consider to be most important.

- Discuss your PSAT score with your counselor.

- Begin narrowing down your college choices. Find out if the colleges you are interested in require the SAT, ACT, or SAT Subject Tests for admission.

- Register for the SAT and additional SAT Subject Tests, which are offered several times during the winter and spring of your junior year. You can take them again in the fall of your senior year if you are unhappy with your scores.

- Register for the ACT, which is usually taken in April or June. You can take it again late in your junior year or in the fall of your senior year, if necessary.

- Begin preparing for the tests you've decided to take.

- Have a discussion with your parents about the colleges in which you are interested. Examine financial resources, and gather information about financial aid.

- Set up a filing system with individual folders for each college's correspondence and printed materials.

Spring

🕐 Meet with your counselor to review senior-year course selection and graduation requirements.

🕐 Discuss ACT/SAT scores with your counselor. Register to take the ACT and/or SAT again if you'd like to try to improve your score.

🕐 Discuss the college essay with your guidance counselor or English teacher.

🕐 Stay involved with your extracurricular activities. Colleges look for consistency and depth in activities.

🕐 Consider whom you will ask to write your recommendations. Think about asking teachers who know you well and who will write positive letters about you. Letters from a coach, activity leader, or an adult who knows you well outside of school (e.g., volunteer work contact) are also valuable.

🕐 Inquire about personal interviews at your favorite colleges. Call or write for early summer appointments. Make necessary travel arrangements.

🕐 See your counselor to apply for on-campus summer programs for high school students. Apply for a summer job or internship. Be prepared to pay for college applications and testing fees in the fall.

🕐 Request applications from schools you're interested in by mail or via the Internet.

Summer

🕐 Visit the campuses of your top five college choices.

🕐 After each college interview, send a thank-you letter to the interviewer.

🕐 Talk to people you know who have attended the colleges in which you are interested.

🕐 Continue to read books, magazines, and newspapers.

Practice filling out college applications, and then complete the final application forms or apply online through the Web sites of the colleges in which you're interested.

Volunteer in your community.

Compose rough drafts of your college essays. Have a teacher read and discuss them with you. Polish them, and prepare final drafts. Proofread your final essays at least three times.

Develop a financial aid application plan, including a list of the aid sources, requirements for each application, and a time-table for meeting the filing deadlines.

TWELFTH GRADE

Fall

Continue to take a full course load of college-prep courses.

Keep working on your grades. Make sure you have taken the courses necessary to graduate in the spring.

Continue to participate in extracurricular and volunteer activities. Demonstrate initiative, creativity, commitment, and leadership in each.

To male students: You must register for selective service on your eighteenth birthday to be eligible for federal and state financial aid.

Talk to counselors, teachers, and parents about your final college choices.

Make a calendar showing application deadlines for admission, financial aid, and scholarships.

Check resource books, Web sites, and your guidance office for information on scholarships and grants. Ask colleges about scholarships for which you may qualify.

Give recommendation forms to the teachers you have chosen, along with stamped, self-addressed envelopes so your teachers can send them directly to the colleges. Be sure to fill out your name, address, and school name on the top of the form.

Talk to your recommendation writers about your goals and ambitions.

🕐 Give School Report forms to your high school's guidance office. Fill in your name, address, and any other required information. Verify with your guidance counselor the schools to which transcripts, test scores, and letters are to be sent. Give your counselor any necessary forms at least two weeks before they are due or whenever your counselor's deadline is, whichever is earlier.

🕐 Register for and take the ACT, SAT, or SAT Subject Tests, as necessary.

🕐 Be sure you have requested (either by mail or online) that your test scores be sent to the colleges of your choice.

🕐 Mail or send electronically any college applications for early decision admission by November 1.

🕐 If possible, visit colleges while classes are in session.

🕐 If you plan to apply for an ROTC scholarship, remember that your application is due by December 1.

🕐 Print extra copies or make photocopies of every application you send.

Winter

🕐 Attend whatever college-preparatory nights are held at your school or by local organizations.

🕐 Send midyear grade reports to colleges. Continue to focus on your schoolwork!

🕐 Fill out the Free Application for Federal Student Aid (FAFSA) and, if necessary, the PROFILE®. These forms can be obtained from your guidance counselor or go to www.fafsa.ed.gov/ to download the forms or to file electronically. These forms may not be processed before January 1, so don't send them before then.

- Mail or send electronically any remaining applications and financial aid forms before winter break. Make sure you apply to at least one college that you know you can afford and where you know you will be accepted.

- Meet with your counselor to verify that all forms are in order and have been sent out to colleges.

- Follow up to make sure that the colleges have received all application information, including recommendations and test scores.

Spring

- Watch your mail between March 1 and April 1 for acceptance notifications from colleges.

- Watch your mail for notification of financial aid awards between April 1 and May 1.

- Compare the financial aid packages from the colleges and universities that have accepted you.

- Make your final choice, and notify all schools of your intent by May 1. If possible, do not decide without making at least one campus visit. Send your nonrefundable deposit to your chosen school by May 1 as well. Request that your guidance counselor send a final transcript to your college in June.

- Be sure that you have received a FAFSA acknowledgment.

- If you applied for a Pell Grant (on the FAFSA), you will receive a Student Aid Report (SAR) statement. Review this notice, and forward it to the college you plan to attend. Make a copy for your records.

- Complete follow-up paperwork for the college of your choice (scheduling, orientation session, housing arrangements, and other necessary forms).

Summer

- Receive the orientation schedule from your college.

- Get housing assignment from your college.

- Obtain course scheduling and cost information from your college.

- Congratulations! You are about to begin the greatest adventure of your life. Good luck.

Classes to Take if You're Going to College

Did you know that classes you take as early as the ninth grade will help you get into college? Make sure you take at least the minimum high school curriculum requirements necessary for college admission. Even if you don't plan to enter college immediately, take the most demanding courses you can handle. Talk with your guidance counselor to select the curriculum that best meets your needs and skills.

Of course, learning also occurs outside of school. While outside activities will not make up for poor academic performance, skills learned from jobs, extracurricular activities, and volunteer opportunities help you become a well-rounded student and can strengthen your college or job application.

GETTING A HEAD START ON COLLEGE COURSES

You can take college courses while still in high school so that when you're in college, you'll be ahead of everyone else. The formal name is "postsecondary enrollment." (In Texas, the formal names are "dual credit"—academic credit and articulated credit—and "Tech-Prep.") What it means is that some students can take college courses and receive both high school and college credit for the courses taken. It's like a two-for-one deal!

Postsecondary enrollment is designed to provide an opportunity for qualified high school students to experience more advanced academic work. Participation in a postsecondary enrollment program is not intended to replace courses available in high school but rather to enhance the educational opportunities available to students while in high school. There are two options for postsecondary enrollment:

Option A: Qualified high school juniors and seniors take courses for college credit. Students enrolled under Option A must pay for all books, supplies, tuition, and associated fees.

Option B: Qualified high school juniors and seniors take courses for high school and college credit. For students enrolled under this option, the local school district covers the related costs, provided the student completes the selected courses. Otherwise, the student and parent are assessed the costs.

Certain preestablished conditions must be met for enrollment, so check with your high school counselor for more information.

6 Study Skills That Lead to Success

1. **Set a regular study schedule.** No one at college is going to hound you to do your homework. Develop the study patterns in high school that will lead to success in college. Anyone who has ever pulled an all-nighter knows how much you remember when you are on the downside of your fifth cup of coffee and no sleep—not much! Nothing beats steady and consistent study habits.

2. **Save everything.** To make sure your history notes don't end up in your math notebook and your English papers don't get thrown at the bottom of your friend's locker, develop an organized system for storing your papers. Stay on top of your materials, and be sure to save quizzes and tests. It is amazing how questions from a test you took in March can miraculously reappear on your final exam.

3. **Listen.** Teachers give away what will be on the test by repeating themselves. If you pay attention to what the teacher is saying, you will probably notice what is being emphasized. If what the teacher says in class repeats itself in your notes and in review sessions, chances are that material will be on the test. So really listen.

4. **Take notes.** If the teacher has taken the time to prepare a lecture, then what he or she says is important enough for you to write down. Develop a system for reviewing your notes. After each

class, rewrite them, review them, or reread them. Try highlighting the important points or making notes in the margins to jog your memory.

5. **Use textbooks wisely.** What can you do with a textbook besides lose it? Use it to back up or clarify information that you don't understand from your class notes. Reading every word may be more effort than it is worth, so look at the book intelligently. What is in boxes or highlighted areas? What content is emphasized? What do the questions ask about in the review sections?

6. **Form a study group.** Establish a group that will stay on task and ask one another the questions you think the teacher will ask. Compare notes to see if you have all the important facts. And discuss your thoughts. Talking ideas out can help when you have to respond to an essay question.

THE COLLEGE SEARCH

The Best Resources

There are thousands of colleges and universities in the United States, so before you start filling out applications, you need to narrow down your search. There are a number of sources that will help you do this.

YOUR GUIDANCE COUNSELOR

Your guidance counselor is your greatest asset in the college search process. He or she has access to a vast repository of information, from college bulletins and catalogs to financial aid applications. She knows how well graduates from your high school have performed at colleges across the country and has probably even visited many of the colleges to get some firsthand knowledge about the schools she has recommended. The more your guidance counselor sees you and learns about you, the easier it is for her to help you. So make sure you stop by her office often, whether it's to talk about your progress or just to say "hi."

YOUR TEACHERS

Use your teachers as resources, too. Many of them have had years of experience in their field. They have taught thousands of students and watched them go off to college and careers. Teachers often stay in contact with graduates and know about their experiences in college and may be familiar with the schools you are interested in attending. Ask your teachers how they feel about the match between you and your choice of schools and if they think you will be able to succeed in that environment.

YOUR FAMILY

Your family needs to be an integral part of the college selection process, whether they are financing your education or not. They have opinions and valuable advice. Listen to them carefully. Try to absorb all their information and see if it applies to you. Does it fit with who you

f **www.facebook.com/find.colleges**

are and what you want? What works and what doesn't work for you? Is some of what they say dated? How long ago were their experiences, and how relevant are they today? Take in the information, thank them for their concern, compare what they have said with the information you are gathering, and discard what doesn't fit.

COLLEGES AND UNIVERSITIES

Don't forget to go to college fairs. Usually held in large cities in the evening, they are free and sponsored by your local guidance counselors' association and the National Association of College Admission Counseling (NACAC). The admissions counselors of hundreds of colleges, vocational/career colleges, and universities attend college fairs each year. Whether your questions are as general as what the overall cost of education is at a particular institution or as specific as how many biology majors had works published last year, the admissions office works to assist you in locating the people who can answer your questions. Bring a shopping bag for all the information you will get.

Admissions officers also visit high schools. Don't forget to attend these meetings during your junior and senior years. In general, college admissions counselors come to a school to get a general sense of the high school and the caliber and personality of the student body. Although it is difficult to make an individual impression at these group sessions, the college counselors do take names on cards for later contact, and you will occasionally see them making notes on the cards when they are struck by an astute questioner. It is helpful to attend these sessions because consistent contact between a student and a college is tracked by colleges and universities. An admissions decision may come down to examining the size of your admissions folder and the number of interactions you have had with the school over time.

College and university brochures and catalogs are a good place to look, too. After reading a few, you will discover that some offer more objective information than others. You will also start to learn what information colleges think is essential to present. That's important. If one college's brochure does not present the same information as most of the other college brochures, you have to ask yourself why. What might this say about the college's academic offerings, athletic or extracurricular programs, or campus life? What does the campus look like? How is the campus environment presented in the brochure? The brochures should present clues to what schools feel are their important majors, what their mission is, and on which departments they are spending their budgets. Take the time to do these informational resources justice. They have a great deal to say to the careful reader.

A college's Web site can give you a glimpse of campus life that does not appear in the college's brochure and catalog. It is true that the virtual tour will show you the shots that the college marketing department wants you to see, highlighting the campus in the best light, but you can use the home page to see other things, too. Read the student newspaper. Visit college-sponsored chat rooms. Go to the department in the major you are investigating. Look at the Course Bulletin to see what courses are required.

Online Help

To help you find two-year and four-year colleges or universities, check out the following online resources for additional information on college selection, scholarships, student information, and much more.

The National Association for College Admission Counseling. This site offers information for professionals, students, and parents: www. nacacnet.org.

U.S. Department of Education. This federal agency's National Center for Education Statistics produces reports on every level of education, from elementary to postgraduate. Dozens are available for downloading. You can find these and other links at http://nces.ed.gov.

Campus Visits

You've heard the old saying, "A picture is worth a thousand words." Well, a campus visit is worth a thousand brochures. Nothing beats walking around a campus to get a feel for it. Some students report that all they needed to know that they loved or hated a campus was to drive through it. Then there is the true story of the guy who applied to a school because it had a prestigious name. Got accepted. Didn't visit, and when he arrived to move into the dorms, discovered to his horror it was an all-male school. A visit would have taken care of that problem.

The best time to experience the college environment is during the spring of your junior year or the fall of your senior year. Although you may have more time to visit colleges during your summer off, your observations will be more accurate when you can see the campus in full swing. Open houses are a good idea and provide you with opportunities to talk to students, faculty members, and administrators. Write or call in advance to take student-conducted campus tours. If possible, stay overnight in a dorm to see what living at the college is really like.

Bring your transcript so that you are prepared to interview with admission officers. Take this opportunity to ask questions about financial aid and other services that are available to students. You can get a good snapshot of campus life by reading a copy of the student newspaper. The final goal of the campus visit is to study the school's personality and decide if it matches yours. Your parents should be involved with the campus visits so that you can share your impressions. Here are some additional campus visit tips:

- Read campus literature prior to the visit.
- Ask for directions, and allow ample travel time.
- Make a list of questions before the visit.
- Dress in neat, clean, and casual clothes and shoes.
- Ask to meet one-on-one with a current student.
- Ask to meet personally with a professor in your area of interest.
- Ask to meet a coach or athlete in your area of interest.
- Offer a firm handshake.

- ☑ Use good posture.

- ☑ Listen, and take notes.

- ☑ Speak clearly, and maintain eye contact with people you meet.

- ☑ Don't interrupt.

- ☑ Be honest, direct, and polite.

- ☑ Be aware of factual information so that you can ask questions of comparison and evaluation.

- ☑ Be prepared to answer questions about yourself. Practice a mock interview with someone.

- ☑ Don't be shy about explaining your background and why you are interested in the school.

- ☑ Ask questions about the background and experiences of the people you meet.

- ☑ Convey your interest in getting involved in campus life.

- ☑ Be positive and energetic.

- ☑ Don't feel as though you have to talk the whole time or carry the conversation yourself.

- ☑ Relax, and enjoy yourself.

- ☑ Thank those you meet, and send thank-you notes when appropriate.

After you have made your college visits, rank the schools in which you're interested. This will help you decide not only which ones to apply to, but also which one to attend once you receive your acceptance letters.

The College Interview

Not all schools require or offer an interview. However, if you are offered an interview, use this one-on-one time to evaluate the college in detail and to sell yourself to the admission officer. The following list of questions can help you collect vital information you will want to know.

- ☑ How many students apply each year? How many are accepted?

- ☑ What are the average GPA and average ACT or SAT score(s) for those accepted?

- ☑ How many students in last year's freshman class returned for their sophomore year?

- ☑ What is the school's procedure for credit for Advanced Placement high school courses?

- ☑ As a freshman, will I be taught by professors or teaching assistants?

- ☑ How many students are there per teacher?

- ☑ When is it necessary to declare a major?

- ☑ Is it possible to have a double major or to declare a major and a minor?

- ☑ What are the requirements for the major in which I am interested?

- ☑ How does the advising system work?

- ☑ Does this college offer study abroad, cooperative programs, or academic honors programs?

- ☑ What is the likelihood, due to overcrowding, of getting closed out of the courses I need?

- ☑ What technology is available, and what are any associated fees?

- ☑ How well equipped are the libraries and laboratories?

- ☑ Are internships available?

- ☑ How effective is the job placement service of the school?

- ☑ What is the average class size in my area of interest?

- ☑ Have any professors in my area of interest recently won any honors or awards?

- ☑ What teaching methods are used in my area of interest (lecture, group discussion, fieldwork)?

- ☑ How many students graduate in four years in my area of interest?

- ☑ What are the special requirements for graduation in my area of interest?

- ☑ What is the student body like? Age? Sex? Race? Geographic origin?

- ☑ What percentage of students live in dormitories? In off-campus housing?

- ☑ What percentage of students go home for the weekend?

- ☑ What are some of the regulations that apply to living in a dormitory?

- ☑ What are the security precautions taken on campus and in the dorms?

- ☑ Is the surrounding community safe?

- ☑ Are there problems with drug and alcohol abuse on campus?

- ☑ Do faculty members and students mix on an informal basis?

- ☑ How important are the arts to student life?

- ☑ What facilities are available for cultural events?

- ☑ How important are sports to student life?

- ☑ What facilities are available for sporting events?

- ☑ What percentage of the student body belongs to a sorority/fraternity?

- ☑ What is the relationship between those who belong to the Greek system and those who don't?

- ☑ Are students involved in the decision-making process at the college? Do they sit on major committees?

- ☑ In what other activities can students get involved?

- What percentage of students receive financial aid based on need?
- What percentage of students receive scholarships based on academic ability?
- What percentage of a typical financial aid offer is in the form of a loan?
- If a family demonstrates financial need on the FAFSA (and PROFILE®, if applicable), what percentage of the established need is generally awarded?
- How much did the college increase the cost of room, board, tuition, and fees from last year?
- Do opportunities for financial aid, scholarships, or work-study increase each year?
- When is the admission application deadline?
- When is the financial aid application deadline?
- When will I be notified of the admission decision?
- Is a deposit required and is it refundable?

Keep in mind that you don't need to ask all these questions—in fact, some of them may have already been answered for you in the catalog, on the Web site, or in the interview. Ask only the questions for which you still need answers.

Should You Head for the Ivy League?

Determining whether to apply to one of the eight Ivy League schools is something about which you should think long and hard. Sure, it can't hurt to toss your application into the ring if you can afford the application fee and the time you'll spend writing the essays. But if you want to figure out if you'd be a legitimate candidate for acceptance at one of these top-tier schools, you should understand the type of student that they look for and how you compare. Take a look at these statistics:

- On average only 15 percent or fewer applicants are accepted at Ivy League colleges each year.

- Most Ivy League students have placed in the top 10 percent of their class.

- Because Ivy League schools are so selective, they want a diverse student population. That means they want students who represent not only the fifty states but also a wide selection of other countries.

Being accepted at an Ivy League school is a process that starts in the ninth grade. You should select demanding courses and maintain good grades in those courses throughout all four years of high school. Get involved in extracurricular activities as well, and, of course, do well on your standardized tests. When it comes time to apply for college, select at least three schools: one ideal, one possible, and one shoe-in. Your ideal can be an Ivy League if you wish.

While the ultimate goal is to get the best education possible, students are sometimes more concerned about getting accepted than with taking a hard look at what a school has to offer them. Often, a university or college that is less competitive than an Ivy may have exactly what you need to succeed in the future. Keep that in mind as you select the colleges that will offer you what you need.

Minority Students

African American, Hispanic, Asian American, and Native American high school students have a lot of doors into higher education opening for them. In fact, most colleges want to respond to the social and economic disadvantages of certain groups of Americans. They want to reflect the globalization of our economy. They want their student populations to look like the rest of America, which means people from many different backgrounds and ethnic groups. You'll find that most colleges have at least one member of the admissions staff who specializes in recruiting minorities.

One of the reasons college admissions staff are recruiting minorities and want to accommodate their needs is because there are more minorities thinking of attending college—and graduating. Let's put

www.facebook.com/find.colleges

some numbers to these statements. A November 2006 report from the American Council on Education (ACE) found that minority enrollment at U.S. colleges and universities over the ten years between 1993 and 2003 increased by 50.7 percent. In 2003, there were 4.7 million minority students, constituting 27.8 percent of all students.

ACADEMIC RESOURCES FOR MINORITY STUDENTS

In addition to churches, sororities and fraternities, and college minority affairs offices, minority students can receive information and assistance from the following organizations:

American Indian Higher Education Consortium (AIHEC)

AIHEC's mission is to support the work of tribal colleges and the national movement for tribal self-determination through four objectives: maintain commonly held standards of quality in American Indian education; support the development of new tribally controlled colleges; promote and assist in the development of legislation to support American Indian higher education; and encourage greater participation by American Indians in the development of higher education policy.

121 Oronoco Street
Alexandria, Virginia 22314
703-838-0400
www.aihec.org

ASPIRA

ASPIRA's mission is to empower the Puerto Rican and Latino community through advocacy and the education and leadership development of its youth.

1444 Eye Street, NW, Suite 800
Washington, D.C. 20005
202-835-3600
www.aspira.org

Gates Millennium Scholars (GMS)

The Gates Millennium Scholars, funded by a grant from the Bill & Melinda Gates Foundation, was established in 1999 to provide out-standing African American, American Indian/Alaska Natives, Asian Pacific Islander Americans, and Hispanic American students with an opportunity to complete an undergraduate college education in all discipline areas and a graduate education for those students pursuing studies in mathematics, science, engineering, education, or library science. The goal of GMS is to promote academic excellence and to provide an opportunity for thousands of outstanding students with significant financial need to reach their fullest potential.

P.O. Box 10500
Fairfax, Virginia 22031-8044
877-690-4677 (toll-free)
www.gmsp.org

Hispanic Association of Colleges & Universities (HACU)

The Hispanic Association of Colleges & Universities is a national asso-ciation representing the accredited colleges and universities in the United States where Hispanic students constitute at least 25 percent of the total student enrollment. HACU's goal is to bring together colleges and universities, corporations, government agencies, and individuals to establish partnerships for promoting the developing Hispanic-serving colleges and universities; improving access to and the quality of postsecondary education for Hispanic students; and meeting the needs of business, industry, and government through the development and sharing of resources, information, and expertise.

8415 Datapoint Drive, Suite 400
San Antonio, Texas 78229
210-692-3805
www.hacu.net

Hispanic Scholarship Fund (HSF)

The Hispanic Scholarship Fund is the nation's leading organization supporting Hispanic higher education. HSF was founded in 1975 with a vision to strengthen the country by advancing college education among Hispanic Americans. In support of its mission, HSF provides

the Latino community with college scholarships and educational outreach support.

55 Second Street, Suite 1500
San Francisco, California 94105
877-473-4636 (toll-free)
www.hsf.net

INROADS

A national career-development organization that places and
develops talented minority youth (African American, Hispanic
American, and Native American) in business and industry and
prepares them for corporate and community leadership.

10 South Broadway, Suite 300
St. Louis, Missouri 63102
314-241-7488
www.inroads.org

National Action Council for Minorities in Engineering (NACME)

An organization that aims to provide leadership and support for
the national effort to increase the representation of successful
African American, American Indian, and Latino women and
men in engineering and technology and math- and science-
based careers.

440 Hamilton Avenue, Suite 302
White Plains , New York 10601-1813
914-539-4010
www.nacme.org

National Association for the Advancement of Colored People (NAACP)

The purpose of the NAACP is to ensure the political, educational, social, and economic equality of all citizens; to achieve
equality of rights and eliminate race prejudice among the
citizens of the United States; to remove all barriers of racial discrimination through democratic processes; to seek enactment
and enforcement of federal, state, and local laws securing civil

rights; to inform the public of the adverse effects of racial discrimination and to seek its elimination; and to educate persons as to their constitutional rights and to take all lawful action to secure the exercise thereof, and to take any other lawful action in furtherance of these objectives, consistent with the efforts of the national organization.

4805 Mt. Hope Drive
Baltimore, Maryland 21215
877-NAACP-98 (toll-free)
www.naacp.org

The National Urban League

The National Urban League's Campaign for African American Achievement is a community-based movement that embodies the values of academic achievement, social development, and economic independence. Among children and youth, the Campaign will foster positive attitudes about academic achievement, consistent and enthusiastic participation in school, commitment to meeting and exceeding education standards, increased social polish and improved navigational skills, and a heightened sense of history, community, and self-worth.

120 Wall Street
New York, New York 10005
212-558-5300
www.nul.org

United Negro College Fund (UNCF)

The UNCF serves to enhance the quality of education by raising operating funds for its 39 member colleges and universities, providing financial assistance to deserving students, and increasing access to technology for students and faculty at historically black colleges and universities.

8260 Willow Oaks Corporate Drive
P.O. Box 10444
Fairfax, Virginia 22031-8044
800-331-2244 (toll-free)
www.uncf.org

Students with Disabilities Go to College

The Americans with Disabilities Act (ADA) requires educational institutions at all levels, public and private, to provide equal access to programs, services, and facilities. Schools must be accessible to students, as well as to employees and the public, regardless of any disability. To ensure such accessibility, they must follow specific requirements for new construction, alterations or renovations, academic programs, and institutional policies, practices, and procedures. Students with specific disabilities have the right to request and expect accommodations, including auxiliary aids and services that enable them to participate in and benefit from all programs and activities offered by or related to a school.

To comply with ADA requirements, many high schools and universities offer programs and information to answer questions for students with disabilities and to assist them both in selecting appropriate colleges and in attaining full inclusion once they enter college. And most colleges and universities have disabilities services offices to help students negotiate the system. When it comes time to apply to colleges, write to the ones that you're interested in to find out what kinds of programs they have in place. When it comes time to narrow down your choices, request a visit.

WHAT IS CONSIDERED A DISABILITY?

A person is considered to have a disability if he or she meets at least one of three conditions. The individual must:

1. have a documented physical or mental impairment that substantially limits one or more major life activities, such as personal self-care, walking, seeing, hearing, speaking, breathing, learning, working, or performing manual tasks; or

2. have a record of such an impairment; or

3. be perceived as having such an impairment.

The following quotes are from students who attend a college that offers services for learning disabled students.

"I have delayed development. I need help getting things done, and I need extra time for tests. As long as I'm able to go up to teachers and ask questions, I do well on tests."

—Anita

"I have dyslexia. I thought the term 'disabilities services' was for people with visual and hearing impairments. But when I got here, I found it covered a variety of disabilities. It was like Christmas. You got everything you wanted and more."

—Debra

"I am hard of hearing. I was always afraid I wouldn't be able to hear what [teachers] said. It's hard to read lips and listen at the same time. With note takers, I still get what I need even if the teacher moves around. They want you to make it through."

—Jeannette

Physical disabilities include impairments of speech, vision, hearing, and mobility. Other disabilities, while less obvious, are similarly limiting; they include diabetes, asthma, multiple sclerosis, heart disease, cancer, mental illness, mental retardation, cerebral palsy, and learning disabilities.

Learning disabilities refer to an array of biological conditions that impede a person's ability to process and disseminate information. A learning disability is commonly recognized as a significant deficiency in one or more of the following areas: oral expression, listening comprehension, written expression, basic reading skills, reading comprehension, mathematical calculation, or problem solving. Individuals with learning disabilities also may have difficulty with sustained attention, time management, or social skills.

If you have a disability, you will take the same steps to choose and apply to a college as other students, but you should also evaluate each college based on your special need(s). Get organized, and meet with campus specialists to discuss your specific requirements. Then, explore whether the programs, policies, procedures, and facilities meet your specific situation.

It is usually best to describe your disability in a letter attached to the application so the proper fit can be made between you and the school. You will probably need to have your psychoeducational evaluation and testing record sent to the school. Some colleges help with schedules and offer transition courses, reduced course loads, extra access to professors, and special study areas to help address your needs.

Remember, admission to college is a realistic goal for any motivated student. If you invest the time and effort, you can make it happen.

TIPS FOR STUDENTS WITH DISABILITIES

- ☑ Document your disability with letters from your physician(s), therapist, case manager, school psychologist, and other service providers.

- ☑ Get letters of support from teachers, family, friends, and service providers that detail how you have succeeded despite your disability.

- ☑ Learn the federal laws that apply to students with disabilities.

- ☑ Research support groups for peer information and advocacy.

- ☑ Visit several campuses.

- ☑ Look into the services available, the pace of campus life, and the college's programs for students with disabilities.

- ☑ Ask about orientation programs, including specialized introductions for, or about, students with disabilities.

- ☑ Ask about flexible, individualized study plans.

- ☑ Ask if the school offers technology such as voice synthesizers, voice recognition, and/or visual learning equipment to its students.

- ☑ Ask about adapted intramural/social activities.

- ☑ Ask to talk with students who have similar disabilities to hear about their experiences on campus.

- ☑ Once you select a college, get a map of the campus and learn the entire layout.

- ☑ If you have a physical disability, make sure the buildings you need to be in are accessible to you. Some, even though they comply with the ADA, aren't as accessible as others.

- ☑ Be realistic. If you use a wheelchair, for example, a school with an exceptionally hilly campus may not be your best choice, no matter what other accommodations it has.

APPLYING TO COLLEGE

Once your list is finalized, the worst part is filling out all the forms accurately and getting them in by the deadlines. Because requirements differ, you should check with all the colleges that you are interested in attending to find out what documentation is needed and when it is due.

What Schools Look for in Prospective Students

As if you were sizing up the other team to plan your game strategy, you'll need to understand what admissions committees want from you as you assemble all the pieces of your application.

Academic record. Admission representatives look at the breadth (how many), diversity (which ones), and difficulty (how challenging) of the courses on your transcript.

Grades. You should show consistency in your ability to work to your potential. If your grades are not initially good, colleges look to see that significant improvement has been made. Some colleges have minimum grade point averages that they are willing to accept.

Class rank. Colleges may consider the academic standing of a student in relation to the other members of his or her class. Are you in the top 25 percent of your class? Top half? Ask your counselor for your class rank.

Standardized test scores. Colleges look at test scores in terms of ranges. If your scores aren't high but you did well academically in high school, you shouldn't be discouraged. There is no set formula for admission. Even at the most competitive schools, some students' test scores are lower than you would think.

Extracurricular activities. Colleges look for depth of involvement (variety and how long you participated), initiative (leadership), and creativity demonstrated in activities, service, or work.

f www.facebook.com/find.colleges

Recommendations. Most colleges require a recommendation from your high school guidance counselor. Some ask for references from teachers or other adults. If your counselor or teachers don't know you well, you should put together a student resume, or brag sheet, that outlines what you have done during your four years of high school. You'll find a worksheet that will help you put together your resume in this chapter.

College interview. An interview is required by most colleges with highly selective procedures.

Admission Procedures

Your first task in applying is to get application forms. That's easy. You can get them from your high school's guidance department, at college fairs, or by calling or writing to colleges and requesting applications. The trend, however, is leaning toward online applications, which are completed on the school's Web site. Admission information can be gathered from college representatives, catalogs, Web sites, and directories; alumni or students attending the college; and campus visits.

WHICH ADMISSION OPTION IS BEST FOR YOU?

One of the first questions you will be asked on applications for four-year colleges and universities is which admission option you want. What this means is whether you want to apply early action, early decision, deferred admission, etc.

Four-year institutions generally offer the following admissions options:

Early admission. A student of superior ability is admitted into college courses and programs before completing high school.

Early decision. A student declares a first-choice college, requests that the college decide on acceptance early (between November and January), and agrees to enroll if accepted. Students with a strong high school record who are sure they want to attend a certain school may want to consider early decision admission. (See "More on Early Decision," on the next page.)

Early action. This is similar to early decision, but if a student is accepted, he or she has until the regular admission deadline to decide whether or not to attend.

Early evaluation. A student can apply under early evaluation to find out if the chance of acceptance is good, fair, or poor. Applications are due before the regular admission deadline, and the student is given an opinion between January and March.

Regular admission. This is the most common option offered to students. A deadline is set for when all applications must be received, and all notifications are sent out at the same time.

Rolling admission. The college accepts students who meet the academic requirements on a first-come, first-served basis until it fills its freshman class. No strict application deadline is specified. Applications are reviewed and decisions are made immediately (usually within two to three weeks). This method is commonly used at large state universities, so students should apply early for the best chance of acceptance.

Open admission. Virtually all high school graduates are admitted, regardless of academic qualifications.

Deferred admission. An accepted student is allowed to postpone enrollment for a year.

If you're going to a two-year college, these options also apply to you. Two-year colleges usually have an "open-door" admission policy, which means that high school graduates may enroll as long as space is available. Sometimes vocational/career colleges are somewhat selective, and competition for admission may be fairly intense for programs that are highly specialized.

MORE ON EARLY DECISION

Early decision is a legally binding agreement between you and the college. If the college accepts you, you pay a deposit within a short period of time and sign an agreement stating that you will not apply to other colleges. To keep students from backing out, some colleges mandate that applicants' high school counselors cannot send transcripts to other institutions.

In many ways, early decision is a win-win for both students and colleges. Students can relax and enjoy their senior year of high school without waiting to see if other colleges have accepted them. And colleges know early in the year who is enrolled and can start planning the coming year.

When Is Early Decision the Right Decision?

For good and bad reasons, early decision is a growing trend, so why not just do it? Early decision is an excellent idea that comes with a warning. It's not a good idea unless you have done a thorough college search and know without a shred of doubt that this is the college for you. Don't go for early decision unless you've spent time on the campus, in classes and dorms, and you have a true sense of the academic and social climate of that college.

Early decision can get sticky if you change your mind. Parents of students who have signed agreements and then want to apply elsewhere get angry at high school counselors, saying they've taken away their rights to choose among colleges. They try to force them to send out transcripts even though their children have committed to one college. To guard against this scenario, some colleges ask parents and students to sign a statement signifying their understanding that early decision is a binding plan. Some high schools now have their own form for students and parents to sign acknowledging that they completely realize the nature of an early decision agreement.

The Financial Reason Against Early Decision

Another common argument against early decision is that if an institution has you locked in, there's no incentive to offer applicants the best financial packages. The consensus seems to be that if you're looking to play the financial game, don't apply for early decision.

However, some folks argue that the best financial aid offers are usually made to attractive applicants. In general, if a student receives an early decision offer, they fall into that category and so would get "the sweetest" financial aid anyway. That doesn't mean that there aren't colleges out there using financial incentives to get students to enroll. A strong candidate who applies to six or eight schools and gets admitted to all of them will look at how much money the colleges throw his or her way before making a decision.

Before You Decide...

If you're thinking about applying for early decision at a college, ask yourself these questions first. You'll be glad you did.

- ☑ Why am I applying early decision?
- ☑ Have I thoroughly researched several colleges and do I know what my options are?
- ☑ Do I know why I'm going to college and what I want to accomplish there?
- ☑ Have I visited several schools, spent time in classes, stayed overnight, and talked to professors?
- ☑ Do the courses that the college offers match my goals?
- ☑ Am I absolutely convinced that one college clearly stands out above all others?

More Mumbo Jumbo

Besides confusing terms like deferred admission, early decision, and early evaluation, just discussed, you'll most likely stumble upon some additional terms that might bamboozle you. Here, we explain a few more:

ACADEMIC CALENDAR

Traditional semesters. Two equal periods of time during a school year.

Early semester. Two equal periods of time during a school year. The first semester is completed before Christmas.

Trimester. Calendar year divided into three equal periods of time. The third trimester replaces summer school.

Quarter. Four equal periods of time during a school year.

4-1-4. Two equal terms of about four months separated by a one-month term.

ACCREDITATION

Accreditation is recognition of a college or university by a regional or national organization, which indicates that the institution has met its objectives and is maintaining prescribed educational standards. Colleges may be accredited by one of six regional associations of schools and colleges and by any one of the many national specialized accrediting bodies.

Specialized accreditation of individual programs is granted by national professional organizations. This is intended to ensure that specific programs meet or exceed minimum requirements established by the professional organization. States may require that students in some professions that grant licenses graduate from an accredited program as one qualification for licensure.

Accreditation is somewhat like receiving a pass/fail grade. It doesn't differentiate colleges and universities that excel from those that meet minimum requirements. Accreditation applies to all programs within an institution, but it does not mean that all programs are of equal quality within an institution. Accreditation does not guarantee transfer recognition by other colleges. Transfer decisions are made by individual institutions.

AFFILIATION

Not-for-profit colleges are classified into one of the following categories: state-assisted, private/independent, or private/church-supported. The institution's affiliation does not guarantee the quality or nature of the institution, and it may or may not have an effect on the religious life of students.

State-assisted colleges and universities and private/independent colleges do not have requirements related to the religious activity of their students. The influence of religion varies among private/church-supported colleges. At some, religious services or study are encouraged or required; at others, religious affiliation is less apparent.

ARTICULATION AGREEMENT

Articulation agreements facilitate the transfer of students and credits among state-assisted institutions of higher education by establishing transfer procedures and equitable treatment of all students in the system.

One type of articulation agreement links two or more colleges so that students can continue to make progress toward their degree, even if they must attend different schools at different times. For example, some states' community colleges have agreements with their state universities that permit graduates of college parallel programs to transfer with junior standing.

A second type of articulation agreement links secondary (high school) and postsecondary institutions to allow students to gain college credit for relevant vocational courses. This type of agreement saves students time and tuition in the pursuit of higher learning.

Because articulation agreements vary from school to school and from program to program, it is recommended that students check with their home institution and the institution they are interested in attending in order to fully understand the options available to them and each institution's specific requirements.

CROSS-REGISTRATION

Cross-registration is a cooperative arrangement offered by many colleges and universities for the purpose of increasing the number and types of courses offered at any one institution. This arrangement allows students to cross-register for one or more courses at any participating host institution. While specific cross-registration program requirements may vary, typically a student can cross-register without having to pay the host institution additional tuition.

If your college participates in cross-registration, check with your home institution concerning any additional tuition costs and request a cross-registration form. Check with your adviser and registrar at your home institution to make sure that the course you plan to take is approved, and then contact the host institution for cross-registration instructions. Make sure that there is space available in the course you want to take at the host institution, as some host institutions give their own students registration priority.

To participate in cross-registration, you may need to be a full-time student (some programs allow part-time student participation) in good academic and financial standing at your home institution. Check with both colleges well in advance for all of the specific requirements.

The Complete Application Package

Freshman applications can be filed any time after you have completed your junior year of high school. Colleges strongly recommend that students apply by April (at the latest) of their senior year in order to be considered for acceptance, scholarships, financial aid, and housing. College requirements may vary, so always read and comply with specific requirements. In general, admission officers are interested in the following basic materials:

- A completed and signed application and any required application fee.

- An official copy of your high school transcript, including your class ranking and grade point average. The transcript must include all work completed as of the date the application is submitted. Check with your guidance counselor for questions about these items. If you apply online, you must inform your guidance counselor and request that he or she send your transcript to the schools to which you are applying. Your application will not be processed without a transcript.

- An official record of your ACT and/or SAT scores.

- Other items that may be required include letters of recommendation, an essay, the secondary school report form and midyear school report (sent in by your guidance counselor after you fill out a portion of the form), and any financial aid forms required by the college.

Make sure you have everything you need before you send out your application.

FILLING OUT THE FORMS

Filling out college applications can seem like a daunting task, but there are six easy steps to follow for the successful completion of this part of the process.

Step 1: Practice Copies

Make a photocopy of each application of each college to which you plan to apply. Since the presentation of your application may be considered an important aspect in the weighting for admission, you don't want to erase, cross out, or use white-out on your final application. Make all your mistakes on your copies. When you think you have it right, then transfer the information to your final original copy or go online to enter it on the college's electronic application. Remember, at the larger universities, the application packet may be the only part of you they see.

Step 2: Decide on Your Approach

What is it about your application that will grab the admission counselor's attention so that it will be pulled out of the sea of applications on his or her desk for consideration? Be animated and interesting in what you say. Be memorable in your approach to your application, but don't overdo it. You want the admissions counselor to remember you, not your Spanish castle made of popsicle sticks. Most importantly, be honest and don't exaggerate your academics and extracurricular activities. Approach this process with integrity every step of the way. First of all, it is the best way to end up in a college that is the right match for you. Second, if you are less than truthful, the college will eventually learn about it. How will they know? You have to supply support materials to accompany your application—things like transcripts and recommendations. If you tell one story and they tell another, the admissions office will notice the disparity—trust us!

Step 3: Check the Deadlines

In September of your senior year, organize your applications in chronological order. Work on materials with the earliest due date first.

Step 4: Check the Data on You

You need to make sure that the information you will be sending to support your applications is correct. The first thing to double check is your transcript. This is an important piece because you must send a transcript with each application you send to colleges. Take a trip to the guidance office and ask for a "Transcript Request Form." Fill out the request for a formal transcript, indicating that you are requesting a copy for yourself and that you will pick it up. Pay the fee if there is one.

When you get your transcript, look it over carefully. It will be several pages long and will include everything from the titles of all the courses that you have taken since the ninth grade along with the final grade for each course and community service hours you have logged each year. Check the information carefully. It is understandable that with this much data, it is easy to make an input error. Because this information is vital to you and you are the best judge of accuracy, it is up to you to check it. Take any corrections or questions you have back to your guidance counselor to make the corrections. If it is a questionable grade, your counselor will help you find out what grade should have been posted on your transcript. Do whatever needs to be done to make sure your transcript has been corrected no later than October 1 of your senior year.

Step 5: List Your Activities

When you flip through your applications, you will find a section on extracurricular activities. It is time to hit your computer again to prioritize your list of extracurricular activities and determine the best approach for presenting them to your colleges. Some students will prepare a resume and include this in every application they send. Other students will choose to develop an "Extracurricular, Academic, and Work Experience Addendum" and mark those specific sections of their application as "See attached Addendum."

If you are a powerhouse student with a great deal to say in this area, it will take time to prioritize your involvement in activities and word it succinctly yet interestingly. Put those activities that will have the strongest impact, show the most consistent involvement, and demonstrate your leadership abilities at the top of the list. This will take time, so plan accordingly. If you feel you have left out important information because the form limits you, include either an addendum or your resume as a back-up.

Step 6: Organize Your Other Data

What other information can you organize in advance of sitting down to fill out your applications?

The Personal Data Section

Most of this section is standard personal information that you will not have any difficulty responding to, but some items you will need to think about. For example, you may find a question that asks, "What special college or division are you applying to?" Do you have a specific school in mind, like the College of Engineering? If you are not sure about your major, ask yourself what interests you the most and then enter that college. Once you are in college and have a better sense of what you want to do, you can always change your major later.

The application will provide an optional space to declare ethnicity. If you feel you would like to declare an area and that it would work to your advantage for admission, consider completing this section of the application.

You are also going to need your high school's College Entrance Examination Board (CEEB) number. That is the number you needed when you filled out your test packets. It is stamped on the front of your

SAT and ACT packets, or, if you go to the guidance department, they'll tell you what it is.

The Standardized Testing Section

Applications ask you for your test dates and scores. Get them together accurately. All your College Board scores should be recorded with the latest test results you have received. Your latest ACT record will only have the current scores unless you asked for all your past test results. If you have lost this information, call these organizations or go to your guidance department. Your counselor should have copies. Be sure the testing organizations are sending your official score reports to the schools to which you're applying. If you are planning to take one of these tests in the future, the colleges will want those dates, too; they will wait for those scores before making a decision. If you change your plans, write the admissions office a note with the new dates or the reason for canceling.

The Senior Course Load Section

Colleges will request that you list your present senior schedule by semester. Set this information up in this order: List any AP or honors-level full-year courses first, as these will have the most impact. Then list other required full-year courses and then required semester courses, followed by electives. Make sure you list first-semester and second-semester courses appropriately. Do not forget to include physical education if you are taking it this year.

YOUR RECOMMENDATION WRITERS

Most schools will require you to submit two or three letters of recommendation from adults who know you well.

Guidance Counselor Recommendations

Nearly all colleges require a letter of recommendation from the applicant's high school guidance counselor. Some counselors will give students an essay question that they feel will give them the background they need in order to structure a recommendation. Other counselors will canvass a wide array of individuals who know a student in order to gather a broader picture of the student in various settings. No one approach is better than the other. Find out which approach is used at your school. You will probably get this information as a handout at one of those evening guidance programs or in a classroom presentation by your school's guidance department. If you are still not sure you know what is expected of you or if the dog has eaten those papers, ask your guidance counselor what is due and by what date. Make sure that you complete the materials on time and that you set aside enough of your time to do them justice.

Teacher Recommendations

In addition to the recommendation from your counselor, colleges may request additional recommendations from your teachers. Known as formal recommendations, these are sent directly to the colleges by your subject teachers. Most colleges require at least one formal recommendation in addition to the counselor's recommendation. However, many competitive institutions require two, if not three, academic recommendations. Follow a school's directions regarding the exact number. A good rule-of-thumb is to have recommendations from teachers in two subject areas (e.g., English and math).

Approach your recommendation writers personally to request that they write for you. They may agree. On the other hand, you may be met with a polite refusal on the order of "I'm sorry, but I'm unable to write for you. I've been approached by so many seniors already that it would be difficult for me to accomplish your recommendation by your due dates." This teacher may really be overburdened with requests for recommendations, especially if this is a senior English teacher, or the teacher may be giving you a signal that someone else may be able to write a stronger piece for you. Either way, accept the refusal politely, and seek another recommendation writer.

How do you decide whom to ask? Here are some questions to help you select your writers:

- ☑ How well does the teacher know you?

- ☑ Has the teacher taught you for more than one course? (A teacher who taught you over a two- to three-year period has seen your talents and skills develop.)

- ☑ Has the teacher sponsored an extracurricular activity in which you made a contribution?

- ☑ Do you get along with the teacher?

- ☑ Does the college/university indicate that a recommendation is required or recommended from a particular subject-area instructor?

- ☑ If you declare an intended major, can you obtain a recommendation from a teacher in that subject area?

Other Recommendation Writers

Consider getting recommendations from your employer, your rabbi or pastor, the director of the summer camp where you worked for the last two summers, and so on—but only if these additional letters are going to reveal information about you that will have a profound impact on the way a college will view your candidacy. Otherwise, you run the risk of overloading your application with too much paper.

WRITING THE APPLICATION ESSAY

Application essays show how you think and how you write. They also reveal additional information about you that is not in your other application material. Not all colleges require essays, and those that do often have a preferred topic. Make sure you write about the topic that is specified and keep to the length of pages or words. If the essay asks for 300 words, don't submit 50 or 500. Some examples of essay topics include:

Tell us about yourself. Describe your personality and a special accomplishment. Illustrate the unique aspects of who you are, what you do, and what you want out of life. Share an experience that made an impact on you, or write about something you have learned from your parents.

Tell us about an academic or extracurricular interest or idea. Show how a book, experience, quotation, or idea reflects or shapes your outlook and aspirations.

Tell us why you want to come to our college. Explain why your goals and interests match the programs and offerings of that particular school. This question requires some research about the school. Be specific.

Show us an imaginative side of your personality. This question demands originality but is a great opportunity to show off your skills as a writer. Start writing down your thoughts and impressions well before the essay is due. Think about how you have changed over the years so that if and when it comes time to write about yourself, you will have plenty of information. Write about something that means a lot to you, and support your thoughts with reasons and examples. Then explain why you care about your topic.

The essay should not be a summary of your high school career. Describe yourself as others see you, and use a natural, conversational style. Use an experience to set the scene in which you will illustrate something about yourself. For example, you might discuss how having a disabled relative helped you to appreciate life's simple pleasures. Or you may use your athletic experiences to tell how you learned the value of teamwork. The essay is your chance to tell something positive or enriching about yourself, so highlight an experience that will make the reader interested in you.

Outline in the essay what you have to offer the college. Explain why you want to attend the institution and how your abilities and goals match the strengths and offerings at the university. Write, rewrite, and edit. Do not try to dash off an essay in one sitting. The essay will improve with time and thought. Proofread and concentrate on spelling, punctuation, and content. Have someone else take a look at your essay. Keep copies to save after mailing the original.

Admission officers look for the person inside the essay. They seek students with a breadth of knowledge and experiences, someone with depth and perspective. Inner strength and commitment are admired, too. Not everyone is a winner all the time. The essay is a tool you can use to develop your competitive edge. Your essay should explain why you should be admitted over other applicants.

As a final word, write the essay from the heart. It should have life but not be contrived or one-dimensional. Avoid telling them what they want to hear; instead, be yourself.

Special Information for Athletes

If you weren't a planner before, but you want to play sports while in college or go to college on an athletic scholarship, you'd better become a planner now. There are many regulations and conditions you need to know ahead of time so that you don't miss out on possible opportunities.

First, think about whether or not you have what it takes to play college sports. It's a tough question to ask, but it's a necessary one. In general, playing college sports requires both basic skills and natural ability, a solid knowledge of the sport, overall body strength, speed, and sound academics. Today's athletes are stronger and faster because of improved methods of training and conditioning. They are coached in skills and techniques, and they begin training in their sport at an early age. Remember, your talents will be compared with those from across the United States and around the world.

Second, know the background. Most college athletic programs are regulated by the National Collegiate Athletic Association (NCAA), an organization that has established rules on eligibility, recruiting, and financial aid. The NCAA has three membership divisions: Division I, Division II, and Division III. Institutions are members of one or another division according to the size and scope of their athletic programs and whether they provide athletic scholarships.

If you are planning to enroll in college as a freshman and you wish to participate in Division I or Division II athletics, you must be certified by the NCAA Eligibility Center (https://web1.ncaa.

FROM THE GUIDANCE OFFICE

Q: What's a big mistake high school athletes make when thinking about college?

A: Some athletes think that their athletic ability alone will get them a scholarship and do not believe that their academics must be acceptable. The Division I or II schools cannot offer scholarships if the student has not met the academic standards required by the school for admission. Our counselors start reminding students in the freshman year and every year after that the courses they take do make a difference in how colleges view their transcripts. Students can't start preparing in their senior year of high school.

Sue Bradshaw
Guidance Counselor
Sterling High School
Baytown, Texas

org/eligibilitycenter). The Center was established as a separate organization by the NCAA member institutions to ensure consistent interpretation of NCAA eligibility requirements for all prospective student athletes at all member institutions.

You should start the certification process when you are a junior in high school. Check with your counselor to make sure you are taking a core curriculum that meets NCAA requirements. Also, register to take the ACT or SAT as a junior. Submit your Student Release Form (available in your guidance counseling office) to the Center by the beginning of your senior year.

INITIAL ELIGIBILITY OF FRESHMAN ATHLETES FOR DIVISION I AND II

Students who plan to participate in NCAA Division I or II college sports must obtain the Student Release Form from their high school, complete it, and send it to the NCAA Eligibility Center. This form authorizes high schools to release student transcripts, including test scores, proof of grades, and other academic information, to the Center. It also authorizes the Center to release this information to the colleges that request it. The form and corresponding fee must be received before any documents will be processed. (Fee waivers are available in some instances. Check with your counselor for fee waiver information.)

Students must also make sure that the Center receives ACT and/or SAT score reports. Students can have score reports sent directly to the Center by entering a specific code (9999) printed in the ACT and SAT registration packets.

Once a year, high schools will send an updated list of approved core courses, which lists each course offering that meets NCAA core course requirements. The Center personnel will validate the form. Thereafter, the Center will determine each student's initial eligibility. Collegiate institutions will request information from the Center on the initial eligibility of prospective student-athletes. The Center will make a certification decision and report it directly to the institution.

Additional information about the Center can be found in the *Guide for the College-Bound Student-Athlete*, published by the NCAA. To get a copy of this guide, visit the NCAA Web site at www.ncaa.org.

NATIONAL ASSOCIATION OF INTERCOLLEGIATE ATHLETICS (NAIA) REGULATIONS

The National Association of Intercollegiate Athletics (NAIA) has different eligibility requirements for student-athletes. To be eligible to participate in intercollegiate athletics as an incoming freshman, two of the following three requirements must be met:

1. Have a minimum overall high school grade point average of 2.0 on a 4.0 scale.

2. Have a composite score of 18 or higher on the ACT or an 860 total score or higher on the SAT Critical Reading and Math sections.

3. Have a top-half final class rank in his or her high school graduating class.

Student-athletes must also have on file at the college an official ACT or SAT score report from the appropriate national testing center. Results reported on the student's high school transcript are not acceptable. Students must request that their test scores be forwarded to the college's admission office.

If you have additional questions about NAIA eligibility, contact them at:

NAIA
1200 Grand Boulevard
Kansas City, Missouri 64106-2304
816-595-8000
www.naia.org

Auditions and Portfolios

If you decide to study the arts, such as theater, music, or fine arts, you may be required to audition or show your portfolio to admissions personnel. The following tips will help you showcase your talents and skills when preparing for an audition or portfolio review.

MUSIC AUDITIONS

High school students who wish to pursue a degree in music, whether it is vocal or instrumental, typically must audition. If you're a singer, prepare at least two pieces in contrasting styles. One should be in a foreign language, if possible. Choose from operatic, show music, or art song repertories, and make sure you memorize each piece. If you're an instrumentalist or pianist, be prepared to play scales and arpeggios, at least one etude or technical study, and a solo work. Instrumental audition pieces need not be memorized. In either field, you may be required to do sight-reading.

When performing music that is sight-read, you should take time to look over the piece and make certain of the key and time signatures before proceeding with the audition. If you're a singer, you should bring a familiar accompanist to the audition.

"My advice is to ask for help from teachers, try to acquire audition information up front, and know more than is required for the audition," says one student. "It is also a good idea to select your audition time and date early."

"Try to perform your solo in front of as many people as you can as many times as possible," says another student. "You may also want to try to get involved in a high school performance."

Programs differ, so students are encouraged to call the college and ask for audition information. In general, music departments seek students who demonstrate technical competence and performance achievement.

Admission to music programs varies in degree of competitiveness, so you should audition at a minimum of three colleges and a maximum of five to amplify your opportunity. The degree of competitiveness also varies by instrument, especially if a renowned musician teaches a certain instrument. Some colleges offer a second audition if you feel you did not audition to your potential. Ideally, you will be accepted into the music program of your choice, but keep in mind that it's possible to not be accepted. You must then make the decision to either pursue a music program at another college or consider another major at that college.

DANCE AUDITIONS

At many four-year colleges, an open class is held the day before auditions. A performance piece that combines improvisation, ballet, modern, and rhythm is taught and then students are expected to perform the piece at auditions. Professors look for coordination, technique, rhythm, degree of movement, and body structure. The dance faculty members also assess your ability to learn and your potential to complete the curriculum. Dance programs vary, so check with the college of your choice for specific information.

ART PORTFOLIOS

A portfolio is simply a collection of your best pieces of artwork. A well-developed portfolio can help you gain acceptance into a prestigious art college and increase your chances of being awarded a scholarship in national portfolio competitions. The pieces you select to put in your portfolio should demonstrate your interest and aptitude for a serious education in the arts and should show diversity in technique and variety in subject matter. You may show work in any medium (oils, photography, watercolors, pastels, etc.) and in either black-and-white or color. Your portfolio can include classroom assignments as well as independent projects. You can also include your sketchbook.

Specialized art colleges request that you submit an average of ten pieces of art, but remember that quality is more important than quantity. The admission office staff will review your artwork and transcripts to assess your skill and potential for success. Some schools have you present your portfolio in person; however, some schools allow students to mail artwork if distance is an issue. There is no simple formula for success other than hard work. In addition, there is no such thing as a "perfect portfolio," nor any specific style or direction to achieve one.

Tips for Pulling Your Portfolio Together

☑ Try to make your portfolio as clean and organized as possible.

☑ It is important to protect your work, but make sure the package you select is easy to handle and does not interfere with the viewing of the artwork.

☑ Drawings that have been rolled up are difficult for the jurors to handle and view. You may shrink-wrap the pieces, but it is not required.

☑ Avoid loose sheets of paper between pieces. Always spray fixative on any pieces that could smudge.

☑ If you choose to mount or mat your work (not required), use only neutral gray tones, black, or white.

☑ Slides should be presented in a standard 8 x 11 plastic slide sleeve.

☑ Label each piece with your name, address, and high school.

THEATER AUDITIONS

Most liberal arts colleges do not require that students audition to be accepted into the theater department unless they offer a Bachelor of Fine Arts (B.F.A.) degree in theater. You should apply to the college of your choice prior to scheduling an audition. You should also consider spending a full day on campus so that you may talk with theater faculty members and students, attend classes, meet with your admission counselor, and tour the facilities.

Although each college and university has different requirements, you should prepare two contrasting monologues taken from plays of your choice if you're auditioning for a B.F.A. acting program. Musical theater requirements generally consist of one up-tempo musical selection and one ballad, as well as one monologue from a play or musical of your choice. The total of all your pieces should not exceed

5 minutes. Music for the accompanist, a resume of your theater experience, and a photo are also required.

Tips to Get You Successfully through an Audition

- ☑ Choose material suitable for your age.

- ☑ If you choose your monologue from a book of monologues, you should read the entire play and be familiar with the context of your selection.

- ☑ Select a monologue that allows you to speak directly to another person; you should play only one character.

- ☑ Memorize your selection.

- ☑ Avoid using characterization or style, as they tend to trap you rather than tapping deeper into inner resources.

For more information about visual and performing arts colleges, check out *Peterson's College Guide for Visual Arts Majors* and *Peterson's College Guide for Performing Arts Majors,* available everywhere books are sold.

WHAT TO EXPECT IN COLLEGE

No one can fill in all the details of what you'll find once you begin college. However, here's some information about a few of the bigger questions you might have, such as how to choose your classes or major and how you can make the most of your life outside the classroom.

Choosing Your Classes

College is designed to give you freedom, but at the same time, it teaches you responsibility. You will probably have more free time than in high school, but you will also have more class material to master. Your parents may entrust you with more money, but it is up to you to make sure there's enough money in your bank account when school fees are due. The same principle applies to your class schedule: You will have more decision-making power than ever, but you also need to know and meet the requirements for graduation.

To guide you through the maze of requirements, all students are given an adviser. This person, typically a faculty member, will help you select classes that meet your interests and graduation requirements. During your first year or two at college, you and your adviser will choose classes that meet general education requirements and select electives, or non-required classes, that pique your interests. Early on, it is a good idea to take a lot of general education classes. They are meant to expose you to new ideas and help you explore possible majors. Once you have selected a major, you will be given an adviser for that particular area of study. This person will help you understand and meet the requirements for that major.

In addition to talking to your adviser, talk to other students who have already taken a class you're interested in and who really enjoyed how a professor taught the class. Then try to get into that professor's class when registering. Remember, a dynamic professor can make a dry subject engaging. A boring professor can make an engaging subject dry.

As you move through college, you will notice that focusing on the professor is more important than focusing on the course title. Class titles can be cleverly crafted. They can sound captivating. However, the advice above still holds true: "Pop Culture and Icons" could turn out to be awful, and "Beowulf and Old English" could be a blast.

When you plan your schedule, watch how many heavy reading classes you take in one semester. You don't want to live in the library or the dorm study lounge. In general, the humanities, such as history, English, philosophy, and theology, involve a lot of reading. Math and science classes involve less reading; they focus more on solving problems.

Finally, don't be afraid to schedule a fun class. Even the most intense program of study will let you take a few electives. So take a deep breath, dig in, and explore!

Choosing Your Major

You can choose from hundreds of majors—from accounting to zoology—but which is right for you? Should you choose something traditional or select a major from an emerging area? Perhaps you already know what career you want, so you can work backward to decide which major will best help you achieve your goals.

If you know what you want to do early in life, you will have more time to plan your high school curriculum, extracurricular activities, jobs, and community service to coincide with your college major. Your college selection process may also focus upon the schools that provide strong academic programs in a certain major.

WHERE DO I BEGIN?

Choosing a major usually starts with an assessment of your career interests. Picture yourself taking classes, writing papers, making presentations, conducting research, or working in a related field. Talk to people you know who work in your fields of interest and see if you like what you hear. Also, try reading the classified ads in your local newspaper. What jobs sound interesting to you? Which ones pay the salary that you'd like to make? What level of education is required in the ads you find interesting? Select a few jobs that you think you'd like and then consult the following list of majors to see which major(s) coincide. If your area of interest does not appear here, talk to your counselor or teacher about where to find information on that particular subject.

MAJORS AND RELATED CAREERS

Agriculture

Many agriculture majors apply their knowledge directly on farms and ranches. Others work in industry (food, farm equipment, and agricultural supply companies), federal agencies (primarily in the Departments of Agriculture and the Interior), and state and local farm and agricultural agencies. Jobs might be in research and lab work, marketing and sales, advertising and public relations, or journalism and radio/TV (for farm communications media). Agriculture majors also pursue further training in biological sciences, animal health, veterinary medicine, agribusiness management, vocational agriculture education, nutrition and dietetics, and rural sociology.

Architecture

Architecture and related design fields focus on the built environment as distinct from the natural environment of the agriculturist or the conservationist. Career possibilities include drafting, design, and project administration in architectural, engineering, landscape design, interior design, industrial design, planning, real estate, and construction firms; government agencies involved in construction, housing, highways, and parks and recreation; and government and nonprofit organizations interested in historic or architectural preservation.

Area/Ethnic Studies

The research, writing, analysis, critical thinking, and cultural awareness skills acquired by area/ethnic studies majors, combined with the expertise gained in a particular area, make this group of majors valuable in a number of professions. Majors find positions in administration, education, public relations, and communications in such organizations as cultural, government, international, and (ethnic) community agencies; international trade (import-export); social service agencies; and the communications industry (journalism, radio, and TV). These studies also provide a good background for further training in law, business management, public administration, education, social work, museum and library work, and international relations.

Arts

Art majors most often use their training to become practicing artists, though the settings in which they work vary. Aside from the most obvious art-related career—that of the self-employed artist or craftsperson—many fields require the skills of a visual artist. These include advertising; public relations; publishing; journalism; museum work; television, movies, and theater; community and social service agencies concerned with education, recreation, and entertainment; and teaching. A background in art is also useful if a student wishes to pursue art therapy, arts or museum administration, or library work.

Biological Sciences

The biological sciences include the study of living organisms from the level of molecules to that of populations. Majors find jobs in industry; government agencies; technical writing, editing, or illustrating; science reporting; secondary school teaching (which usually requires education courses); and research and laboratory analysis and testing. Biological sciences are also a sound foundation for further study in medicine, psychology, health and hospital administration, and biologically oriented engineering.

Business

Business majors comprise all the basic business disciplines. At the undergraduate level, students can major in a general business administration program or specialize in a particular area, such as marketing or accounting. These studies lead not only to positions in business and industry but also to management positions in other sectors. Management-related studies include the general management areas (accounting, finance, marketing, and management) as well as special studies related to a particular type of organization or industry. Management-related majors may be offered in a business school or in a department dealing with the area in which the management skills are to be applied. Careers can be found throughout the business world.

Communication

Jobs in communication range from reporting (news and special features), copywriting, technical writing, copyediting, and programming to advertising, public relations, media sales, and market research. Such positions can be found at newspapers, radio and TV stations, publishing houses (book and magazine), advertising agencies, corporate communications departments, government agencies, universities, and firms that specialize in educational and training materials.

Computer, Information, and Library Sciences

Computer and information science and systems majors stress the theoretical aspects of the computer and emphasize mathematical and scientific disciplines. Data processing, programming, and computer technology programs tend to be more practical; they are more oriented toward business than to scientific applications and to working directly with the computer or with peripheral equipment. Career possibilities for computer and information science majors include data processing, programming, and systems development or maintenance in almost any setting: business and industry, banking and finance, government, colleges and universities, libraries, software firms, service bureaus, computer manufacturers, publishing, and communications.

Library science gives preprofessional background in library work and provides valuable knowledge of research sources, indexing, abstracting, computer technology, and media technology, which is useful for further study in any professional field. In most cases, a master's degree in library science is necessary to obtain a job as a librarian. Library science majors find positions in public, school, college, corporate, and government libraries and research centers; book publishing (especially reference books); database and information retrieval services; and communications (especially audiovisual media).

Education

Positions as teachers in public elementary and secondary schools, private day and boarding schools, religious and parochial schools, vocational schools, and proprietary schools are the jobs most often filled by education majors. However, teaching positions also exist in noneducational institutions, such as museums, historical societies, prisons, hospitals, and nursing homes, as well as jobs as educators and trainers in government and industry. Administrative (nonteaching) positions in employee relations and personnel, public relations, marketing and sales, educational publishing, TV and film media, test development firms, and government and community social service agencies also tap the skills and interests of education majors.

Engineering and Science Technology

Engineering and science technology majors prepare students for practical design and production work rather than for jobs that require more theoretical, scientific, and mathematical knowledge. Engineers work in a variety of fields, including aeronautics, bioengineering, geology, nuclear engineering, and quality control and safety. Industry, research labs, and government agencies where technology plays a key role, such as in manufacturing, electronics, construction communications, transportation, and utilities, hire engineering as well as engineering technology and science technology graduates regularly. Work may be in technical activities (research, development, design, production, testing, scientific programming, or systems analysis) or in nontechnical areas where a technical degree is needed, such as marketing, sales, or administration.

Foreign Language and Literature

Knowledge of foreign languages and cultures is increasingly recognized as important in today's international world. Language majors possess a skill that is used in organizations with international dealings as well as in career fields and geographical areas where languages other than English are prominent. Career possibilities include positions with business firms with international subsidiaries; import-export firms; international banking; travel agencies; airlines; tourist services; government and international agencies dealing with international affairs, foreign trade, diplomacy, customs, or immigration; secondary school foreign language teaching and bilingual education (which usually require education courses); freelance translating and interpreting (high level of skill necessary); foreign language publishing; and computer programming (especially for linguistics majors).

Health Sciences

Health professions majors, while having a scientific core, are more focused on applying the results of scientific investigation than on the scientific disciplines themselves. Allied health majors prepare graduates to assist health professionals in providing diagnostics, therapeutics, and rehabilitation. Medical science majors, such as optometry, pharmacy, and the premedical profession sequences, are, for the most part, preprofessional studies that comprise the scientific disciplines necessary for admission to graduate or professional school in the health or medical fields. Health service and technology majors prepare students for positions in the health fields that primarily involve services to patients or working with complex machinery and materials. Medical technologies cover a wide range of fields, such as cytotechnology, biomedical technologies, and operating room technology.

Administrative, professional, or research assistant positions in health agencies, hospitals, occupational health units in industry, community and school health departments, government agencies (public health, environmental protection), and international health organizations are available to majors in health fields, as are jobs in marketing and sales of health-related products and services, health education (with education courses), advertising and public relations, journalism and publishing, and technical writing.

Home Economics and Social Services

Home economics encompasses many different fields—basic studies in foods and textiles as well as consumer economics and leisure studies—that overlap with aspects of agriculture, social science, and education. Jobs can be found in government and community agencies (especially those in education, health, housing, or human services), nursing homes, child-care centers, journalism, radio/TV, educational media, and publishing. Types of work also include marketing, sales, and customer service in consumer-related industries, such as food processing and packaging, appliance manufacturing, utilities, textiles, and secondary school home economics teaching (which usually requires education courses).

Majors in social services find administrative positions in government and community health, welfare, and social service agencies, such as hospitals, clinics, YMCAs and YWCAs, recreation commissions, welfare agencies, and employment services.

Humanities (Miscellaneous)

The majors that constitute the humanities (sometimes called "letters") are the most general and widely applicable and the least vocationally oriented of the liberal arts. They are essentially studies of the ideas and concerns of human kind. These include classics, history of philosophy, history of science, linguistics, and medieval studies. Career possibilities for humanities majors can be found in business firms, government and community agencies, advertising and public relations, marketing and sales, publishing, journalism and radio/TV, secondary school teaching in English and literature (which usually requires education courses), freelance writing and editing, and computer programming (especially for those with a background in logic or linguistics).

Law and Legal Studies

Students of legal studies can use their knowledge of law and government in fields involving the making, breaking, and enforcement of laws; the crimes, trials, and punishment of law breakers; and the running of all branches of government at local, state, and federal levels. Graduates find positions of all types in law firms, legal departments of other organizations, the court or prison system, government agencies (such as law enforcement agencies or offices of state and federal attorneys general), and police departments.

Mathematics and Physical Sciences

Mathematics is the science of numbers and the abstract formulation of their operations. Physical sciences involve the study of the laws and structures of physical matter. The quantitative skills acquired through the study of science and mathematics are especially useful for computer-related careers. Career possibilities include positions in industry (manufacturing and processing companies, electronics firms, defense contractors, consulting firms); government agencies (defense, environmental protection, law enforcement); scientific/technical writing, editing, or illustrating; journalism (science reporting); secondary school teaching (usually requiring education courses); research and laboratory analysis and testing; statistical analysis; computer programming; systems analysis; surveying and mapping; weather forecasting; and technical sales.

Natural Resources

A major in the natural resources field prepares students for work in areas as generalized as environmental conservation and as specialized as groundwater contamination. Jobs are available in industry (food, energy, natural resources, and pulp and paper companies), consulting firms, state and federal government agencies (primarily the Departments of Agriculture and the Interior), and public and private conservation agencies. See the "Agriculture" and "Biological Sciences" sections for more information on natural resources–related fields.

Psychology

Psychology majors involve the study of behavior and can range from the biological to the sociological. Students can study individual behavior, usually that of humans, or the behavior of crowds. Students of psychology do not always go into the obvious clinical fields, the fields in which psychologists work with patients. Certain areas of psychology, such as industrial/organizational, experimental, and social, are not clinically oriented. Psychology and counseling careers can be in government (such as mental health agencies), schools, hospitals, clinics, private practice, industry, test development firms, social work, and personnel. The careers listed in the "Social Sciences" section are also pursued by psychology and counseling majors.

Religion

Religion majors are usually seen as preprofessional studies for those who are interested in entering the ministry. Career possibilities for religion also include casework, youth counseling, administration in community and social service organizations, teaching in religious educational institutions, and writing for religious and lay publications. Religious studies also prepare students for the kinds of jobs other humanities majors often pursue.

Social Sciences

Social sciences majors study people in relation to their society. Thus, social science majors can apply their education to a wide range of occupations that deal with social issues and activities. Career opportunities are varied. People with degrees in the social sciences find careers in government, business, community agencies (serving children, youth, and senior citizens), advertising and public relations, marketing and sales, secondary school social studies teaching (with education courses), casework, law enforcement, parks and recreation, museum work (especially for anthropology, archaeology, geography, and history majors), preservation (especially for anthropology, archaeology, geography, and history majors), banking and finance (especially for economics majors), market and survey research, statistical analysis, publishing, fundraising and development, and political campaigning.

Technologies

Technology majors, along with trade fields, are most often offered as two-year programs. Majors in technology fields prepare students directly for jobs; however, positions are in practical design and production work rather than in areas that require more theoretical, scientific, and mathematical knowledge. Engineering technologies prepare students with the basic training in specific fields (e.g., electronics, mechanics, or chemistry) that are necessary to become technicians on the support staffs of engineers. Other technology majors center more on maintenance and repair. Work may be in technical activities, such as production or testing, or in nontechnical areas where a technical degree is needed, such as marketing, sales, or administration. Industries, research labs, and government agencies in which technology plays a key role—such as in manufacturing, electronics, construction, communications, transportation, and utilities—hire technology graduates regularly.

STILL UNSURE?

Relax! You don't have to know your major before you enroll in college. More than half of all freshmen are undecided when they start school and prefer to get a feel for what's available at college before making a decision. Most four-year colleges don't require students to formally declare a major until the end of their sophomore year or beginning of their junior year. Part of the experience of college is being exposed to new subjects and new ideas. Chances are your high school never offered anthropology. Or marine biology. Or applied mathematics. So take these classes and follow your interests. While you're fulfilling your general course requirements, you might stumble upon a major that appeals to you, or maybe you'll discover a new interest while you're volunteering or participating in other extracurricular activities. Talking to other students might lead to new options you'll want to explore.

CAN I CHANGE MY MAJOR IF I CHANGE MY MIND?

Choosing a major does not set your future in stone, nor does it necessarily disrupt your life if you need to change your major. However, there are advantages to choosing a major sooner rather than later. If you wait too long to choose, you may have to take additional classes to satisfy the requirements, which may cost you additional time and money.

The Other Side of College: Having Fun!

There is more to college than writing papers, reading books, and sitting through lectures. Your social life plays an integral part in your college experience.

MEETING NEW PEOPLE

The easiest time to meet new people is at the beginning of something new. New situations shake people up and make them feel just uncomfortable enough to take the risk of extending their hand in friendship. Fortunately for you, college is filled with new experiences. There are the first weeks of being the newest students. This can be quickly followed by being a new member of a club or activity. And with each passing semester, you will be in new classes with new teachers and new faces. College should be a time of constantly challenging and expanding yourself, so never feel that it is too late to meet new people.

But just how do you take that first step in forming a relationship? It's surprisingly easy. Be open to the opportunities of meeting new people and having new experiences. Join clubs and activities. Investigate rock-climbing. Try ballet. Write for the school paper. But most of all, get involved.

CAMPUS ACTIVITIES

College life will place a lot of demands on you. Your classes will be challenging. Your professors will expect more from you. You will have to budget and manage your own money. But there is a plus side you probably haven't thought of yet: college students do have free time.

The average student spends about three hours a day in class. Add to this the time you will need to spend studying, eating, and socializing, and you will still have time to spare. One of the best ways to use this time is to participate in campus activities.

Intramural Sports

Intramurals are sports played for competition between members of the same campus community. They provide competition and a sense of belonging without the same level of intensity in practice schedules. Anyone can join an intramural sport. Often there are teams formed by dormitories, sororities, or fraternities that play team sports such as soccer, volleyball, basketball, flag-football, baseball, and softball. There are also individual intramural sports such as swimming, golf, wrestling, and diving. If you want to get involved, just stop by the intramural office. Usually it is located near the student government office.

Student Government

Student government will be set up in a way that is probably similar to your high school. Students form committees and run for office. However, student government in college has more power than in high school. The officers address all of their class's concerns directly to the President of the college or university and the Board of Trustees. Most student governments have a branch responsible for student activities that brings in big name entertainers and controversial speakers. You may want to get involved to see how such contacts are made and appearances negotiated.

Community Service

Another aspect of student life is volunteering, commonly called community service. Many colleges offer a range of opportunities. Some allow you to simply commit an afternoon to a cause, such as passing out food at a food bank. Others require an ongoing commitment. For example, you might decide to help an adult learn to read every Thursday at 4 p.m. for three months. Some colleges will link a service commitment with class credit. This will enhance your learning, giving you some real-world experience. Be sure to stop by your community service office and see what is available.

Clubs

There are a variety of clubs on most college campuses spanning just about every topic you can imagine. Amnesty International regularly meets on most campuses to write letters to help free prisoners in foreign lands. Most college majors band together in a club to discuss their common interests and career potential. There are also clubs that are based on the use of certain computer software or that engage in outdoor activities like sailing or downhill skiing. The list is endless. If you cannot find a club for your interest, consider starting one of your own. Stop by the student government office to see what rules you will need to follow. You will also need to find a location to hold meetings and post signs to advertise your club. When you hold your first meeting, you will probably be surprised at how many people are willing to take a chance and try a new club.

Greek Life

A major misconception of Greek life is that it revolves around wild parties and alcohol. In fact, the vast majority of fraternities and sororities focus on instilling values of scholarship, friendship, leadership, and service in their members. From this point forward, we will refer to both fraternities and sororities as fraternities.

Scholarship

A fraternity experience helps you make the academic transition from high school to college. Although the classes taken in high school are challenging, they'll be even harder in college. Fraternities almost always require members to meet certain academic standards. Many hold mandatory study times, keep old class notes and exams on file for study purposes, and make personal tutors available. Members of a fraternity have a natural vested interest in seeing that other members succeed academically, so older members often assist younger members with their studies.

Friendship

Social life is an important component of Greek life. Social functions offer an excellent opportunity for freshmen to become better acquainted with others in the chapter. Whether it is a Halloween party or a formal dance, there are numerous chances for members to develop poise and confidence. By participating in these functions, students enrich friendships and build memories that will last a lifetime. Remember, social functions aren't only parties; they can include such activities as intramural sports and Homecoming.

Leadership

Because fraternities are self-governing organizations, leadership opportunities abound. Students are given hands-on experience in leading committees, managing budgets, and interacting with faculty members and administrators. Most houses have as many as ten officers, along with an array of committee members. By becoming actively involved in leadership roles, students gain valuable experience that is essential for a successful career. Interestingly, although Greeks represent less than 10 percent of most undergraduate student populations, they often hold the majority of leadership positions on campus.

Service

According to the North-American Interfraternity Council, fraternities are increasingly involved in philanthropies and hands-on service projects. Helping less fortunate people is a major focus of Greek life. This can vary from work with Easter Seals, blood drives, and food pantry collections to community upkeep, such as picking up trash, painting houses, or cleaning up area parks. Greeks also get involved in projects with organizations such as Habitat for Humanity, the American Heart Association, and Children's Miracle Network. By being involved in philanthropic projects, students not only raise money for worthwhile causes, they also gain a deeper insight into themselves and their responsibility to the community.

Roommates

When you arrive on campus, you will face a daunting task: to live peacefully with a stranger for the rest of the academic year.

To make this task easier, most schools use some type of room assignment survey. This can make roommate matches more successful. For example, two people who prefer to stay up late and play guitar can be matched, while two people who prefer to rise at dawn and hit the track can be a pair. Such differences are easy to ask about on a survey and easy for students to report. However, surveys cannot ask everything, and chances are pretty good that something about your roommate is going to get on your nerves.

In order to avoid conflict, plan ahead. When you first meet, work out some ground rules. Most schools have roommates write a contract together and sign it during the first week of school. Ground rules help eliminate conflict from the start by allowing each person to know what is expected. You should consider the following areas: privacy, quiet time, chores, and borrowing.

When considering privacy, think about how much time alone you need each day and how you and your roommate will arrange for private time. Class schedules usually give you some alone time. Be aware of this; if your class is cancelled, consider going for a cup of coffee or a browse in the bookstore instead of immediately rushing back to your room. Privacy also relates to giving your roommate space when he or she has had a bad day or just needs time to think. Set up clear hours for quiet time. Your dorm may already have some quiet hours established. You can choose to simply reiterate those or add additional time. Just be clear.

Two other potentially stormy issues are chores and borrowing. If there are cleaning chores that need to be shared, make a schedule and stick to it. No one appreciates a sink full of dirty dishes or a dingy shower. Remember the golden rule: do your chores as you wish your roommate would. When it comes to borrowing, set up clear rules. The safest bet is to not allow it; but if you do, limit when, for how long, and what will be done in case of damage.

Another issue many students confront is whether or not to live with a best friend from high school who is attending the same college. Generally, this is a bad idea for several reasons. First, you may think you know your best friend inside and out, but you may be surprised by his or her personal living habits. There is nothing like the closeness of a dorm room to reveal the annoying routines of your friend. Plus, personalities can change rapidly in college. Once you are away from home, you may be surprised at how you or your friend transforms from shy and introverted to late night partygoer. This can cause conflict. A final downfall is that the two of you will stick together like glue in the first few weeks and miss out on opportunities to meet other people.

Armed with this information, you should have a smooth year with your new roommate. But just in case you are the exception, most colleges do allow students who absolutely cannot get along to move. Prior to moving, each student must usually go through a dispute resolution process. This typically involves your Resident Adviser, you, and your roommate trying to work through your problems in a structured way.

Living with a roommate can be challenging at times, but the ultimate rewards—meeting someone new, encountering new ideas, and learning how to compromise—will serve you well later in life. Enjoy your roommate and all the experiences you will have, both good and bad, for they are all part of the college experience.

Commuting from Home

For some students, home during the college years is the same house in which they grew up. Whether you are in this situation because you can't afford to live on campus or because you'd just rather live at home with your family, some basic guidelines will keep you connected with campus life.

By all means, do not just go straight home after class. Spend some of your free time at school. Usually there is a student union or a coffee shop where students gather and socialize. Make it a point to go there and talk to people between classes. Also, get involved in extracurricular activities, and visit classmates in the dorms.

If you drive to school, find other students who want to carpool. Most schools have a commuters' office or club that will give you a list of people who live near you. Sharing a car ride will give you time to talk and form a relationship with someone else who knows about the challenges of commuting.

Commuters' clubs also sponsor a variety of activities through-out the year—give them a try! Be sure also to consider the variety of activities open to all members of the student body, ranging from student government to community service to intramural sports. You may find this takes a bit more effort on your part, but the payoff in the close friendships you'll form will more than make up for it.

What if You Don't Like the College You Pick?

In the best of all worlds, you compile a list of colleges, find the most compatible one, and are accepted. You have a great time, learn a lot, graduate, and head off to a budding career. However, you may find the college you chose isn't the best of all worlds. Imagine these scenarios:

- Halfway through your first semester of college, you come to the distressing conclusion that you can't stand being there for whatever reason. The courses don't match your interests. The campus is out in the boonies, and you don't ever want to see another cow. The selec-tion of extracurricular activities doesn't cut it.

- You have methodically planned to go to a community college for two years and move to a four-year college to complete your degree. Transferring takes you nearer to your goal.

- You thought you wanted to major in art, but by the end of the first semester, you find yourself more interested in English lit. Things get confusing, so you drop out of college to sort out your thoughts and now you want to drop back in, hoping to rescue some of those credits.

- You didn't do that well in high school—socializing got in the way of studying. But you've wised up, have gotten serious about your future, and two years of community college have brightened your prospects of transferring to a four-year institution.

- Circumstances shift, people change, and, realistically speaking, it's not all that uncommon to transfer. Many people do. The reasons why students transfer run the gamut, as do the institutional policies that govern them. The most common transfers are students who move from a two-year to a four-year university or the person who opts for a career change midstream.

- Whatever reasons you might have for wanting to transfer, you will be doing more than just switching academic gears. Aside from potentially losing credits, time, and money, transferring means again adjusting to a new situation. This affects just about all transfer students, from those who made a mistake in choosing a college to those who planned to go to a two-year college and then transferred to a four-year campus. People choose colleges for arbitrary reasons. That's why admissions departments try to ensure a good match between the student and campus before classes begin. Unfortunately, sometimes students don't realize they've made a mistake until it's too late.

The best way to avoid transferring is to extensively research a college or university before choosing it. Visit the campus and stay overnight, talk to admissions and faculty members, and try to learn as much as you can.

Cool Colleges Index

ALPHABETICAL LISTING OF COLLEGES

Notes

Notes

Notes